24.95   E

1995

Isolationism Reconfigured

Isolationism
Reconfigured

AMERICAN FOREIGN POLICY
FOR A NEW CENTURY

Eric A. Nordlinger

PRINCETON UNIVERSITY PRESS

PRINCETON, NEW JERSEY

Library of Congress Cataloging-in-Publication Data

Nordlinger, Eric A.
Isolationism reconfigured : American foreign policy for a
new century / Eric A. Nordlinger.
p.   cm.
Includes bibliographical references and index.
1. United States—Foreign relations—1989–
2. Neutrality—United States.   I. Title.
E840.N65   1995   327.73'009'049—dc20   94—43137
ISBN 0-691-04327-2
ISBN 0-691-02921-0 (pbk.)

This book has been composed in Sabon

Second printing, and first paperback printing, 1996

Printed in the United States of America
by Princeton Academic Press

2   4   6   8   10 9   7   5   3

To my wife "Sam"

———————————————

CONTENTS

FOREWORD AND ACKNOWLEDGMENTS

ERIC NORDLINGER completed *Isolationism Reconfigured* just prior to his untimely death from illness in June 1994. Had he lived even a short while longer, he would have been able to compose a preface to this book and to acknowledge the support and assistance he received from many quarters in its preparation, drafting, and revision. We can hope to provide only a rough and surely incomplete approximation of the acknowledgments Eric would have wished to make, using secondhand knowledge and a perusal of Eric's records of written correspondence.

From the beginnings of this project, Eric relied heavily on support and advice from Samuel P. Huntington and from Robert Jervis, whom Eric had known for many years, originally through various mutual affiliations at Harvard's Center for International Affairs. Sam and Bob read from multiple drafts of the manuscript as it evolved, and Sam's John M. Olin Institute for Strategic Studies helped finance its preparation. Since Eric had written his previous books in various nonsecurity fields such as comparative politics, political sociology, political development, political theory, and even urban politics, he knew he would come under careful scrutiny by security specialists when this work finally appeared. The chance to preview his controversial argument with Sam and Bob was an obvious scholarly benefit, and, we know, a source of deep personal collegial satisfaction.

A number of other colleagues were helpful and supportive in the preparation of this work over the years. However, because Eric relied on his memory more than on written files, we can name with confidence only a few of those whom Eric would have wished to thank for providing thoughtful, insightful comments. Among them are Ted Galen Carpenter, Stephen D. Krasner, and Richard Ned Lebow. Richard Smoke and Tonm Gleason are among the colleagues at Brown University and the Watson Institute for International Studies whose advice Eric sought.

Nancy L. Rosenblum, Eric's friend and colleague at Brown, not only provided him with an ongoing forum for debate while they traveled together between Boston and Providence, she gave Eric extraordinary support during his final semester of teaching and the resources to complete this manuscript. In my own capacity as a colleague and a close personal friend, I too, had opportunities to react to earlier versions of this work over the years. I was honored when Eric requested my assistance toward the end of his illness in seeing the final manuscript through to publication.

Institutional debts are also acknowledged. Eric received support along the way from the Olin Institute, the Cato Institute, and from the Center for Foreign Policy Development at Brown University. Grace de Magistris at the Olin Institute expertly typed many manuscript drafts for Eric, as did Margaret Soares, who typed the final manuscript at Brown. Matthew Woods, a graduate student in Brown's political science department, helped complete references and provided generous assistance at a critical time.

Thanks are also owed to Princeton University Press for accommodating the circumstances that attended the final book editing and production. Eric took enormous satisfaction from knowing, before his death, that *Isolationism Reconfigured* would get Princeton's trademark professional treatment. Although he knew that I would be helping to oversee that process, he could not have known that Princeton would eventually ask Marianne Perlak, who is my wife, to help design the book. He would have approved, since Marianne was also a friend, and the designer of a previous book he published.

Eric's wife, Carol Uhl-Nordlinger, knew better than anyone the importance of bringing this project to a successful completion. For her large role in doing so and the strength she gave to all, we are most in debt.

Robert L. Paarlberg
Cambridge, Massachusetts
August, 1994

Isolationism Reconfigured

Chapter I

INTRODUCTION

THIS BOOK develops a national security strategy and compares it with the security designs of strategic internationalism in both its adversarial and conciliatory variants. It does so by way of two encompassing questions. How do the alternative security strategies compare in protecting America's security, its highest political, material, and survival values, from any and all external threats? And since all security strategies are consequential beyond the security realm, how do they stack up in promoting America's extrasecurity values—at home and abroad, material and ideal, political and economic? These questions are primarily addressed with respect to the Cold War period and after. But the preceding years, extending back to the early Republic, are hardly neglected. The answers to the security and extrasecurity questions take the form of a sharply revisionist interpretation of historical isolationism, an encompassing critique of adversarial and conciliatory internationalism from 1950 to the present, whose five strategic tenets form a radical policy prescription for the coming years.

A national strategy entails a near reversal of strategic internationalism's great commonalities. Instead of strategic engagement—a geographically wide-ranging and effortful political-military activism for shaping the behavior of opponents with varying combinations of forcefulness and accommodation—there is strategic nonengagement. In part 1 of the book, a national strategy is seen to maximize America's security. It promises the most security whether the opponent's intentions tend toward the hostile-aggressive or fearful-defensive, whatever strategy of forceful, political, or economic expansionism it adopts, and however great or small its military, economic, and ideological capabilities. And all this despite— or largely because of—the exceptionally narrow security perimeter that a national strategy draws around North America. Other than protecting the international sea- and air-lanes to and from the water's edge, the strategy demands a true minimum of security-centered involvements beyond North America.

Part 2 of this book considers the nation's extrasecurity values as they have been and might be affected by the alternative security strategies. Here too a national strategy promises more than any variant of strategic internationalism. It heightens the effectiveness of a foreign policy design for the promotion of our international ideals and economic interests. The concurrent design is three-tiered in its activism: The minimally effortful national strategy in the security realm; moderately activist policies to advance our liberal ideals among and within states; and a fully activist economic diplomacy on behalf of free trade, possibly modified by fairly managed trade relations with Europe and Japan. The promotion of America's ideals and economic interests abroad is much advantaged by disentangling them from just about all security concerns and policies. The divorce allows for the autonomy with which to pursue them and the most efficacious application of power, leverage, and accommodation.

Domestically, the national strategy can contribute more than any other security strategy to the nation's economic and social welfare. Its radically lower defense budgets allow for the greater satisfaction of material needs and wants, public and private, while promoting economic growth by way of more flexible macroeconomic policies and the devotion of a larger proportion of defense budgets to productive expenditures. A minimal political-military activism also affords more room on the political and policy agendas for the pursuit of economic and social projects. In addition, the national strategy promises more than any variant of strategic internationalism in preserving America's liberal and constitutional ideals—from respect for the civil liberties of citizens through the lawful and principled conduct of presidents and other executive officials. As it is embedded in the concurrent foreign policy, the national strategy offers yet one other "domestic" benefit: America can thereby best define and attain its much desired reputation as a world actor—both potent and principled. President Reagan's depiction of an assertive America, "standing tall," can be fulfilled at a lower level of confrontation, cost, or risk.

This last claim is developed in the final chapter, which considers the political appeal of the concurrent design, the possible adoption of something very much like it. The discussion focuses upon the fit between policy and culture—the long-standing beliefs, values, expectations, and norms regarding the world beyond the United States and our relations with it. America's foreign policy culture is made up of several dualistic orientations that range from the incompatible to the contradictory, only beginning with the well-known isolationist-internationalist dualism. Although the fit is by no means perfect, the concurrent foreign policy turns out to be considerably more congruent in form and consonant in substance with this culture than full-blown isolationism, realist internationalism, or internationalism with a conciliatory cast. In this basic, politically salient sense the design may be characterized as a decidedly American foreign policy.

These are far-reaching claims in their substantive scope and temporal range, especially since the security claims run directly counter to the conventional wisdom after 1945. The assumptions of strategic internationalism, with their viselike grip upon foreign policy officials, elites, analysts, and scholars, began to loosen up only in the mid-1980s. What then of the still pejorative I-word? Is not a national strategy at one with the isolationism that was sorely dangerous in the 1930s, yet more so after the United States was laid open by the advent of nuclear-tipped missiles, and something between totally irrelevant and irredeemable throughout the twentieth century, with its great and growing global interdependencies? And what of isolationism's close association with appeasement, retreat, naïveté, economic protectionism, and an inordinately self-serving nationalism? Is there any warrant for the more vituperative interventionists to have called those who opposed the war against Iraq "proisolationist" and "isolationist chicken?" Was Anthony Lake, President Clinton's national security adviser, justified in dismissing any proposed shift away from the globalism paradigm as "the rhetoric of neo-know-nothings?"

Much of this book is a response to these questions. Reconfiguring isolationism begins by correcting for the epithets that have been foisted upon it. Its true meanings are found in the summary terms used by its advocates: "No entangling alliances," "masterly inactivity," "continentalism," and "national reserve" in the nineteenth century; "fortress America," "impregnability," and "the policy of the free hand" in the middle of the twentieth century; "disengagement," "unilateralism," "noninterventionism," and "strategic independence" in recent years.

The strategic vision of historical and contemporary isolationism is one of quiet strength and national autonomy. Its advocates have confidently opted for a strong, self-denying strategy, a purposefully considered choice not to go abroad politically and militarily. This has been unnecessary to improve upon the nation's security, prove its strength, or maintain its reputation for resolve. In fact, going abroad for these reasons can be depicted as weakness, conceptualized as a loss of autonomy. For we have indeed been much constrained by others, opponents, allies, and clients alike, in bearing sizable costs and risks—from expensive military forces, through support for ethically unpalatable regimes, unto intermittent interventions and wars. It is strategic internationalism, not isolationism, that could involve appeasement—making major concessions or reneging on defense commitments so as to buy time and buy off the adversary. It was Britain and France, not a disengaged America, that pressured Czechoslovakia to concede much of its territory to Hitler at Munich. Without being at all bellicose, isolationism does not involve significant concessions to opponents, with whom there are few interactions and few political-military treaties and agreements.

To give way to rhetorical temptation, the metaphorical aviary of security studies, which already includes hawks, doves, chicken hawks, owls, and putative ostriches, should be expanded to include eagles. They are powerful, keen sighted, high-flying, remotely perched, and thus eminently well-protected birds. Symbolizing strength and freedom, the bald-headed eagle also happens to be America's national bird. Although the eagle became an endangered species, it is we ourselves who killed and allowed them to be destroyed, having only lately come to appreciate their distinctive value. They are now on their way to insured survival, possibly a good deal more.

The national strategy is neither naive nor simplistic. It extends and specifies strategic isolationism's fundamental maxims: Going abroad to insure America's security is unnecessary; doing so regularly detracts from it. They are fully developed in the form of five strategic propositions. The first broadens what was once referred to as America's military impregnability into a concept of strategic immunity that addresses any and all threats to America's security, including its economic and energy security. The United States is strategically immune in being insulated, invulnerable, impermeable, and impervious and thus has few security reasons to become engaged politically and militarily. The other four doctrinal tenets indicate why activist policies cannot improve upon minimalist ones and why the former bring on security risks and deflations. The four propositions compare a national strategy's record and promise with those of adversarial and conciliatory internationalism along all the possible paths leading to America's insecurity—from the problematics of tailoring a strategy to the challenger's intentions to the risks of strategic mismanagement. These propositions constitute a full-blown security doctrine, a grand strategy that speaks to the distant and recent past as well as the discernible future.

Isolationism has always been first and foremost a security strategy. Like any other, its significance for America's other foreign policies relates to the promotion of our international ideals and economic interests. Contrary to the epithets of protectionism that have been foisted upon it, free-trade practices and principles have been a venerable part of the isolationist tradition. The infamous Smoot-Hawley tariff of 1930 is the single exception, and it was passed by isolationists and internationalists alike under the exigencies of economic depression. Since the early 1980s some isolationists—and internationalists—have advocated the raising of retaliatory and nontariff barriers, a shift from free-trade policies to equitably managed trade relations, or both. But these are usually acknowledged as second-best solutions—the barriers as threat and leverage with which to move Europe and Japan toward free-trade principles; fairly managed trade arrangements partly on the expectation that these trading partners cannot be moved toward free trade.

Isolationists continue to reject virtually all military, economic, and political efforts on behalf of America's international ideals. The isolationist epithet was first used in the 1840s against those who opposed the breaking of diplomatic relations with Austria in support of Hungarian self-determination. For past and present isolationists, our liberal and peaceful values are only to be advanced by having America serve as an example of what is possible, a model to inspire and a guiding beacon—"like a city upon the hill" in Puritan imagery. No matter how good the cause, to interfere in the affairs of others is variously ineffectual, counterproductive for others, and overly costly for us. Moreover, since 1945 the joining of activist idealism with strategic internationalism has often eventuated in morally unacceptable actions. Demonstrably illiberal regimes have been supported, even in the service of secondary and tertiary security concerns acknowledged as such.

The singular—and crucial—difference between full-blown isolationism and the concurrent dispensation is found in the latter's moderately activist, reasonably ambitious promotion of liberal and peaceful causes abroad. But it should also be noted that the two designs' underlying rationales are not nearly as divergent as their policies. According to the concurrent doctrine, the United States can further its international ideals by serving as an exemplar, but only when it is also seen to be actively committed to them. Isolationists are right in pointing to the folly of a vaulting idealism; however, a crusading spirit and vast undertakings are also rejected by the great majority of internationalists. Isolationists are correct in stressing strategic internationalism's illiberal means and consequences, yet it has also made major contributions to democratization and international security. Setting security concerns aside creates room for an autonomously defined liberal project. It allows for the moderated, unilateral, and multilateral pursuit of a principled, focused, well-leveraged, and thus reasonably beneficial liberal idealism.

This is isolationism reconfigured. Devoid of misleading epithets and characterizations, isolationism is taken and considered as its advocates have always meant for it to be. The national strategy and the concurrent foreign policy take the best that isolationism has to offer, develop and build upon it, and revise the rest.

The next part of this introductory chapter clarifies the basic concepts of strategy and security. A brief discussion is needed because all of their definitions have been imbued with internationalist biases. The following section outlines the ways in which the case for the concurrent design is to be made across the temporal span from the late eighteenth century to the beginning of the twenty-first. The final section turns to contemporary politics. It delineates the emergence of the new isolationism that took hold in the 1980s. It ranges across the entire partisan spectrum, linking up with four distinct foreign policy and domestic visions.

I

Strategy and security are simple concepts. There is no difficulty in defining them in straightforward, meaningful, strategically neutral terms. Yet each of the differing conceptions is invested with internationalist meanings; they underscore the deep and abiding bias with which security issues have been treated. Traditional, contemporary, and postmodern definitions of strategy and security cannot be properly used in assessing a minimally activist security strategy. In fact, if taken as stated, as seriously as intended, some definitions obviate nonengagement as a strategic option from the outset. Others assume away the possibility of a secure America if it were implemented. When strategy refers exclusively to a state's purposeful interactions with others, it becomes almost a contradiction in terms to speak of a minimally activist strategy. On the expansive usages of security, a state is almost definitionally insecure unless it is making great international efforts. Conceptions of strategy thus need to be broadened, those of security delimited.

The narrowest meaning of *strategy* is found in Michael Howard's essay "The Classical Strategists," where it refers to the threatened or actual use of force. Economic, covert, diplomatic, propagandistic means are included under its rubric only when they "are combined with force." In Raymond Aron's discussion, "Modern Strategic Thought," this traditional focus is marginally expanded. Strategy refers to policies of force and those in which "force is not excluded" from the outset.[1] Contemporary conceptions have been appropriately extended with the diversification of security threats and the varied ways for meeting them. In one national security text, strategy encompasses military, diplomatic, and economic means as they "vary from cooperation and persuasion, at one extreme, to violent coercion at the other end."[2] Another text appears to include any and all means when it refers to security policy as "the creation of national and international conditions" for dealing with "existing and potential adversaries."[3] Currently, the widely accepted definition is of the kind offered by Barry Posen. "A grand strategy is a political-military, means-end chain, a state's theory about how it can best 'cause' security for itself" by relying upon military, economic, and "other remedies."[4]

All these definitions are overly restrictive in implicitly downplaying policies of nonengagement, inaction, and national reserve. These are largely ruled out when strategy revolves around the threat or use of force,

the "creation" of favorable conditions, policies that vary from "cooperation . . . to violent coercion," and implicitly negated when strategy refers
to "means" and "remedies." Activist efforts could certainly be necessary
in providing for the nation's security. But an empirical assumption surely
has no place in a definition. It may not be (fully) valid, while imparting a
decided bias to strategic design and evaluation.

Activist assumptions are so deeply inbred into strategic studies that
they intrude into its most basic analytical formulations, the "purest" of
theory-building approaches. Game theory begins with the separate strategic choices of two actors who have both conflictual and shared interests;
maximizing both culminates in rational explanations and predictions of
interactive outcomes. Each state is allowed only two choices. In the stag
hunt, the prisoner's dilemma, and the game of "chicken" the players can
either defect or cooperate, the equivalent of choosing between adversarial
and conciliatory internationalism. Yet there is a third strategic option—
of not selecting either of the activist ones, of choosing not to play the
game, of purposefully disengaging.

Robert Jervis is probably the one writer who has recognized that "the
policy of isolation" expresses neither defection nor cooperation. He also
notes that "In many cases [game theory's] most interesting choices" extend beyond its dichotomous options.[5] This comment not only questions
the two-choice restriction that constitutes the analytical foundation of all
formal and strategic theorizing; it also suggests that there are not one, but
two important dimensions along which to array and analyze strategic
choices. Running perpendicular to the defection-cooperation, firmness-
flexibility, hawk-dove continuum, there is the activist-inactivist, engage-
ment-nonengagement dimension. Thomas Schelling does not quite rule
out its analytical presence. But he denies its significance by rejecting the
possibility of successful nonengagement. "If you are . . . invited to play
chicken and you say you would rather not, you have just played"—and
lost.[6] That this is not always the case, almost certainly not for a strategically immune state, is suggested by some simple parallels of the kind that
Schelling is fond of. Is it weakness and failure or strength and success for
addicts to "Just say no" to drug pushers? Is the big kid on the block
demonstrating self-confident strength or a credibility-deflating yellow
streak by ignoring the public taunts of the little kids? And thus how are
states likely to react to a strategically immune America that adopts a self-
denying nonengagement posture in a visibly unconstrained, self-confident
manner? On the historical record, others have never viewed an isolationist America as weak-kneed or irresolute, as anything like a loser in choosing not to play in their international games.

As used here, a security strategy brings together policy and doctrine. It
refers to any broad-gauged policies that a state may adopt for the preser-

vation and enhancement of its security. It also includes the doctrinal rationale—the "means-end chain"—that indicates how and why one set of policies is expected to succeed or prove more successful than the others. Being entirely open-ended, this simple definition encompasses all the others, leaving room for purposeful decisions not to act, inactive "means," and the possible negation of activist doctrine. And it does so without introducing any biases in this or any other direction.

National security should also be an unproblematic term in referring to what is to be protected against what sorts of danger. However, moving from its traditional, through its modern, and unto its postmodern usage is to witness a steady inflation in the number and diversity of activist meanings associated with the nation's security. From the seventeenth-century beginnings of the European state system down to about the middle of the nineteenth century, security referred to the preservation of a state's sovereignty and territorial integrity in the face of external military threats. This traditional variant turned out to be too narrow when nations, not just kings and princes, became the reference point. They upheld additional security goals, which then also entailed a heightened activism in warding off a greater diversity of external threats.

In its modern meaning national security refers to the preservation of the country's highest values as these are purposefully threatened from abroad, primarily by other states, but by other external actors as well. The nation's highest values may encompass much more than the protection of its territorial integrity and sovereignty insofar as they pass the standard litmus test—a widespread willingness to accept great costs and known risks in seeking to preserve them.

The modern definition of national security, which is the one used here, is eminently appropriate. The problem lies with its oftentimes inflated and thus unwarranted usage. In one well-regarded national security text the term encompasses the protection of some unspecified "vital national values" *and* their "extension abroad."[7] According to an unusually sophisticated text, national security policies are designed to "protect and extend national values," including the "promotion or protection of the nation's ideology" throughout the world.[8] Nothing is said about these being limited to our highest values.

Such usage not only violates the basic, oft noted distinction between security and "milieu goals." On the conventional indicator of our highest values—the willingness to accept high costs and known risks on their behalf—there is virtually no evidence that these include the global protection, much less the extension, of our liberal values. Widespread support for foreign intervention in a liberal cause has appeared only when it was also thought necessary to preserve the nation's security. The politically attractive conflation of ideal and security interests can be left to partisan supporters of activist security ventures. For others it is misleading and sidesteps the relevant question: How do minimally and maximally activist security strategies compare in furthering freedom, human rights, democracy, and peace within and among states?

The modern definition of national security has recently been challenged by a postmodern version, one that literally multiplies the number of values that are to be preserved and the array of possible threats to them. In Richard Ullman's formulation, national security refers to the preservation of any widespread public value, any aspect of the country's "quality of life," from any and all threats, external and internal, purposeful and unintended, man-made and natural. The nation's security is thereby diminished by the American government's assault upon domestic liberties, homegrown economic recessions, the illegal influx of Mexican immigrants, and inadequate earthquake warnings.[9]

The evocative, consensus-building usage of national security language has its political attractions. It is also afflicted with the glaring problem of indiscriminateness. Its meaning is so inclusive that it is practically left without a meaning. When the safeguarding of so many diverse values from any and all risks are involved—from the deterrence of a missile attack upon the United States to the defense of civil liberties against our own government's intrusiveness—it is hard to imagine what the design and study of "national security" policies would look like. As used here, the modern definition of national security does not downgrade the importance of what is included in the postmodern variant. Nor does it exclude consideration of much of what it takes in. With national security defined in a meaningful, coherent manner, it is used in assessing the alternative security strategies' impact upon civil liberties and other political abuses, high oil prices, economic recessions, and a variety of policies that bear directly upon quality-of-life issues.

II

Having cleared away the definitional underbrush, there is the crucial question of evidence: How can this study's security and extrasecurity claims be made persuasive over a two-hundred-year time span? It may be that they extend beyond the supporting evidence, that the past, present, and future are being overgeneralized. But probably not by very much, after taking three considerations into account. First, the years from 1796 to 1896 are demonstrably easy ones in which to make the case for the national strategy's security and extrasecurity record. For there is virtually no disagreement about isolationism's having served the country exceptionally well throughout the nineteenth century. Its most damning critics do not extend their mildest criticisms back into the 1800s. Second, there is a great difference in the plausibility attaching to the national strategy's security and extrasecurity arguments. It is only the former that run up squarely against the established scholarly wisdom. Third, it has to be acknowledged that the security case cannot be made all that confidently with regard to the years just after World War II.

An assessment of the isolationists' counsels and warnings between 1900 and 1950 does not necessitate anything like a year-by-year analysis. It hinges upon the times of America's shift toward internationalism, the turning points of an increasingly ambitious political-military interventionism. It was then that the isolationists took their public stand, concomitantly being vociferously attacked by their internationalist contemporaries, their arguments dismissively criticized by subsequent historians and political scientists. Thus the focus is upon the years just before and after the Spanish-American War, when the United States first diverged from the isolationist path in assuming the mantle of a major power; America's intervention in World War I, when it took on the "responsibilities" of a world power; the years before World War II, which far more than any others discredited the isolationist tradition; and the immediate postwar period, when isolationism was thoroughly rejected in favor of Cold War internationalism.

With the benefits of hindsight the reasonableness to full validity of most of the isolationist arguments can be readily argued. Over and above the historical appropriateness of a revisionist interpretation in and of itself, that of the 1930s in particular should mitigate the sharply prejudicial views that have contributed so much to the rejection of the isolationist option after 1945. In addition, a reassessment of 1930s isolationism should allow for some extrapolation. As of December 1941 Japan controlled much of China and was about to attack the European colonies in Southeast Asia. Germany dominated all of Eastern and Western Europe except for the British Isles. The Red Army was still retreating after a succession of major defeats. If the isolationists' security claims are seen to be at least plausible in these decidedly difficult circumstances, they should help validate the comparable arguments that were made during the earlier years and to some extent the later ones as well.

Most of the evidence for appraising the national strategy comes from the Cold War era. All of its strategically significant events and developments are considered, as are all the major doctrinal arguments and concerns that justified America's effortful engagement with the Soviet Union. They include interpretations of Soviet motivations, the military, geographic, domino, and credibility rationales for containment, the concerns for America's dependencies upon oil, trade, and strategic minerals, assessments of the Soviet Union's expansionist capabilities and successes, the several ways in which detente and arms control agreements were said to promote peace, and the arguments about nuclear superiority and parity as effective deterrents. The claims for a national strategy in the Cold War context are developed in contradistinction to those of both adversarial and conciliatory internationalism.

Due to their special significance, three Cold War periods warrant some comments at this point. The immediate postwar years in Western Europe were the riskiest ones in which to rely upon a national strategy. Here was a world power center with the potential for determining the East-West military and economic balance for years to come, exposed to external attack and susceptible to mass turbulence from within. The Soviet Union was in firm control of Eastern Europe, its military forces were orders of magnitude larger than those of Western Europe, and dozens of Red Army divisions were stationed on and near the East-West dividing line. The economies of Western Europe were variously at a standstill, dislocated, and shattered. The strength of the French and Italian communist parties were at their historic highs, and they were willing to act on Moscow's directives.

From the perspective of a national strategy, one response to these circumstances is to suggest that the dangers were inflated and that America's security was not enhanced by the NATO alliance. Another response refers back to Washington's Farewell Address, the isolationist touchstone that allows for "temporary alliances for extraordinary emergencies." Given the uncertainties and fluidity of the late 1940s, it may never be possible to determine which position was warranted at the time.

In suggesting that the dangers were possibly much exaggerated, there are the facts of the USSR having suffered much more than Western Europe in World War II. It lost over 20 million soldiers and civilians. Most of its industrial base was destroyed. Not until the mid-1950s did the economy attain its pre-1939 levels, which were about the same as those of 1914. The USSR probably did not intend to expand its protective corridor beyond Eastern Europe after 1947 since it had not done so when Western Europe lay prostrate. Stalin did not order the French and Italian communists to carry out the general strikes that would have been thoroughly disruptive economically and perhaps worse politically. He demobilized half the Red Army and posted its most successful generals far from Eastern Europe (and Moscow). The dangers were brought on by encircling Russia with alliance partners, stationing U.S. troops abroad, and implicitly threatening an atomic attack. These actions heightened its strategic insecurities, exacerbated tensions, created hazardous flash points, and brought on an arms race.

Of America's military, economic, and political efforts in "saving" Europe, the Marshall Plan has consistently received the most credit. It might just have received too much credit. Detailed investigations have led a few historians to question its necessity and impact. The Europeans' economic objectives, political revitalization, and governing coalitions would have been about the same in its absence.[10] In any case, while the Marshall Plan was first and foremost inspired by security concerns, it could also have been supported by the concurrent foreign policy's second and third tiers. With the American economy inching toward overproduction and given Europe's great potential as a trading partner, large-scale export assistance was an eminently advantageous part of an affirmative economic internationalism. Considering our strong attachments to Europe and the connections between its economic and democratic good health, the Marshall Plan could also have been justified in terms of America's international ideals.

Moreover, if America's security did require a deep involvement in the defense of Western Europe in the late 1940s, it could have been phased out starting in the late 1950s. By then the democracies were politically secure, economically rejuvenated, militarily capable, and likely to generate still larger forces if left on their own. In fact, the Truman administration originally allowed that U.S. forces were only to serve as a short-term expedient until Western Europe could stand on its own feet economically and militarily. Speaking as supreme commander of NATO forces, Dwight D. Eisenhower stated that they would remain only on a "temporary or emergency basis." As president, he occasionally expressed the hope of bringing them home in three or four years.[11]

The 1970s should also present a severe test for the national strategy alternative. At the beginning of the decade we suffered the first military defeat in the country's history. The Arab oil embargo was followed by economic stagnation. The starting point of America's relative economic decline is dated from our going off the gold standard. (It should, however, be noted that the "imperial overstretch" arguments of Paul Kennedy and the other declinists are not used in making the security case for a national strategy.)[12] By the middle of the decade the Soviets were said to have achieved an impressive "geopolitical momentum" in the Third World—from supplying military advisers and weapons to several dozen states to moving into southern Africa along with forty thousand Cuban troops. The Soviets also transformed a coastal-defense force into a blue-water navy, bolstered the size and firepower of their already larger Warsaw Pact forces, and attained an advantage on some limited measures of strategic power. The decade ended with the invasion of Afghanistan—the Soviets' only military action outside Eastern Europe, one that placed them closer to Middle Eastern oil supplies. President Carter depicted the attack as potentially "the greatest threat to world peace since 1945."

It should also be particularly hard to make the case for a national strategy during the 1980s. Total success followed in the wake of adversarial and conciliatory internationalism. While the Reagan administration was pursuing a sharply hawkish strategy in the early 1980s the Soviets' Third World expansionism came to a halt. Their "good behavior" was marred only by continuing military shipments to current clients. When the administration adopted a much more conciliatory posture after 1985, the Cold War spiraled downward towards its 1990 demise. How then could a national strategy have improved upon this record?

While some evidence can be found to support just about any plausible proposition, the most telling kind comes from the difficult cases, those that are least likely to support it.[13] Considering the hurdles to be overcome in establishing the security-maximizing promise of a national strategy during the 1970s and 1980s, the supporting evidence and arguments should go an especially long way in doing so. They are yet more persuasive in that these two decades stack the cards against the claims of a national strategy in nearly opposite ways, by way of relative American weakness and great internationalist success. Nor does the case for a national strategy rely upon the hindsight provided by the Soviet Union's economic debilities, which became more pronounced and fully evident in the late 1980s, or upon its subsequent political implosion and collapse. It refers only to the knowledge that was readily available, if generally unappreciated, at the time.

The post–Cold War era to date is considered primarily in terms of its most important conflict, the Persian Gulf War, and its central security agenda. On its face, the Persian Gulf War constitutes a strong case for strategic internationalism. The United States was able to put together a sizable international coalition and attain an easy victory. The war against Iraq was fully in accord with the two central security aims of the post–Cold War period. First, U.S. defense commitments and troop deployments are to guard against nuclear proliferation. They are to reassure allies of their security, sufficiently so for them to forgo the nuclear temptation. Arms control treaties, forceful threats, and possibly interventions are to stop others from acquiring the weapons. Second, the United States is to maintain its global primacy. It is to remain "number one" on all the dimensions of power—military, economic, and political—especially with regard to potential challenges from Japan and Europe. Given the great attractiveness of this goal and the possibilities for realizing it, how can a national strategy promise more?

III

With the Korean War and its crystallization of global containment, isolationist ideas went into a near-total political eclipse until the 1980s. But despite their removal from the political agenda, they retained considerable underground support. Well before Vietnam, throughout the years of the Cold War "consensus," about one-quarter of the population consistently registered its isolationist support in public opinion surveys.[14] "What never really died [after 1945] was populist isolationism—the sentiment among the poor and poorly educated that however noble America's purposes, most things it does for the rest of the world are wasteful, pointless, unappreciated and tragic."[15]

The Vietnam War was and was not clearly implicated in the emergence of the new isolationism. Among all the heavy-handed and disparate criticisms of U.S. policy, there were preciously few calls for strategic disengagement. The arguments against the war were decidedly limited in their geographic scope and doctrinal substance. We were only to withdraw from Vietnam or Southeast Asia. Elsewhere we were to practice a less militarized, costly, strident, and intrusive form of containment. And this largely because we were overextended militarily and economically, not because containment's underlying premises were questioned. The leading doves—Hans Morgenthau, George Kennan, George Ball, and Senators Eugene McCarthy, Robert Kennedy, and George McGovern— did not doubt that U.S. security required the maintenance of a favorable balance of power throughout much or most of the world.

In fact, only two isolationist writings appeared in the wake of Vietnam. Robert W. Tucker's *A New Isolationism: Threat or Promise?* gained considerable attention in academic circles.[16] He argued that America was largely self-reliant economically and totally safe behind the nuclear deterrent. Alliances and other external involvements only decreased its security by way of regional wars and the risks of their escalation. A decline in U.S. "influence" was the one entry on the negative side of the isolationist ledger. Yet shortly after the book's publication, the Arab oil embargo prompted Tucker to modify his political-military isolationism; he even spelled out the conditions under which the United States should intervene militarily to secure the Middle East oil fields.

In a *Foreign Affairs* article Earl Ravenal set out the "The Case for Strategic Disengagement."[17] "Instead of deterrence and alliance," he advanced a strategy of "war-avoidance and self-reliance." The analysis parallels Tucker's in pointing to alliances as possible "transmission belts" for nuclear war, and thus to the advisability of "quarantining" regional conflicts. It takes the argument further by stressing the "unmanageable diffusion of power," America's (and Russia's) declining ability to affect the behavior of challengers and allies. In addition, America was not willing—and on a cost-benefit calculation should not try—to generate the necessary military power to contain communism in the Third World. The Soviet attainment of strategic parity destroyed the credibility of NATO's first-use nuclear threat in warding off a European war. Ravenal was slightly less sanguine than Tucker in regarding the disadvantages of disengagement. He acknowledged the need to hedge, to become more self-reliant economically, and to accept occasional embargoes and the expropriation of American firms.

Although Vietnam did not bring on anything like a resurgence of isolationist thinking and support, in shattering the Cold War consensus it did much to move the country away from global containment—at the time and for future times. Containment was practiced in a more contingent, circumscribed, and circumspect manner long after the Nixon doctrine, which promised to do so, was forgotten. The 1970s saw the emergence of a sizable strategic "school" advocating the affordability and advisability of some form of delimited containment, moderated interventionism, or "selective engagement."[18] Popular support for containment became less exuberant and confident. The proportion of the population that favored isolationist policies may have risen from about one-quarter to one-third.[19] Slivers of isolationist ideas were adopted at the highest rungs of the educational, occupational, and income ladders. Based on the responses from survey samples drawn from *Who's Who in America* (1976 and 1980), "Many traditional isolationist themes were no longer confined to the outer fringes of the nation's political landscape. . . . Isolationist ideas have achieved a degree of respectability and support unknown since before Pearl Harbor."[20]

During the late Carter years the country came close to flagellating itself for its weaknesses, most intensely so because of Washington's inability to negotiate the freedom of or to rescue the diplomat-hostages in Iran. In turning the country around subjectively, Ronald Reagan laid a necessary foundation for the new isolationism, subsequently much reinforced by developments within the Soviet Union. America's self-confidence was revived by presidential candidate Reagan's excoriating America for its muscular atrophy and by his subsequent arms buildup and public stridency—the rhetoric of "standing tall" and "getting tough" with the "evil empire." Only after the sharp abatement of our anxieties and fears was it possible to consider the great advantages of staying home. In the mid-1980s the country's sense of security was further bolstered by Mikhail Gorbachev's publicly acknowledging the USSR's domestic debilities and international constraints. By 1988 the Soviet economy was seen to be in such dire straits that there was no doubting its further decline before things might get at all better.

This new sense of security allowed isolationist sentiments to be politically rekindled by frustration and anger with our major allies. The attractions of the unilateralism that is central to a national strategy were heightened by the Europeans who were less than enthusiastic supporters of U.S. security policies. They held up, criticized, or negated American efforts involving the installation of intermediate-range missiles in Europe, the invasion of Grenada, military aid for the Nicaraguan contras, the bombing of Libya, restrictions upon advanced technology exports to the USSR, the building of a natural gas pipeline from the USSR into West Germany, and prohibitions on chemical and nuclear weapons sales to Third World countries. Irving Kristol, an arch cold warrior, strongly objected to the allies' pusillanimous restraints upon American boldness. He proposed a withdrawal from NATO and other alliances in favor of "global unilateralism."[21] Another cold warrior published *How NATO Weakens the West*, advocating a complete withdrawal from NATO and a strategic shift to Asia.[22]

More important, economic problems and resentments were focused on the allies. The budget deficit, the trade imbalance, and the foreign debt were attributed to the refusal of wealthy European and Japanese allies to carry their fair share of the common defense burden and their departures from the principles of free trade. We were defending countries to whom "we owed money for defending them," who were free riding on our military expenditures, who refused to accept a "level playing field" in trade competition, and to whom we were a "free trade patsy." Sam Nunn, chairman of the Senate Armed Services Committee and a leading Atlanticist, introduced an amendment in 1984 that would have reduced U.S. troop deployments in Europe by one-third unless the Europeans increased their defense spending. The measure was defeated only after intensive lobbying by the Reagan administration. Unlike the similar Mansfield amendment that was proposed several times during the 1970s, on this occasion the opposition did not use isolationist epithets, arguing only that the Nunn amendment was a dangerous first step down that slippery slope.

The significant shift toward something approximating a national strategy was unhappily acknowledged in a 1985 article on "Isolationism, Left and Right." Charles Krauthhammer observed that the movement has "regained its voice. . . . The political monopoly enjoyed by postwar internationalism is at an end."[23] As the Cold War wound down in a soft landing, isolationist sounding voices were more widely heard. Almost half the respondents in a 1988 survey subscribed to the view "that we should bring our troops home and limit our military involvement to defending only our own borders—that we should gradually end our treaty commitments and let allies take care of themselves." Three-quarters of those interviewed in another survey said that "We can't afford to defend so many nations," while another 80 percent advocated reduced defense commitments. In a 1991 survey 59 percent agreed that "Our allies are perfectly capable of defending themselves, and they can afford it," up from the 48 percent who offered this reply in 1988. In one poll sizable majorities favored bringing U.S. troops home from Western Europe (60 percent) and South Korea (74 percent). Without any major external challengers in sight, domestic engagement became a serious competitor to strategic engagement; three-quarters of the population favored a reduction of "involvements in world politics to concentrate on problems at home." Nearly 90 percent attributed America's economic failures to our "helping others" rather than putting "America's needs first." Most striking, in a 1991 poll 44 percent endorsed the outright isolationist position that "the U.S. should mind its own business internationally and let other countries get along as best they can on their own."[24]

The elite stratum has been consistently far more internationalist than the public since 1945. Although still so, here too the Cold War's demise helped engender isolationist proclivities. A 1992 survey of more than two thousand opinion leaders in a variety of occupations elicited majority agreement with two isolationist verities. Fifty-nine percent and 56 percent respectively agreed with these statements: "Our allies are perfectly capable of defending themselves and they can afford it, thus allowing the U.S. to focus on internal rather than external threats to its well-being"; "The best way to encourage democratic development in the Third World is for the U.S. to solve its own problems." In addition, 42 percent said that U.S. troops should be brought home from Europe, and 23 percent went so far as to agree that "What we need is a new foreign policy that puts America first, and second and third as well."[25]

Magazine articles—in *Harper's*, the *New Yorker*, the *New York Times Magazine*, the *Atlantic*, and others—supported strategic options for the "devolution" of NATO military responsibilities to Europe and for a narrowly circumscribed "interest-based" foreign policy. Sitting at the center of the foreign policy establishment, the editor of *Foreign Affairs* urged "partial disengagement," something like an 80 percent reduction in our European forces. The allies were to take over ground defenses, while we provided air and naval support and nuclear weaponry.[26] He was seconded (or more than that) by articles appearing in other international affairs journals: *National Interest* on the right, *Foreign Policy* around the center, and the *World Policy Journal* on the left. In scholarly writings isolationism was introduced into and respectfully discussed in several strategic typologies.[27] As hawkish a strategist as Colin Gray criticized interpretations of Cold War disengagement as a failure of will, as a retreat; he devoted several pages to the several ways in which the fortress America idea enjoys "some abstract merit"—before indicating why it should nevertheless be rejected.[28]

The flavor of the new thinking was captured by Strobe Talbot. He summarized

> a spate of recent articles and speeches that all say the same thing: Come home, America. Now that the Red Menace is history and the Emir of Kuwait is back on his throne, many of Bush's constituents would like him to do more

to save their schools, hospitals, banks, jobs, and pensions. In a fire-breathing cover story in the July *Atlantic*, Alan Tonelson . . . says [that the U.S.] should junk the idea of "exercising something called leadership" and "insulate" itself from the disasters of the Third World. . . . William Hyland, editor of *Foreign Affairs*, wrote a guest column for the *New York Times* calling on the U.S. to "start selectively disengaging" from overseas commitments, "a psychological turn inward" and a Marshall Plan "to put our own house in order." Four weeks later, *The Times's* own James Reston argued that "the main threat to our nation's security [comes] from within" and urged Bush to build a "new American order." Meanwhile, Peter Peterson, chairman of both the Council on Foreign Relations and the Institute for International Economics, is advocating "the primacy of the domestic agenda." . . . Thomas Jefferson's warning against entangling alliances is back in fashion. Reston endorses John Quincy Adams' injunction to go "not abroad in search of monsters to destroy."[29]

The end of the Cold War prompted a score of writings delineating the policy alternatives for the new era. Most of them include the isolationist option and treat it respectfully—strategically and politically. Some are striking in their limited and less-than-relevant reasons for rejecting it. Charles Maynes, the editor of *Foreign Policy*, set out the strengths and weaknesses of three possible foundations for a new foreign policy: "National interest, democratic values, and global partnership."[30] He objects to the first of these "grand options" because prudence requires that "at least in its early stages the coming retrenchment not be too sweeping." It certainly does, but no advocate of strategic disengagement has suggested otherwise. This option's only other problem is that the United States is not "capable of following a foreign policy grounded in a strict (i.e., a geographically narrow) definition of national interest." Too many "popular sympathies for the underdog," "ethnic empathies," and economic interests among the public stand in the way. Whatever its possible merits, this is not a strategic argument. Nothing is said about possible security risks or strategic drawbacks deriving from a more tightly restricted political-military perimeter.

Robert Tucker's grand alternatives are continued strategic internationalism, a much moderated ("modest") internationalism, and isolationism.[31] In favoring the second over the third he notes that "Great powers are not in the habit of voluntarily relinquishing the role to which they have become accustomed, and this despite the fact that the circumstances initially prompting the assumption of the role have changed." But this is a prediction about what the United States is likely to do rather than a strategic assessment. And our foreign policy culture is sufficiently distinctive to question the generalization, as seen in the quick reversion to isolationism after World War I. Tucker himself observed that once it becomes apparent that "we now live in a very different world, the advantage (in the current foreign policy debate) that is conferred by the force of the habitual will erode. The advocates of change will then have their day." As in Maynes's article, the only other argument is that of "caution and conservatism," which should be satisfied by a gradual disengagement.

The widespread support for some form of disengagement is only partly belied by the Persian Gulf War. Not only was the war option opposed by many normally interventionist members of the foreign policy elite, it was exceptionally easy for large majorities to favor the economic embargo and blockade against Iraq absent any significant American sacrifices. Just before the war began, slightly less than half the country favored immediate military action. Support in the opinion polls decreased marginally on the stated assumption that one thousand U.S. soldiers would die (44 percent in favor of war and 53 percent opposed). It declined further (to 35 percent in favor and 61 percent opposed) if ten thousand troops were killed.[32] The circumstances favoring war also happened to be truly unusual. Saddam Hussein was the perfect enemy, having been likened to Hitler because of his use of chemical weapons against Kurdish villagers and unprovoked aggression against tiny Kuwait. Our ideal interests were involved in protecting Israel from Iraqi missiles, deterring others from blatant aggression, and stemming nuclear proliferation. They were crystallized in Bush's promise that collective UN action would usher in a "new world order." And the administration further justified the war by linking oil supplies to "jobs, jobs, jobs" during an economic recession. Moreover, President Bush unilaterally placed so many ground troops in Saudi Arabia that they would have to be used or ignominiously withdrawn.

By the late 1980s proponents of full-blown or quasi isolationism were found across the entirety of the political spectrum—not surprisingly, for its minimal demands permit an open-endedness on other foreign policy issues and all domestic ones. Contrary to the common identification of isolationism with political conservatism, it was exclusively so only just prior to and after World War II. Before 1939 isolationists populated the ranks of Republicans and Democrats, eastern Progressives and midwestern and southern Populists, and throughout the nineteenth century they were consensually regnant. In recent years, the extrasecurity commonalities of the liberals and conservatives who favor complete or substantial disengagement have been limited to putting defense savings to good (albeit very different) uses and pressuring Europe and Japan on trade issues.

These and full-blown strategic isolationists of a liberal persuasion divide into a left and a populist stream. The former are distinguished by their interest in using defense savings for the needy and the country's economic renewal via government funding for education and research, renovation of the infrastructure of roads, airports, and housing, and as financial incentives to increase productive investments. Rejecting full-blown isolationism because it ignores our liberal international ideals, and rejecting the imperialist premises of strategic internationalism, we are to pursue a wide-ranging multilateralism—in maintaining quasi-global peace, safeguarding human rights, promoting democracy, providing economic relief for endemically poor countries, and in addressing the ecological issues of the global commons. This is the political world of Jesse Jackson's campaign for the Democratic Party's 1988 presidential nomination, the editors of the *Nation*, the World Policy Institute, and such policy writers as Lester R. Brown and Richard J. Barnet.[33]

The liberal populist variant has a special appeal for the blue-collar and middle-class strata. It is partly inspired by economic resentments toward allies and clients. Speaking as a candidate for the Democratic party's 1988 presidential nomination, Congressman Richard Gephardt took strong exception to our maintaining a "global defense financed with dollars borrowed from creditors who are the very countries being protected. In 1987 we actually owe the West Europeans and the Japanese money for defending them."[34] While working Americans suffered financially, Washington has wasted huge sums on defense, foreign aid, and on trade credits for vastly exaggerated security needs, as well as adhering to free trade policies that are not practiced by others. These notes were struck by Gephardt and in Senator Tom Harkin's quest for the Democratic party's 1992 presidential nomination. Alan Tonelson stridently argued for a largely isolationist, interest-based foreign policy that would serve the "manifest (if seldom articulated) wishes of the great majority of Americans, rather than those of the small, privileged caste of government officials, former government officials, professors, think-tank denizens, and journalists whose dreamy agenda has long dominated [our] foreign policy. . . . For surely [it] was conducted with utter disregard for the home front largely because it has been made by people whose lives and needs have almost nothing in common with those of the mass of their countrymen."[35]

On the conservative side of the partisan spectrum, advocates of isolationism also divide into two streams, those of normality and nationalism and of libertarianism. Regarding the former, it was reported that "Many mainstream conservatives are reverting to the isolationism that characterized traditional Republicanism before the rise of the 'Red Menace.' "[36] A senior (and dissenting) editor of the *National Review* opposed intervention against Iraq by urging that America "just get back to normal." With the unraveling of the Soviet Union "conservatives ought to be redoubling their efforts to achieve the domestic goal of restoring a limited republic, not sacrificing this purpose to global empire."[37] Jeane Kirkpatrick, who had stridently articulated Reagan's adversarial internationalism, offered a manifesto for "A Normal Country in a Normal Time."[38] There are only two reasons for going abroad, those of "negotiating rules under which American business can compete effectively" and the constitutional requirement to "provide for the common defense." With most alliance obligations now outdated, "there is no pressing need for heroism and sacrifice." Without a "mystical American 'mission'" to democratize the world, and unable to do so in any case, we should only "encourage democratic institutions wherever possible." The time has come to "give up the dubious benefits of superpower status and become again an unusually successful, open American republic," a normal country that takes "care of pressing problems of education, family, industry, and technology."

The nationalist note was most starkly struck by Patrick Buchanan, a member of the Nixon and Reagan staffs and a candidate for the 1992 Republican presidential nomination. "What we need is a new nationalism, a new patriotism, a new foreign policy that puts America first, and, not only first, but second and third as well." With peaceful neighbors and vast oceans for protection there is no need to "seek permanent entanglement in other people's quarrels." No crucial interests were threatened by Iraq's control of Kuwait. As an island-continent and as the "greatest trading nation on earth . . . [America] should use her economic and technological superiority to keep herself permanent mistress of the seas, first in air, first in space." As for democracy, involvement in the political arrangements of other countries "contradicts history and common sense . . . [It is] a formula for interminable meddling and endless conflict." Buchanan's nationalism speaks to normality by way of huge defense and foreign aid savings making for tax reductions; the working and middle classes can then live according to their "American values." His nationalism goes further in allowing that immigration is ruining the country. It approximates the virulent nativism of 1930s isolationism in this linkage between foreign and domestic affairs: "When we say we will put America first, we mean also that our Judeo-Christian values are going to be preserved, and our Western heritage is going to be handed down to future generations, not dumped into some landfill called multiculturalism."[39]

The libertarian variant, revolving around the benefits of small, minimally activist government, is the most thoroughly isolationist. It is well represented in Ravenal's strategic writings, which also feature codas on disengagement's extrasecurity benefits. These include a "more reserved, less extensive government," respect for our civil liberties and "accustomed freedoms," fiscal sobriety and national solvency, and the overall "integrity of our constitutional system." For Ted Carpenter, the director of foreign policy studies at the Cato Institute, "strategic independence" would sharply curtail the individual and institutional abuses carried out in the name of national security; the "imperial presidency" would give way to the constitutionally prescribed balance of executive-legislative power. Drastic defense cuts would encourage economic growth and allow for more private choices. Neither during the Cold War nor much less so now should the government be able to sacrifice and risk the "lives, freedoms, and financial resources of the American people. . . . It does not have a right to implement the political elite's conception of good deeds internationally any more than it has a right to do so domestically." Without subscribing to nationalist exuberance or intolerance, libertarian isolationism roundly rejects the activist pursuit of our ideals—unilaterally or through the United Nations. Its vision is one of independent states cooperating and competing—especially economically—as in an open and fair market. For Ravenal, America is to relinquish its "honorable pretensions" for maintaining world order, "to live modestly, like other nations." In international politics "the desire to do good often leads to objective harm. Private virtues are often public vices; national virtues are often international vices . . . [E]ven the private vice of indifference to disorder might, in this imperfect world of fragmented sovereignties, translate into the public virtue of preserving national integrity and respecting external reality." For Carpenter, this position is reinforced by our having associated with and succored repugnant and repressive regimes for security reasons. Although it is "essential that a post-Cold War strategy contain an element of idealism," the latter can best be served by "emphasizing the potent example of America's economic and political values."[40]

The spread of isolationist ideas was and was not evident in the first presidential election of the post–Cold War era. The major candidates proceeded as usual, Bill Clinton talking the language of multilateral internationalism and George Bush that of strategic internationalism with hegemonic overtones. They barely differed regarding moderate reductions in the size of the 1990s military; the United States should maintain the capability to fight two regional wars simultaneously. On the other hand, isolationist notes were sounded by one candidate for the Democratic presidential nomination (Harkin), one for the Republican candidacy (Buchanan), and by the independent candidate (Ross Perot). While it is unclear how much electoral benefit they derived in doing so, their positions were in line with the electorate's overt concern with economic issues, its disinterest in foreign policy questions, and what one opinion analyst saw as a "pervasive mood of isolationism."[41] With so many voters chafing under the heavy burdens of world leadership, absent the Soviet or any other major security threat, both Clinton and Bush were diffident about their internationalism. The president had little to say about foreign policy issues, despite this being his once proud strong suit.

Clinton picked away at him for having accorded too much attention to the world beyond America, while Perot went much further, sometimes sounding distinctly isolationist. It is only a partial exaggeration to say that "the three candidates pledged to reverse cold war practice and focus on America."[42]

Absent any pressing security threats during its first year and a half, the Clinton administration sought to concentrate on the domestic agenda of resuscitating the economy and legislating health care reforms. Liberal internationalism yes, but of a muted, ad hoc, somewhat muddled kind, exhibiting neither exuberance nor ambition. The electoral campaign subtheme of an activist idealism was diluted. Little more was heard of a "global democratic alliance" and the use of force when the "conscience of the international community" is defied—even with regard to the bloody and cruel "ethnic cleansing" of Bosnia. After the Somali operation momentarily turned from humanitarian food dispersal and peacekeeping toward peacemaking, resulting in the deaths of eighteen U.S. soldiers, the president adopted a thoroughly centrist posture. He denounced the "poison" of isolationism while scolding the UN for overextension; he opposed demands for an immediate troop withdrawal from Somalia yet announced a firm date for the operation's termination. However, "Bill Clinton will spend more on defense than Richard Nixon two decades ago: $260 billion as against $230 billion in inflation adjusted dollars."[43]

The political emergence of the isolationist security alternative and the collapse of communism have done much to unhinge strategic internationalism. The U.S. is standing at a historic crossroads. Yet a full-blown debate about America's position in the world and its strategic relations has not taken place.[44] The reasons for its absence range from intellectual crustifications through the usual gamut of vested interests—political, bureaucratic, and economic. But paradoxically, perhaps the most important one relates to the isolationist centerpiece: The country is at minimal risk from external threats. Living securely in a post–Cold War world that is far more dangerous for many others, the Clinton administration and most Americans have not been moved to reexamine the premises governing forty years of strategic internationalism.

There are three possibilities for a shift to something like a national strategy. One involves a slowly growing understanding of our truly privileged position of strategic immunity, along with an appreciation of the extrasecurity costs, especially economic ones, of going abroad politically and militarily. Another possibility entails a different kind of learning exercise. A sizable handful of "destabilizing" developments occur over the next ten years—some combination of distant coups, internal wars, nuclear acquisitions, aggressive acts, and international wars. In each instance the United States seriously contemplates and perhaps takes some first steps on an interventionist course. In each case it concludes that the costs and risks are excessive or that success is unlikely. In an ad hoc manner we will then have moved a long way toward a national strategy and become convinced of its appropriateness. On the other possibility, some "vital" interest, an "entangling alliance," or the detonation of nuclear weapons brings the United States up to some kind of conflictual abyss. After (we hope) avoiding it or after emerging from it comes the shock of recognition—of the limits, counterproductive consequences, and dangers of going abroad for security reasons. The three possibilities are not mutually exclusive.

PART ONE

America's Security

THERE ARE ONLY two fundamental doctrinal bases for the design of any broad-gauged set of security policies: Capabilities writ large and the challenger's intentions. Doctrine shapes policy according to assessments of relative military, economic, and political capabilities and according to interpretations of the opponent's intentions, which can vary from the hostile and implacably expansionist to the insecure and fearful. Variations in these encompassing and irreducible criteria allow for three and only three "pure" grand strategies: Adversarial engagement, conciliatory engagement, and nonengagement.

Adversarial and conciliatory internationalism are at one in their highly activist policies and their derivation from both capabilities and intentions. Capability (or power) assessments underscore the need for activist security measures. Interpretations of intentions determine whether these measures are firm or flexible, hard or soft. The great differences between adversarial and conciliatory internationalism, between hawkish and dovish policies, are primarily due to divergent understanding of the opponent's intentions. Strategic nonengagement's minimal policy activism derives from an assessment of capabilities and an agnostic position with regard to intentions. A country that is strategically immune to the opponent's capabilities need not engage him in order to maximize its security.

The United States has adopted each of these grand strategies: Nonengagement from the end of the eighteenth to the close of the nineteenth centuries, fairly rapid shifts among nonengagement and both types of engagement throughout the first half of the twentieth century, and adversarial engagement punctuated by periods of modest conciliatory engagement during its second half. There is no doubting the appropriateness of nineteenth-century isolationism, its effectiveness in maximizing security. Nonengagement's appropriateness in the twentieth century has been regularly questioned, its effectiveness often vehemently denied on the basis of great changes. Among these are the enormous growth of American economic and military power, the distant spread of economic interests and the threats to them, the German Empire's challenge to the balance of power in Europe, great advances in military technology, Nazi Germany's control of Western Europe, Japanese hegemony in the Pacific, the enormous power of the Soviet Union and its worldwide expansionism, the advent and proliferation of nuclear weapons, and an array of great and growing global economic interdependencies. Each of these changes has been taken as a major, manifestly persuasive reason for turning to or continuing with an effortful, highly activist security strategy.

The reality of these developments has not at all been denied by the historical isolationists or contemporary ones. They are not strategic ostriches. However, twentieth-century developments do not necessarily call for an internationalist strategy. The changes cannot be said to bear significantly upon America's security without also considering its strategic immunity and comparing the security-enhancing promises of strategic engagement and nonengagement.

Chapter II

A NATIONAL STRATEGY:
CONTEMPORARY CONTOURS AND THE
HISTORICAL RECORD

EVERY GRAND STRATEGY has its characteristic and distinctive features, the elements that bind it together and distinguish it from others. These can be most clearly adumbrated by placing them within a comprehensive typology of security strategies. The first part of this chapter delineates the most basic classificatory scheme for ordering all security strategies. Placing adversarial and conciliatory internationalism within it brings out their great policy and doctrinal commonalities. Opposing these commonalities are the central features of a national strategy.

The second part of the chapter describes the national strategy's policy and doctrinal contours. The most distinctive policy, and the one that allows for and largely orders the others, is the drawing of an exceptionally narrow security perimeter, beyond which political-military activism is limited to a bare minimum. The doctrine of strategic nonengagement takes the form of five propositions or strategic tenets. They are summarized and their policy implications fleshed out at this point. The following five chapters develop and substantiate them for the years since 1950.

The third section reviews isolationist security arguments from the end of the eighteenth century to the demise of the old isolationism in the middle of the twentieth. Contrary to the severe criticisms to which they have been subjected by historians and political scientists, this historical review shows them to be invariably reasonable and plausible. It also shows that critiques of strategic internationalism were regularly warranted. The review can be read in conjunction with the first parts of chapters 8, 9, and 10, which discuss the historical isolationists' extrasecurity arguments regarding America's international ideals, domestic political ideals, and economic and social welfare.

I

Most security typologies are one-dimensional. They are limited to what is variously referred to as the hawk-dove, adversarial-conciliatory, firmness-flexibility, and hard line–soft line continuum. But a second continuum ranging from low to high activism, is equally basic. Taken together, these two dimensions depict the irreducible and comprehensive dimensions of any security strategy.

It is commonly forgotten that choosing between a firm or flexible policy involves not one, but two strategic choices: Whether to interact with the other side at all, and if so, whether to do so in a hawkish or dovish manner. In fact the activism dimension has analytical, if not also empirical, priority. Firmness or flexibility is contingent upon the decision to interact with the other side in the first place. Only then does it matter whether this is to be done in an adversarial or conciliatory manner.

This point comes through in Albert Hirschman's influential study *Exit, Voice, and Loyalty*, an analysis of the alternative reactions to the poor performance of firms, organizations, and governments on the part of consumers, clients, members, and citizens.[1] Why is a dissatisfied customer, for example, likely to exit by switching to another brand, voice a complaint to the company, or remain a loyal customer? Hirschman's analytical framework is broad enough to encompass a great diversity of circumstances, including those of a status quo state's reactions to the poor performance—the security-threatening actions—of a challenger. But these need not be elaborated in order to appreciate the argument that exit, voice, and loyalty are not comparable decisions, that they do not reside at the same analytical level. Those actors who voice their complaints, as well as those who remain loyally silent, have already made a prior decision. They chose to remain actively engaged; not to exit.[2]

To suggest that the activist dimension must be included in *the* typology of security strategies, it is necessary to ask how it stacks up against any other possibility. How do the alternatives to activism compare with it as one of the two elementary and inclusive dimensions of a strategic typology?

During the 1970s and early 1980s there was a growing appreciation of the possibility of an inadvertent nuclear war between America and Russia. Avoiding such a war served as the impetus for the development of a strategic dimension focused upon the "rationality" of policy choice. The "owlish" concerns of Graham Allison, Albert Carnesale, and Joseph Nye highlighted inadvertent decisions and actions—rushed, careless, faulty, unauthorized, and accidental. While hawks and doves are said to work on the rational premise that the rival's decisions are the product of self-conscious, calculated, reasonably accurate beliefs and assessments, owls "focus primarily on loss of control and nonrational factors in history. In this view, a major war would not arise from careful calculations, but from organized routines, malfunctions of machines or of minds, misperceptions, misunderstandings, and mistakes," most egregiously so with Europe's stumbling into World War I.[3]

These owlish concerns are undeniably important, yet they are too narrow if the "primary focus is [the] triggering of a war in a crisis."[4] The rationality dimension is then much too circumscribed to serve as a fundamental one in a strategic typology for it does not address the entire range of security issues. The rationality continuum could be understood in a much broader fashion to refer to just about all misperceptions, mistaken assessments, breakdowns in command and control, and other "nonrational" actions as they help bring on and exacerbate conflicts. But then this dimension loses its distinctiveness. Insofar as these concerns are shared by hawks, doves, and eagles, the rationale for a separate continuum falls by the wayside. (It is seen to do so in chapters 4 through 7.) Indeed, chapter 7 goes one step further, showing eagles to be much better able than the internationalist species to guard against inadvertence or mismanagement.

Only two other—largely overlapping—policy variations have been used as dimensions along which to array alternative security strategies. States can adopt a multilateral or unilateral strategy, relying upon others or upon themselves in providing for their security. And similarly, when balancing against the challenger they can choose to do so externally or internally. Both sets of options vary along the activist continuum, in their substance and degree. Rather than constituting alternative dimensions, they underscore its greater compass. Whether multilateralism involves a reliance upon allies (as patrons or clients), regional institutions, or a collective security organization, it involves at least a considerable degree of activism. Unilateralism may be activist in engaging the contender or minimally so as part of a national strategy. External balancing against the threat involves the acquisition of allies in meeting it, whereas internal balancing relies upon a buildup of one's own military and economic capabilities. Both kinds of balancing policies are at least substantially activist.

Together the firmness and activist dimensions thus form the comprehensive, irreducible strategic typology whose variations are depicted in figure 1. Adversarial and conciliatory engagement strategies are arrayed along the upper reaches of the typology; they vary from high to low degrees of firmness at consistently high levels of activism. The nonengagement strategy is located at the low end of the activism dimension and around the midpoint of the firmness continuum. Balanced engagement is situated around the strategic center. It is doubly balanced in combining a moderate ranking on the firmness and activist dimensions. It could serve as a long-term strategy or as a transitional one, the latter by way of testing and calming the international waters while gradually shifting from strategic engagement to nonengagement.

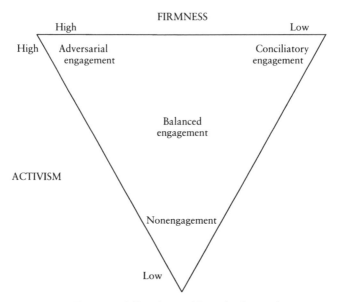

Figure 1. A Typology of Security Strategies

Nonengagement's location at the bottom of the schematic triangle depicts its equidistance from adversarial and conciliatory engagement, with regard to both levels of activism and degrees of firmness. There is a symmetrical narrowing of the classificatory space in moving toward the lower end of the activism dimension; fewer and fewer efforts to influence the opponent's behavior preclude more and more of both hawkish and dovish options. It is difficult to imagine decidedly adversarial or conciliatory forms of nonengagement.

Having set out the elementary policy variations of the alternative security strategies, the discussion turns to their doctrinal content—the theories, beliefs, and perceptions that engender the various policy positions within the classificatory scheme. Because of the one-dimensional, exclusively internationalist debate between Cold War hawks and doves, their shared features have received very little attention. In fact, the number of adversarial-conciliatory commonalities is much greater than their differences. There is only one major doctrinal divergence—the very different interpretations of the challenger's intentions. They are largely responsible for driving hawks and doves to their different perches on the firmness-flexibility continuum.

Adversarial and conciliatory policies derive first and foremost from the common assumption of America's vulnerability. Most, if not nearly all, expansions of an opponent's territorial influence or control and military capabilities are thought to have adverse security consequences—if not directly and immediately, then indirectly and over the foreseeable future, if not via the threat or use of force, then politically and economically, if not geographically and materially, then symbolically and subjectively."

Hawks are more sensitive than doves to the ways in which the opponent's territorial successes and military improvements impinge upon the nation's security. But the differences are all too easily exaggerated. The global scope of the hawkish containment perimeter during the Cold War was only somewhat wider than its dovish counterpart. And the sharp differences in forceful and accommodating means for convincing the contender not to undertake expansive actions should not obscure this crucial commonality: If he did so successfully, hawks and doves would usually be at one in assessing its adverse security impact. Their assessments of vital, central, and secondary interests converge; divergent judgments are limited to the territorial peripheries and the military edges. The disagreements about the consequences of an improvement in the rival's position have more to do with intentions—why the opponent undertook an expansive venture and what he expects to do with his gains—than with assessments of the gains themselves.

As a case in point, of the territorial issues that surfaced during the 1980s, hawks and doves disagreed most with regard to Central America. At bottom they differed about the nature of the Marxist movements, their ideology and the meaning of reformist and defensive pronouncements. The differences in assessments of the security stakes were not all that striking, as with Soviet and Cuban arms shipments to the Marxist insurgents in El Salvador. Hawks and doves largely shared a concern with the possibility of an insurgent victory. Their divergence disappeared entirely when they contemplated the prospects of El Salvador as a Marxist-Leninist dictatorship or a Soviet client. Similarly, the disagreements regarding the security consequences of Cuban and Soviet small arms shipments to the Sandinista regime in Nicaragua diminished sharply when regarding the possible arrival of Soviet tanks and planes and evaporated entirely when envisaging a Soviet military presence and Nicaragua's possible military actions against its neighbors.

Because internationalists view most or all of the challenger's expansive successes as deflating security, they converge on the need to ward off the probable and possible ones by adopting a full range of activist policies. The opponent must be dissuaded or persuaded not to expand his influence-control and military forces by a continuous stream of political-military efforts, signals, initiatives, responses, and preparations. The comprehensive resort to activist measures is seen in the paucity of instances in which inaction is warranted. Adversarial counsels of inaction are limited to those in which military resources are overextended and to those in which the opponent's accommodating initiatives are seen as deceptive ploys. Dovish inaction is called for only when the challenger's expansive ventures are thought to be prompted by legitimate security concerns and grievances, and then there is still a dispatch of clarifying messages, calming diplomatic activity, and possibly negotiations.

Adversarial internationalism tends to be seen as substantially more activist than its conciliatory counterpart, probably because of the great notoriety and consequences of forceful measures. Yet a somewhat larger security perimeter, more frequent interventionist threats, and strivings for greater military advantage do not necessarily make for a more activist strategy. Conciliatory internationalism features a bevy of comparable measures: Continuous interactions with allies throughout the world, the stationing of troops abroad, the maintenance of sizable strategic forces, the laying down and occasional manipulation of deterrent threats, the provision of military and economic assistance to dozens of states, and ongoing programs of weapons research and development. And then there are the doves' distinctive varieties of diplomatic activism: proposals, discussions, conferences, bargaining, compromises, informal understandings, and formal agreements. Substantively, they involve arms ceilings and reductions, geographic limits upon the scope of the rivalry, rules for avoiding and managing crises, the settlement of political and territorial disputes, and the facilitation of trade.

Activist policies are directed at a variety of targets, but adversarial and conciliatory internationalism are at one in focusing upon the opponent's "hearts and minds"—his short- and long-term intentions as shaped by his values, perceptions, and calculations. For these are the immediate determinants of the other side's actions, of its decisions to undertake or forgo expansive actions. The single leader, government officials, political elites, and/or publics that determine the opponent's policies must somehow be dissuaded or persuaded not to infringe upon America's vulnerability. And that means a great program of continuing communication.

Strategic engagement is largely about communications, the sending of signals. Since even straightforward messages may be garbled, ignored, misinterpreted, or disbelieved, constant efforts are needed to insure that they are received, understood, and believed. Adversarial messages are primarily of a deterrent kind. They are to be communicated in ways that insure their clarity and credibility and highlight the costliness of the threatened action. Conciliatory messages are about reassurance and accommodation. They must convince the contender of the guardian state's nonthreatening intentions, of shared interests, or of both.

To communicate effectively is not necessarily to communicate successfully. The messages may be clear and convincing—but wrong. Hawks and doves agree that correct messages must take full account of the opponent's underlying motivations, values, and beliefs. They then also agree that it is crucial to get "into" the other side's heart and mind. In fact, as seen in chapter 4, they rely upon the same kinds of reasoning and indications, often the very same pieces of evidence, in coming to their understandings of the rival's aims. Some hawks and doves recognize the problems in identifying the challenger's aims; they sometimes acknowledge their inability to do so with confidence. But it is still taken for granted that intentions can usually be known, and when not, an educated assessment is required.

The shared doctrinal logic of adversarial and conciliatory internationalism culminates in the matching up of the substance of policy with an opponent's aims and motivations. Strategic engagement entails tailoring policies to fit his hegemonic aspirations, implacable hostility, revisionist ambitions, opportunistic expansionism, legitimate grievances, defensive concerns, and/or security fears. The safest, indeed the only effective, security posture is shaped in accordance with a correct interpretation of the challenger's intentions. This is also to say—and is said by hawks and doves when they criticize each other—that if the mix of firm and flexible policies derives from a mistaken interpretation, the consequences will range from the ineffective, through the counterproductive, to the disastrous.

Characterizing hawks and doves as driven apart primarily by their differing interpretations of intentions is likely to encounter objections from both sides. It is sometimes said that adversarial policies derive at least as much from assessments of capabilities as of intentions; at the extreme, the latter are said to have practically no weight. Although intentions are crucial, the argument goes, sometimes they cannot be confidently interpreted, given the incentives and opportunities for disguising them. And unlike capabilities, they are subject to rapid change, as when a new leadership emerges overnight. Security policies are thus to be matched up with capabilities rather than intentions. To do so is also essential. When there is no doubting the challenger's capabilities for undertaking expansive actions, it is safest to assume the worst—that it could well be necessary to deter and defend against them.

It is one thing to acknowledge the problematics of ascertaining intentions. It is quite another to deny that adversarial policies are shaped by the possible presence of hostile intentions. To make policy "as if" these were present, to take the rival's aggressive inclinations as a "working premise," to prepare for "worst-case scenarios"—all this is certainly to tailor policies to hostile intentions. And it is to do so almost as closely as if intentions were confidently known. Moreover, the justification for worst-case thinking is manifestly incomplete without a recourse to intentions. Since doves are also well aware of the other side's capabilities, it is

not possible to account for hawkish worst-case thinking through reference to capabilities alone. This leaves intentions as the only other explanation for matching policies to the opponent's potentially threatening
means. Whether explicit or not, interpretations of the opponent's hostility and ambitions go a very long way in generating adversarial policies.

Conciliatory internationalism does not deny the derivation of reassuring policies from the challenger's grievances, defensive aims, and security
concerns. Yet dovish policies are sometimes also said to be shaped by the
limited applicability, questionable effectiveness, and the unintended consequences of military measures. Coercion and violence are especially difficult to calibrate, overly blunt means with a distinct tendency to backfire.
It is usually safer and surer to rely upon diplomatic, political, and economic measures, along with a willingness to work out compromise and
offers of accommodating carrots. On this understanding of conciliatory
doctrine, policy divisions are attributable to the doves' doubts and the
hawks' relative confidence in the effectiveness of forceful measures.

There is no denying this characterization of the dovish position as far
as it goes. However, it does not go far enough in addressing the bottom-
line issue, the reasons for questioning the utility of force. The singular
importance of intentions in conciliatory doctrine would have to be quali-
fied if these reasons involved only the relationship between the application of forceful measures and their expected results—if they revolved
around palpable limits and difficulties, such as the logistic problems of a
military intervention or gaps in the information that is needed to execute
a surgical bombing run. Without denying the import of these concerns,
more important considerations have to do with the other side's heart and
mind as these mediate his response. Whether force will succeed or fail is
first and foremost dependent upon the rival's intentions. It is unnecessary
or counterproductive when he is motivated by security fears, defensive
concerns, mistrust, and legitimate grievances—perhaps by any aims other
than those of an aggressive kind.

The centrality of intentions in shaping adversarial and conciliatory
policies is brought out by the issue that animated the military debate of
the 1980s: What kind of nuclear forces are needed to deter the Warsaw
Pact from exploiting its conventional advantages by attacking Western
Europe? Is retaliatory sufficiency, overall parity, or some degree of superiority needed? The issues debated were about capabilities—the significance of missile throw weights, the wartime sustainability of command
and control networks, the ability to communicate with missile-launching
submarines, the targetability of mobile missiles, and the survivability of
intelligence satellites during a protracted nuclear conflict. Yet hawks and
doves were not primarily driven apart by these military issues.

Whether it is possible to communicate with a submerged submarine,
for example, does say a great deal about the number of missiles that could

be fired at the Soviet Union. There is, however, a prior and deeper issue: What kind of threatened destruction is needed to deter the Soviets from attacking Western Europe? The purely military questions attain their salience only after this central one has been settled. Some may not come into play at all. And resolution of the issue does not hinge on capability and the utility of force, but on the Soviet leadership's aims, values, and priorities. Did it assign a higher value to its own survival, continuing control over the population, and the maintenance of great military might, or to the preservation of the country' population and industrial centers? The former answer pointed to the need for an advantaged war-fighting force with which to threaten thousands of missile sites, command bunkers, troop concentrations, military installations, and weapons factories. The latter answer allowed for a much smaller force capable of destroying a few hundred cities and industrial centers. Richard Betts has observed that "The physical balance of military forces should logically be estimated independently from beliefs about adversary intentions, but pessimism about technical stability tends to vary directly with pessimism about political stability. Those who see the Soviet Union as aggressive also tend to see the military balance as unfavorable, while those who see the Soviets' intentions as less malevolent and their political gains as less impressive have more confidence in Western capabilities."[5] In another analysis he was more specific: "Observers who assume Soviet malevolence focus on analyses that emphasize missile throw-weight and gross megatonnage (Soviet advantages); those who assume more benign Soviet intentions focus on analyses that emphasize missile accuracy and numbers of warheads (U.S. advantages)."[6]

All parts of both adversarial and conciliatory doctrine culminate in full-blown engagement—a purposeful, continuous, multifaceted, and effortful involvement with the challenger. With nearly all his expansive actions impinging adversely upon the nation's security, the threat must be actively addressed, the rival and the rivalry continuously managed. It is necessary not only to communicate with the contender, but to send messages that are sufficiently "forceful" so as to alter his aims. To do so successfully it is necessary to identify them, ideally by getting "into" his mind set. Security policies are then closely tailored to these understandings. Given this logic, it becomes readily understandable how those who subscribe to incompatible interpretations of the contender's intentions are driven to very different positions on the firmness-flexibility continuum.

II

Reversing the commonalities of adversarial and conciliatory engagement practically defines the central doctrinal and policy components of a national strategy. First and foremost, its minimal political-military activism translates into an exceptionally narrow security perimeter, the narrowest one that can provide for the nation's security. The opponent's actions in, around, and against this core perimeter are unacceptable; they are most certainly to be deterred and defended against. His possible and actual expansive actions outside it do not call for activist preparations and responses. There are no allies and clients to be defended, no threats of extended deterrence, interventions, negotiated settlements, military and economic assistance programs, and only a few arms control treaties.

The contours of the narrowest possible core perimeter are empirically—not dogmatically—determined on the basis of America's intrinsic and extrinsic security interests. The former include all that is most highly valued in and of itself. The latter take in the areas that are instrumental for the protection of these unrivaled intrinsic interests.

A state is included within the core perimeter on intrinsic grounds if its value approximates that which is accorded to the United States itself. Our attachments to it are sufficient to warrant great costs and known risks in warding off any threats to its security. The standard litmus test of a country's sufficiently high intrinsic value is the same one that is applied in identifying all other components and aspects of the nation's most highly valued security interests—the willingness to risk or to go to (nuclear) war on their behalf. And that willingness obtains over and above any contributions that such a country might make to the preservation of America's own security. We are prepared to risk war on its behalf even against a third state that is not threatening us. This is indeed a stringent standard, but an analytically, strategically, and politically appropriate one. To apply it is to conclude that there is probably no country that falls within the core perimeter on intrinsic grounds. Some may appear to do so. Canada, Great Britain, and Israel look to be the leading candidates. However, no more than a minority of Americans have valued the security of these countries anywhere nearly as much as that of the United States. Our willingness to defend them derives primarily from their instrumental, extrinsic security value as determined by the logic of strategic internationalism.

Thus on intrinsic grounds the core perimeter is limited to the continental United States, Alaska, Hawaii, Puerto Rico, several small U.S. islands in the Caribbean and the Pacific, American ships and planes in international waters and air space, and American citizens traveling and living abroad.

To circumscribe the core perimeter of a national strategy on extrinsic grounds is to identify the smallest one that can insure the security of the nation's most valued intrinsic interests. Delimiting it depends on the answers to two questions. Given an opponent's capabilities and advantages, to what extent is he able to realize any expansionist objectives in America's political-military absence? To what extent would these successes then infringe upon America's security? Insofar as the challenger is incapable of making significant gains despite our not opposing him, or insofar as expansionist successes do not have security-deflating consequences, the United States is strategically immune. To venture beyond the lines within which we are immune is unnecessary. It should be noted that in principle this formulation conforms to that of most strategic internationalists. They do not advocate our going abroad for security reasons beyond the point at which it is necessary and advantageous to do so—where the rival is unable to expand and where the gains would not detract from America's security. The radically different compass of a national and internationalist security perimeter derives from very different empirical conclusions regarding the extent of America's strategic immunity, at any one time and over the forseeable future.

As circumscribed here, the extrinsically derived security perimeter is yet narrower than that of the historical isolationists and many contemporary ones. Since the Monroe Doctrine, theirs has extended down the length of Latin America, included for reasons of military propinquity—in the belief that unfriendly forces in the Southern Hemisphere would threaten the Northern Hemisphere.[7] Here the core perimeter does not encompass the Caribbean islands, Central America, and South America. The only land areas it includes for extrinsic security reasons are Canada and Mexico. American ships and planes in international waters and air space are included as intrinsic interests. A related extrinsic interest is the free movement of all non-U.S. shipping to and from North America, which means passage through nearby waters (the Caribbean) and distant ones (the Persian Gulf).

Strategic nonengagement's central feature having been set out, it is appropriate to delineate its doctrinal rationale, the five strategic propositions that indicate how and why America's security is maximized by a minimal activism around the narrow core. They are summarized here along with the ways in which they fit together. Presenting them together underscores the comprehensiveness of the national design, the ways in which it addresses any and all kinds of security threats.

According to the first doctrinal tenet, America enjoys a privileged position in being strategically immune within the narrow security perimeter. Beyond it, a challenger's expansive territorial ventures and military improvements would fail to attain their immediate objectives and any successful ones would not have significant security-deflating consequences. Because of the diverse ways in which an opponent might put our security at risk, the comprehensive immunity concept is made more manageable by breaking it down into its component parts. The United States is shown to enjoy a high immunity ranking in terms of its insulation, invulnerability, impermeability, and imperviousness.

The meaning of the immunity concept can be highlighted metaphorically. A state is militarily, economically, and politically immune to a rival in the same ways that an individual is physiologically immune to certain bacteria and viruses. In both instances there is a potential threat. Yet the "foreign agents" do not detract from or endanger the body's physical well-being, political constitution, and economic good health. A state and an individual are immune to the extent that they are resilient or unsusceptible. The "attackers" fail to enter the national body or are rendered harmless if they do as the immunizing agents neutralize their adverse effects. The kinds of immunity that are relevant here parallel those that are inherited or acquired with a single inoculation, as opposed to frequent, costly, and painful injections.

Immunity-enhancing conditions of great scope and potency are necessary for a national strategy to be affordable and maximally effective. Yet their presence is by no means a sufficient reason to disengage. The United States could also capitalize upon its privileged position in mounting an overwhelming adversarial effort, diminishing the risks of an inordinately conciliatory one, or in adopting a centrist internationalism. The other four propositions are of a generalized kind; they indicate how and why national policies engender greater security for any strategically immune state than do the variants of strategic internationalism.

Turning to intentions, the second proposition offers a fundamental, decidedly debilitating critique of the strategic internationalism that is consistently and necessarily premised upon them. To tailor a strategy's overall hawkish-dovish thrust to an interpretation of the opponent's intentions as more or less aggressive or defensive is commonly problematic and overly risky. It is usually not possible to ascertain the challenger's aims with all that much confidence—not nearly enough to warrant the adoption of policies that would almost surely have security-deflating consequences if they were shaped in accordance with a mistaken interpretation. To be clear, this agnostic precept does not at all deny the need to address the opponent's intentions. A singular advantage of the national strategy is its ability to respond effectively to the entire spectrum of possible aims without assuming the validity of, or tailoring policies to, any one of them. The third proposition is premised upon the rival's decidedly aggressive aims, the fourth upon largely defensive ones, and the fifth allows for both possibilities. As such, national policies invariably match up with the contender's short- and long-term goals and their underlying motivations, in the present and for the future.

The third proposition refers to the rival's direct challenges to the core perimeter. It does so on the assumption that his intentions are hostile, hegemonic, or expansionist. The proposition also covers the case of a defensively inclined opponent whose insecurities have not been (fully) allayed by the national strategy. On either premise, it is at least as effective as adversarial engagement in warding off any and all unacceptable actions against the narrow core perimeter—be they economic competition and pressures, minor probes, deterrent challenges, coercive threats, or outright attacks. An adversarial internationalism featuring global alliances, frequent credibility-heightening exercises, major and minor interventions, nuclear superiority, and primacist economic and political strivings cannot improve upon a national strategy in these crucial respects, while detracting from our security in some basic, readily predictable ways.

The fourth tenet takes the challenger's intentions to be benign. Security concerns and fears are the primary determinant of its behavior toward the United States, possibly toward other countries as well. National policies are then maximally effective, much more so than activist conciliatory ones, in convincing such a rival that we are no more than a status quo power. They make for more "forceful," extensive, and "automatic" reassuring inactions. Defensively motivated threats to the core perimeter and expansive actions beyond it that relate to the United States are thus unnecessary. Although most bilateral and multilateral accords are rendered disadvantageous or superfluous, strategic nonengagement values the ones that are compatible and effective supplements to it.

The fifth doctrinal tenet addresses the ubiquitous possibilities of strategic mismanagement or inadvertence—those that are unforeseeable and foreseeable, the product of psychologically motivated errors and unmotivated cognitive ones, and those that can and cannot be controlled from the center. A national strategy is maximally effective in guarding against all types of strategic mismanagement, in negating inadvertent security deflations along each of the paths leading up to them. To return to the earlier metaphor, the health of an immune individual or nation is not guaranteed. It may be impaired by mistakenly conceived involvements, uncontrollable environments, and accidental interactions. These risks are truly negligible for a nonengaged America.

Most students of international politics appreciate the security dilemma, the common inability of states to protect themselves without detracting from or appearing to compromise the security of others. Military, political, and economic actions to bolster one state's security elicit another's improvements in an increasingly dangerous upward spiral; both states are compelled to respond after placing a conflictual interpretation upon the other's moves. The security dilemma may be structurally foreordained by geography and technology, comparable to a god-given Greek tragedy, or due to the biases and limitations of particular decision makers, as in the sinful stain of a Christian tragedy. Taking the five propositions together leads to the conclusion that a national strategy can radically alleviate the dilemma, far more so than any variant of strategic internationalism. Nonengagement offers the strategically immune state the most security whether the other side's intentions and "moves" are of the aggressive-defection or defensive-cooperation variety, whether it is eminently powerful or weak, whether the threat is immediate or potential, and whether it is of a military, economic, or political kind.

Despite the interrelatedness of the doctrinal tenets, the strategy need not be accepted or rejected in its entirety. As distinct propositions, any one of them should be amenable to revision in the face of analytical lapses, insufficient evidence, and neglected eventualities. Perhaps the greatest doubts about the strategy revolve around the past, present, and potential gaps in America's strategic immunity. But it should be possible to stop up any holes in the immunity-enhancing umbrella with specific, delimited activist measures rather than rejecting the strategy in toto. And if the scope and potency of the immunity-enhancing conditions are thought to have a moderate rather than a high ranking, it is still not necessary to forgo all of nonengagement's great advantages. As depicted in the previous section's strategic typology, the strategy of balanced engagement stands midway between the national strategy and adversarial and conciliatory internationalism. Had the United States adopted it, or were it to do so, the security perimeter would presumably include Western Europe, Japan, the Persian Gulf, and the Caribbean basin. Balanced engagement can also be adopted contingently and temporarily, as a way in which to test the immunity-enhancing umbrella in the course of fully disengaging.

Along with its minimal activism, the national strategy's other most general feature is its position around the midpoint of the firmness-flexibility continuum. Though not at all distinctive, less important than minimal activism, and partly flowing from the latter, it is nonetheless central to the strategy, most especially so in bolstering the security-enhancing promises of the third and fourth strategic propositions that were just set out. From their centrist vantage point on the firmness-flexibility dimension, national policies are intended to fulfill two objectives. They are to make for sufficient assertiveness and power to safeguard U.S. security interests, while providing for sufficient conciliation and accommodation to reassure opponents of our nonthreatening intentions. Unilateralism, which is regularly associated with adversarial policies alone, is not adversarial as part of a national strategy. For example, regarding the trade disputes with Europe and Japan that bear upon our potential security and immediate prosperity, the absence of allies facilitates the most effective kind of economic diplomacy, one that is both assertive and affirmative.[8]

While nonengagement is far less reliant upon communications with the rival than strategic engagement, it certainly does not negate the sending of crucial deterrent and reassuring messages. To a great extent the security of a nonengaged America depends upon both kinds of messages getting through to the rival. However, they take the form of minimally activist communications. On the deterrent side, there is the clear articulation of the lines that distinguish unacceptable actions from expansive ones. The message is underscored by the deployment of eminently powerful nuclear and conventional forces. The credibility of the threat does not rely upon a panoply of words, commitments, and actions, those that are designed to bolster a reputation for resolve over time and across space as the challenger extrapolates from the defense of interests beyond the core to commitments at the core. Instead of relying upon such a vast signaling exercise, credibility derives from what is, from the manifestly compelling attachments to our highest national values as these are embodied in the core perimeter. On the reassuring side, there is a demonstrably powerful self-denying message: No political-military obligations or interventions beyond the narrow core and no striving for offensive military advantages despite the unquestionable ability to undertake them.

A national strategy features a circumspect and contingent orientation toward security agreements. It obviates those that actively involve the United States beyond the territorial core or constrain the design of a maximally effective and distinctly defensive military configuration. However, other accords are not rejected because of distinctly hawkish attachments to unilateralism, the concerns about their allowing the contender a significant advantage, a consequential opportunity to cheat, or their fostering a lulling effect at home. These criticisms are not well founded. But nor are the positive, consequential results of the nearly two dozen political-military agreements signed by the United States since 1945 especially impressive.[9] They are yet less so compared to the promise of a national strategy. The reassurance of political-military agreements is rendered more or less superfluous by national policies that can accomplish far more in this regard. And with their being undertaken unilaterally, they are fully and consistently implemented, rather than depending upon an undependable mutuality. Still, nonengagement allows for and recognizes the contributions of certain accords. Of these, the 1968 Nuclear Nonproliferation Treaty is the most important, especially if its inspection requirements and procedures are markedly improved at the treaty's 1995 review conference. In fact, it could be characterized as globalizing nuclear nonengagement, and this without obligating U.S. actions against violators.

The deployment of military forces that are capable of deterring and defending while appearing nonthreatening is commonly considered to be inordinately difficult. The problems are central to the security dilemma: States cannot make themselves secure without simultaneously making others less so or, almost as important, appearing to threaten them. However, the dilemma's viselike grip can be released for a strategically immune America situated at great distances from any challengers, one whose security interests are circumscribed by an exceptionally narrow core perimeter.

The appropriate size, firepower, and costs of military forces for a nonengaged America turn out to conform to this rough rule of thumb: They constitute half of strategic internationalism's levels during the Cold War, the early post–Cold War years, and for the near-term future. Up to the collapse of the Soviet Union, isolationists alone advocated such radical defense reductions. With virtually no possibility of a large-scale war against any major Eurasian power, others have now come close to doing so—and this with regard to the planned 1997 Base Force levels, which already involve a 20 percent reduction from those of 1980 and 1990.

The sufficiency of a national military posture costing no more than $150 billion annually is underscored by several proposals in that range that include military missions extending well beyond the core perimeter. William Kaufmann and John Steinbruner propose a $161 billion defense budget that is to suffice for the protection of our security interests in and around U.S. territories, the Atlantic and Pacific sea-lanes, Panama and the Caribbean, north Norway, Central Europe, the Middle East, and South Korea.[10] According to two other assessments, military expenditures of $150 billion would include not only the $104 billion cost of defending something very much like the core perimeter outlined here; it would "still allow the United States to play a global role," including a variety of Third World interventions, a variant of the Desert Storm capability for insuring access to oil supplies, as well as substantial contributions to multilateral undertakings on behalf of international security.[11] Comparable proposals have been put forward by former CIA director William Colby and former defense secretaries Robert McNamara and James Schlesinger.[12]

The radical, 50 percent across-the-board, reduction may appear to err too far on the side of flexibility and conciliation, especially with respect to the Soviet-American rivalry. It does not. The $150 billion limit of a national military posture represents more than three times the past and present defense spending of any other country except for Russia, twelve times that of Iraq prior to the Persian Gulf War. It would easily leave the United States with the world's most powerful navy, in numbers of ocean-going ships, tonnage, firepower, and evasive and defensive capabilities—and would have done so during the Cold War. Conventional military forces are greatly advantaged in defending the core. They can capitalize upon the vast ocean distances that have if anything provided for more protection since the mid-twentieth-century advent of air power. And while nuclear-tipped missiles have obviously made for immeasurably greater vulnerability, it does not at all follow that a huge nuclear armory could mitigate it. In fact, this armory was mostly justified not in terms of basic deterrence, but with regard to the provision of extended deterrence for distant allies.

According to Earl Ravenal's design, a nonengaged America would have been fully protected against the Soviet threat and any current ones with the deployment of general-purpose forces comprising 1.2 million soldiers manning eight land divisions, twenty tactical air wing equivalents, and six aircraft carrier battle groups.[13] On Ted Carpenter's force sizing, a somewhat smaller deployment is sufficient, with no major power now challenging the United States.[14] Here the eight army and marine divisions feature a mix of heavy armor, light infantry, and airborne forces, plus the army, navy, and air force's special operations units. Half of the twenty air wing equivalents, each with more than seventy deployable aircraft, meet the services' highest air support standard of one hundred planes per land division. The other half can then be devoted to independent air-ground operations. Most of the strategic bomber force is also capable of dropping and launching conventional munitions. Each of the six aircraft carrier battle groups deploy some eighty planes, two missile-launching cruisers, two frigates, and two attack submarines.[15] Additional ships—destroyers, submarines, minesweepers, and supply and repair vessels—total close to two hundred.

These eminently powerful forces are sufficient for building up larger ones on the chance that they are needed, for contingencies requiring a rapid response, for guarding the sea-lanes, for attacking a rogue nuclear state threatening the United States, and for protecting American citizens abroad. Despite their impressive absolute and relative size, these forces form a distinctly defensive configuration. America's readily evident intrinsic and extrinsic interests extend into the vast ranges of several oceans, and the forces deployed on those oceans need not be part of an offensive design. They only became that with the Reagan administration's adoption of the provocative maritime strategy, the planned use of carrier battle groups to cut off Soviet submarines from deep Arctic waters during a crisis and to attack Soviet land bases in wartime.[16]

During the Cold War the United States deployed a huge nuclear force of nearly twelve thousand strategic weapons. Within the context of a national strategy, a force of about six thousand weapons would have best satisfied the requirements of deterrence, stability during a crisis, and limitation of damage to the United States in the event of war—all the more so on two further changes. Vulnerable land-based missiles would have been eliminated in favor of the dyad of submarine-launched missiles and standoff bombers carrying cruise missiles. The deterrent threat would not have been the hawkish one of attacking all military and leadership targets or the "dovish" one of destroying Soviet cities. The targets would have been limited to conventional military forces and installations situated at some distance from major population centers.[17] There is no doubt about the defensive distinctiveness of such a nuclear strategy. It would also have been much more effective than the alternatives as a credible deterrent and damage-limiting force in the event of war. Currently, in the absence of a major nuclear rival, there is relatively little strategic basis for deciding among deployment options ranging from thirty-five hundred to one thousand weapons. The number of three thousand proposed by isolationists would appear to be roughly appropriate within the context of national strategy.[18]

The issue of strategic defenses has recently gone through several phases. In 1983 President Reagan proposed the Strategic Defense Initiative (SDI) so as to make nuclear weapons "impotent and obsolete." Space-based defenses were to provide a fully protective umbrella, a veritable population shield. Many or most hawks embraced "Star Wars"; the doubters among them were not opposed to it in principle, but questioned its technical and financial feasibility. Nearly all doves subjected SDI to several additional criticisms. The testing and deployment of space-based defenses would make the Soviets unduly fearful of American strategic superiority, be seen to allow for an American first-strike with SDI defending against a ragged retaliatory attack, rule out negotiated reductions in offensive forces by subverting the Anti-Ballistic Missile Treaty that prohibits strategic defenses, and thereby bring on a new round of arms racing in offensive, defensive, or both types of weapons. These criticisms are well taken, but they need not be taken especially far in the context of a national strategy that is decidedly defensive to begin with. A nonengaged America might well have tested and deployed SDI without sharply increasing Soviet anxieties and mistrust. Having denied itself alliance outposts and cut its nuclear forces in half, it would not appear to be building defenses to gain a coercive advantage or a first-strike opportunity.

SDI lost most of its salience after 1986. Most hawks and all doves recognized that the design, development, and deployment problems could not be overcome. The enormously demanding, exquisitely fine-tuned weapon could never be fully tested, the Soviets could overwhelm it by building relatively cheap offensive missiles, and countermeasures and weapons were already available for getting through and under the defensive shield (e.g., low-trajectory, submarine-launched missiles). SDI was replaced on the policy agenda by a system providing for point defense rather than population defense. It was supported by many hawks as a way of improving upon the deterrent threat. The doves argued that protecting land-based ICBMs was unnecessarily provocative, and secondarily, that there were more efficacious and cost-effective means of doing so.

A national strategy turns this issue into a nonissue: Missile defenses are superfluous since nonengagement's strategic dyad does not include the land-based missiles that are to be protected.

At present, the issue of defenses centers around the building of an anti-ballistic missile system to protect the United States from an accidental or unauthorized launch and a limited salvo of up to two hundred warheads. Even its dovish opponents acknowledge that it is possible to guard against these risks by building a "thin" or "light" ground-based ABM system.[19] Although a nuclear device can always be smuggled into America or placed on a ship moored in our seaports, a thin ABM deployment would maximize the security of our very highest values. While non-engagement does as much as possible to insure that the United States is not the target of nuclear states and terrorists, there are no guarantees on this score or on the absence of an unintended or "mad" launch. A thin ABM system being thoroughly defensive, Russia should be willing to renegotiate the 1973 ABM treaty that prohibits its deployment.[20] In 1992 Moscow and Washington set up a high-level group to develop an acceptable treaty revision that allows for ground- but not space-based interceptors.

A national strategy does not entail any less of a commitment to research and development than strategic internationalism. Without it there is no knowing how science and technology can make for yet greater security, and it is the only way to guard against others forging beyond us in ways that could detract from our security. The absence of a major rival suggests two changes from past practices.[21] The proportion of funds devoted to basic technology should be significantly increased relative to those assigned to weapons systems. And promising weapons should not be taken beyond the development or testing stages unless they provide for a manifest military need or a distinctly defensive advantage over current ones.

These then are the major policy outlines of a national strategy as it would have been practiced in the recent past and as it promises to maximize our security and extrasecurity values over the discernible future.

III

Moving well back from nonengagement's contemporary contours, this section considers its antecedents from the founding of the Republic to circa 1950, when the old isolationism died out. The centerpiece of isolationism, the unnecessary hazard of going abroad, has remained the same, while the strategy has responded to great changes in the world and America's position within it. The isolationists' security doctrine, policies, and critiques of internationalism have been consistently reasoned and reasonable. At the least, this revisionist interpretation should cut loose the contemporary version of strategic isolationism from the influential prejudices against its historical antecedents.

Nearly all historians and political scientists who have examined historical isolationism assess its two periods differently. The consensus is extraordinarily positive regarding isolationist policies from the late eighteenth to the late nineteenth century: They maximized the nation's security and minimized the risks in providing for it. The consensus view takes a negative turn circa 1900, surely one of the very sharpest U-turns in American historical and political scholarship. Twentieth-century isolationism and its advocates have been characterized as irrelevant, complacent, naive, immature, traditionalist, unthinking, utopian, irresponsible, and dangerous. Most recently, Terry Deibel maintains that "The oldest approach devised by Americans to serve their physical security seems hardly worthy of being called a strategy at all." Isolationism was a "realistic strategy when risks from overseas threats were slight," but "Americans failed to abandon it when the conditions required for its success disappeared at the beginning of the twentieth century," after which it became a "dangerous illusion."[22]

The counsels of strategic prudence in George Washington's Farewell Address, heavily shaped by Alexander Hamilton and secondarily so by James Madison, did not emanate from complacency about the country's security or from some naive view of international politics. The isolationist injunction was the product of a comparison, a studied appreciation of the fit between American interests and international realities.[23] It was also a forthright expression of realist thinking.[24]

In Washington's stentorian words, "Europe has a set of primary interests, which to us have none, or very remote relation. Hence she must be engaged in frequent controversies, the cause of which are essentially foreign to our concerns. Hence, therefore, it must be unwise for us to implicate ourselves, by artificial ties, in the ordinary vicissitudes of her politics, or the ordinary combinations and collisions of her friendships, or enmities." There is no need for, or advantage to be gained from, noncommercial involvements with Europe. Given America's "distant and detached position" and a "respectably defensive posture," it can well afford to remain disengaged. America can "defy material injury from external annoyance" and "cause the neutrality we may at any time resolve upon to be scrupulously respected." Washington did not expect that belligerent states would somehow be in short supply, but "under the impossibility of making acquisitions upon us, they will not lightly hazard the giving us provocation."[25]

Washington could then ask rhetorically: "Why forego the advantages of so peculiar a situation? Why, by interweaving our destiny with that of any part of Europe, entangle our peace and our prosperity in the toils of European ambition, Rivalship, Interest, Humor, or Caprice?" Why not adopt the appropriate triumvirate of security principles for capitalizing upon America's situation, those of unilateralism, conflict avoidance, and defensive preparation? "The Great Rule of Conduct for us, in regard to foreign nations is in extending our commercial relations, to have with them as little *political* connection as possible. . . . Tis our true policy to steer clear of permanent alliances." Conflict and war are to be avoided by policies of "Harmony, liberal intercourse with all nations . . . [Even] our commercial policy should hold an equal and impartial hand . . . diffusing and diversifying by gentle means the streams of commerce, but forcing nothing." It is, of course, still necessary to protect the United States and its commercial rights. "Taking care always to keep ourselves, by suitable establishments, on a respectably defensive posture, we may safely trust to temporary alliances for extraordinary emergencies," while choosing "peace or war, as our interests guided by justice shall counsel." On occasion war might be necessary, but only in the manifest absence of any other acceptable recourse.

Washington's measured self-confidence was not intended to disguise the facts of America's weaknesses—its internal divisions, minor military capabilities, and encirclement by Europe's colonial outposts. But without ignoring them, he fully expected the country to realize the full benefits of his counsels in a "period not far off" if only "we remain one People, under an efficient government." A year earlier, he was yet more optimistic in maintaining that "twenty years of peace, with such an increase of population and resources as we have a right to expect, added to our remote situation from jarring British power, will in all probability enable us, in a just cause, to bid defiance to any power on earth."[26]

Washington's counsels closely guided the United States for a century. They were considered on a par with the Constitution and the Declaration of Independence in their political wisdom. The "great rule" of political-military detachment served as the "country's most fundamental theory of foreign policy." Not a single administration throughout the nineteenth century had reason to diverge from it, and were the temptation present, none dared to act upon it.[27] The peaceful acquisitions, imperialism, and military expansionism of the nineteenth century, involving France, Spain, Britain, Mexico, and Native Americans, were obviously of enormous significance. But they were continental, exclusively North American actions. Up to to 1861 U.S. foreign policy was governed by the "absorption" of neighboring territories. In contrast, Washington and his successors warned against the security risks of becoming involved *overseas*, in European affairs, not against the material ambitions and beliefs of an expanding settler society in Manifest Destiny.

Toward the end of the nineteenth century the United States attained the demonstrably impressive resources and potential capacities of a major power: a quasi-continental territory, a large population, abundant natural resources, extensive commercial wealth, great industrial capabilities, and advanced military technology. It began to act like a major power with the building of a world-class navy, war with the "decrepit" Spanish empire over Cuba, followed by the annexations of the Philippines, Hawaii, and a few small Pacific islands.

According to the advocates of these first internationalist ventures, an America that did not actively seek to protect its interests would only encourage and enable other states—a newly powerful Germany and Japan in particular—to put them at risk. Although the putative British threat before 1898 was supplanted by good relations after then, Britain was losing its outright naval predominance, and the United States was no longer anything like an infant country dependent on others. The acquisition of defensive outposts in the Pacific was necessary to protect trade routes, insure the open door to China, and maintain the country's freedom of action. According to Theodore Roosevelt, Alfred Thayer Mahan and other naval strategists, and the commercial expansionists who advanced these arguments, naval stations were needed at Pearl Harbor, Midway, Guam, Wake Island, and the Philippines—where military actions at the cost of five thousand American deaths put down a hostile population and an armed independence movement. The twentieth-century globe was shrinking rapidly. As Theodore Roosevelt told Congress, "The increasing interdependence and complexity of international political and economic relations render it incumbent on all civilized and orderly powers to insist on the proper policing of the world."[28]

The isolationist critique was forcefully presented by an impeccably respectable coalition featuring William James, Mark Twain, William Dean Howells, Samuel Gompers, William Graham Sumner, Andrew Carnegie, William Jennings Bryan, and former president Grover Cleveland. It was organized into the Anti-Imperialist League, formed in the aftermath of the Spanish-American War as the country's first organized interest group devoted exclusively to foreign affairs. The isolationists maintained that expansionist ventures in the Far East would not promote the country's security, but rather embroil it in a military competition for empire with the European powers. Given America's favored geographic position, annexations would break the country's "ocean belt of security." Placing the flag at a great distance from its shores would make America vulnerable to intimidation or attack. For Carl Schurz, the reforming Republican senator from Missouri, to engage in overseas expansion was to surrender our major noninterventionist benefits. "In our present condition we have over all the great nations of the world one advantage of incalculable advantage. We are the only one not under any necessity of keeping up a large armament either on land or water for the security of its possessions, the only one that can turn all the energies of its population to productive employment, and the only one that has an entirely free hand. This is a blessing . . . [that] should not lightly be jeopardized."[29]

These isolationist arguments were consistently rejected in scholarship after 1950. Robert Osgood's major work on the idealist and realist traditions in American foreign policy argues that isolationists after 1900 "largely failed to make a mature adjustment" to changing realities.[30] Those realities appear on the first page of Foster Rhea Dulles's history of *America's Rise to World Power: 1898–1954*. By the beginning of the twentieth century "a rapidly contracting world, impending shifts in the European balance of power, and the growth of American economic and industrial strength created a situation that made impossible a continued aloofness from international affairs."[31] According to Selig Adler, the historian who drew the most detailed and unflattering portrait of the isolationists, it was not at all accidental that the first wave of internationalism appeared circa 1900. It was a response to the power shift toward America, the German challenge to Britain's preeminent position in Europe and on the oceans that had previously provided for America's safety, and Japan's victory over Russia, which marked the beginning of the end of European dominance in Asia. Adler contrasted Theodore Roosevelt's "realistic insights" with his isolationist contemporaries' naive and irresponsible views of international affairs, their "mood of self-complacency."[32]

These years did witness major changes. However, they did not require or justify the rejection of strategic isolationism. The new realities did not put America's strategic immunity at risk. Britain lost its unchallenged naval dominance, which thereby cut back on our free security in the Western Hemisphere. Yet if this gap was precarious, it was already filled by Roosevelt's "great white fleet," which if necessary, could have been further expanded. In fact, the changing technology of warfare made a challenge to the Western Hemisphere yet more difficult. On the basis of data that were then publicly available, it "simply could not occur."[33] Steam-powered battleships with their fueling and service requirements reduced naval cruising ranges and imparted a defensive advantage to the U.S. fleet, as did the complexities of moving mechanized armies. Germany and Japan had become major military powers, and their trade with China was expanding. But the China trade never had more than minor commercial significance for the United States, and by 1900 the economy was actually far less dependent upon trade than during the golden age of isolationism.

The United States certainly acquired the geographic, demographic, industrial, and technological resources of a major power. Yet how does it follow that these endowments somehow *require* a state to take up the activist mantle of strategic internationalism? The internationalists of the time and their subsequent scholarly defenders voiced a truly paradoxical argument: The resources of a great power make for constraint rather than autonomy, the need for effortful involvements rather than (more) safety at home. It is one thing for a status quo state to exercise its newfound power when actually threatened by others. It is quite another to do so reflexively, to ignore the ways in which greater capabilities enhance the country's strategic immunity along with the long-standing conditions that still insure it. Theodore Roosevelt was wrong in flatly asserting what became the conventional internationalist wisdom: "We have no choice as to whether or not we shall play a great part in the world. All that we can decide is whether we shall play it well or ill."[34]

There is, of course, a very strong association between great power and widespread external involvements. But apropos of America during the early part of the twentieth century, the connections probably had relatively little to do with the realities of national security. They were largely cultural connections—cultural insofar as power resources were translated into activist power relations via the unquestioned application of international norms and foreign policy conventions.

Great power endows nations with great potential status in their own eyes and those of others. According to convention, its full realization requires an internationalist strategy. Widespread vital and lesser interests, order-maintaining responsibilities, and forceful policing ventures are necessary demonstrations of high standing, of well-deserved accreditation. An activism that is traditionally quite simply expected of a powerful state is not part of a strategically respectable, reasoned internationalism. In fact, it allows internationalists to be depicted as "unthinking traditionalists." There is a close association between the power of states to affect remote international outcomes and their perceived interest in doing so. What may even be acknowledged as distant threats to a powerful state's security elicit immediate, effortful responses. But this could be mainly due to the ability to do something about them; policy is driven by available capabilities rather than considered security concerns. Bernard Brodie concluded that the United States has acted like a world power since 1900 for just this reason—because it has had the necessary capabilities, simply because it "feels itself able to do something effective about a (security) threat that remains as yet indirect or remote."[35]

Of the substantial majority who favored America's intervention in the war to make the "world safe for democracy," only a minority maintained that a German victory would seriously impinge upon the nation's security. The immediate, most widely supported interventionist cause was not widely thought to bear upon it. Germany's turn to unrestricted submarine warfare—its desperate gamble to cut off American shipping to Britain and France and thereby defeat them before U.S. forces could take the field in 1918—was seen as an unacceptable challenge to our neutral rights, national honor, principled commitment to the freedom of the seas, and the responsibility for upholding the latter as the country with the world's third largest navy.

The chief hawk, Senator Henry Cabot Lodge, laid out the security argument for intervention as early as 1915. He feared that "unarmed, unready, undefended, we offer a standing invitation to aggression and attack." Harkening back to his position of twenty years earlier, Lodge maintained that the "ocean barrier which defended us in 1776 and 1812 no longer exists. Steam and electricity have destroyed it."[36] The isolationists rejected the security argument for intervention by underscoring the continued salience of great oceanic distances, America's overwhelming defensive power, and thus the absence of a threat in the event of a German victory. The submarine attacks were said to have been brought on by the overt American tilt toward Britain and France. Along with most of the internationalists, they viewed the shipping losses as having little tangible importance for the United States. Besides, U.S. naval forces alone could have done what they actually did in destroying the U-boats without sending ground troops to Europe.

In hindsight, intervention could have made a significant security contribution only on one possible scenario. In the absence of U.S. expeditionary forces there was the distinct possibility that the 1918 German offensive would have reached Paris. This victory would have ended the war, followed by a dictated peace settlement that insured German preeminence in Europe, which would then have endangered a well-prepared America. In the actual scenario, America's intervention did nothing to constrain—indeed, by moving Germany toward unconditional surrender it allowed for—the harsh terms of the Versailles peace treaty, which helped bring on the rise of Hitler and World War II. Taking the story one step further, it is often said that the interwar period would have turned out differently had the isolationists not prevented the United States from joining the League of Nations after the war. This claim is doubly problematic. The internationalists of a balance-of-power persuasion, led by Senator Lodge, contributed at least as much to the League's rejection as the isolationists. And considering Britain's ambivalence toward Hitler, along with Britain and France's deep reluctance to fight another devastating war, it is not at all clear that America as a member of the League would have made a telling difference.

The isolationists who continue to be held in worst repute are, of course, the opponents of American involvement in the late 1930s and intervention during the European war years of 1939–41. In Hans Morgenthau's judgment, "isolation was [seen to be] a natural state and only needed to be left undisturbed in order to continue forever. Conceived in such terms, it was the very negation of foreign policy." Isolationists were "oblivious to political reality"[37] It was illusionary to believe that Nazi Germany was not a great threat to our security given its expansionist intentions and capabilities. It could only be warded off by becoming a full belligerent after 1939. Otherwise Britain and the USSR would have been defeated. Dominating all of Europe, Hitler would then have further enlarged his huge war machine, established bridgeheads in South America, and then moved against the United States.

The isolationist position hinged primarily upon the country's "impregnability." By virtue of distance, economic resources, and armaments, neither aggressive expansionism nor war in Europe would put the country's security at risk. Writing as the country's foremost historian, in *Giddy Minds and Foreign Quarrels* Charles Beard concluded that without any direct military threat to the North American continent George Washington's concept of defensive security remained singularly persuasive. "Not until some formidable European power comes into the western Atlantic, breathing the fire of aggression and conquest, need the United States become alarmed about the ups and downs of European conflicts, intrigues, aggressions, and war." According to the politically prominent America First Committee, the country is so invulnerable and powerful that no foreign power, no group of powers, can successfully attack a *prepared* America.[38] Thousands of miles of ocean, naval superiority in our home waters, the industrial capacity to outbuild other countries, an air force and navy that make the transport of huge forces across the ocean exceptionally problematic, and the creation of an army that could defend both coasts simultaneously—these were more than adequate safeguards. Charles Lindbergh convincingly showed that the emergence of air power had actually buttressed America's defensive position in North and South America. Bombers could start attacking German troop transports a thousand miles from U.S. shores.

Many isolationists doubted that the great German war machine would succeed in conquering all of Europe. They were duly impressed with what Germany could not do. Despite its control of most of Europe by 1940 it was still unable to breach the narrow English Channel to attack England. And if U.S. security were somehow challenged, if it ever became necessary to defend America, the isolationists were at one in thinking that this could best be done from a position of strength, from around its own well-protected waters and shores, where its military superiority would be overwhelming and the enemy's military might was sharply circumscribed by geography. These geostrategic advantages and defensive capabilities would be fretted away by becoming involved in a European war. In 1941 the president of the University of Chicago rejected the argument that the United States should fight now, that if we waited any longer Britain would be lost and America would have to face the world on its own. For Robert Hutchins the argument was untenable because it rested "on a pyramid of assumptions, hypotheses, and guesses." They run through the fall of Britain and the British empire, the survival of the present totalitarian rulers into the postwar period, their then wanting to make war on the United States, their being in a position to do so rather than having to hold down the conquered nations, and their being able to attack us. The latter issue would not be decided, as President Roosevelt and many other internationalists repeatedly insisted, by the "flying time between Africa and Brazil, or Europe and America. . . . The issue is what will be at the western end of the line? This will depend on our moral and military preparedness."[39]

At a minimum, these are surely more than illusionist claims. In chapter 4 it is seen that Germany's aggressive, hegemonic aims could not have been confidently known prior to six months before the beginning of the war. All internationalists allow that America would only have been threatened after the defeat of Britain and Russia. That they would not have been defeated—the most questionable isolationist claim—can actually be well supported. Germany would not have been victorious in America's absence as a full belligerent despite some telling facts. The alliance with Italy was cemented and Austria and Czechoslovakia were incorporated into the Third Reich before World War II. By the time of Pearl Harbor, Germany was in control of France, Belgium, the Netherlands, Denmark, Norway, nearly all of Eastern Europe, and the western (industrialized) parts of the USSR. The British Expeditionary Force had been roundly defeated on the continent, its weapons left behind at Dunkirk. The Red Army had experienced a series of costly defeats and retreats. By December 1941 Germany had failed in only one regard. It did not gain control of the air over England.

The case for Germany's conquest of all of Europe had the United States not come to the rescue rests upon these facts as of 1941. However, the salient year is 1942. The decisive question is how and why the Nazi war machine was actually stopped. Could it be that American belligerency did not play a significant part, perhaps none at all?

Bruce Russett has made this argument fully and directly: "Hitler had already lost his gamble to control Europe" by the time Pearl Harbor brought us into the war. On the Western front, Germany's failure to defeat the Royal Air Force in the Battle of Britain was crucial. The invasion of England was put off, and not just temporarily, since the British air force would first have had to be destroyed. By December 1941 Britain was producing its own and receiving more than enough aircraft, ships, armored vehicles, and artillery from the United States to protect herself. In 1940 it was already building more aircraft than Germany and deployed the world's largest navy. On the Eastern front, Germany's surprise attack along with its far better leadership and organization produced the stunning Soviet defeats of 1940 and 1941. But by late 1941 Germany's early advantages had lost their sway; outright Soviet superiority in troops, tanks, and planes became dominant. The Germans failed to capture Moscow, the lines held, and the infamous Russian winter came into play. "Looking back," Russett sees "that *this* was in fact the hinge of fate; the more visible turning point a year later (Germany's costly defeat at Stalingrad) was more nearly the outward sign of a predetermined shift." And even if Stalingrad was the real turning point that placed the military initiative in Soviet hands, the U.S. war effort cannot be credited with any direct assistance or in drawing significant German forces away from the Eastern front.[40]

Many isolationists acknowledged that neither Britain nor Russia could have held off Germany without the sizable amounts of U.S. military and economic aid that were provided under the armed neutrality legislation. This fits with Russett's conclusion: Britain and Russia would have survived if the United States had limited itself to "twilight belligerence." Instead of a German victory, there would have been a stalemate. It is not necessary to speculate about its contours, such as the degree of mutual exhaustion, the geographical lines of division in Eastern Europe, and the emergence of an informal truce or peace settlement. For whatever the specifics of the stalemate, neither South America nor the United States would have been imperiled by a Germany that was not only worn down, but penned in both in the East and West.

The isolationists' confidence in the great Atlantic barrier is clearly supported by the noncrossing and crossing of the English Channel. When a Germany in control of continental Europe could not breach it, surely there was no way for its forces to cross thousands of miles of ocean to threaten a many times over more formidable opponent than Great Britain. The allies' Normandy invasion succeeded only after creating a huge supply base in close-by southern England, winning control of the air, and completely dominating the seas. Satisfying these conditions against a fully prepared America across four thousand miles of ocean would have been many orders of magnitude more demanding.

The critics of isolationism neglect the Pacific side of World War II. Its origins cannot be used to fault the isolationists. The attack on Pearl Harbor was prompted by policies of deterrence and compellence that were opposed by the isolationists who knew of them and those who were suspicious of the Roosevelt administration's involvements. Japan's decision for war was a calculated gamble on the least bad option, given its irreducible aims and Washington's demands, coercive actions, and threats.

Japan was indeed intent upon expanding into Southeast Asia. This was the one way for it to become self-sufficient in rice, minerals, and especially oil, and to become a world power, the military equal of the United States and the Soviet Union in Asia. Japan's hopes for moving into Southeast Asia without prompting American intervention on behalf of the British, French, and Dutch colonies ran up against Washington's security concerns. More or less explicit deterrent threats were laid down by establishing military ties with the colonial powers, supplying munitions and arms to the colonies, and by keeping the fleet closer to them at Pearl Harbor rather than at its usual West Coast ports. Washington also sought to deny Japan the core of its East-Asian Co-Prosperity Sphere, which it had already acquired, attempting to compel an evacuation from those parts of China that had been conquered during almost ten years of war. U.S. compellence aims—and deterrent signaling—were pursued by embargoing scrap iron and the oil shipments that made up 80 percent of Japan's fuel supplies, freezing Japanese assets in the United States, and by refusing to negotiate with Tokyo until it had agreed to a troop withdrawal from China.

Most members of the Roosevelt administration appreciated the provocativeness of the threats. They were laid down mainly as a bluff, since the administration was not at all optimistic about the country's willingness to go to war with Japan. Yet Tokyo took them most seriously. After agonizing over their alternatives for two years, the Japanese decided upon war with the United States as a desperate solution. It has been compared to a risky medical operation that alone might save a patient with a threatening illness. For Tokyo knew that the war would be lost unless a settlement was negotiated within a year of its inception.[41]

Rather than adding anything to the anti-isolationist interpretation of U.S. policy in the years before World War II, the Pacific side of the story brings out the isolationists' prescience in predicting that U.S. demands and pressures would bring on a war with Japan. It also brings out the potential miscalculations and dangers of adversarial engagement. Roosevelt erred in "not fully recognizing how American steadfastness would provoke rather than deter the Japanese."[42] The events leading up to Pearl Harbor demonstrate "how a policy of deterrence can fail even if the force capabilities are robust and the threats are credible . . . The Tokyo government believed that the United States *might* be persuaded to accept a negotiated settlement (after the start of hostilities) rather than a total war. But this assessment was more a hope than an expectation, and Japanese leaders chose to attack the United States despite being highly pessimistic about the prospects of victory."[43] In short, as a principle cause of the war, interventionism backfired.

The isolationists who died out politically around 1950 were criticized as severely as those of the interwar years. The very idea of strategic isolationism was seen as patently deficient, egregiously so, in an interdependent world whose West European and American centers were sorely threatened by the USSR.[44] The isolationists were depicted as blind to these self-evident facts due to their unthinking traditionalism, as having a "fixation" upon ideas dating back over 150 years, as clinging "tenaciously to a faith in the unchangeability of our changing world."[45] George Washington's word's were said to be "sanctified and encrusted with tradition until they were no longer 'counsels of prudence.' They were hardened into iron rules of conduct." Kenneth Thompson enlarged upon this charge in disparaging the substance of isolationist doctrine and analysis as no more than a central idea, that of national autonomy, retaining "command of our fortunes," and "the free hand," furthered by "creeds and dogmas" such as "noninterference in European affairs," "avoidance of joint action," and "insulation against entanglement." Instead of being derived from consistent first-order principles attuned to the vicissitudes of international politics, strategic detachment was the product of preciously little ordered analysis. "Seldom has the isolationist proceeded from an objective appraisal of our vital interests, distribution of power in the world, and the resulting threat to American security."[46]

While fully consistent with the Farewell Address, the isolationist critique of American globalism during the early postwar years did not simply repeat the old arguments. They were revised and expanded in response to the new conditions in a reasoned and plausible manner. Because of the nation's impregnability, Soviet limitations, and possibly Soviet intentions, we could well forgo the containment of Moscow and its communist offshoots. To try to police the world was fraught with security risks, as well as counterproductive in exacerbating the Soviet-American conflict. The nation's capabilities were also decidedly inadequate for the task.

America's impregnability was said to have remained intact after 1945 notwithstanding the rapid reduction in our conventional land forces. Manifest superiority in strategic air and naval power was more than adequate to guarantee control over both oceans, rendering impossible any significant threat to the Western Hemisphere. And there was the additional check provided by the atomic arsenal and its ability to destroy the Soviet war machine before it could be employed against the United States. While some isolationists saw the Soviet Union as capable of overrunning Western Europe, they thought it foolhardy to dissipate America's power by trying to extend defense perimeters across the Atlantic. Given its geostrategic and military advantages, U.S. defenses should be concentrated in the Western Hemisphere.

Containment policies could also be set aside due to Soviet limitations. Where, it was asked, is the evidence to suggest that a communist-dominated government in Greece would be able to extend communism into other parts of the Mediterranean or spread confusion and disorder throughout the Middle East? Soviet expansion would probably succeed at the outset, yet the likely targets of further aggression would thereby be put on warning and probably balance against Moscow. Nor would the extension of Moscow's influence and domination redound to its great benefit. The communist world could be expected to fracture with the addition of nationalist, difficult-to-control Marxist regimes and movements. Yugoslavia and the Chinese communists had already refused to accept Stalin's directives. Client states would find communism's totalitarian ideology unacceptable. Soviet military power and economic resources would waste away in maintaining an empire in the face of national resistance and localized revolts. On this analysis, a few isolationists even discerned the USSR's eventual collapse as a world power.[47]

Consistently staving off expansionist successes was unnecessary, and we were incapable of doing so given our distant geographic position and much smaller conventional capabilities than those of the USSR and Marxist movements in the Third World. Senator Robert A. Taft, "Mr. Republican" and the most prominent isolationist, was not entirely averse to warding off communist aggression. However, a state with 6 per cent of the world's population "cannot send armies to block a Communist advance in every far corner of the world." A land war in Asia was entirely out of the question; even a successful outcome would result in America's "complete exhaustion" because it was so greatly outnumbered. In Taft's oft echoed words, "Nothing can destroy this country except the over-extension of our resources." Former president Hoover maintained that we could not keep a foothold in both Europe and Asia; to fight wars on the European and Asian mainlands would eventuate in the country's "exhaustion." The Western Hemisphere was to serve as the "Gibraltar of Western Civilization."[48]

If America did underwrite widespread defense commitments, they would expand and exacerbate the rivalry, bringing on minor and major wars by way of provocativeness and the inadvertence and willfulness of allies. Interference in Eastern Europe, aid to Greece and Turkey, and the Truman Doctrine's assertion of global responsibilities all bore too great a resemblance to the policies that had brought on the war with Japan. The specific risks included Syria, Iraq, Palestine, India, China, Korea, as well as Eastern and Western Europe. Just as Washington would consider Soviet political, economic, or military involvements in Latin

America unacceptable, Moscow would react comparably to U.S. interference in Eastern Europe, as many isolationists foresaw. Taft maintained that if "we assume a special position in Greece and Turkey, we can [no] longer reasonably object to the Russians continuing their dominance in Poland, Yugoslavia, Rumania, and Bulgaria." Aiding the anticommunist Greek guerrillas might lead Moscow to go to war, "just as we might be prompted to go to war if Russia tried to force a Communist government on Cuba." Some isolationists argued that rather than being inexorably expansionist, Moscow was consolidating the sphere of influence in Eastern Europe that was assigned to it at the Yalta conference.[49]

Taft made the most comprehensive case against the North Atlantic Treaty. He claimed that Russia was not bent upon military aggression. Not having attacked a prostrate Europe soon after 1945, it most probably never intended to do so. In the 1949 Senate debate on the treaty he characterized it as provocative. "Every good defense includes elements of offense. We cannot have an adequate armament for defense which cannot be converted overnight into a weapon of offense . . . no matter how defensive an alliance may be, if it carries the obligation to arm it means the building up of competitive offensive armaments. This treaty, therefore, means inevitably an armament race, and armament races in the past led to wars." He warned that the Soviets could only view the alliance and the stationing of American soldiers in Europe as an attempt to encircle and destroy them, as "ringing them about with armies for the purpose of taking aggressive actions when the time comes." Moreover, the Atlantic alliance would involve America "in every cloud which crosses the political sky in Europe, in every incident which could be the cause of war." To allow the alliance to vitiate the "free hand" in deciding whether to go to war required an astounding faith in the judgment of eleven other nations.[50]

Rather than being "fixated" upon the Farewell Address, post-1945 isolationism featured an immediately textured relevance and considerable prescience. None of its security arguments and prognostications have been vitiated by subsequent development. Most of them are amply supported in the next five chapters.[51]

Chapter III

AMERICA'S STRATEGIC IMMUNITY

A NATIONAL STRATEGY begins with a general statement and a specific question. To the extent that a country—any county—is strategically immune it can well afford to dispense with its activist security policies. What is the narrowest security perimeter that makes for America's strategic immunity, that which safely allows it to forego political-military involvements beyond the perimeter?

The strategic immunity concept is encompassing in its scope and diversity. Just as there is no shortage of health-threatening bacteria and viruses, there are numerous military, geostrategic, economic, and political challenges—aggressively and defensively motivated—that could threaten the nation's immunity. Breaking down this concept analytically helps insure that all the potentially threatening actions of all opponents will be identified, that none will escape the finer mesh of its component parts. Being more precise and more manageable, they also facilitate a systematic assessment of America's greater or lesser immunity. And if it turns out that there are some holes in one or another panels of the country's immunizing umbrella, these can be repaired without collapsing an otherwise perfectly good form of protection.

A country's strategic immunity is broken down into four components by first distinguishing between the rival's attempts to expand his space and to expand his muscle. Territorially, he may try to extend his span of influence and control over other countries. Militarily, he could attempt to build up his armed forces. One type of expansive action could, of course, be used to make gains with regard to the other, yet this commonly used distinction is fundamental and reasonably clear. Given all the uses to which territorial expansionism can be put, along with military improvements they exhaust all but one kind of potentially threatening actions—the economic ones involving trade and finance that might detract from our material well-being, if not also our military security. As it relates to Japan and Europe this possibility is taken up in chapter 5 when critiquing America's primacist strivings—the aim of remaining number one in the world militarily, politically, and economically—and in chapter 9's discussion of trade relations.

The opponent's expansive actions are also distinguished according to their consequences. Immunity obtains insofar as they fail to attain their immediate territorial or military aims, or any successful ones do not have

EXPANSIVE ACTION OUTCOME

	Failure	Inconsequential Success
Territorial Extensions	Insulation	Invulnerability
Force Improvements	Impermeability	Imperviousness

EXPANSIVE
ACTION
TYPE

Figure 2. An Analytic Breakdown of Strategic Immunity

significant security-deflating consequences. For example, a challenger does not succeed in its attempt to gain control over Persian Gulf oil, or its success in doing so does not detract from America's economic security.

These two distinctions are brought together in figure 2. The types of expansive actions are located on the vertical axis, their outcomes on the horizontal one. Any country's strategic immunity is seen to depend upon its insulation, invulnerability, impermeability, and imperviousness. (These abstract categories may seem analytically overblown, but each needs to encompass a diversity of actual and possible actions and outcomes.) A state is insulated insofar as the rival's efforts to extend his territorial sphere of influence-control prove to be unsuccessful. It is invulnerable to the extent that successful geographic extensions do not have a security-deflating impact, either in impairing its deterrent-defensive capacities for protecting the core or its economic good health. A country is impermeable if the opponent's force additions and improvements do not translate into superiority. They do not give him a quantitative or qualitative advantage, either strategically or conventionally. And it is impervious when the contender cannot exploit the military imbalance. His bigger and/or better armed forces are neither effective for purposes of coercion nor for fighting in and around the core.

According to the national strategy's *first doctrinal tenet*, the United States has been and will continue to be strategically immune into the foreseeable future within and around the narrow core perimeter whose North American and oceanic bounds were outlined in the previous chapter. The encompassing scope and great potency of numerous immunity-enhancing conditions make for a high ranking with regard to each of its four components. The need for activist adversarial and conciliatory efforts is sharply curtailed since America enjoys a great deal of extra insurance; in most (not all) respects it is doubly immune in that a rival's expansive actions are unlikely to attain their objectives and any successful ones are not about to detract from the nation's security. The immunity-enhancing umbrella may not be fully leakproof, part of the case for one of its analytical panels may be unpersuasive. However, the country would still be effectively immune unless the *same* territorial or military ventures succeeded and proved to be consequential.[1]

When laid alongside Cold War internationalism, the first doctrinal proposition renders most of its defensive efforts superfluous. Other than the possible defense of Western Europe until the late 1950s, the material justifications for the global containment perimeter—military, geostrategic, and economic—are directly called into question by America's insulation and invulnerability. The justifications for most of the strivings for military superiority, advantage, and parity—nuclear and conventional— are negated by America's impermeability and imperviousness. The major exceptions involve the maintenance of superior naval power and advanced weapons research and development. (Containment's nonmaterial, political "half"—its credibility-heightening rationale—does not fall within the strategic immunity concept. Its superfluousness as a means for protecting our material interests is discussed in chapter 5.)

I

The United States is insulated insofar as any opponent's attempts to expand his territorial influence-control are unsuccessful. The failures are due to some combination of his limitations and the resilience of third states, the expansionist targets of the rival and his allies. They are sufficiently resilient to serve as buffers and barriers, deflecting and negating each of the expansionist means at the rival's disposal: ideological appeal and propaganda, political infiltration and subversive actions, economic rewards and coercion, diplomatic carrots and sticks, military assistance for governments and their opponents, as well as the use of conventional forces and the nuclear threat. There is admittedly a problem in fully demonstrating America's post-1945 insulation given its continuous, widespread political-military involvements. These must be factored out, showing that the opponent's expansionist failures were due to its own limitations and the resilience of others. Still, sufficient evidence is available with which to circumvent the problem.

Starting in the mid-1950s Moscow pursued its expansive interests in the Third World with almost all the means at its disposal. It began with an ideological offensive supported by an impressive, globe-spanning propaganda machine that effectively exploited powerful anti-imperialist resentments and anticapitalist sentiments. A substantial number of former colonies expressed an affinity for the Soviet Union in their foreign policies, adopted a centralized economic-planning model, and embraced a socialist political ideology. The Soviets took up the cause of the neutral states, lauding them as a "beneficial and positive" force as well as including them in an "extensive zone of peace" along with the socialist states themselves. By the late 1950s these efforts were proving so effective that Nikita Khrushchev announced a bandwagoning movement in enlisting Third World states as Soviet allies.[2] Many Americans considered the Soviet Union's ideological attractiveness a greater threat than its military power.

Yet Soviet successes were soon reversed. The USSR as a model and the communist ideology were discredited with little if any help from the United States. In the early 1960s the appearance of socialist unity suffered when China openly challenged the Soviet Union. Moscow's ideological bonds with Algeria, Ghana, Mali, and Indonesia were so shallow that immediately after the personalistic leaders of these countries were overthrown in the mid-1960s the Soviet connections were severed. As the postindependence euphoria waned, the unenviable record of the states that subscribed to socialist political ideals and centralized economic planning became widely evident. Contrary to Moscow's predictions, by the late 1970s Russia's slow economic growth eventuated in widening disparities with the U.S. economy. Unflattering comparisons were drawn with the economic performance of such "underdeveloped" countries as South Korea and Brazil. The continuously expanding recognition of Russia, not as the fervent advocate of peace, self-determination, and socialism, but as just another great power with imperialist designs became widespread in the Moslem world with the invasion of Afghanistan. By the end of the Cold War Marxism-Leninism had taken firm hold only where it was able to build upon strong nationist foundations, as in China, Vietnam, and Cuba. Only some dozen Third World regimes identified with the Soviet Union ideologically.[3]

Around 1955 Moscow also began using material incentives to extend its influence in the Third World. However, these were never more than marginally successful due to the Soviet economy's manifest limitations in supporting effective programs of trade and aid.[4] Its autarkic features, inconvertible currency, hard-currency shortages, and shoddy manufactured goods precluded extensive economic relations and thus any trade-based dependencies. In the 1960s the Third World conducted 5 percent of its total trade with the Soviet bloc. In the 1980s it was 6 percent, one-fifteenth of its trade with the developed capitalist countries.[5] The visible Soviet presence in a few large development projects—notably the Aswan Dam and the Helwan steel complex in Egypt—could not compare with that of thousands of Western subsidiaries and joint ventures. Soviet aid programs were generally inflexible—tied to second-rate products and machinery that often took years to deliver—and often promised more than they could deliver. Moscow disappointed friendly regimes, such as those of Salvador Allende in Chile and Michael Manley in Jamaica, that were desperately seeking aid and trade to offset their dependence upon the West. By the early 1980s its clients were encouraged to look to the West for assistance.[6]

In the late 1950s the Soviets began using military aid to extend their influence and control in the Third World. By the 1970s sales agreements reached $10 billion a year. Weapons were given to a number of national liberation movements who were engaged in guerrilla or full-blown civil wars. Low-cost, attractively financed, easy-to-maintain, and quickly obtainable weapons were supplied to some fifty governments. By the end of the 1970s Moscow had replaced Washington as the leading arms supplier to the Third World, providing more arms in every category other than subsonic aircraft. Between 1970 and 1979 the number of Eastern bloc military personnel expanded from ten thousand to eighteen thousand advisors, technicians, and palace guards to defend against coup-minded officers.[7] In addition, the USSR financed and transported some forty thousand Cuban combat troops to Angola. Besides multiplying the Soviets' presence, military assistance was more or less instrumental in producing Soviet successes in Vietnam, Angola, Mozambique, South Yemen, Somalia, Ethiopia, and Nicaragua. They were Moscow's greatest Third World successes.

Then in 1979 the USSR employed its own forces to attack a Third World state. But after years of fighting it failed to attain any more control over Afghanistan than it had prior to the introduction of some 300,000 troops. American arms supplies to the Mujahidin guerrillas—especially the handheld missiles for use against helicopter gunships—were important in accounting for the stalemate. Still, the Soviet Union also enjoyed the most unusual advantage of being able to conduct a war just across its border. The only other possibilities—Iran, Turkey, and China—would have been yet more problematic targets. Although every Third World country was patently outclassed militarily, it does not follow that the Soviets could have absorbed the enormous costs of acquiring more than a few, whose governance would probably have required a substantial military presence in combatting drawn-out insurgencies. By way of comparison, Moscow had to intervene militarily in three Eastern European countries that should have been relatively easy to manage—they being variously close to or on the Soviet border, hosts for the Red Army, and intertwined with the Soviet economy.

Partly because the invasion of Afghanistan had turned the huge Moslem world away from Moscow, by the mid-1980s it renewed its propagandistic strivings with a decided twist. Instead of seeking to spread the socialist ideology throughout the Third World, the aim was the much more limited one of establishing friendly relations with some dozen influential "nationalist" regimes. The "peace offensive" was directed at such countries as Brazil, Mexico, Saudi Arabia, Morocco, India, Indonesia, and Thailand. They were courted with trade agreements, cultural exchanges, high-level visits, and effusive commendations to garner diplomatic support, to put a greater distance between them and the United States, and to attain an influential role in regional conflicts.

Bilateral relations were warmed up, but beyond that dubiously significant gain there was no evidence of tangible results. There was little to offer the nationalist regimes, certainly not enough to offset their pervasive mistrust of Moscow. The case of Soviet-Indian relations is especially telling since Moscow referred to them as a model for its dealings with others. Soviet trade with India was much greater than with any other Third World country, and it received the most high-level attention under Gorbachev. It relied upon Soviet arms shipments and support in its conflicts with China and Pakistan. Yet New Delhi refused basing rights for the Soviet navy, rejected Gorbachev's proposed Asian security conference, and generally showed itself to be independent in its political and economic dealings with other countries.[8]

Moscow's attempts to expand its influence-control in the Third World were thus no more than moderately successful, the most impressive gains deriving from various forms of military assistance during the 1970s. The case for the Soviets' limited capabilities and the Third World's resilience in the face of their expansionism is further developed by considering two central justifications for the containment strategy. A single major success or a handful of secondary ones would snowball by way of falling dominoes and pro-Soviet bandwagoning. And once the Soviets had established their presence militarily, ideologically, economically, or with palace guards, it would translate into influence and control.[9]

If expansionist successes did lead to toppling dominoes among nearby states and bandwagoning with the USSR to avoid becoming the next target, these effects should certainly have appeared in the 1970s. Besides the already noted string of successes that made up the Soviets' "geopolitical momentum" and Brzezinski's "arc of crisis" from the Horn of Africa through Southeast Asia, the USSR attained nuclear parity, acquired force projection capabilities and a blue-water navy, and confidently announced a decisive shift to socialism in the global "correlation of forces." Developments on the American side should have further encouraged bandwagoning: The major defeat in Vietnam, the economic shock of the Arab oil embargo, containment's mild retrenchment (the Nixon doctrine), the public bemoaning of our weakness (America as "a pitiful giant" in

Nixon's words), and the influential alarmism of the Committee on the Present Danger.

Yet where were the falling dominoes (other than Laos and Cambodia) and the bandwagoning states?[10] In fact, during the 1970s there was a good deal of balancing against the USSR as the increasingly powerful state, as the more threatening state, or both. Various Third World states ordered out its advisors, heightened their resolve, upgraded their defenses, and formed defensive alliances. Moscow suffered rejections and losses in Egypt, the Sudan, Somalia, Uganda, Equatorial Guinea, Guinea-Bissau, Chile, and pre-1979 Afghanistan. Of these, perhaps only Egypt and Chile are marginally attributable to American involvements. The one comprehensive review of Third World changes between 1970 and 1980 found no increase in the total number of countries in which Moscow enjoyed substantial influence or control.[11] When defeat was imminent in South Vietnam, the nearby countries of Southeast Asia, the "next" targets, were discernibly less anxious about the threat to their security than was the United States. In response to the complete North Vietnamese victory in 1975 and Vietnam's invasion of Cambodia in 1978, the Association of Southeast Asian Nations (ASEAN) coalesced and balanced against Vietnam. The Nixon administration's reduction of U.S. troops in South Korea and the Carter administration's proposed complete withdrawal led it to balance by tripling defense outlays between 1976 and 1980.[12]

The Soviets themselves did not evince especially optimistic expectations of Third World developments during the late 1970s. Soviet analysts recognized the balancing behavior of China, Japan, Thailand, and South Korea, while severely limiting any expectations of falling dominoes to Laos and Cambodia. In their speeches, including hortatory ones to Third World audiences, Soviet leaders did not voice expectations of culminating gains even following from the communist victory in Vietnam.[13]

Soviet expansionism would render America's insulation problematic if, as was commonly assumed, the Soviet presence made for influence and control, insofar as allies and clients were managed and put to good use. However, it is one thing for the Soviets to enlarge their political, economic, and military presence, most extensively with arms sales to some fifty Third World states; it is quite another for these to eventuate in palpable influence, real leverage, no less control. Soviet success in this regard was sharply limited throughout the Cold War because of the resilience of Marxist and "fraternal" regimes.

During the late 1950s and early 1960s, when Marxist socialism and the Soviet model had their greatest appeal in the Third World, Khrushchev was forced to accept a bevy of unpalatable ideological developments and political setbacks. Moscow had to stop supporting local communist parties, put up with the jailing and shooting of their leaders, and show respect for the syncretic nationalist ideologies of African socialism and pan-Arabism. Throughout the Khrushchev era Cuba was the only ally to adopt orthodox Marxism-Leninism as its governing ideology.[14] Starting in the mid-1960s, the Soviets were sometimes simply told to depart, to remove the military, political, and economic apparatus they had shipped abroad. Their continued presence elsewhere was usually conditional, depending upon convergent strategies for the realization of common objectives. "When a Third World leader perceives the USSR as being overbearing or unsupportive, the question 'what have you done for me recently?' is more relevant to him than 'what did you do for me in the past?'. . . . The status of the Soviet Union typically has not been [so much] that of imperial overlord but of guest worker."[15]

Clients asserted their independence despite being exceptionally dependent on Moscow's support. The Angolan regime relied upon more than forty thousand Cuban troops and Soviet largesse to assure its very survival, while refusing base rights for the Soviet navy, signing a nonaggression accord with South Africa that was mediated by Washington, declining to mesh its economy with the East, and maintaining extensive ties with the West. During the nearly twenty years in which Egypt depended upon Moscow as its largest donor of economic aid and only important source of military equipment, it imprisoned local communists, rejected the Rogers Peace Plan, and began the War of Attrition and the 1973 Mideast war, all contrary to Soviet advice and pressure.[16] By 1976 Iraq had received more than $1 billion in Soviet aid and more military equipment than any other Middle Eastern client. Yet Moscow's influence was "very limited," Iraq giving "relatively little in the way of political obedience in return."[17]

Throughout the Cold War Moscow's considerable leverage was limited to Mongolia, Cuba, North Vietnam, and probably Ethiopia, South Yemen, Cambodia-Kampuchea, and Laos. Only after years of pressure did Ethiopia's ruling Dergue finally assent to the formation of a vanguard worker's party. "Mengistu Haile Mariam and the other military leaders of Ethiopia understood full well the Soviet motives in pressing for a vanguard party and resisted the idea for as long as they did precisely to avoid giving Moscow an extra source of leverage."[18] Beyond Ethiopia and the other half dozen clients it is hard to discern more than an occasional instance in which the Soviets prevailed on a major internal or external issue—at least when voting correctly at the United Nations and restraint in condemning the invasion of Afghanistan are not considered major issues.

Some part of the Soviets' limited Third World successes was certainly due to the active counterefforts of the United States, perhaps also to

America's likely support for states who might come under the Soviet gun. But Cold War internationalism does not at all account for Moscow's inability to translate its presence into influence, leverage, or control. Washington made virtually no attempts to move Moscow's allies and clients out of its embrace. The few partial successes in this regard resulted from Washington's diminished adversarial pressures. As with Mozambique and Angola, they could then reduce their dependencies on Moscow. For the most part dependencies upon the USSR were heightened by our tightly drawn bipolar lines.[19] In several instances—China, Cuba, Vietnam, and Nicaragua—American intervention, economic embargoes, and support for anti-Marxist insurgents heightened the need for their patron's support.

Instead of being in a self-congratulatory mood at this superpower zenith during the late 1970s, some Soviet academics and officials at the middle levels of the governmental, party, and military hierarchies recognized the independence of the "fraternal" Third World states. And their explanations minimized U.S. involvements. The outer empire was seen to be highly resilient to Moscow's guidance and leverage. "Progressive" military regimes, "socialist-oriented" states, as well as overtly Marxist ones were no longer viewed as sufficiently stable or ideologically committed to make the transition to socialism in the near future. Nor could they serve as a durable basis for the consolidation of Soviet influence. Even the hegemony of Leninist "vanguard parties" was downgraded into a "prerequisite" for the realization of these goals. Along with much skepticism about the effectiveness and affordability of military and economic assistance, limited Soviet influence was explained by enduring nationalist, ethnic, and religious attachments. Explanations focusing upon neocolonial economic dependencies and imperialist-backed insurgencies against Marxist regimes were deemphasized.[20] These assessments subsequently led squarely into Gorbachev's "new thinking" about international affairs.

Turning to Western Europe, would American nonengagement have resulted in its Finlandization? Without U.S. troops and the nuclear deterrent, could Europe have deterred and defended against a Warsaw Pact invasion? To offer a considered "no" is to claim that Europe's resilience and thus America's insulation were far higher than almost invariably assumed in Washington and academia. Much of the evidence is necessarily speculative given America's full-blown, continuously powerful presence. However, the conventional thinking on these questions is equally so. The present claim—if the United States had disengaged, Europe would not have fallen under the influence or control of an expansionist Soviet Union—parallels this equally hypothetical claim: Without the American alliance the consequences would have been Finlandization or far, far worse. Both are counterfactuals.

Characterizations of the Finnish experience emphasizing weakness and subjection were central to American anxieties about its extension into the rest of Western Europe. However, the real Finland is the small country that refused Moscow's demands for territorial concessions in 1939, that threw the Red Army back into Russia during the Winter War of 1939–40 with only minor territorial losses of its own, that attacked Russia in 1941 to regain those areas, that mobilized a population of four million in meeting the Soviet counterattack sufficiently well to have to cede only a few small tracts of territory. Moreover, Finland was among the only three European countries (along with Britain and Russia) that fought against Nazi Germany without suffering an occupation. It was one of four (along with Britain and neutral Sweden and Switzerland) that maintained its democratic institutions during World War II. It is an exaggeration to say that Finland has been "Finlandized" since 1945.[21] It is more accurate to say that it has cleverly and prudently fended off Moscow's military intimidation to become markedly autonomous as a neutral state, only somewhat more subject to Moscow's demands than Sweden and Austria.

To try to generalize Finlandization raises several additional questions. If a small country subject to immediate Soviet intimidation eventuates in "Finlandization," how account for Yugoslavia? During the late 1940s Soviet troops were deployed close to its border and Stalin viciously attacked Marshal Tito and the Yugoslav communists. Yet the "little cold war" with Belgrade did not at all compromise the country's independence. And what of Norway? It not only resisted Soviet attempts to dissuade it from becoming part of NATO; they helped move it into the alliance. Since Europe also includes a few large countries, why not take France as an alternative to the Finlandization model for a Europe without America? "The transformation of French political culture induced by de Gaulle's policy of resisting both superpowers suggests how Western Europe is likely to behave (after America's disengagement). Neutralism, pacifism, and the nuclear allergy are conspicuously absent."[22] And what of those developments about which the United States was most anxious— Charles de Gaulle's vision of a Europe poised and mediating between the superpowers, Willy Brandt's *Ostpolitik* for overcoming the East-West divide, and the late 1970s specter of Eurocommunism prompted by communist electoral gains in Spain, Portugal, and Greece? None of them made for any kind of neutralism, much less a shift toward Moscow.

A vision of Finlandization in America's absence runs up squarely against the European states' long-standing communist antipathies and wariness of Moscow's peaceful wiles, valued national traditions and strong democratic institutions, as well as their size and economic wherewithal. Western Europe had nearly one and a half times as many people as the USSR; the population of the USSR and Eastern Europe together was only slightly larger than Western Europe's. Even on the old, much inflated figures the Soviet GNP was never more than half the size of Western Europe's; West Germany's alone stood at nearly 40 percent of the Soviet Union's. An assessment of the future has a good deal of resonance for the earlier possibility of Finlandization: If Western Europe were to become politically cohesive, it "would have the population, resources, economic wealth, technology and actual and potential military strength to be the *preeminent* power of the 21st century."[23]

A vision of Finlandization also requires some rough-hewn scenario, some realism regarding Moscow's leverage. Undoubtedly the biggest carrot was that of German reunification, at least for the Federal Republic. But that possibility could not be taken past the semicosmetics of "reassociation" given Moscow's worst-case fears of a resurgent Germany. The other possibilities are found in Paul Nitze's 1980s concerns for a West Germany that "could be particularly vulnerable to a carrot-and-stick approach." As carrots, the USSR "can offer to continue and to expand its deliveries of natural gas. The Warsaw Pact countries can continue to service their debt obligations (to West German banks). The German Democratic Republic can expand permitted contacts between its citizens and those of the Federal Republic. The Soviet Union can offer unilaterally to place limits on its and the Warsaw Pact's military buildup facing Germany." As for sticks, these "would be the implied or actual threat to do the reverse of all these things."[24]

There are several problems with such an analysis. The most important one should be obvious: The value that West Germany set upon these carrots and sticks did not compare with the other side of the ledger—the security risks of giving up NATO membership and the possible economic withdrawal from the European Economic Community. Second, the lines of economic dependency ran far more deeply from East to West, thereby mitigating the leverage Moscow might have derived from the manipulation of energy, trade, and financial policies. Third, what kind of palpable leverage could Moscow have exerted upon West Germany or Western Europe after the first and second rounds of offers and pressures were simply ignored? It could have resorted to intimidation by placing more troops on the inter-German border and by placing more warships astride the North Atlantic sea-lanes. But this would probably have been politically counterproductive for Europe's shift to the East, while leading to a possible cutoff of trade, technology transfers, and credits to the Soviet Union. This may be why Moscow never even hinted at these possibilities.

NATO military forces were apparently sufficient to deter a presumptively expansionist Soviet Union, and perhaps to have defended successfully against a conventional Warsaw Pact invasion.[25] But would Europe on its own have been sufficiently resilient militarily? Would Europeans have maintained forces whose size and special advantages would have made them capable of deterring and defending against the Warsaw Pact at least as well without America as with it? They did, in fact, have the will, resources, and some special advantages to compensate fully for the American contribution.

This claim is developed with reference to the mid-1980s, after the relatively favorable balance of the early 1960s was gradually lost. Warsaw Pact ground forces had been enlarged and modernized during the 1970s, the Soviets had just deployed the SS-20 intermediate range missiles that prompted so much consternation in the West, and America's European and strategic forces were at their numerical and qualitative peaks. Specifically, the Europeans would have had to compensate for the annual $135 billion that we were spending on our forces in Europe and those oriented toward it in the event of a war, the 320,000 U.S. military personnel stationed in Europe, the 130,000 to be transported across the Atlantic in wartime, and the U.S. nuclear forces targeted upon the USSR that were more than ten times larger than Britain's and France's together.[26]

Circa 1985 America was devoting 6.8 percent of its GNP to defense compared to NATO Europe's 3.8 percent.[27] But the latter's lower level was at least substantially due to America's higher level. NATO Europe was acting "rationally" as a free or cheap rider; its self-interests were maximized by not spending more so long as we were there to make up for the shortfall in the common defense. That its expenditures would have risen markedly with an American downsizing is seen in the responses to our lower NATO contributions during and after the Vietnam War. Between 1970 and 1979 the Europeans nearly doubled their share of total NATO expenditures, as well as doubling their total contributions in constant dollars.[28] The political feasibility of Europe's much greater financial contributions is also suggested by a comparison of per capita defense spending. Where it spent $263 per person, the annual U.S. per capita outlay was $1,077.[29] To fully make up for U.S. expenditures of $135 billion the European figure would have had to be doubled. Yet its per capita contribution would still have been only half that of our own.

The 450,000 U.S. troops stationed in and slated for Europe should be set against NATO Europe's 3,338,000, plus reserves. Of the ready forces on the continent, the Europeans fielded more than 90 percent of the ground troops and armored divisions, 86 percent of the air forces, and 75 percent of the tanks.[30] It should have been politically possible to make up for all U.S. forces. The proportion of the U.S. population serving in the military was 0.96 percent; for NATO Europe it was 1.0 percent, with Belgium at the highest level of 1.1 percent.[31] Adding 450,000 military personnel to NATO Europe would have required an increase from its one soldier per one hundred population to a 1.14 ratio, which was virtually level with Belgium's actual contribution.

Nor would Europe have had to make up the entire financial, personnel, and weapons deficits resulting from a U.S. withdrawal. Four considerations point to the sufficiency of a smaller effort while still retaining the equivalent deterrent and defensive potency of the American alliance. According to David Calleo, a full $135 billion replacement of the American contribution would not have been at all necessary; such a spending requirement is "preposterous," and not for any debatable military reasons. "America's ratio of military expenditures to military forces is notoriously inferior to Western Europe's—a result that reflects not only America's vast inefficiencies in procurement, management, and weapons acquisition, but also its inherent comparative disadvantage in deploying large conventional forces overseas."[32] French francs, German marks, and British pounds buy more defense capabilities than their dollar equivalents.

Unlike the American force, the European one had the special advantage of proximity to the battlefield—a truly crucial advantage in defending against the Warsaw Pact's plans for a blitzkrieg attack. Thus how important was it to replace all of the 130,000 troops who would not arrive in their entirety until three months after a NATO mobilization? If none of this force were lost to submarine attacks in the Atlantic, and if it were able to disembark with its heavy equipment despite the destruction of port cities, no more than half of it would have arrived in time for the critical first ten days of defending against a blitzkrieg invasion.[33] This is also to say that an expansion of European reservists would probably have served as the "functional equivalent" of ready U.S. forces stationed across the Atlantic.

Throughout the Cold War there was a readily available opportunity to negate a substantial part of the Warsaw Pact's numerical advantage. While a West Germany with U.S. backing refused to build defenses along the inter-German border, without America it might well have overcome its strong political distaste for symbolically reinforcing the division of the two Germanies. Antitank ditches, antitank fortifications, prechambered bridges, and other preparations would have served as exceptionally cheap and effective defenses. According to one study, a $5 billion investment in fortifications (plus $3.5 million in annual operating expenses) would have been the defensive equivalent of ten additional divisions.[34] Relying upon standard military data, William Kaufmann estimated that "such barriers would decrease the relative effectiveness of a given offensive force by as much as 40 percent." They would have allowed seventeen divisions to halt a concentrated attack by as many as thirty Pact divisions—and this on the cheap, as it were.[35]

Britain and France each possessed a small force of submarine-launched missiles and nuclear-tipped ground- and air-launched cruise missiles totaling some one thousand warheads capable of striking the USSR. Leaving aside any American farewell presents of nuclear weapons, the nuclearization of Germany, or the likely enlargement of this force, it might well have deterred a Warsaw Pact invasion as effectively as a huge U.S. arsenal. Most of the one thousand British and French missiles were nearly indestructible in their impossible-to-locate submarines, and sufficient in number to threaten every large and medium-sized Soviet city. The U.S.-led NATO deterrent ran up against the central credibility issue: How could we believably threaten to defend Frankfurt by going nuclear when this meant the likely destruction of Chicago? The credibility deficit would have been significantly reduced by replacing extended deterrence with basic deterrence, by and for Europe. What Robert Tucker wrote about America's missiles also applied to Europe's. "So long as it is clear that they are employed only in the direct defense of the homeland, they confer a physical security that is virtually complete," one that a loss of allies cannot alter. Even inferior nuclear forces would still impart "maximum credibility" to America's deterrent threat in and around the homeland.[36] As for the possible disadvantages of a much smaller force in limiting damage and fighting a war, in chapter 5 it will be seen that these are barely, if at all relevant.

On the other side of the world, what of Japan's resilience to Soviet efforts at Finlandization, coercion, or outright attack? While U.S. officials and analysts expressed streams of anxiety about the safety of Europe, there has been a trickle over Japan's. If the minimalist fears for Japan were not due to its resilient posture, they should have been. Any notions of Finlandization would immediately have run up against its sharp anti-communism, cohesive political institutions, and powerful nationalist proclivities. Other than returning the small northern islands, Moscow was without any carrots or sticks with which to attain some leverage over Tokyo. Economic means were out of the question in light of Japan's larger GNP, more advanced technology, and exclusive trade links with the West. Only Moscow's control of Middle Eastern oil would have offered some potential leverage. Japan is a readily defensible island country. It already had a sizable navy and would surely have doubled or tripled its size and quite possibly armed it with nuclear weapons in America's absence. And any serious Soviet moves against Japan would have elicited a strong deterrent reaction from China, possibly eminating in a Sino-Japanese alliance.

In the post–Cold War era the question of America's insulation was most sharply raised by Iraq's 1990 invasion of Kuwait as it bore upon our energy security. How would other states have reacted had the United

States not organized, led, and largely manned the coalition forces used against Saddam Hussein? Clearly no others would have tried to force a withdrawal from Kuwait. But Kuwait and its oil were not a significant security or economic issue. The prominent concern was Iraq's next likely move against or into Saudi Arabia and the other Persian Gulf states. It would then have gained control of one-fifth of the noncommunist world's oil production, two-thirds of proven world reserves.

The Iraqi case apparently points to the limits of America's insulation. There were no indications that the Middle Eastern countries would form a coalition to protect the Persian Gulf on their own. They joined the U.S.-UN coalition only at Washington's effortful diplomatic behest. Iran, Syria, and Egypt were divided among themselves and without an obvious leader to organize a balancing movement. Still, the possibility should not be ruled out, given the well-established tendency of states to balance against threats. We rushed right in, committed ourselves to the protection of Saudi Arabia within two days of the Iraqi invasion of Kuwait. Others thus had much less reason to do so; they might have after having some time to digest the attack that surprised literally everyone and to contemplate the Iraqi threat to themselves. And there were reasons for thinking that a balancing coalition could form without America's involvement.

Countries are especially likely to balance, to deter and defend if necessary, under several conditions: When the expanding state has not yet attained its major objectives, when it is outclassed militarily and internally divided, when it has acted in a manner that is patently threatening, when this occurs amid an ongoing rivalry and feelings of enmity, and when other states are willing to defray the military costs of balancing. These conditions were all satisfied in the Iraqi case. The invasion of Kuwait was a blatant act of aggression. An Iraq enjoying the entire Gulf's oil revenues would have had the means to build up yet more powerful forces. In his attempts to head up a pan-Arab coalition and spread the Baathist ideology, Hussein had become the nemesis of Iran, Syria, and Egypt. These states held an overwhelming preponderance of power. Their forces outnumbered Iraq's one million troops by nearly two to one, somewhat more so in aircraft and tanks. An Iraqi attack upon Saudi Arabia would have left it—and Baghdad—exposed to attacks from Syria in the West. Iran would have encouraged and assisted a Shiite uprising within southern Iraq, and the Kurds would have revolted in the north. Saudi Arabia and Kuwait would have bankrolled the Egyptian and Syrian military just as they did the American. And if these states thought it necessary, or perhaps simply advantageous, they would have invited the Israeli air force—easily the region's most powerful—to do its major part. None of this would have escaped the attention of an Iraq contemplating a move into Saudi Arabia.

II

The United States was and is militarily and economically invulnerable. It is militarily invulnerable insofar as the contender's expansionist successes do not provide an advantageous geostrategic position from which to attack or coerce the core; the capabilities of his newly acquired allies and clients do not significantly alter the military balance; and these states do not control resources that the United States needs for building weapons and fueling them in wartime. The latter condition also speaks to the country's economic invulnerability.

At one time or another American officials invested just about all Third World states with substantial geostrategic importance—Sri Lanka, for instance, due to its "strategic location off southeastern India as a crossroads in sea and air transport"; Libya was said to be "vital to the defense of north Africa and the southern flank of NATO." Geostrategic importance was regularly derived from such concepts as bridges, island chains, barriers, and flanks. Robert Johnson has pointed out that these concepts often lack meaning and discriminateness. "[I]t has been said that the Persian Gulf region has great importance as a 'bridge' between Europe and all of Asia. The Persian Gulf is unquestionably important, but how is it a bridge and for what purposes and under what circumstances? Why the Persian Gulf rather than Egypt, Suez, and the Red Sea? Moreover, since the globe is a piece with every area ultimately connected to every other, it does not take a great deal of ingenuity to develop a geostrategic rationale for the importance of almost any country."[37] Thus during the Vietnam era officials asserted that Soviet bases in Southeast Asia could control crucial American sea- and air-lanes. The Reagan administration warned that any Soviet installations in Central America would strangle critical sea-lanes and oil shipments.[38]

Geostrategic indiscriminateness may have occasional warrant in protecting far-flung allies, but not with regard to the core perimeter. Then the Caribbean and Central American countries are the only ones that might constitute pieces of strategic real estate. No Soviet bases within the area, as our "backyard" or "frontyard," constituted the "irreducible minimum security interest." Yet neither the loss of American positions in the Caribbean basin nor the appearance of Soviet clients and bases within it would have impaired our invulnerability. The U.S. naval station at Guantanamo served mainly as an irritant to the Cuban government. The Panama Canal's military importance was limited to the resupply of U.S. forces fighting overseas, rather than the movement of warships, which are too big to pass through its locks. Except for the minor advantage of increasing their submarines' on-station time, Soviet bases and forces in the Caribbean might have been a liability since they could not be defended or resupplied in wartime.[39] The surprise launching of missiles from nearby locations would have created serious coordination problems for the Soviets and offered few, if any, overall benefits. And there was clearly no way in which conventional Soviet forces could threaten the United States, given our many times over conventional air, sea, and land-based superiority in the area. For many officials the Caribbean made only for our "sea-lane vulnerability" with respect to a conventional war in Europe.[40]

Soviet territorial gains elsewhere, including any involving the loss of U.S. naval bases, would not have appreciably threatened our sea lines of communication. Except for the Diego Garcia base in the Indian Ocean, the loss of all others would require only a few extra off-station days every two months to return to American island bases and home ports for supplies and repairs. As for the crucial American shipping lanes, no Third World territories lie between us and Japan. Cuba and the Caribbean islands, the only ones astride the European routes, could be bypassed by using our East Coast ports. Sea routes from the Persian Gulf do lie adjacent to large Third World territories. Yet only one possible choke point—the Strait of Hormuz running past Iran and Oman—is unavoidable. Any Soviet bases elsewhere could have been given a wide berth. Soviet and hostile bases "would matter more if Third World areas straddled key American sea lanes in the way that Denmark, Turkey and Japan straddle Soviet sea lanes, but only the Strait of Hormuz comes close on this score."[41] Extensive claims have been made for the importance of American bases and the threat from Soviet ones.[42] Yet none of them belie any of these arguments for a nonengaged America's sure command of the seas with its markedly superior naval forces.

In considering the Soviets' translation of territorial extensions into military power there is this crucial fact: The United States enjoyed an enormously wide margin of actual and potential military superiority over every state other than the USSR. That margin was greater than that enjoyed by every major power over any other but its chief rival since the seventeenth-century beginnings of the modern state system. China underscores America's military invulnerability. The adverse security consequences were indiscernible after China's one-quarter of the world population shifted into the communist camp in 1949, except for the attack upon U.S. forces in Korea, which was brought on by their movement right up to the Chinese border. Nor was our security notably enhanced after China changed sides again circa 1970, this time along with a small nuclear capability. Ranking third in the world in military expenditures during the 1980s, China's were still less than one-fifth of ours.[43]

With industrial resources as the primary basis of military power, what would it have taken for Soviet expansionism to eventuate in a military advantage? Our GNP was fifteen times larger than Brazil's, the Third

World country with the largest GNP. It was fully twice that of the entire
Third World, the wealthy oil-producing states included. If Moscow had
controlled Japan, Germany, France, and Italy—the world's wealthiest
countries after the superpowers—it would have acquired somewhat more
than the equivalent of America's economic resources. In order to have
twice as much it would have had to dominate the entire Eurasian land
mass.[44] And then it is not at all likely that the United States would have
become vulnerable by being "spent into the ground." The conventional
force requirements for protecting the core are readily manageable, and
nuclear weaponry is relatively inexpensive.

Moreover, the military importance of territory, population, and industrial resources has been substantially reduced by the nuclear revolution.
Much more will be said to establish the reality of the revolution, one in
which the subjective balance of interests, resolve, and credibility are much
more important than the balance of strategic power. Here it is sufficient
to quote Stephen Van Evera. "The nuclear revolution has devalued the
strategic importance of all conquered territory . . . even huge conquests
would not give the conqueror enough technical or material assets to give
it decisive nuclear superiority over another great power. Thus even if the
Soviet Union gained control of all the industrial regions in Eurasia, and
even if these regions remained as productive as they are now, the Soviets
would still lack sufficient industrial superiority to gain nuclear superiority over the United States."[45]

To turn to America's economic vulnerability is to face the pervasive
aura of "interdependence"—that it is great, growing, and thus heavily
constraining. But this term should not be simply taken to refer to the
amount of trade or exchange. Not all that much about a country's true
dependence, the degree to which it is economically constrained, is determined solely by the amount of its trade. Two countries that exchange
great quantities of goods need not be equally dependent upon one another, or dependent at all. Dependence is about the losses, opportunity
costs, and economic harm to be suffered if others can threaten or cut back
on their trade with us or sharply raise the prices of their products.

On this standard usage,[46] which is the meaning given to economic vulnerability here, we are not totally invulnerable. This would only be the
case under conditions of near autarky, if we were as economically self-
sufficient as was the USSR. However, the United States continues to rank
high on each of the other determinants of invulnerability. A country is
invulnerable insofar as its trading partners, exporters and importers, are
markedly more dependent upon it for the satisfaction of their economic
needs than vice versa, thereby negating their potential leverage. It is invulnerable to the extent that there is a diversity of current and potential
trading partners, the loss or hostility of some being offset by the avail-

ability of others. A state is also invulnerable when affordable substitutes for crucial imports are domestically available or capable of being developed at prices that are not substantially higher than imports. And it is invulnerable if stockpiles are adequate to see it through an emergency situation and over the near term.[47]

A singularly important fact is regularly overlooked in writings about America's trade dependencies (or vulnerabilities). With two exceptions, no country has refused to do economic business with the United States since 1945, even after Washington severed diplomatic relations and lent military support to insurgent movements. It is we who have cut trade relations for security reasons, to squeeze opponents, and to punish them. When we indicated a willingness to resume them, the offers were always quickly taken up. And no group of countries has formed a successful cartel—not for bauxite, copper, tin, iron ore, or for oil. As for the exceptions—the 1973–74 Arab oil embargo and Albania—we brought on one by intervening politically and militarily on Israel's side in the 1973 Mideast war. The other is irrelevant because of its size and refusal to trade with anyone.

America has been characterized as heavily dependent with regard to total trade, strategic minerals, and oil. During the first half of the Cold War the proportion of GNP deriving from exports and imports did not reach a minimal 5 percent. It then grew steadily to 14 percent toward its conclusion. In assessing the trade invulnerability of a nonengaged America, the percentage of GNP based on trade should immediately be reduced by 25 percent, the proportion of total trade conducted with Canada and Mexico. The trade-based GNP generated with these, our first and fourth most important trading partners, would enjoy certain protection within the core perimeter. The trade-based U.S. GNP generated from beyond the core perimeter would be little more than 10 percent of total GNP, and much of that could be shifted into the core at low cost. The proportion of GNP deriving from trade ranges from 22 to 44 percent among Britain, Germany, France, Italy, and Japan.[48]

With some fluctuations, about one-third of U.S. exports went to and one-third of our imports came from the Third World.[49] Although weighted toward Latin America and the oil exporters, this trade was highly diversified. It included nearly one hundred countries differing widely in location and political complexion. Nearly all of them were far more dependent upon us than vice versa. The United States continues to have much more of what they very much want in the way of export markets, investment capital, and advanced technology. These dependencies are supplemented by the financial leverage accruing to an America with a special, often dominant, position within the World Bank and the International Monetary Fund.[50]

What then of the approximately 40 percent of our trade conducted with Western Europe and Japan? Here there are no "redeeming" or off-setting features, even after this figure has been appropriately reduced to 30 percent to take account of that one-quarter of fully secured trade with Canada and Mexico. We would not have been invulnerable if the USSR had gained control of Europe and Japan—by way of Finlandization or war—and then imposed a trade cutoff with the United States. Had the loss of both Europe and Japan occurred at one fell swoop, the very worst scenario, the United States would have lost 3 to 4 percent of its total GNP. In the short run it would have been impossible to find other trading part-ners or to make domestic arrangements to take up all the economic slack. Still, no one has ever supposed that any Soviet acquisition of Europe and Japan would occur overnight. A nonengaged America would have had considerable time to prepare for the possible loss of its chief trading part-ners if this looked to be a real possibility, including the time to create a free trade area in North and possibly South America.

Nonfuel minerals—from ordinary bauxite to titanium—are critical to civilian and defense industries alike. Dependencies upon strategic miner-als should be examined during the early 1980s. Members of the Reagan administration then spoke of a possible "resource war" with the Soviet Union, one that Secretary of State Alexander Haig and some writers thought we might "lose." We were importing more than 50 percent of annual consumption of twenty different minerals; some were irreplace-able in the steel and defense industries; and the sources of the most impor-tant ones were concentrated in the volatile southern African states.[51]

Assessing a nonengaged America's vulnerability on this score begins within the core. Canada was the major supplier of eight of the twenty strategic minerals, the second-ranking source of another, and Mexico was among the chief suppliers of four. The unimportance of the Third World in its vast entirety is highlighted by the fact that the major sup-pliers of seventeen of these minerals were found within the core, Western Europe, and Japan.[52]

Cobalt and chromium were singled out as the most alarming supply vulnerabilities by the Joint Chiefs of Staff, the National Materials Ad-visory Board, and academic analysts.[53] 95 percent of cobalt was im-ported; the biggest suppliers were "unstable" Zaire and Zambia; these two countries held 50 percent of current world reserves; and the Soviet Union and Cuba were the next largest producers. Yet 40 percent of cobalt consumption was neither irreplaceable nor critical; Canada was the third-ranking supplier and the world's fifth biggest producer; the nickel sup-plied chiefly by Canada could serve as a substitute in the crucial alloys; projects were under way to develop nickel and ceramic substitutes for cobalt's other applications; and stockpiles were fully adequate for critical defense and industrial needs.[54] Seventy-three percent of chromium was imported; the chief suppliers were South Africa, Zaire, Zimbabwe, Yugoslavia, and Turkey; and the only other large sources were located in the USSR and Albania. Yet other minerals could immediately replace one-third of chromium in some of its applications; more than half of chromium supplies were used for making stainless steel, for which there are a wide variety of substitutes; only one-fifth of stainless steel was put to uses that require its special properties; and chromium stockpiles were equal to five years of consumption requirements.[55]

In 1979 Congress enacted a requirement for the stockpiling of sufficient minerals to meet military and civilian needs on the contingency of a three-year conventional war and a total trade disruption. The Reagan administration that highlighted the dangers of a resource war proposed the downward revision of several target levels and the sale of some current stocks. It explained that "strategic materials needs will be sharply reduced in a future war by cutbacks in civilian consumption, keeping the sea lanes open to reliable overseas sources, encouraging substitutions, and stimulating more recycling."[56] The proposed levels were fully warranted, even when discounting the six-to-twelve-month inventories in industry hands. In any case, even the 1979 stockpile levels could have been quickly reached with an expenditure of between $5 and $7 billion. Mineral dependencies could have been further reduced by policies to encourage the opening of old mines and research on substitutability, recycling, and conservation.[57]

What then of the energy concerns that have governed so much of U.S. security policy? Oil is critical to every part of the economy. In 1977 and at present close to one-half of the annual oil supplies have been imported. Much of it has come from the Middle East. The region harbors two-thirds of the world's proven reserves. And this politically volatile area has been threatened by the Soviet Union, Iran, and Iraq. Despite these obviously good reasons for concern, reviewing the years from the 1973–74 Arab oil embargo to the 1991 war against Iraq suggests that America's oil vulnerability has been greatly exaggerated.

The Arab embargo of the United States, and more importantly the production cutback, eventuated in a rapid fourfold increase in the world market price of oil and sorely hurt the U.S. economy. Concerns about a future attempt at economic strangulation were deep enough to prompt proposals for U.S. forces to seize the oil fields if the threat materialized.

As the West Europeans recognized before and after 1973, energy concerns could best be alleviated by something other than the overt political-military support for Israel that brought on the embargo. As demonstrated since then, the only issue that could unite the Middle Eastern oil producers, and just about the only one that could turn most of them against

the United States, is the Arab-Israeli conflict. Once Washington's emphasis shifted from a thoroughly pro-Israeli policy in guarding against
Moscow's incursions and those of its clients to a mediating, human rights
focus on the Palestinian question, Arab oil as a political weapon lost its
entire raison d'être. As it bears upon a national strategy, the quadrupling
of oil prices in 1974 depends upon its explanation. Was it due to a supply
shortage or to market conditions and consumer psychology? It is mainly
the former that points to a political-military rationale for U.S. protection
of the oil fields. And there was only a minor, temporary reduction in
world oil supplies.[58] Non-Arab producers quickly took the opportunity
to take up the slack. The sharp price rise occurred when the Arab producers "almost inadvertently" realized that a politically inspired cutback
allowed for it, demand for oil being strong and inelastic in the short run.
The increase was further fueled by speculative market panic and consumer anxieties about future supplies.[59] Indeed, some economists argue
that the fourfold rise simply brought oil costs into line with past price
increases in other commodities.[60]

The second oil shock came in 1979. Prices rose 170 percent over a
fifteen-month period as the growing fundamentalist opposition to the
shah's regime disrupted and then ended oil production in Iran, the second
largest producer in OPEC (the Organization of Petroleum Exporting
Countries). The Arab members of OPEC did not bring on the price rise.
Nor was it primarily due to a supply shortage relative to demand. Saudi
Arabia immediately increased production, leaving only a small, temporary shortfall in supplies. Most of the 170 percent price rise was the result
of stock building, hoarding, and speculation. The industrialized countries' (incorrect) anticipation of future shortages led them to augment
their reserve stocks. Prices continued to spiral upward due to hoarding
and inventory profits in the expectation of yet further increases.[61]

Strategic internationalism obviously did not prevent the shah's overthrow, which brought on the second oil shock. And a nonengaged America would most probably have been better positioned to temper the supply, price, and hoarding consequences of the Iranian revolution. Relying
far more upon ourselves than upon others—including the shah as America's "chief policeman" in the Middle East—the Strategic Petroleum Reserve would have contained much more than its 100,000 barrels of oil.
Filled to its billion-barrel capacity, it would have held the near equivalent
of a year's supply of oil imports from the entire Persian Gulf.[62]

Circa 1980 energy concerns were of three kinds. The steep rise in oil
prices was expected to continue as the OPEC cartel exacted further increases. The Iran-Iraq war that began in 1980—a war between two major
oil-producing countries, with Iran also in control of the Strait of Hormuz,
the "oil life line of the West"—bolstered those expectations. And the

1979 invasion of Afghanistan placed Soviet forces on the Iranian border, hundreds of miles closer to its oil.

Each of these concerns was misplaced. In fact, the 1980s might be labeled the energy security decade. Oil prices declined sharply from $34 a barrel in 1981 to the $10 to $15 range in the mid-1980s, then rose and remained at $18 per barrel. Adjusted for inflation, 1990 prices were about 60 percent below those of 1981. Average gasoline prices dropped from $1.38 a gallon in 1981 to $.93 in 1986 and then rose to $1.16 by 1990, more than a 40 percent decline when adjusted for inflation. Non-OPEC oil production increased annually, and when OPEC was not in disarray, it was dominated by Saudi Arabia and the Gulf states that favored moderate prices. With small populations, relatively undemanding revenue needs, and large oil reserves, these states adhered to a long-run pricing strategy. Despite its destructiveness, the Iran-Iraq war did not cut supplies below demand. Only a small number of tankers were sunk in the Strait of Hormuz—and not because of the subsequent introduction of Western naval forces, after which the attacks on shipping increased by 60 percent. The Soviet threat never raised its head beyond an unconquerable Afghanistan. If the Iranian oil fields had somehow been seized in America's absence, Moscow would barely have had enough supply leverage to affect world prices, much less extort the West economically and politically with about one-quarter of Middle Eastern production.[63]

U.S. imports declined from about 8 million barrels of oil per day in 1980 to 5 million in 1985, and then moved back to the 8 million level by 1990. The temporarily high prices had encouraged a turn to alternative energy sources, more efficient energy use, and publicly mandated and privately undertaken conservation programs. In 1980 nearly 40 percent of all imported oil came from the Middle East; it varied between 10 and 15 percent after 1985. Transportation takes up to two-thirds of oil consumption. Yet a miniscule 0.5 percent of gasoline came from the Middle East; in burning 549 gallons of fuel a year during the late 1980s the average car used 2.7 gallons of its oil. At the time the Strategic Petroleum Reserve held some 550 million barrels. At still only half of capacity this was equivalent to one year's imports from the entire Middle East—and this with total imports again reaching 45 percent of annual consumption. Moreover, the largest and fourth largest oil suppliers (Mexico and Canada) lay within the core perimeter. Beyond it, the six largest ones, Venezuela, Saudi Arabia, Nigeria, Great Britain, Algeria, and Indonesia in descending order,[64] featured great geographic and political diversity.

If Iraq had gained control of all the oil fields in the Gulf it would have acquired one-fifth of world production and two-thirds of proven reserves. President Bush announced that "our jobs, our way of life, our own freedom" would suffer "if control of the world's great oil reserves falls into the hands of Saddam Hussein."[65] It would certainly have triggered a sharp run up in prices. But just how long would they have remained at their new levels? Over the near term they would have been partly brought down by the release of supplies from the Strategic Petroleum Reserve and additional pumping by other oil producers. (Prices actually fell after the cutoff of oil from Kuwait and Iraq.) Nor is it at all clear that Iraq's new-found oil would have been kept off the market so as to maintain high prices. Iraq was almost completely dependent on oil revenues. It would have seen other producers (including Iran) reaping the benefits of higher prices. And it would have had to ignore the lesson of the 1980s: High prices eventuate in lower demand as consumers turn to conservation measures and alternative fuels, especially the abundant natural gas, which is a particularly good substitute for oil.

Still, assuming that Iraq would have tried to fully exploit its newfound control of 20 percent of world production, the "monopoly" price effect may be gauged by this observation: With its responsibility for guarding against monopolies and oligopolies "the U.S. Department of Justice approves mergers of that magnitude every year."[66] Economists as different as Milton Friedman and James Tobin were at one with David Henderson's calculations. If Iraq had wanted to drive up the price of oil to maximize revenues, it would have reduced Gulf production by about 40 percent, equivalent to a 7 percent cut in world output. Given oil's −0.15 inelasticity this would have translated into a 50 percent price increase, from a precrisis $20 a barrel to $30 a barrel. Assuming pessimistically— "and contrary to common sense and evidence," as Henderson remarks— that America continued to import as much oil as it did at the lower price, the loss would have amounted to an annual $30 billion a year, or one-half of 1 percent of GNP. It would have cost each American about $112 a year, including an added twenty-four cents for gasoline at $1.33 per gallon. Such a loss "is surely not what [Treasury Secretary] James Baker had in mind when he asserted that Saddam could 'strangle' the world economy."[67]

There are two undeniable points to be made about an Iraq in control of two-thirds of the world's proven oil reserves. They include a lot of oil "that no one would contemplate pumping for 40 or 50 years—long after Saddam will have become nothing but a bad memory."[68] In fact, any lasting price increase would have extended the life of all reserves by reducing consumption and prompting additional drilling that was unprofitable at the lower price. And the concept of proven world reserves does not have all that much significance in the short run. They have been consistently underestimated; changes in exploration technology and geological knowledge have regularly driven estimates upward. Between 1985 and 1990 proven resources increased from 700 billion barrels to nearly 1 trillion barrels. With respect to the crucial number, world reserves concurrently total nearly fifty times that of annual consumption—the highest ratio ever.[69] With the introduction of new technologies for finding and pumping oil, it could rise yet further.

With respect to a national strategy in particular, what was said before the invasion of Kuwait applies equally well to our future oil invulnerability: "The most important actions the United States can take to protect itself from a supply squeeze and sudden price increases must be taken at home within U.S. territory. They relate to maintenance of adequate strategic oil reserves, conservation measures, tax policies and the like."[70] This injunction takes on special relevance considering the military costs of protecting Middle Eastern oil supplies. The Rapid Deployment Force (later the Central Command) has cost more than $40 billion a year to protect $14 billion of current oil imports from the Persian Gulf. Besides being economically skewed, the $40 billion a year could have been better invested in energy security at home.

Another kind of concern for the country's economic vulnerability has become relatively more prominent since the end of the Cold War. U.S. alliances are necessary to preserve the "peace and stability" upon which our trading relations depend. In Secretary of Defense Dick Cheney's words, "We are a trading nation, and our prosperity is linked to peace and stability . . . the world wide market that we're part of cannot thrive where regional violence, instability, and aggression put it at risk."[71] Proponents of limiting defense commitments to Europe, Japan, and the Persian Gulf also subscribe to this alliance rationale.[72] Severing our alliances would at least marginally increase the likelihood of conflicts and wars that would cut deeply into our commercial relations. Disengagement can "conceivably" allow for a general war in Europe that "would harm America's prosperity by destroying America's European trade partners and disrupting trans-Atlantic commerce."[73]

It was just seen that beyond Western Europe, Japan, and the Persian Gulf, no part of the world is of special economic importance to the United States. And a fifty-year record disconfirms the instability-trade connection. As many as two hundred military coups, violent governmental changes, insurgencies, civil wars, and regional wars have occurred since 1945. But except for the nationalization of a few American companies in the 1950s and the Arab oil embargo, it is practically impossible to see where and how these developments have affected U.S. trade, no less the economy.

Europe is our chief trading partner and a relatively fertile area of war. However, the former consideration applies to Western Europe and the latter to its Eastern half. The possibility of war in Western Europe absent the trans-Atlantic alliance is truly miniscule, for reasons ranging from its economic integration to the powerful disinclination of democracies to go to war with one another.[74] Eastern Europe and the Commonwealth of Independent States are a different matter. The actualities and potentialities of ethnic hatreds, civils wars, hypernationalism, irredentist movements, border disputes, and arms races could eventuate in more than one war, perhaps involving Germany.[75] Except for the latter possibility, however, U.S. trade is not about to be affected, given commercial relations with Eastern Europe that are of no more than tertiary significance. And it is very difficult to foresee a war there spilling over into Western Europe and substantially disrupting our trade relations with it.

III

Besides an opponent's expansive territorial ventures and their consequences, there are the improvements in his military capabilities that bear upon the nation's security. A state is strategically immune to them depending upon its impermeability and imperviousness.

Impermeability means that the rival's force improvements fail to make for a quantitative or qualitative military advantage. They are still inadequate for purposes of intimidation, coercion, terrorism, or combat—a limited naval or land action around the core, a surprise strike against it, or any kind of success in a conventional or nuclear war. This is also to say that there is virtually no chance of a telling quantitative surge or qualitative breakthrough that would not be recognized early enough to be neutralized with dispatch.

Cold War anxieties about America's strategic impermeability have appeared with some regularity: The Soviets' launching of Sputnik, the bomber and missile "gaps," the "window of vulnerability," and the greater throw weight of their heavy missiles. There are similarities among these "periods of peril." According to Robert Johnson, "Like myths, the period of peril theory is a self-contained system of thought. If its basic assumption of technological determinism and its projections of Soviet capabilities are accepted, there is almost no way that it can be invalidated. . . . [The Soviets] are generally perceived as going well beyond anything that can be justified on any concept of defense."[76]

The factual bases for some of these anxieties were soon seen to be nonexistent; the others were subsequently put to rest, convincingly shown not to entail a strategic advantage for the USSR. Since 1960 high-powered reconnaissance satellites have provided ample warning time, allowing for the production and deployment of weapons to neutralize any potential Soviet advantages. And with a GNP that was twice the Soviets' (on the old, inflated Soviet figures) and technological-scientific resources that outstripped theirs, how could the research and development programs of a national strategy have failed to produce weapon prototypes at least comparable—in speed, accuracy, firepower, maneuverability, and survivability?

The qualitative strategic advantages that the Soviets almost certainly could not have achieved are barely imaginable in effective conventional forces. Given America's geographic position, bolstered by naval and air interdiction capabilities, the success of conventional actions around the core was always out of the question. The Soviets were less capable of doing what Germany never came close to doing in World War II— severing the Atlantic, no less crossing it.[77] It would have been about equally impossible in the case of a nonengaged America with half its Cold War land and air power—even with some Soviet bases in South America and the Caribbean, since they could not have been resupplied from the USSR in wartime. For with Nazi Germany, in control of nearly all of Europe, unable to manage a cross-channel invasion against England in 1940–41, how could a Soviet force cross an ocean to attack North America? How was the Soviet navy to concentrate for such an attack when thoroughly outclassed in numbers of blue-water ships, their size and survivability, nuclear and conventional firepower, and speed and cruising ranges?[78]

At the present and for the discernible future the major threats to America's impermeability are widely taken to be those of nuclear proliferation and nuclear terrorism. Some states and perhaps political movements are likely to improve their military capabilities by acquiring weapons and devices of mass destruction. Although a national strategy may be able to do little more than strategic internationalism in curbing or minimizing nuclear spread, it does far more to avoid American targeting. These points are taken up in chapter 5. Here the relevant issues are our safety and noncoercibility on the double-barreled premise of nuclear weapons being acquired by one or more opponents who are (somehow) contemplating their use against a nonengaged America.

A national strategy is as capable as strategic internationalism in making us impermeable, in dealing with small nuclear forces trained on, and nuclear devices being smuggled into, the United States. The strategies feature equally effective capabilities—intelligence, air power, and special operations forces—for deterring the acquisition and if necessary destroying the (nearly deployed) nuclear weapons of threatening states. The national design includes the "light" ballistic missile defenses that can also be part of an international strategy. Less can be done to prevent a rogue nuclear state or terrorist movement from detonating a device in an American city, for example, or to stop its being set off in a port after being brought in by ship. But whatever is to be done can and should be done to the same extent by any security strategy.

What then if an opponent enjoyed a military advantage? A country is impervious insofar as the contender's bigger and/or better forces are not usable or ineffective if used. The military imbalance does not translate into a forceful advantage. It does not adversely affect the potency or credibility of the deterrent threat, the results of a coercive deal, the damage suffered if attacked, or the outcome of a war.

Most importantly for present purposes, how secure would a non-engaged America have been with nuclear forces half the size of the Soviets'? In a world of mutually assured massive damage there would have been preciously little doubt about our imperviousness. When war entails vast mutual destruction it is not the military balance, but the balance of resolve that determines the effectiveness of deterrent and coercive threats and a war's outcome. Since resolve is visibly at its maximum when it bears directly upon the homeland, the resolve behind and the credibility of the deterrent are almost bound to be greater than the rival's threats.[79] Since individuals regularly place greater value upon preserving what they have than upon what they hope to gain, the defending state is less reluctant to run escalatory risks.[80] Since the contender is attempting to alter the status quo, he is saddled with the last clear chance to avert a mutually destructive war.[81] Since both sides are able to destroy the other in wartime, the outcome will depend upon subjective levels of unacceptable damage and mutual perceptions in this regard, rather than upon the number of prewar and intrawar weapons on each side.[82] All but the last consideration favors even a militarily disadvantaged America.

Rather than fleshing out these claims here, they are taken up in the more realistic "reverse" context. In chapter 5 it is argued that America's huge strategic arsenal and capability of fighting a nuclear war did not make, and that nuclear superiority would not have made, us more secure, more impermeable. And this before, during, and after a war. The same arguments for the superfluousness of strategic superiority in protecting the United States apply to the irrelevence of America's strategic inferiority under the auspices of a national strategy.

This chapter's strong implications for the foreseeable future should be clear. America was markedly immune to many diverse threats when facing an enormously powerful, globe-straddling Soviet Union.[83] In some respects it was doubly so: Soviet expansive actions did not and could not obtain their immediate objectives for reasons unrelated to our political-military involvements; and had they succeeded, our security would still not have been adversely affected. Without a threat on the horizon that at all approximates the Soviet one in scope and power, the United States is consequently far more immune than in the recent past. The world could well turn out to be a more dangerous place than it was before 1990, yet there can be no doubting that it is a much safer one for the United States. Put differently, were some of this chapter's Cold War arguments found less than persuasive, the overall case for America's security within the narrow core perimeter should still be persuasive over the discernible future.

Chapter IV

TAILORING POLICIES TO INTENTIONS:
PROBLEMATICS AND HAZARDS

STATES DIFFER enormously in the range of their aggressive-defensive intentions. Intentions are the most immediate, if not also the most fundamental, explanation of their hostile to benign behavior. The success of any security strategy is heavily dependent upon its addressing the other side's actual intentions.

There is no doubting the validity of these tenets. But it does not follow that it is necessary or advisable to act on them. In chapter 2 it was seen that strategic internationalism recognizes their full import and shapes its hawkish or dovish policies accordingly. A national strategy also appreciates the fundamentals of intentions, without however expressing them in activist policies or modulating the latter in accordance with intentions. It assumes an agnostic position—atheism is out of the question—toward an understanding of the contender's short- and long-term aims, concomitantly adopting largely invariant policies in addressing them. To do otherwise is unnecessary. In explicating America's strategic immunity not a single reference was made to the intentions lying behind the rival's actual and possible expansive and unacceptable actions. Taken together, the following three chapters show that national policies can more fully and consistently address the opponent's intentions than any set of internationalist policies—and this even if the latter were to match up with the contender's actual intentions. This chapter considers the problematics and hazards of trying to tailor policies to those intentions.

According to the *second doctrinal proposition*, the identification of the opponent's intentions regularly lies somewhere between the unreliably known and the inherently unknowable; mistaken interpretations are at least as common as those that come reasonably close to the mark. Faulty understandings generate policies that consistently detract from the nation's security. Tailoring policies to intentions is thus a problematic and hazardous security exercise. Nor is it possible for any activist strategy to escape from the interpretative problematics. To shape activist policies solely in accordance with the opponent's capabilities or behavior more broadly is unworkable, hazardous, or both.

Although this chapter is exclusively devoted to a critique of strategic internationalism, it is no less significant in making the case for a national strategy. The second doctrinal tenet elaborates upon what is the central, most consequential debility of strategic internationalism. Since security policies can only be premised upon intentions or capabilities writ large, to show that the former focus is decidedly problematic goes a long way in supporting the latter. Given the heavy dependence of adversarial and conciliatory engagement upon a reasonably accurate understanding of intentions, the security deflations brought on by faulty ones highlight nonengagement's relative effectiveness. To demonstrate the unmanageability and dangers of an activist strategy based entirely upon the challenger's capabilities and behavior (the reciprocated responsiveness of the tit-for-tat strategy), closes out the one other alternative to strategic nonengagement—that of an activist strategy that is not focused upon intentions.

I

Activist policies premised upon mistaken understandings of the other side's intentions regularly eventuate in security deflations. This claim need not be much elaborated. It has been most extensively developed and documented in Robert Jervis's analysis of the characteristic risks entailed by deterrence theory and the spiral model, somewhat modulated by Charles Glaser's refinements. The claim was also set out and systematically tested in the comparison of hard-liners and soft-liners by Glenn Snyder and Paul Diesing.[1] In fact, hawks and doves themselves are agreed that policies based upon faulty interpretations of the challenger's aggressively ambitious or defensive aims are thoroughly counterproductive. Advocates of adversarial activism highlight the dangers of policies that are overly flexible or accommodating; proponents of conciliatory activism underscore the risks of overly demanding or firm ones. During the Cold War the former frequently alluded to the coming of World War II while the latter singled out World War I in making the same point: To base policies upon a misreading of the rival's intentions is to court disaster.[2]

According to adversarial doctrine, overly accommodating policies that are not congruent with the challenger's actual aims make for perceived and actual weaknesses. The opponent's expansionist ventures and direct challenges are not just permitted, but encouraged and facilitated by a decline in the credibility of deterrent threats and the defensive capabilities for meeting them. The contender comes to expect that he is not about to be (fully) opposed by the guardian state, and along with newly acquired advantages and capabilities, he may believe that it is possible to overcome the opposition that might materialize. Excessive flexibility also encourages the rival's opportunistic expansionism on the expectation of being able to revive good relations in the aftermath of limited moves; "salami tactics" are to be deterred from the outset. Hard-line measures are to remain in place when the challenger is evidently weakened and on his good behavior. As with U.S. policies toward the Soviet Union in the mid-1980s, an accommodating breathing spell would permit a future renewal of its power and the resuscitation of revisionist goals. The demonstration of power and resolve should also discourage potential challengers, as with the current thinking about maintaining U.S. primacy vis-à-vis Japan and Germany.

Conciliatory internationalism is focused upon the unnecessary creation, exacerbation, and escalation of conflicts. The status quo state must reassure the other side that it is no more than that, overcoming its defensive anxieties and fears, rather than acting in ways that engender and reinforce suspicions, antagonisms, and insecurities. Overly adversarial activism eventuates in a defensive expansionism, arms racing, tests of resolve, and confrontations, possibly in an action-reaction cycle that spirals toward war. A "radical" dovish analysis assigns American policies major responsibility for the onset of the Cold War by way of a self-fulfilling prophecy. After 1945 Washington was inordinately insensitive to Moscow's security-motivated requirements and actions in Eastern Europe, thus becoming mistakenly convinced of its expansionist designs upon Western Europe. The subsequent adoption of adversarial measures convinced the Soviets of our deep hostility, prompting their adoption of (defensive) measures that then threatened America's security. It has also been argued that the Kennedy administration's decision to quadruple nuclear forces when the USSR was sorely outclassed increased the Kremlin hardliners' opposition to Khrushchev's minimum-deterrent doctrine and his calls for cutbacks in conventional forces. It thereby contributed to his downfall and the Soviets' own massive buildup.[3]

Invariable and total success cannot be expected of a security strategy. However, it should certainly be capable of recognizing and rectifying its errors. Both adversarial and conciliatory engagement are ill equipped for correcting policies based upon a misinterpretation of the contender's intentions.

Once excessively adversarial measures have been implemented, there are very few actions on the opponent's part that would disconfirm their interpretive foundations. Deterrence failures tend to be attributed to inadequately threatening measures in confronting an implacably revisionist state. The fault lay with insufficient firmness and power. Little if any consideration is given to the possibility that the adversarial posture engendered defensive fears and a perceived need for expansive actions on the part of a contender that was more benignly motivated than had been presumed. With mistakes unrecognized, they are not about to be rectified. Adversarial policies are almost reflexively judged successful by their proponents when the rival does not undertake security-threatening actions, without seriously entertaining the alternative possibility—that he never intended to. If so, "successful" deterrence was a costly waste that could have eventuated in an action-reaction spiral.

A conciliatory strategy is open to the parallel error. Defections that follow in the wake of accommodative efforts, compromise agreements, concessions, and other reassurances are attributed to insufficiently reassuring efforts. Moreover, once a sufficiently loud warning bell is sounded, once the opponent is correctly seen to have threatening intentions, it may be too late. Policy changes are too late if the rival achieved some consequential, possibly irreversible, territorial gains and military advantages. He cannot be stopped from exploiting them. A guardian state that seeks to recoup its losses or restore its strength may, by that much-warranted shift, trigger an immediate challenge. Knowing that the future will be less advantageous for carrying out his ambitious ventures than the present, the challenger has an incentive to capitalize upon his recently acquired advantages before the impending strategic shift rescinds them.

The security-deflating consequences of policies shaped in accordance with mistaken understandings of the contender's intentions are thus real and exceptionally difficult to recognize and correct. To be sure, the hazards are substantially mitigated if the rival is roundly outclassed. A benignly motivated challenger who is dealt with as a potential aggressor may well be incapable of carrying out seriously threatening actions despite his feeling beleaguered. In the case of a weak opponent with revisionist ambitions who is treated as benignly motivated, there should be sufficient time and opportunity to discover and rectify the mistaken policies. But these considerations then point to the diminished need for engaging a weak opponent from the outset.

II

The claim that it is inordinately difficult to identify the intentions of most opponents with a reasonably high degree of confidence—a degree that can justify the basic thrust of a security strategy—is supported by three telling cases: Nazi Germany, the Soviet Union, and Saddam Hussein's Iraq.

At the time and since then, the American, French, and the British governments have been sharply criticized for not recognizing Hitler's vaulting ambitions. The criticism has cut so deeply partly because of the common belief that his intentions were readily evident. Yet even in this putatively clear-cut case, one whose lessons have had an enormous impact upon our post-1945 foreign policy, there was no way in which German aims could have been confidently known until March 1939, only six months before the beginning of World War II.

Up to the occupation of the non-German-speaking parts of Czechoslovakia in March 1939 Hitler's actions were consistent with the prevalent
manner in which they were widely understood, as those of a peculiar,
ranting nationalist, fully intent upon restoring Germany to its rightful
place after the great injustices inflicted upon it at the Versailles peace
conference. How could it have been known that Hitler had always been
serious about the maniacal claims and aims in *Mein Kampf*? His government was only demanding a restoration of Germany's pre-1914 entitle-
ments as a fully sovereign state and a great European nation. The *An-
schluss* (union) with Austria, the entry of German forces into their own
Rhineland, the rearmament of a sovereign state, and "self-determination" in annexing the German-speaking parts of Czechoslovakia—these
actions could readily be seen as the rectification of Versailles's inequities,
as a nationalist revivalism and restoration prompted by them. Hitler's
words and Nazi propaganda consistently portrayed them in just these
terms. Moreover, there were virtually all the people around Hitler to consider. While all were committed to Germany's resurgence, few civilians
and officers even thought of going to war with France and Britain to
achieve it. Yet fewer were willing to do so in order to achieve German
hegemony over Western and Eastern Europe. The German general staff
took exception to most of Hitler's moves, in the belief that he was leading
the country into a disastrous war. Had France and Britain stood firm, the
generals would probably have moved against him.

If an opponent's intentions are knowable, it is hardly unreasonable to
expect them to be known in the case of a forty-year rivalry. But with
American publics, academics, and foreign policy elites subscribing to
very different, irreconcilable understandings of Soviet aims and values
throughout the Cold War, many or most were thoroughly mistaken.

On one interpretation, the Soviets were implacably bent upon expanding to the limits of their enormous capabilities, vanquishing the United
States politically and extending their influence-control and the communist ideology globally. The dictates of totalitarianism, the leadership's
legitimacy requirements, and its ideological ambitions—not any threats
to Soviet security—imparted shape and substance to a relentless imperialism.[4] Others characterized the USSR as opportunistically expansionist
or as aiming to achieve its rightful superpower equality with the United
States. Revisionist aims were certainly present, but not relentlessly compelling. They were to be translated into expansionist gains only when
the costs and risks were on the low side. The Soviet Union was seen to
have the ambitions of any major power—flexing its muscles and striving
for more power and influence—while appreciative of external (and later
of internal) limitations and the risks of nuclear war.[5] Then there is the
view of the USSR as defensively oriented, deeply insecure, striving to

protect itself and its protective empire by fending off the West to the maximum extent of its capabilities. Soviet insecurities, alternatively the quest for maximum security, were a product of the experience and memories of past invasions, ideological depictions of capitalist hostility, internal weaknesses, and America's threatening nuclear arsenal and global interventionism.[6]

An ineluctable conclusion follows. As a collective entity the United States did not understand Soviet intentions. They were indeterminate for an interpretively divided America. At any given time many or most Americans were thoroughly mistaken in their understandings of the Soviet Union, without there being any way to determine which of them were on, wide of, or totally off the mark. Those who advocated one or another of the three irreconcilable interpretations did not possess some secret intelligence, special information, or better intellectual credentials to give them a leg up on, and certainly not a monopoly on, the truth.

Another point about America's inability to identify Soviet intentions pertains to the second half of the Cold War. Between circa 1970 and 1985 Washington subscribed to five different interpretations. It is possible that Moscow sharply revised its intentions four times over within some fifteen years. But it is hardly plausible. Soviet power and behaviors did not fluctuate that widely or often. The same Leonid Brezhnev and Politburo coterie—a "conservative" one at that—were in power during nearly the entire period.

The rapidity and depth of the supposed changes should thus elicit skepticism about one or more of Washington's interpretations. Under Nixon's and Ford's auspices, Moscow was thought to have quasi-global ambitions of an opportunistic kind. During the first year or two of the Carter administration the USSR was seen in a cautiously benign light, and then according to a flashing red one. In the early 1980s Reagan moved yet further in this direction. The USSR was an "evil empire," aiming for "world revolution and a one-world Socialist or Communist state," and reserving unto itself "the right to commit any crime, to lie, to cheat." Then in 1985, within four days of Mikhail Gorbachev's ascension, Reagan claimed that the Soviets are "in a different frame of mind than they've been in the past."[7] A few months later the White House announced what turned out to be an effusively warm 1985 Geneva summit, followed by the 1986 Iceland summit, by which time Reagan had so much more trust in Moscow's intentions that he urged Gorbachev to agree to the elimination of all nuclear weapons.

The failure to discern Saddam Hussein's aggressive intentions vis-à-vis Kuwait was not only total, it occurred in the face of a diverse handful of telling aggressive indications. Saddam had previously invaded Iran, fought an utterly bloody war with it, showed his ruthlessness in attacking

Iraq's Kurdish population (sometimes with chemical weapons), voiced his Baathist ideological aims for the entire Middle East, expressed grandiose hegemonic ambitions for the region, and maintained a one-million-man army, by far the largest in the region and featuring the highest ratio of military manpower to population size of any modern state. As noted in chapter 10, the Bush administration knew of Iraq's chemical and nuclear weapons programs. Iraq publicly expressed its grievances against tiny Kuwait. They had to do with its islands controlling access to Iraq's only port, its pumping operations from the Rumaila oil field that lay partly under Iraq, its refusal to forgive the huge debt incurred in the war against the common Iranian threat, and its exceeding OPEC oil-production quotas ("an act of war"). In early 1990 Saddam began to spell out a collision course with the United States as an enemy of the Arab world. Two weeks prior to the attack he accused Kuwait and the United Arab Emirates of purposefully lowering oil prices as a "Zionist plot" in the service of U.S. imperialism. He appended this threat: "If words fail to afford us protection, then we will have no choice but to resort to effective action to put things right and ensure the restitution of our rights."[8]

The most that can be said on behalf of Washington's understanding of Saddam's intentions is this: It recognized his grand ambitions, and two weeks before the invasion there was some concern that he might act upon them in the not-too-distant future. However, the main lines of analysis and policy were very different. The Bush administration "generated plausible defensive interpretations for Saddam's moves: he feared another Israeli strike as in 1981, so his threats against Israel were deterrents; the Romanian experience of revolution and the Voice of America's broadcast of prodemocratic messages to Iraq unnerved him with regard to domestic stability and American intentions; and his economic problems at home led him to seek foreign policy grandeur."[9] The National Security Council never discussed Iraq. The White House continued to assist it financially and allowed dual-use exports for its nuclear and missile programs. President Bush was fairly optimistic that Saddam would be benignly influenced by such assistance and the diplomatic message that we sought "better relations" with him. And as Iraqi troops massed on the day before the invasion, the National Security Council and the CIA concluded that it would be limited to the small islands and the slice of Kuwaiti territory over the disputed oil field.[10]

The American failure might be partly explained away in that no other government foresaw Iraq's resort to force. As our ambassador to Baghdad later noted, "Obviously, I didn't think—and nobody else did—that the Iraqis were going to take all of Kuwait. Every Kuwaiti and every Saudi, every analyst in the Western world, was wrong too."[11] Although this mitigates Washington's failure, it simultaneously underscores the problematics of interpreting a challenger's intentions, even on the part of governments that are much closer to the scene. And this with so many consistent indications pointing to Saddam's ruthlessness in the service of relentless ambitions.

III

These three telling cases help make for a persuasive, but not a conclusive, argument. The latter requires a demonstration of intentions being regularly indeterminate.

Unlike the opponent's capabilities, which are directly discernible and thus frequently known with considerable reliability and exactitude, as purely subjective phenomena intentions are not observable and thus not directly knowable. There are two and only two approaches to take in identifying them. The opponent's aggressive-defensive aims and motivations can be discovered from the top down by inferring them from his observable behaviors. They can be discovered from the bottom up by explaining their formation, preservation, and alteration. The policymakers, analysts, and academics who rely upon one approach do not deny the other's premises. Without any incompatibilities between them, they can be used together as checks and corroborations.

Yet both the top-down and the bottom-up approaches are regularly afflicted with deep, even irresolvable difficulties. They cannot be circumvented. It is usually not possible to do much more than mitigate them. Beginning with George Kennan as the chief intellectual architect of the containment strategy, through the recent integrated application of the two approaches in a methodologically self-conscious manner, the countless efforts to understand Soviet intentions have failed to clear several high hurdles.

The bottom-up approach does make good sense. To explain a state's intentions is to identify them. Like all other subjective phenomena, they derive from some potentially knowable sources. This approach does not place any a priori restrictions on the explanatory candidates. They may feature domestic and international conditions, long-standing and situational circumstances, historical experiences and memories of them, structural and cultural patterns, and the political, material, and institutional interests of individuals, groups, and sectors. The exercise may be pursued in a holistic or positivist manner, by focusing upon a country's "richly detailed cultural, social, and historical context" in accordance with the "actor's subjective understanding," or by developing and applying generalizable (if, then) hypotheses while holding extraneous factors constant.[12]

One problem with the positivist exercise is the paucity of well-established generalizations. Only one is well established—democratic states do not go to war with others of the same ilk.[13] It says nothing about non-democratic states and thus about the USSR and America's other opponents. It is often said that governments adopt expansionist goals in order to compensate for the loss of domestic support. But this is still only a tendency statement, and it is silent with regard to regimes that do not face a legitimacy deflation and those that can substitute forceful coercion for public support. The argument that the latter kind of regime, especially a totalitarian one, tends to be aggressively expansionist overgeneralizes the Nazi case. It is belied by others, most strikingly perhaps by years of governmental repression in Burma and Albania coupled with their uncompromising insularity.

One problem with the holistic exercise is not a scarcity, but an overly large number, of plausible explanatory candidates. Without cross-national generalizations as a guide, how is it to be known which of them are in fact the important ones? In the Soviet case, some dozen explanatory candidates have been put forward. These include the centuries-long history ("the tradition") of czarist expansionism, memories of having been attacked four times in the twentieth century and devastated twice, Joseph Stalin's paranoia, the size and resources of a world power, the universalist communist ideology, Leninism's "attacking" culture, the elite's culturally ingrained risk aversiveness, China's ideological challenge as the fount of socialist orthodoxy, the regime's totalitarian origins and structure, a decided sense of national inferiority, the leaders' political insecurities, potential challenges to their legitimacy, the institutional and professional interests of the military-industrial complex, economic debilities and modernizing constraints, and the presence of a powerful NATO and China on the country's borders.

Moreover, some formative conditions are decidedly indeterminate. They could about as plausibly shape aggressive as defensive intentions, which is also to say possibly both, among different individuals and groupings. For example, there is often insufficient evidence to determine whether the experience of having been devastated by another state helped engender revengeful ambitions or deep anxieties, whether economic weakness prompts an acquisitive expansionism or a concentration upon domestic development, or whether powerful neighbors engender aggressive resentments or defensive insecurities. Such indeterminateness parallels a psychobiography of individual leaders in which painful childhood experiences can eventuate in their imitative embrace or a reaction formation against them.

These difficulties afflict the most influential interpretation of Soviet intentions, set out by George Kennan at the beginning of the Cold War. Soviet conduct is "the product of ideology and circumstances: ideology inherited by the present Soviet leaders from the movement in which they had their political origin, and circumstances of the power which they have exercised for nearly three decades in Russia." Kennan concluded that the Soviet leaders "had come to believe implicitly in the truth and soundness of the Marxian-Leninist teachings," the innate class conflict within and among states out of which socialism would ultimately triumph. The regime's "outstanding circumstance" is the failure to complete the "process of political consolidation. . . . The men in the Kremlin have continued to be predominantly absorbed with the struggle to secure and make absolute the power which they seized in November 1917." The insecurities created by the leadership succession question and the need to justify full-blown dictatorial rule at home reinforced the vision of a powerful external threat.[14]

But what of the validity of this plausible interpretation? Kennan only sought to establish half the case: the reasons for thinking it valid, not those for rejecting the alternatives. Except for one terse assertion, he did not consider, no less persuasively downgrade or reject, the other plausible possibilities that were just noted. The analysis also tends toward the indeterminate. An ideologically inspired leadership could have adopted hegemonic aims in the conviction of capitalism's ultimate demise and the need to provide a forceful, culminating push. It could also have embraced defensive aims on capitalism's unbending hostility, great strengths, and its encirclement of the USSR. The "inevitability of war" thesis could have led to expansionist undertakings so that the destruction would take place far beyond the homeland, to a protective quest via an all-out bolstering of defenses within the USSR and around it within the inner empire, or to both. As for the succession anxieties of rival leaders, after the regime was stabilized and legitimized circa 1965, Soviet aims should have shifted toward the benign end of the spectrum on Kennan's reasoning. Yet political security and popular support could have given the Politburo the opportunity, confidence, and encouragement to move across the world stage as the leaders of a great imperial power.

The bottom-up approach sometimes requires some further steps, demanding, possibly insuperable ones. They are required when the challenger is not governed by a single, virtually dominant leader or a leadership that is (somehow) known to be like-minded. Under Stalin the people around him subscribed to only slightly different views—a Molotov versus a somewhat more conciliatory Malenkov, for example—and they invariably deferred to his. But after Stalin's death in 1953 the explanatory exercise had to be carried out for each set of influential political actors, extending considerably beyond the Politburo after circa 1970. What were their foreign policy aims as formed by their particular generational memories, ideological beliefs, factional commitments, and organizational and professional interests? The hard-liners and moderates' policy preferences then had to be aggregated into a more or less coherent collective position. This required considerable inside knowledge of the distribution and relative weight of their political resources, as well as their mediation by the contours and interstices of a closed decision-making process.

Rather than explanation, the more commonly used top-down approach relies upon inferences drawn from observable behaviors. Since a state's intentions are the most immediate determinants of its actions, the latter serve as the evidence that reveals them—directly or when placed in their international context. Economists, psychologists, sociologists, historians, intelligence officers, public officials, pollsters, and just about everyone else regularly draws conclusions about people's intentions from their behavioral manifestations, often with considerable confidence and agreement.[15] In the case of an external opponent the commonly used behavioral indicators include more or less frequent interventions, their location at greater or lesser distances from the homeland, the size of military deployments, and their offensive-defensive configuration, military assistance programs, the negotiation of meaningful arms accords, and threatening or accommodating words. Other potentially revealing behaviors include announcements of ideological revisions, official and unofficial writings and speeches, production rates of industrial and consumer goods, foreign trade and aid policies, along with all sorts of purloined information.

Success varies with the wider or narrower, more or less distorting gap between the behavioral evidence and its motivational source. Even with all the open information at their disposal and their analytical simplifications, economists have been partly stymied in their understandings of "revealed preferences."[16] Compared to just about all other subjects, the inferential bridging operation is orders of magnitude more tenuous when it involves an international rival. Its actions are all too readily susceptible to Janus-faced interpretations: The very same undisputed facts can all too easily be read as evidence of aggressive aims or defensive vulnerabilities; they lend themselves to about equally persuasive contradictory conclusions without there being any general or contextually specific decision rules for resolving them. The interpretive difficulties stem from the security dilemma, the difficulties in distinguishing between actions and reactions in a complex relationship, and the incentives and opportunities for purposeful dissembling.

Given the security dilemma, what could be made of Moscow's using all its strengths and situational chances to expand its influence and control? Perhaps all that could be confidently inferred is the implacability of its expansionist objectives, not whether the underlying intentions were of an aggressive or defensive kind. What the Red Army did in occupying Eastern Europe and invading Hungary, Czechoslovakia, and Afghanistan does not compare with American actions in Central America. However, the differences could have been due to greater protective necessities and deeper fears for the preservation of Russia's immediate geostrategic space. In the 1970s the Soviets extended their presence thousands of miles beyond the homeland. But since the United States had also globalized the rivalry, those distant intrusions could have been due to the perceived need to compete for equal power and influence, to demonstrate that the Soviet's defensive resolve was no less than America's, or both. Washington certainly sought to demonstrate the resolve to defend Western Europe and the Middle East by way of protecting the peripheries despite and because of their evident material unimportance.

Nor is it clear that Moscow consistently capitalized upon its expansionist capabilities and opportunities. The Red Army was withdrawn from Czechoslovakia, Bulgaria, and Finland after 1945; no aid was given to the communist revolutionaries in postwar Greece; the huge French and Italian communist trade unions were not ordered to carry out a general strike when this would have greatly disrupted Western Europe's political and economic rehabilitation; Mao Tse-tung was told to compromise with Chiang Kai-shek rather than strive for a victory that was manifestly in his grasp; hardly any arms were transferred to national liberation movements in southern Africa whose successes might have interrupted Western access to strategic minerals; no assistance was given to the secessionist Kurds during the years in which Iran served as America's chief security pillar in the Gulf region; when Washington was giving arms to North Yemen in its 1979 war with Marxist South Yemen, the latter only received a trickle of Soviet help. True, Moscow may have had tactical or constraining reasons not to act expansively in these instances. However, this cannot be determined without first knowing what the Soviets were thinking, which simply recasts and adds to the intentions problem in terms of their calculations without at all resolving it.

Parallel problems of interpretation deriving from the security dilemma bear upon Soviet strategic capabilities. The hundreds of underground shelters for national and regional leaders were viewed as evidence of Soviet intentions to launch a first strike against the United States in the vortex of a deep crisis. They were also taken as indicative of the leadership's primary concern with its own survival and political-military control after a nuclear war brought on by its expansionism. However, the hard shelters could also have been built for defensive reasons. By negating a decapitating strike that would prevent Soviet retaliation and by limiting Soviet losses, they would better deter a U.S. first strike.[17] An interpretation of capabilities also has to contend with the possibility that their numbers, design, and configuration are unrelated to intentions.

> Does the bigness of Soviet missiles indicate greater capability, or a Soviet inability to design lighter and more compact missile payloads, and more efficient rocket engines, as some analysts suggest? Does the large number of Soviet systems indicate a Soviet force of greater diversity and strength, or does it demonstrate a Soviet political incapacity to prevent Soviet design bureaus from deploying samples of their less successful products? Does the number of new Soviet systems suggest Soviet strategic momentum, or an inability to modernize efficiently by upgrading existing systems, as the United States has done (for instance, with Minuteman III)?[18]

The organizational and bureaucratic politics explanations that have so often been used in explicating American weapons decisions could well apply on the Soviet side.

The rival's recent behavior is commonly used as evidence with which to assess its possibly altered intentions, to detect any changes that would warrant a revision of an interpretation based on the earlier record. When that behavior constitutes a major divergence from a past pattern, the question takes on special importance: Is the departure best understood as a "new" action stemming from altered intentions, or as a reaction, a response to a previous move on the part of the guardian state? It is no simple matter to disentangle the messy skeins of an ongoing relationship when the present is enmeshed in a fast-paced, several-sided rivalry. The Soviet missile emplacement in Cuba is a telling case of the interpretive complexities. As a direct challenge to the United States and a sharp departure from past Soviet behavior, the decision was presumably taken with a clear set of objectives in mind. The facts of the case—the number, range, and deceptive installation of the missiles—were not in doubt. President Kennedy's advisers on the Excom certainly appreciated the importance of identifying Moscow's objectives. Yet some were unable to fathom them, and the others were divided. And this uncertainty has persisted despite 1962 being distant enough in time to allow for relatively detached assessments, and the appearance of several excellent studies of the missile crisis. Nor has it been resolved by open discussions among some of the Americans and Russians who were then sitting in and around the seats of power.[19]

The question remains: Were the missiles intended to gain a strategic advantage by placing U.S. bombers at risk of destruction on the ground, to press Washington to make some concessions on the Berlin issue, and to impress the Third World, Latin America in particular, with Soviet audaciousness and momentum? Alternatively, were the missiles deployed to

deter an American attack against Cuba and to give an immediate boost to
the Soviets' deterrent threat of second-strike retaliation? If the latter, it
would have been a reaction to the likelihood of an American invasion of
Cuba after the halfhearted Bay of Pigs attempt and to the Kennedy administration's decision to quadruple the number ICBMs within the next
few years, despite its knowledge of a "missile gap in reverse," a five-to-
one U.S. advantage. The Soviet participants in the recent dialogues all
said that Nikita Khrushchev's intentions were defensive. Some claimed
that the fear of a U.S. invasion of Cuba was his uppermost concern;
others were equally certain that the major (or single) purpose was that of
partly redressing the huge strategic imbalance by placing intermediate
range missiles within striking range of the United States. They also suggested an interpretation that was not considered by Kennedy and the
Excom. Khrushchev was said to be motivated by "a complex emotional
dimension that sprang from frustration at the exposure by the United
States of Soviet strategic inferiority and the collapse of his Berlin policy,
resentment of the U.S. deployment of Jupiter missiles in Turkey, and concern over mounting foreign policy problems."[20]

A contender's actions stand in starkest contrast with those of a buyer
of fixed-price goods. Consumer behavior is fully transparent to retailers,
producers, and economists; there are no incentives to hide or disguise
purchasing motivations and calculations. Understanding the challenger's
intentions runs up against considerable, sometimes irremediable departures from these transparencies. With states regularly having the opportunity to shroud their real aims and their variable reasons to do just that,
the interpretive exercise immediately raises the issue of whether or not
such an incentive is present. The usual focus is upon the possibility of
cooperative actions being used to create a false impression of benign intentions and a misleading sense of security. There is also another side to
the coin: The contender may threaten, swagger, and exaggerate his power
because of defensive vulnerabilities and anxieties; he is trying to ward off
the coercive actions of a guardian state that is thought to harbor unsavory
designs. Without first having identified his intentions how is it then to be
known whether the challenger has an incentive to dissemble, and if so, in
which direction?

Stalin's vitriolic condemnations of the West and inflammatory talk of
"world revolution" could be taken at their face value, or as a protective
cover for a war-torn country facing a hostile America with a nuclear monopoly producing close to half of the world's GNP. Khrushchev's peaceful talk of "competitive coexistence" and proposals for conventional
arms reductions could have been an attempt to split off Western Europe
from the United States after Stalin's threats had united them, or they may
have been prompted by an appreciation of the nuclear risks to the Soviet

homeland. Similarly, his braggadocio and "we will bury you" claim might have been inspired by the country's rapid economic growth and impressive ideological gains in the Third World, or used to hide and compensate for its markedly inferior strategic forces. Leonid Brezhnev may have signed on to detente in good faith as a formula for peaceful competition, or promoted it as a stratagem for surpassing the United States strategically and defusing U.S. opposition to Third World expansionism. During his first year or two in power Gorbachev might have abstained from expansionist ventures to focus all his energies on the deteriorating economy, concomitantly fostering the idea of a "common European home" for the sake of peace, or to obtain a much needed breathing spell prior to the next round in the Cold War.

Lastly, the most basic premise of the top-down approach may not obtain in some instances. There is no knowing the contender's intentions if they are unknown to himself. They are nonexistent in any strategically meaningful sense when the opponent has not determined whether he has any aims beyond the defensive realm. It would not be surprising if an ambitious expansionism was neither embraced nor rejected by a powerful, yet considerably weaker challenger. He has little or no reason to come to some sort of grand decision when current policies would not be affected. Prior to the emergence of some equal balance of power and advantages, policies designed to buttress the opponent's security could easily be the same as those for paving the way to a revisionist future. The occasion and need for choice are absent, the knowledge for sorting through the future costs and risks of expansionism is meager, and the leadership may have more to lose than to gain by putting the question of future aims on the agenda.

Overall, the USSR was discernibly disadvantaged vis-à-vis the United States throughout their rivalry, achieving strategic parity alone around 1970. And if Khrushchev's exaggerated claims are set aside as bluster, it would seem that the Soviet leaders did not disagree. In chapter 3 it was seen that many on the Soviet side were decidedly unimpressed with their "geopolitical momentum" of the 1970s. Moscow publicly acknowledged its secondary position in the 1980s. It is thus entirely possible that the Politburo neither subscribed to nor rejected an ambitious expansionism; striving for hegemony was a nonissue, without policy-guiding import. Even a confident socialist triumphalism need not have entailed the policy-guiding embrace of great revisionist aims prior to the achievement of superpower equality. Marxism-Leninism foresaw the victory of socialism, without, however, predicting time schedule, while explicitly warning against the dangers of excessive haste. And as recognized by nearly all analysts, an appreciation of the hazards of acting before conditions were sufficiently ripe was central to the Soviet leaders' well-imbued risk aversiveness, their rejection of "adventurism."[21] Thus ambitious wishes and optimistic expectations may simply have been laid aside, rather than shaping the ongoing round in the East-West conflict or Moscow's future plans.

The weaknesses of the bottom-up and top-down approaches might be remedied by using them together. Since they proceed from opposite starting points, their coming to a similar conclusion should lend it considerable credence. Since each has its distinctive weaknesses, those of one may be checked or offset by the strengths of the other. However, these potential improvements do not markedly mitigate the interpretive problematics. For the two approaches' characteristic strengths do not address each other's weaknesses, and thus there is no special reason to expect them to come to similar conclusions.

These points come out most clearly in Jack Snyder's methodologically self-conscious assessment of Soviet intentions regarding the wartime use of nuclear weapons.[22] His analysis focuses upon a highly salient and specific set of intentions whose implementation required considerable advanced planning. As such they should have been relatively easy to identify. Snyder addresses the contingency of a conventional war in Europe, NATO forces are about to be overrun, prompting them to carry out their declared policy of limited nuclear attacks upon military targets in Eastern Europe and the USSR. He then uses the top-down and bottom-up approaches to determine whether Moscow planned to fight a controlled, counterforce nuclear war or to execute an all-out attack upon the United States and its allies.

The top-down perspective provides several reasons to believe that once nuclear weapons were fired Moscow would respond with a full-scale attack upon those who used them first. This was inferred from the civilian leadership's public declarations and statements about the need to curtail the damage inflicted upon the Soviet Union by totally destroying the enemy. These pronouncements were at one with Soviet military doctrine, which highlighted the practical impossibility of executing a series of limited nuclear exchanges and of maintaining intrawar deterrence. The doctrine's presumptive validity and implementation were reinforced by the Warsaw Pact force posture.

Yet Snyder did not simply take these behavioral facts at their face value. The public statements could have been designed to demonstrate the inevitability of massive devastation once any nuclear weapons were fired. NATO's resolve to be the first to do so would then be degraded, leaving it at a conventional disadvantage. Dissension would also be sown into the alliance. Washington's leadership would be challenged, since it was more strongly committed to fighting a counterforce nuclear war than the Europeans, they much preferring that the superpowers carry out any nuclear strikes over their heads, against one another alone. As for the Warsaw Pact deployments, these turned out to be indeterminate. The capabilities and posture for fighting a limited nuclear war did not differ significantly from those needed for a coordinated, all-out disarming attack against the NATO countries.

Snyder then turned to the bottom-up approach. His effort is devoted to explaining the Soviet military's wartime doctrine, determining whether the stated rejection of the option of a limited nuclear war portrayed its actual plans. This is done on the premise that military doctrine, "like any belief system, is rooted in the sociological characteristics, historical experiences, and parochial outlook of the people who develop it." As applied to the Soviet officer corps, this premise consistently "predicts" the presence of a "strategic culture" that rejects the idea of limited war. The military doctrine is used to explain and thus corroborate its authoritatively embraced all-out wartime plans.

But with what degree of confidence? Snyder concludes by recommending a "research strategy for checking these findings with and against further work on the theoretical (premise) and on its application to the Soviet case. Is it true that military professionals are usually hostile to limited-war doctrines? What accounts for exceptions to this rule? Does the Soviet case fit the patterns of these exceptions?"[23] Besides this forthright caution about the bottom-up approach being able to resolve the uncertainties surrounding Soviet intentions, there is some reason for skepticism about the generalization as it applies to the planned use of *nuclear* weapons. The military's institutional interests in larger and better arsenals, and possibly its combat values, plausibly point toward the adoption of a limited-use, nuclear war strategy. Of the few cases against which to check Snyder's generalization, the only one that is adequately comparable—the U.S. military with its large and secure nuclear forces—diverged from it in the 1970s and 1980s.

<h1 style="text-align:center">IV</h1>

This leaves the question of whether an activist political-military strategy can still be largely salvaged, whether its policies can be designed without interpreting the opponent's intentions. There are only two overlapping ways to pursue an activist strategy without relying upon a knowledge of the other sides' aims.

A focus upon the opponent's capabilities alone is, of course, the approach favored by some hawks. They acknowledge that intentions are sometimes unfathomable, that capabilities are observable and crucial, and that activist measures should therefore be shaped in accordance with them. However, in chapter 2 it was seen that this is not how adversarial policies are actually formulated. Knowingly or not, assumptions and tentative hypotheses about the rival's intentions are imported into the analysis that shapes policy. And this is usually done by using worst-case possibilities that further distort a supposedly neutral exercise with regard to intentions.

Strategic reciprocation, as in the game of tit-for-tat, focuses upon capabilities as well as any other kinds of relevant behavior. In some considerable measure the United States has conducted itself in just this way vis-à-vis the USSR. At any one time the guardian state's security policies are solely responsive to the opponent's latest move. If the latter is adversarial so too is the response, and vice versa, without attempting to decipher the opponent's intentions. As most extensively elaborated by Robert Axelrod, this kind of strategy is "nice" in calling for cooperation on the very first move, and "forgiving" in responding positively to a cooperative move despite a long string of defections. It is realistically governed by the "long shadow of the future." Since the players expect the conflict to continue beyond the foreseeable horizon, the next move is far from being the last or a crucial one that could spell victory or defeat; neither player thus has a special to overwhelming reason to defect in the present. The guardian state is not at risk in reciprocating cooperatively, while consistently offering the contender an incentive to cooperate and a disincentive against defection. Over time a hostile opponent should learn that defection does not pay, while a benign one is reassured that cooperation is safe. Axelrod offers an impressive array of computer simulation data showing that the players who adhere to this gaming strategy are nearly always successful when playing against others using some other strategy. There are no losers when both adhere to it.[24]

Tit-for-tat is an excellent activist strategy in principle. In practice it is afflicted with enormous, commonly prohibitive complications, along with the distinct risk of an upward conflictual spiral. In severely simplified gaming situations, defection and cooperation are standardized and seen as substantively equal opposites. In international politics, identical responses to the other's latest move are sometimes unavailable or unacceptable. Moreover, identical responses, and especially the equivalent ones undertaken in lieu of them, are unlikely to be accorded equal value and consequentiality by both sides.

Strategic reciprocation immediately raises the issue of America's response to the opponent's use of force against another state. A defensive effort could be too late, too dangerous, or too costly. The use of comparable American force elsewhere may be unacceptable due to normative, alliance, or escalatory considerations. Washington searched for, but did not begin to come up with, an equivalent response to the Red Army's moves against the Hungarians in 1956 and the Czechs in 1968. Canceling U.S.

participation in the Moscow Olympic games, the grain embargo, and the funneling of weapons to the Mujahidin did not add up to a comparable response to the Soviet invasion of Afghanistan—certainly not considering President Carter's depicting it as potentially the "greatest threat to world peace since 1945." No consideration was given to sending American troops into Afghanistan or invading Cuba as a nearby equivalent of Afghanistan.

Where identical or equivalent moves are available, opting for them is commonly constrained, if not bedeviled by the problem of incomparable gains and losses. Contextual variations generate different utilities, divergent assessments of their relative value. The problem is evident in the nuclear weapons dimension of the Soviet-American rivalry despite its quantitative amenability to reciprocated activism. Many of the disagreements in negotiating symmetrical arms limitation and verification agreements were due to the rivals' dissimilar military postures, weapons development leads, geostrategic positions, and secrecy requirements. With regard to the Soviet heavy missiles that exercised so many on the American side, the rivals placing "a different value on throw-weight versus number of missiles . . . can play havoc with [the tit-for-tat strategy] since neither side can fully understand what the other would view as reciprocity."[25] The comparability problem would have arisen in the simplest hypothetical case, that of the Soviets dismantling five hundred long-, intermediate-, or short-range missiles. Considering NATO's greater reliance upon nuclear deterrence in the face of the Warsaw Pact's larger conventional forces, many or most on the American side would have insisted that following suit constitutes more than equivalent cooperation. Allies raise additional complications. Are their actions always to be counted in the tit-for-tat strategy? Does it matter whether they are (thought to be) carried out at the behest of or contrary to the wishes of the alliance leader? Would allies be willing and able to respond in an identical or equivalent manner?

Strategic reciprocation also features a built-in escalatory risk, the possibility of a single defection setting off subsequent rounds of mutual defection. To compensate for this "echo effect" Axelrod suggests a strategic modification, an extraforgiving rule: The retaliatory move is somewhat less extensive than the other side's latest defection.[26] But not only does a game theoretic analysis show this to be an unsatisfactory (collectively unstable) solution,[27] both sides are likely to view the significance of objectively identical and equivalent, and even extraforgiving, moves through biased lenses that escalate the rivalry.[28] The value accorded their own cooperation and sacrifices is inflated; the significance of their own defections and gains are deflated. They are also prone to downgrade the consequentiality of the other side's accommodative actions while upgrading its adversarial ones. An upward conflictual spiral sets in as one state is or appears to be overcompensating for the other's latest adversarial moves and undercompensating for its cooperative ones. Strategic reciprocation thus turns out to be largely unworkable and possibly hazardous even with a defensively motivated opponent who wants to play by its rules. In short, there is no way for strategic internationalism to escape or circumvent the problematics and hazards of tailoring policies to intentions.

Chapter V

MAXIMIZING DETERRENCE, DEFENSE,
AND ECONOMIC SECURITY

EASILY THE MOST important objective of any security strategy is the protection of America's highest values from direct external threats. Whether the strategy's scope does or does not extend beyond a narrow security perimeter, our intrinsically highest values are physically, politically, and economically embodied within it. Whether the strategy be of a national or international kind, safeguarding them means warding off unacceptable actions around, against, and within the core perimeter, as well as minimizing their hurtful consequences if they were to materialize.

This chapter compares the performance of strategic engagement and nonengagement in safeguarding America's highest values under hawkishly defined premises. The opponent or opponents are taken to have the capabilities to mount a serious military, terrorist, and/or economic challenge. They are also assumed to harbor various hostile intentions. This is not to play down the extent to which America's security may be put at risk by a challenger driven by defensive aims and concerns. What follows can also be read on the premise that the contender's behavior is governed by pronounced security fears that (contrary to the claim of the next chapter) have *not* been allayed by the national strategy's reassuring attributes.

According to the *third doctrinal tenet*, national policies are maximally successful in guarding against an opponent's direct threats to America's highest values. The effectiveness of its deterrent and protective capabilities cannot be improved upon militarily, politically, or economically. The most effortful adversarial strivings on behalf of global interventionism, nuclear predominance, and the retention of our political, military, and economic primacy do not make for greater security than the national strategy. Even when facing eminently powerful contenders with hostile-aggressive intentions and those with the ambitions to challenge the United States economically, adversarial efforts cannot improve upon the national strategy. Adversarial internationalism also makes for potential or predictable security deflations and counterproductive risks. The national strategy obviates them.

This chapter considers each set of adversarial policies as they bear upon any and all direct challenges to the nation's highest values. The next section sharply questions the credibility-enhancing doctrine and policies of global containment. The second section following does so with regard to the credibility and military claims made on behalf of nuclear parity, parity "plus," and outright superiority. It concomitantly supports a claim about America's strategic immunity that was not developed in chapter 3—our imperviousness to the nuclear superiority that the Soviet Union would have enjoyed had we adopted a national strategy. The final part critiques adversarial post–Cold War policies for meeting the specter of nuclear spread and potential challenges to America's across-the-board global primacy from Japan, Germany, and Western Europe.

I

Cold War containment policies were encompassingly determined by a material and geopolitical rationale. The material concerns focused most importantly upon Europe and Japan's industrial might, their current and potential military power, Central America's geographic proximity, the Persian Gulf's oil supplies, and southern Africa's strategic minerals. All of their doctrinal underpinnings (e.g., the translation of the Soviet presence into influence-control) were sharply critiqued in the course of establishing America's strategic immunity, in particular its territorially centered insulation and invulnerability.

The geopolitical rationale for global containment addressed these military and economic concerns by way of image and reputation. Our commitments, resolve, and credibility were taken to be indivisible on a global scale; containment was consistently used as a vast signaling exercise to demonstrate America's high resolve through the media of politics, psychology, and symbols. Despite their material unimportance, the peripheries were protected to bolster America's credibility in protecting itself and its central interests in Western Europe, Japan, the Caribbean basin, the Persian Gulf, and southern Africa. For a country to come within the containment perimeter it need not have any special military, geostrategic, or economic significance, none whatsoever if aggressively threatened by the Soviet Union or its offshoots. To make the point as made by others, it was often not our interests that determined our commitments, but the other way around. A country's importance was not so much determined by us as by Moscow's designs upon it.[1]

The belief that the demonstration of high resolve is globally interconnected and that it must be continually reinforced was the product of 1930s history and straightforward political logic. During the first half of the Cold War, containment policies were shaped by the deeply etched lessons drawn from events leading up to World War II. Not surprisingly so. States respond strongly, sometimes overreact, to their most recent foreign policy crisis. Britain and France had clearly failed to stand up to

Germany, losing their credibility and encouraging its aggression. Expansionist threats must therefore be consistently met with firmness; aggressive actions must invariably be confronted with force. To do any less is to impair our credibility and embolden others to challenge our commitments. Peace, which is also to say U.S. security, is globally indivisible, bound together by perceptions of U.S. resolve.

These lessons led directly into the first major Cold War intervention. The defense of South Korea was first and foremost a credibility-enhancing exercise. It was undertaken despite a studied appreciation of the peninsula's negligible geostrategic, military, and economic value. On two occasions the Joint Chiefs of Staff asked themselves whether South Korea was worth defending in the event of a major war. Both times they answered in the negative, a recommendation that was affirmed by the National Security Council, President Truman, and "announced" by Secretary of State Dean Acheson in excluding South Korea from our Asian defense perimeter.[2] Within twenty-four hours after the North Korean invasion this policy was rendered irrelevant, and not because the attack was far short of a general war.

Truman and his advisers drew a close analogy between this act of aggression and those of Germany, Italy, and Japan prior to World War II. The mistakes of the past must not be repeated. The United States could not afford to select when and where to respond forcefully; no matter how distant and unimportant the stakes, unless aggression was checked everywhere, adversaries would see us irresolute and friends will become less committed to their own defense. Ernest May underscored the impact of the 1930s by showing how a plausible alternative Cold War logic would have produced a very different decision. Since nothing was known about the reasons for the North Korean attack, it could easily be surmised that it was a feint. Stalin encouraged or ordered the invasion so as to tie up American forces in a small peninsula that led nowhere, with a view to attacking a singularly important Western Europe on the other side of the globe. Some American and European officials subscribed to this view. But for the Truman administration to accept it entailed a signal drawback: Sending more military forces to Europe would not address the subjective indivisibility of peace.[3]

To a lesser extent our other major Cold War intervention was also the product of the 1930s. President Johnson announced that the loss of South Vietnam "would encourage and spur on those who seek to conquer all free nations within their reach. . . . This is the clearest lesson of our time. From Munich until today we have learned that to yield to aggression brings only greater threats." The decision to deploy the first large-scale intervention force of 100,000 troops was made (or solidified) in a 1965 meeting between Johnson and his principal national security advisors. Henry Cabot Lodge, Jr., our ambassador to Saigon, summarized the thinking of all but one of his colleagues: "I feel there is a greater threat to start World War III if we don't go in. Can't we see the similarity to our own indolence at Munich?"[4]

America went into Vietnam for the sake of its global credibility. If it "allowed itself to be challenged successfully in any part of the world, then its determination to resist aggression would be called into question everywhere else." John Gaddis elaborates:

> What the Kennedy and Johnson administrations came to fear most, one gathers, was not communism, which was too fragmented, or the Soviet Union, which was too committed to detente, or even China, which was too impotent, but rather the threat of embarrassment, of humiliation, of appearing to be weak. Both men could accept the argument that Eisenhower and Dulles had overextended the United States . . . [But] having committed itself to maintaining the existing distribution of power in the world, the United States could not allow challenges to that distribution even to appear to succeed against its will, because perceptions of power could be as important as the real thing.[5]

This assessment was quantified in a 1965 memorandum by Assistant Secretary of Defense John McNaughton. America's reasons for being in Vietnam were "70%—to avoid a humiliating U.S. defeat [to our reputation as guarantor]. 20%—to keep [South Vietnam and the adjacent] territory from Chinese hands. 10%—to permit the people of [South Vietnam] to enjoy a better, freer way of life."[6]

By 1967 the highest officials knew that anything approximating a successful outcome was unrealizable. Yet American troops remained in Vietnam for another five years and suffered half their total casualties to achieve a cosmetic political settlement, one that was to curtail the damage to our global credibility. In Henry Kissinger's unqualified words, "the commitment of 500,000 Americans has settled the issue of the importance of Vietnam. For what is involved now is confidence in American promises." President Nixon explained the 1970 expansion of the war in similar terms. In announcing the U.S. incursion into Cambodia he maintained that it was not "our power, but our will and character that is being tested." Failing the test, the United States will be seen as "a pitiful, helpless giant," resulting in heightened threats to "free nations around the world."[7] The credibility imperative led us into Vietnam; once the commitment was made, it kept us there in a lost cause.

The lessons of the 1930s were so ingrained that they still resonated for some policymakers in the early 1980s. "Officials of the Reagan administration who formulated the policy of using the Nicaraguan rebels (the contras) to pressure or overthrow the Sandinista regime, saw critics of their policy as 'appeasers' of the Sandinistas. Some, like Jeane Kirkpatrick, argued that Munich, not Vietnam, was the appropriate analogue for the challenge in Nicaragua."[8] What Zbigniew Brzezinski said about the stakes in Central America was often said about most parts of the world. "The United States cannot afford to lose there because of its rivalry with the Soviet Union. . . . A loss would have widespread ramifications for . . . perceptions of international affairs that intangibly merge (and inevitably so) with the realities of international politics."[9]

Reinforced by the experiences and memories of the 1930s, containment was generally justified by what was thought to be the close relationship between America's past behavior and others' beliefs about its likely current and future behavior. Credibility is very much dependent upon a reputation for resolve; commitments and deterrent threats at any one time are assessed on the basis of the status quo state's past record in making and sustaining them. The more frequently the United States undertakes and fulfills defensive obligations, the greater its current credibility. Insofar as the fulfillment of defense commitments involves major efforts and great sacrifices, the other side will be all the more convinced of our high resolve. And by protecting demonstrably secondary and peripheral interests U.S. credibility with regard to the manifestly primary ones becomes all the firmer. The rival will extrapolate from the frequency of America's past actions, their high costliness, and low material stakes to the great likelihood of forceful responses in the present and for the future.

Perhaps no academic was more influential in imbuing several administrations with the reputational rationale than Thomas Schelling; none contributed more to its analytical and tactical development.

> It is often argued that "face" is a frivolous asset to preserve, and that it is a sign of immaturity that a government can't swallow its pride and lose face. It is undoubtedly true that false pride often tempts a government's officials to take irrational risks or to do undignified things—to bully some small country that insults them, for example. But there is also the more serious kind of "face," the kind that in modern jargon is known as a country's "image," consisting of other countries' beliefs (their leaders' beliefs, that is) about how the country can be expected to behave. It relates not to a country's "worth" or "status" or even "honor," but to its reputation for action. If the question is raised whether this kind of "face" is worth fighting over, the answer is that this kind of face is one of the few things worth fighting over. Few parts of the world are intrinsically worth the risk of serious war by themselves, especially when taken slice by slice, but defending them or running risks to protect them may preserve one's commitments; it is a coun-

try's reputation for action, the expectations that other countries have about its behavior. We lost thirty thousand dead in Korea to save face for the United States and the United Nations, not to save South Korea for the South Koreans, and it was undoubtedly worth it.

While acknowledging much of the strategic-immunity claim in writing that "few parts of the world" bear upon American security in any material way, Schelling still insists that most of the globe is central to our security for subjective, political reasons. "Even the commitments not deliberately incurred, and the commitments that embarrass one in unforeseen circumstances, cannot be undone cheaply. The cost is the discrediting of other commitments that one would still like to be credited."[10]

The indivisibility of peace centered around U.S. credibility is a seemingly powerful justification for continuous, far-flung demonstrations of resolve. Yet it is only supported by the events leading up to World War II if they are misread. The geopolitical logic is sound as far as it goes. But it runs up squarely against some yet more salient strategic reasoning supported by much evidence from the Cold War and other times and places. Moreover, a nonengaged America, relieved of the heavy demands of extended deterrence, would have had little reason to worry about its credibility once the security perimeter was defined in terms of our highest intrinsic values. Some forty years of global containment in protecting secondary and tertiary material interests so as to enhance the credibility behind the protection of our central and core interests were thus unjustified, less than efficacious, the grand design and its enormous security sacrifices largely, if not entirely, superfluous.

It is one thing to say that past actions help determine a state's credibility. It is quite another to maintain that the frequent, continuous, or invariable demonstration of resolve is necessary to establish its current resolve. It is the latter conclusion that was drawn from the 1930s, thereby leading America into widespread Third World involvements and interventions. If Britain and France had failed to stand firm once or twice, with Germany then no longer crediting their credibility, there would have been reason to learn to avoid similar mistakes after 1945. However, the actual record does not at all justify the conclusion; in some measure the 1930s actually call the reputational requisite into doubt.

Britain and France failed to stand firm not once or twice, but on five distinct occasions. These failures occurred within the space of a few years, and all but one contravened a formal, fully publicized declaration. The democracies did not resist the military occupation of the Rhineland, German rearmament, the incorporation of Austria, the annexation of the Sudetenland, and then the rest of Czechoslovakia. How then can this record show that resolve must be *continually* demonstrated to translate into credibility? Nor did inactions and appeasement convince Hitler that the democracies would continue to be irresolute, that their reneging on one or more commitments was predictive of similar behavior. France's passivity at the time of the Rhineland's illegal remilitarization did not lead Berlin into believing that Paris would renege on its defense obligation if Germany attacked Czechoslovakia.[11] And despite Britain and France's consistent unwillingness to stand up to Germany, it fully expected them to go to war—although not an all-out one—in response to the invasion of a Poland that they were in no geographic position to defend.

Nor do the 1930s support the argument that the defense of lesser interests bolsters the credibility behind the major ones. The 1930s are silent on this score. For there is no comparison between the importance of Britain's and France's stakes in Central Europe and America's interests in any part of the Third World except for the Persian Gulf. Germany's expansive actions in the geographical heart of Europe had a central bearing upon Britain and France's security. German rearmament threatened all of Europe. The military occupation of the Rhineland weakened France's defensive position. Britain's ceding the German-speaking third of Czechoslovakia at Munich crippled that country's political and military resistance to German aggression. The Sudetenland contained formidable fortifications against a German attack, a defensible mountainous terrain, the world's second biggest and most modern armaments-manufacturing center, and nearly all of Czech heavy industry. Britain's and France's failures to protect these crucial security interests have little if anything to say about America's putative need for defending the Third World as a way of persuading Moscow of its resolve at the center and around the narrow core.

The strength of the relationship between a state's earlier actions and current reputation, the frequency with which it needs to reinforce its credibility, is called into doubt under some readily imaginable circumstances. A state's failure to fulfill a defense commitment or deterrent threat on one occasion could well be explained away by the contender as due to special circumstances. A lapse on the next occasion may be seen as all the less likely, precisely because of the great store that states are thought to place upon their credibility. The credibility-enhancing actions of a state that has frequently shown its determination over some longer or shorter time span are subject to the law of decreasing marginal utility, having less and less impact upon its perceived resolve. And a state that has an excellent record in showing its strength of purpose has already generated a reputation for high resolve that would not be significantly diminished by selectively resting on its laurels.

These circumstances probably explain why the reputational rationale failed to pass a relatively easy test. It did not hold up in the mid-1970s when Moscow should have had especially good reasons to doubt America's continuing high resolve. The United States withdrew from Vietnam in 1973, did very little and failed to stop a pro-Soviet guerilla movement in Angola from defeating two pro-Western ones by 1976, and despite Washington's warnings about the impending collapse of detente, the Soviets actively supported an Ethiopian client against a Somali attack in 1977. Yet, there is Ted Hopf's assessment of the impact of these developments upon Soviet perceptions and expectations of U.S. reactions to current and future challenges.[12] His systematic examination of over five hundred articles and three hundred speeches directed to internal and external audiences clearly indicates that Soviet academics, journalists, and party leaders did "not draw the kind of inferences predicted by deterrence theorists and assumed by American policymakers who believe in the 'lessons of Munich.' . . . Even at the height of culminating gains, after the Paris accords and the fall of Saigon, the Soviets never doubted American elite resolve to resist. Instead, they attributed the American defeat to transitory public and congressional constraints on the government that compelled it to withdraw." This conclusion is tempered in one regard. The Soviets did conclude that "neither the American people, Congress, nor the American ruling elite would ever consciously choose to repeat an intervention on the same scale as Vietnam."[13] Still, this finding does not do much to support the reputational rationale. For at the time the United States itself gave every indication that it did not intend to repeat the Vietnam experience.

Whatever the effect of a state's previous behavior upon its credibility, there is also the present to consider. In comparing the relative importance of historicism and contextualism, the former as reputational rationale suffers markedly relative to the latter in determining a state's credibility. The shadow of the past is regularly overshadowed by the present. What is invariably accented, consistently predominant, is the guardian's immediate actions and reactions, its stakes in the issue at hand, its strengths and weaknesses, along with the prevailing conflict patterns that help interpret them. Moreover, its past and more recent behavior could well be incommensurate with the current issue, ambiguous, lacking in much information, and partly irrelevant due to the accession of new governmental leaders. Compared to memories of the past, present circumstances are also more palpable, offer greater detailed information, allow for "richer" implications to be drawn from them, as well as being psychologically more compelling when estimating the guardian's resolve.

The greater impact of contextualism over historicism is born out by several systematic studies ranging over geographical space and historical time. Alexander George and Richard Smoke carried out a close examination of eleven cases in which the United States sought to deter military attacks upon allies or neutrals between 1948 and 1963. They concluded that it was the interests at stake—not such signaling techniques as a state's past behavior—that had a decided impact upon the credibility of the deterrent threat. "The opponent is likely to pay more attention to strategic, political, economic and ideological factors determining the nature and magnitude of [the] interests than to rhetorical and other signalling devices to enhance credibility."[14] A rigorous analysis of fifteen overt conflicts, half of them Cold War crises, led Glenn Snyder and Paul Diesing to this conclusion: "What stands out is the discrepancy between the little evidence that statesmen *do* infer an opponent's resolve from his past behavior in previous cases and the massive evidence that decision makers think such inferences are made." A state's credibility is far more strongly related to its "inherent resolve," its intrinsic interests, than to its credibility-enhancing efforts.[15]

Similar results emerged from Paul Huth and Bruce Russett's analysis of fifty-four cases of extended deterrence between 1900 and 1980. In each of them a defender threatened to retaliate against an attacking state if it acted, as it seemed about to, against the defender's protégé. The data show that the defender's earlier actions—whether it did or did not previously fight when a protégé was attacked—had no impact upon the attacking state's decision to challenge the current deterrent threat. Successful deterrence was most strongly related to the political, military, and economic ties between the defender and its protégé, that is, by the magnitude of the interests at stake. Relying upon arms sales and trade as indicators of those interests, Huth and Russett found that "if the protégé takes 25 per cent or less of its arms imports from the defender the probability of successful deterrence is just .28, but if the proportion of military imports from the defender exceeds 75 per cent, the probability of successful deterrence rises to .79. Similarly, with no trade between defender and protégé the chances of successful deterrence are just about even, but if as much as 6 per cent of the defender's trade is with its protégé, the chances of effective deterrence rise to about seven out of eight."[16] In a later study using a revised data base (fifty-eight cases between 1885 and 1984), Huth found only a limited impact of the past upon the present. The kind of policy adopted by the defender vis-à-vis the same attacker in their most recent comparable encounter does help explain the next outcome. "Conciliation" and "bullying" behavior on the defender's part in the last parallel encounter lowered the likelihood of successful deterrence in the next one; a previous firm-but-flexible stance had no significant subsequent effect.[17]

Besides critiquing containment in the Third World, this discussion speaks directly to the credibility of a nonengaged America's deterrent threats. The fulfillment of commitments beyond the narrow core does not significantly improve upon the evident resolve to protect the core. To appreciate that our credibility in Europe, Japan, the Caribbean basin, and the Persian Gulf was no more than marginally heightened by demonstrating resolve beyond them, means that it was not and could not be heightened for the core. Given the crucial importance of the immediate context, the eminent visibility and demonstrable weight of a state's highest values is almost invariably sufficient as a demonstration of resolve. If not, it is hard to imagine how distant actions can further maximize the credibility to protect them. In Robert Jervis's words, "when interest is great enough"—as it surely is around the core perimeter—the active demonstration of "commitment is not necessary."[18] For Schelling, the "difference between [protecting] the national homeland and everything 'abroad' is the difference between threats that are inherently credible, even if unspoken, and the threats that have to be made credible."[19]

Over and above America's absolutely high credibility, there is the crucial matter of relative resolve. In deciding whether to cross a line, defy a threat, or escalate a confrontation, the contender will be much concerned with the two sides' comparative resolve. Who will sacrifice more, take greater risks, be less compromising in Schelling's "situations of competitive risk taking?" The stakes embodied within the core make for a decidedly favorable imbalance of actual and perceived resolve. Our stakes embrace the highest values, necessarily higher ones than whatever the challenger is striving to attain. Moreover, avoiding losses is commonly more salient than achieving objectively otherwise comparable gains. America would place greater store upon what it could lose than would the opponent upon what it could gain. Regarding the credibility calculus itself, there is this consideration: If we accept a diplomatic-political-military setback at the core, our future reputation would be more severely deflated than that of a challenger who chose to back down, precisely because it embodies our highest values. This is no secret on both sides.

Nor is it at all implausible to suppose that the national strategy would actually bolster the credibility of deterrent threats against unacceptable actions around the North American and oceanic core perimeter. Disengagement entails a unilateral, unconstrained, purposeful refusal to maintain widespread political-military involvements. It would have been, could be, and should only be undertaken alongside a manifestly visible confidence in our abiding strength and security. Turning to a national strategy follows from the recognition that it is unnecessary to bear the material and human costs of foreign entanglements to make America more secure abroad and at home. Such a great strategic shift would probably occur in the course of a fully publicized consideration of the country's truly privileged security position, a growing appreciation of the great scope and potency of the many conditions that ensure its strategic

immunity. Despite occasional glimmerings of pacifism, historical isolationism has varied between two poles, a quiet, unwavering confidence in
the country's great power and impregnability and a nationalist pugna-
ciousness. Both make for the unquestioning—and historically unquestioned—resolve to deter and fully defend against unacceptable actions.

On the argument up to this point a conclusion follows that is as important as it is incontestable. The defense of materially peripheral areas so as
to reinforce America's credibility with regard to its central and core interests was unnecessary and ineffective. Having entered two major regional
wars and continued one of them primarily as a credibility-signaling exercise, adversarial internationalism thus sorely detracted from our security.
More than 100,000 Americans died in Korea and Vietnam; over 300,000
were wounded. The extent of these losses cannot be mitigated, as they
sometimes are, because they occurred abroad rather than at home, because they were suffered by soldiers rather than civilians. These enormous
casualties detracted as much from our "physical security" as if they had
been suffered in an attack upon the homeland.

The official and public talk about U.S. credibility dropped off sharply
with the withering of the Cold War in the mid-1980s. But at a lower key,
the notion of U.S. security being stitched together around most of the
world by way of our perceived resolve is alive and well. It was very much
present in the decision to go to war against Iraq and constitutes a central
part of the primacist strategy that is discussed below. In fact, with the
interventionist costs and risks of demonstrating our resolve looking to be
far less demanding absent a superpower rival, the credibility imperative
could maintain its place at the forefront of the security agenda. Yet whatever the warrant for a globe-spanning credibility exercise, it loses yet
more of its sway when not facing a globe-spanning rival.

II

Force matters greatly, the balance of military power matters yet more,
and the United States should strive to maintain a decidedly advantageous
balance. There is a great deal to these adversarial maxims. In fact, they
are at one with those of a national strategy regarding the conventional
defense of the core perimeter. However, hawks and eagles divide sharply
on the maxims' applicability to nuclear weaponry. At its deepest, the division is about the existence of the nuclear revolution, whether weapons of
mass destruction against which there is no defense do or do not dictate
changes in the central assumptions governing the uses of conventional
weaponry. Can nuclear forces be put to good use in fulfilling all the objectives of conventional ones? Is nuclear superiority advantageous? Are strategic advantages necessary? These are the military issues on which hawks

and eagles divide. The majority of Cold War doves who took strategic parity as their lodestar are perched somewhere between them.

Any overview of U.S. nuclear policy during the Cold War should highlight this striking pattern: The purposes that were assigned to nuclear weapons increased steadily, the additional ones were more and more demanding, and they ended up encompassing all those requirements that have been assigned to conventional forces.

The atomic monopoly of the late 1940s was solely intended to deter a Soviet attack upon Western Europe. The many-times-over superiority of the 1950s was to deter an invasion of Europe and a surprise nuclear attack upon the United States. During the 1960s, with the Soviets clearly capable of inflicting unacceptable damage upon us, there was much dissatisfaction with the threat of mutual assured destruction (MAD) for protecting Western Europe and Japan. It was losing its credibility and left us without any options. In the 1970s the nuclear armory was thus to be capable of more than the destruction of Soviet industrial and population centers. According to the demanding policy of counterforce targeting, Soviet military sites were to be attacked with enough accuracy to limit widespread collateral damage. Soviet cities would survive as hostages to stave off attacks against America's. Nuclear weapons were also to ensure crisis stability and coercive success, to deter a preemptive Soviet attack in the heat of a confrontation and allow us to determine its resolution. In 1980 President Carter extended the nuclear-deterrence umbrella yet further (over the Middle East) and the strategy for fighting nuclear war was amplified in Presidential Directive (PD) 59. Beyond affirming the targeting of Soviet nuclear forces, deterrence was to be bolstered by threatening to destroy what the Soviet leadership "values most"—its survival, military might, and political control of the population. During the Reagan administration we were to be capable of conducting a limited (or protracted) nuclear war over a period of weeks or months while curtailing the damage to ourselves. The administration adopted the additional goal of prevailing at the end of such a war, that of ending it on relatively favorable terms.[20]

By the mid-1980s nuclear weapons were thus designed to fulfill six distinct purposes. Doing so successfully was thought to hinge upon the military balance, just as in a conventionally armed world, where superiority is trumps. Thus the justification for arms racing with the Soviets, achieving "escalation dominance" at each level of possible conflict, attaining a "margin of superiority," and trying to "spend the Soviets into the ground."

As spelled out in chapter 2, the national strategy would have featured a nuclear force at half the size of its past levels (absent land-based missiles). It would have exclusively targeted Soviet military installations (other than missile fields) situated at some distance from population centers. This design would have been no less effective than the adversarial one in deterring a preemptive strike, allowing us to prevail in a confrontation, and, in the event of war, in limiting destruction to the United States and ending it on relatively favorable terms. (Providing for extended deterrence is not discussed, given its irrelevance for a nonengaged America. However, extending what is said about the other five nuclear objectives could arguably show that there are no special weaknesses attaching to a national strategic posture in this regard.) In claiming maximally attainable security with U.S. strategic forces at about half the size of the Soviets', the national strategy goes much further than the doves' advocacy of parity. However, they are at one in stressing the potential security deflations brought on by strivings for nuclear advantage. The dangers have to do with excessive provocativeness, the Soviets' preemptive fears and temptations, the heightened chances of inadvertent war, the risks of "use them or lose them" weapons, hair trigger, launch-on-warning policies, and the possibilities of sheer accidents.[21] On these claims the national strategic posture substantially exceeds the adversarial one in its security promises.

How then can it be shown that nuclear parity did not promote, and that superiority would not have promoted, any of our strategic purposes? This is done by assessing the connections that were drawn between the military balance and the weapons' intended purposes, the intervening conditions, as it were. The countervailing strategy and an advantaged counterforce were said to bolster American resolve, greatly narrow the credibility gap, and threaten truly unacceptable damage.[22]

Advocates of adversarial internationalism have been much concerned with the problem of self-deterrence, our inadequate resolve in issuing forceful demands and carrying through on them. We held back and might well have held back in extremis, in the knowledge that a movement toward the nuclear brink could spell disaster for the United States. American leaders who were not sufficiently resolute to order the first use of nuclear weapons during a European war or a Soviet invasion of the Middle East would become so when sitting astride a more powerful armory. A nuclear advantage would impart greater determination by promising less than all-out destruction to the homeland in the event of war. The evidence does not, however, support a connection between U.S.-Soviet force ratios and American resolve.

If there were a generalized connection between the strategic balance and American resolve, it should certainly have been present during the Cuban missile crisis, an eyeball-to-eyeball confrontation during which we enjoyed a lopsided five-to-one strategic advantage. Yet President Kennedy and his Excom advisors gave little thought, no less decision-making salience, to it. Marc Trachtenberg's recent investigation reinforces the earlier view that the strategic imbalance "did not have an important direct influence on American policy. The Kennedy administration's fears of escalation [toward nuclear war] substantially cancelled out, in its own mind, whatever benefits it might have theoretically been able to derive from its strategic superiority. The American ability to 'limit damage' [to ourselves] by destroying an enemy's strategic forces did not seem, in American eyes, to carry much political weight."[23]

Nor are there any indications that the resolve of American officials was affected by the later loss of superiority. Throughout the 1970s the Soviets enlarged their strategic forces while U.S. deployments remained largely the same. Hawkish critics of the Carter administration feared that we would experience a failure of nerve in standing up to Moscow if the vulnerability of the land-based missile forces was not corrected. Yet a review of U.S. policy toward Western Europe concluded that our resolve to be the first to use nuclear weapons in the event of a Warsaw Pact invasion was as good as ever.[24] And President Carter took it upon himself to warn Moscow that a move toward the oil fields would elicit an American reaction that would, if necessary, take a nuclear form.

The Reagan administration came to power in the belief that a "window of vulnerability" was currently opening up, one that would allow two hundred Soviet MIRVed missiles, each carrying ten warheads, to destroy nearly all one thousand U.S. land-based ICBMs. This would leave us with the choice of not retaliating or using bombers and inaccurate submarine-launched missiles to destroy Soviet cities, with comparable results for our own. Yet this alarmist strategic disability hardly impaired the administration's resolve; it "stood tall" in its rhetoric while supporting roll-back efforts in Central America, Asia, and Africa. Over the course of the Cold War there was no deterioration in America's high resolve despite the adverse shifts in the nuclear balance. "The risk-maximizing approach toward nuclear coercion" that Richard Betts took to be most characteristic U.S. strategy was not diluted in moving from a nuclear monopoly, to overwhelming preponderance, to superiority, to parity, and then unto marginal inferiority on a few measures.[25]

Since the early 1960s policymakers and hawkish writers have been most often and deeply concerned about the credibility gap. The perceived resolve lying behind a threat is yet more important than actual resolve. It is decidedly problematic when the rivals can retaliate with nuclear destruction. Like other nations, the United States is not given to risking suicide even on behalf of allies who are deemed essential for its own security. Even MAD's most influential advocates acknowledged the deterrent's low credibility.[26] Up to this point hawks, doves, and eagles are largely at one. The advocates of MAD went on to insist that the low credibility of "existential deterrence" was sufficient. The Soviets were not about to take even a low risk of suicide by putting Washington's threats to the test. Those who supported the countervailing strategy maintained that low credibility is not nearly good enough, especially since the inordinately instrumentalist Soviet leadership might well find the possible destruction of its society to be acceptable under certain conditions. Credibility could be enhanced by consistently striving for nuclear advantages that would limit wartime damage to the United States. A favorable force ratio would allow for the destruction of Soviet missiles before they were fired and a counterforce war in which American cities would be spared.

When questioning the impact of a strategic advantage upon U.S. credibility, the Cuban missile crisis represents an especially hard case. Advocates of nuclear superiority hold it up as persuasive evidence for their claims; most studies of the crisis support or do not dispute them. After Washington took firm actions, Moscow started to back off. After the twenty-four-hour warning of impending military action, it backed down. The Soviets were were said to be "profoundly affected" by their nuclear inferiority.[27] However, any one of several plausible possibilities would puncture this argument for hawkish policy conclusions.

The American compellent threat was sufficiently credible; it did bring about a favorable resolution of the crisis. But this does not mean that it was highly credible. Rather than the strategic imbalance imparting such credibility, the existence of nuclear weapons alone (existential deterrence) might surely have been sufficient. The small possibility of the Soviet Union's nuclear destruction determined the outcome, heightened by the perceived risks of the crisis spiraling out of Washington's and/or Moscow's control. Second, whether America's sufficient credibility was high or low, it did not necessarily stem from strategic superiority. When two states with the ability to inflict vast damage upon each other find themselves in situations of competitive risk taking, what matters most is neither the military balance nor the status quo state's credibility. What counts is the balance of perceived resolve.[28] And just as Moscow's was far greater than Washington's when it resorted to force in Eastern Europe in 1953, 1956, and 1968, America's was surely far higher in its Caribbean backyard. Third, there is the argument that it was not nearly so much the strategic, but the yet greater disparity in conventional, forces around Cuba that determined the outcome.[29] If the Soviets had tried to prevail, it was they who would have had to move toward the nuclear brink given their local inferiority; as the demonstrably weaker side in the region there was no way for them to stand firm and avoid a coercive nuclear duel. This interpretation is supported by the previously noted study of fifty-four cases of extended deterrence between 1900 and 1980. It was the local, not the central, balance of forces that explained the defending states' successes and failures in deterring actions against their protégés. This result held up after controlling for variations in the central balance.[30] Moreover, since nearly all the cases were conventional ones, the local balance should be at least as robust when, as in Cuba, nuclear opponents with secure second-strike forces come into conflict.

Were nuclear superiority important in 1962, it could still have had little or no policy import since then. If America's five-to-one missile superiority accounted for success in Cuba, it does not follow that anything like this could have been sustained after 1962. Although the American economy was far larger than the USSR's, the Soviets were rarely more than a few years behind the United States in nuclear technology and design. The Soviet-American rivalry bears out Samuel Huntington's proposition about the differing outcomes of "qualitative" (e.g., nuclear) and "quantitative" arms races: Because the former depends upon relatively free-floating, widely and quickly available scientific and technological developments rather than the near givens of industrial might and population size, they regularly eventuate in parity.[31] The results of the attempt to attain a "margin of superiority" are especially telling. For between 1981 and 1986 U.S. military expenditures doubled. They paid for the development of strategic forces that included the B-1 and Stealth bombers, the ten-warhead MX missile, accurate SLBMs, stealthy cruise missiles, additional aircraft carrier battle groups for attacking the USSR, and reinforced C3I networks. Yet it was widely recognized that the strategic balance had not improved significantly by 1986 because of the continuing modernization of Soviet forces.

Several Cold War patterns fail to support the predicted relationships between the strategic balance and U.S. credibility. An adverse shift in the balance should have decreased our perceived resolve and thus increased the frequency of the Soviets' direct challenges, their resort to nuclear threats, and their success in doing so. However, the number of conventional, near-nuclear, and nuclear crises brought on by Soviet actions was much greater during the first half of the Cold War than after the onset of nuclear parity during the second half—between five and seven from 1945 to 1967 compared to the one crisis at the end of the 1973 Mideast war.[32] Preciously little evidence indicates that Moscow's decisions to "resort to nuclear coercion" were affected by changes in the strategic balance;[33] there was "no congruence between Soviet military capabilities and enhanced Soviet propensities to take risks."[34] These assessments are supported in a study based on a sample of thirty-three incidents between 1946 and 1975 in which Washington used nuclear or conventional forces as a "political instrument," their deployment being altered to signal forthcoming punishments and rewards. The proportion of U.S. successes did not decline as we became progressively less advantaged in missiles, warheads, and bombers. When the analysis is limited to those incidents involving the superpowers alone, and when restricted yet further to those in which Moscow threatened or used force, the proportion of successful U.S. outcomes still did not diminish as the nuclear monopoly gave way to strategic parity.[35]

There is hardly any reason to suppose that the 1979 adoption of the countervailing strategy and its subsequent war-fighting elaborations helped close the credibility gap, or that it could have done so had we enjoyed some substantial strategic advantage. In principle, U.S. credibility could have been bolstered by the ability to destroy Soviet weapons before they could wreak their destruction while sparing Soviet cities—as this would have obviated attacks upon our population and thereby heightened our perceived resolve. The countervailing strategy was, however, inordinately problematic in this regard. It was based upon a conventionalized view of the nuclear world, one in which decision makers expected a nuclear war to be limited, controllable, and winnable. To achieve its goals even in part, this strategy requires that both sides be willing to fight such a war, capable of doing so, and reasonably confident of the other's willingness and ability to do so. If any one of these conditions is not satisfied, the strategy becomes irrelevant at best. It should not be necessary to rehearse all the overwhelming cognitive and physical demands, emotional strains, and the bizarre imponderables of a protracted nuclear war[36]—and whether for these or other reasons, Moscow was apparently unwilling to "cooperate." It regularly denied having any such war-fighting plans, announced its unwillingness to abide by U.S. rules in a war, and both predicted and insisted that any nuclear war would be total. The denials were persuasive enough for hawkish advocates to acknowledge that the Soviets had neither accepted the assured-destruction doctrine nor begun to think about protracted warfare.[37]

As economists are fond of saying, "Assume. . . ." Assuming the absence of any serious problems with the protracted-war scenario, it is still exceptionally difficult to imagine how a nuclear advantage would have affected wartime damage, the war's outcome, and thus prewar deterrence. On the best set of imaginable conditions, the U.S. armory is outrightly superior prior to a war; this disparity remains in place or is widened throughout its controlled course; and cities suffer a minimum of collateral damage as each side holds the other's as hostages. Under these "ideal" conditions the Soviets would still have retained at least several hundred warheads, more than enough to destroy all our large and medium-sized cities.

How then would the pre- or interwar military balance have determined whether cities were ultimately attacked and whether the conflict ended in a draw or with one side prevailing? In all probability the outcome would have been mostly determined by the kinds of subjective variables that governed peacetime actions, namely, the value that each side places on the survival of its (remaining) population and industry, their stakes in the outcome of the conflict, their consequent resolve and success in communicating it, and the resulting balance of perceived resolve. Either side could issue the final threat: End the war (conditionally or unconditionally) or suffer total, unremitting civilian destruction. Which side would do so, and how the other would react, would have had little or nothing to do with the final strategic balance. For in the wake of several nuclear exchanges, would the president (or his replacement) count up the remaining missiles and megatonnage on both sides and then issue the ultimate threat or toss in the nuclear towel because the U.S. was ahead or behind? Before the war, would the Soviets have expected him to do so on this basis? If not, how could the nuclear balance possibly have mattered?

There might have been something to the hawkish claim that deterrence had to be strengthened by threatening the Soviet leaders with truly unacceptable damage. The targeting of industrial-population centers did not promise the level of hurt at which deterrence would hold up under any and all circumstances—not for an extraordinarily instrumentalist, totally self-serving, and ideologically hostile leadership. It had to be threatened with its own destruction, that of its military might, and its control over the population. Given the uncertainties surrounding the interpretation of the rival's intentions, values, and motivations, this claim could not be ruled out. The thousands of deep underground shelters may have been built by Soviet leaders intent upon expansion and their survival at a still powerful national pinnacle. In defending U.S. nuclear efforts on the possibility of a first strike against our vulnerable land-based missiles, Secretary of Defense Harold Brown acknowledged that "it is difficult to imagine any circumstances or expectations that would prompt Soviet leaders to undertake such a self-destructive attack. . . . [However,] the 'rubbish heap of history' is filled with authorities who said something reckless could or would not be done."[38]

The governing assumption of an extraordinarily self-serving Soviet leadership would still not have justified the countervailing strategy. The threat to destroy the leadership was presumably less than believable as well as counterproductive. Its execution directly contradicted the plans to fight a protracted nuclear war. Who then would have been left on the Soviet side to control it, limit it, and end it on favorable terms for the United States? Moreover, if the leadership did, or was allowed to, survive in its deep command and control bunkers, threatening its other highest values was also counterproductive. To destroy its military power and

networks of internal control would have left it with little or no incentive
to spare U.S. cities, almost certainly so on the premise of a totally self-
serving leadership.

On these arguments adversarial nuclear policies most probably did not
contribute to the nation's security. The same ones indicate why outright
strategic inferiority would not have had any adverse consequences for a
nonengaged America. Due to the nuclear revolution, reinforced by the
narrowness of the security perimeter, we would not have been at any
greater risk with strategic forces at half their Cold War levels. There are,
in fact, some reasons for thinking that the hazards would have been
diminished.

III

With the displacement of the Soviet Union from the center of the security
agenda, two others have moved toward that position. Concerns about the
proliferation of nuclear and other weapons of mass destruction have
taken on far more prominence. The long-standing aim of maintaining
America's global primacy has also done so, concomitantly being given a
greater economic emphasis and a competitive cast vis-à-vis the European
and Japanese allies.

According to one characterization of the Bush administration's thinking, proliferation "holds out the most serious threat to American security
in the period ahead. The great object of a policy of intervention is thus
one of keeping weapons of mass destruction from falling into the hand of
aggressive and expansionist states. In the wake of the Gulf crisis, it is
above all the prevention of nuclear proliferation that provides the justification for an interventionist policy."[39] Among the bevy of grand strategies that have been proposed for the post–Cold War era, Robert Art's is
especially noteworthy in this regard. "Taking out additional insurance
against nuclear weapons spread . . . is [now] the prime, indeed the *only*,
security rationale for a continuing military global role for the United
States."[40]

Some twenty states are capable of acquiring nuclear weapons by the
beginning of the next century. More than two dozen are developing or
stockpiling chemical weapons. Eight of these states are capable of or near
to obtaining ballistic missiles to deliver weapons of mass destruction. Five
of them—Iraq, Iran, Syria, Libya, and North Korea—are overtly hostile
to the United States. There are the possibilities of rogue nuclear states,
fanatical leaders, nuclear terrorism on the part of governments and political movements, weapons falling into the wrong hands in the midst of
civil wars and military coups, and accidental launches due to deficient
technical safeguards.[41] In a conventional war a state might use its nuclear

weapons "to dictate the terms of a settlement; to force the intervention of an outside power on its side; to paralyze a conflict or stop the intervention of an outside power on an adversary's side; to destroy and disperse an adversary's military forces, stop or slow down their advance, and interrupt their supply lines; or to terrorize an adversary's cities and populations."[42] And then there are the risks to U.S. forces abroad, of preventive wars, preemptive strikes, unauthorized use, and accidents in the absence of survivable weapons and secure command and control structures in the Third World.

The dangers of nuclear spread bear upon America's ideal of international security and upon its own security. But at this point the discussion focuses upon the latter, with the former being taken up in chapter 8. Strategic internationalism addresses the nuclear threats to the United States in an adversarial and conciliatory manner. The latter, largely revolving around the Nuclear Nonproliferation Treaty, is discussed in the following chapter.

The national strategy offers America far more insurance against nuclear dangers than does adversarial internationalism. The latter is unlikely to prove generally effective, while greatly increasing the possibility of nuclear weapons and "suitcase bombs" being used against U.S. forces abroad and Americans at home. And this is said after acknowledging that the abrogation of alliances would heighten the nuclear temptation for Germany, Japan, South Korea, and Taiwan despite a possibly strengthened nonproliferation regime. Germany faces a nuclear-armed Russia, a Ukraine that could retain its nuclear weapons, and a Poland that might go down the nuclear path if Germany does so. Japan and South Korea must live with China's nuclear armory and probably North Korea's.

A simple, inordinately important consideration is regularly ignored. If nuclear threats are to be directed at the United States, there need be a reason. Reasons plummet with the abrogation of entangling alliances. Maximum safety lies in getting out of harm's way. If conflict avoidance were somehow to prove insufficient, if some sort of attack were in the offing, a national strategy's deterrent, forceful, and punitive responses would not differ from those of an adversarial strategy. They are at one with regard to the use of any and all necessary means to guard the nation's highest values from an immediate threat, which does not, however, require widespread alliance commitments and troop deployments.

The adversarial strategy for guarding against nuclear threats involves defense commitments, the deployment of U.S. forces abroad, deterrent threats, and possible air strikes and interventions. Alliances are to serve as nuclear inhibitors in reassuring friendly countries of their security. During the Cold War we were in Europe primarily to keep the Russians out, but also to "keep the Germans down," to negate their need to build nuclear weapons and to reassure the rest of NATO on this score. This alliance rationale also has some applicability to northeast Asia. As a "nuclear pacifier" for allies, we are to target our several thousand strategic weapons upon "every reasonable adversary"; forces stationed abroad and mobile ones are to prevent the spread of nuclear and other weapons of mass destruction by full-scale interventions if necessary.[43]

Whether defense commitments and troop deployments can overcome nuclear inclinations and temptations depends upon their credibility, their reassuring impact. Among the variables that impinge upon it none is more important than the presence or absence of a shared threat. American security commitments were largely believable during the Cold War when they pertained to the common communist threat. They were sufficiently so to overcome any nuclear ambitions on the part of West Germany, Japan, South Korea, and Taiwan. But reassurance was insufficient for other allies. Israel, Pakistan, South Africa, Brazil, and Argentina did not relinquish the nuclear option. For they were engaged in conflicts outside the Cold War's common perimeters. Pakistan moved well down the nuclear weapons path not because of the Soviet Union or China, but because of its rivalry with India. Having Washington as a staunch ally did not convince Brazil and Argentina to sign the Nuclear Nonproliferation Treaty or to dispense with nuclear efforts directed at one another. With the Arab-Israeli conflict having its decided extra–Cold War dimensions, Israel was nowhere near sufficiently reassured by Washington to forgo a small nuclear armory. And a comparable point applied to South Africa. Along with Brazil and Argentina it has recently reversed course because of the resolution of non–Cold War conflicts.

Given the sharp decline in the number of common threats after 1990, U.S. defense commitments have lost much of their credibility and thus their effectiveness as nuclear pacifiers. There is no more than an occasional substitute for the shared alignment against the USSR, China, and Soviet clients. Current and future conflict lines—ethnic, religious, territorial, economic, and any involving water resources—are politically diverse, fragmenting, and even crosscutting as they involve the United States, its allies, and their opponents. The Greek and Turkish case, in which a U.S. ally has been involved in a severe conflict with another ally, could be replicated in nuclear terms. How then will either ally be sufficiently reassured to forgo the nuclear temptation? If one of them is seen to be more valuable to us, reassurance wanes yet further for the other. Reassurance could easily plummet if one ally or common adversary had already acquired nuclear arms. Would America be willing, and be confidently seen as willing, to put U.S. troops and perhaps the homeland under the nuclear gun? Moreover, defense efforts on behalf of allies might lead neighboring opponents to acquire nuclear weapons. These "common" opponents would thus be at an enormous military disadvantage, if not also seeing themselves as threatened by the United States. The nuclear option could then look like the only one for their defensive or expansionist purposes. This is hardly an implausible interpretation of North Korea's nuclear efforts, especially with South Korea spending twice as much on conventional forces.

As for the forceful, interventionist prevention of nuclear spread, would a military deterrent be resolutely brandished to stop a state from acquiring weapons of mass destruction? Would the threat be credible especially when made primarily on behalf of an ally? Would American resolve and credibility suffice in the case of a state that is not challenging us but threatens to retaliate against U.S. interventionism with any means at its disposal? Would resolve, credibility, and intervention be adequate in the case of a state whose nuclear manufacturing facilities are widely dispersed, underground, and whose chemical weapons are already deployed? Most states in the process of acquiring nuclear weapons are decidedly intent upon doing so and they have probably taken the international costs into account. They are thus not about to be easily deterred.

At first glance the use of force against a heavily armed Iraq and the quick and easy victory underscore the will to intervene and its effectiveness. However, the Gulf War suggests the improbability of a repeat performance, since Saddam was the "perfect enemy." U.S. policy toward Iraq before 1990 raises another kind of nuclear question about strategic internationalism. It was not just that Washington completely failed to buy off or dissuade a client from moving down the nuclear path. Iraq was given economic aid and dual-use technologies that were diverted into nuclear and ballistic missile programs. High officials, including President Bush himself, knew this (see chap. 8). Yet the administration was so concerned about maintaining good relations with its client to offset the Iranian threat that it licensed sensitive exports and urged Congress to provide financial assistance. In fact, at different times Washington has helped or not stood in the way of allies acquiring a nuclear capability, as with Israel, South Africa, Iran, and Pakistan. Thus the question of what is likely to be more important, maintaining good relations with allies and clients so as to protect what are seen to be our many security interests, or to curtail such efforts and carry out sanctions to stop allies from acquiring nuclear weapons? There is also a parallel issue: Will the United States be willing to exert telling pressures on valued allies to dissuade them from commercial sales of nuclear and dual-use technologies? The record with regard to Germany, France, Britain, Israel, and Brazil is not encouraging.

The problematic effectiveness of alliances, deterrence, and interventionism in preventing proliferation and protecting allies from nuclear opponents is out of all proportion to the risks to our security. Yet the latter have been diminished even by those who are most appreciative of them. John Mearsheimer makes a determined theoretical and historical case for a Central and Eastern Europe whose future is "dark" and dangerous despite continuing U.S. security involvements. Over and above the spread of the former Soviet Union's nuclear weapons, he expects them to be acquired by Germany, Poland, and possibly one or two other countries—and for them to be deployed under some thoroughly disconcerting conditions. Central and Eastern Europe will feature precarious conventional deployments, intractable ethnic conflicts, irredentist passions, fragmenting states, hypernationalism, and protofascist movements.[44] Yet prescriptively, Mearsheimer does not at all question whether America's security is well served by maintaining its European involvements. Stephen Rosen has adumbrated regional nuclear war scenarios for the Middle East, south Asia, and northeast Asia. If any were to materialize (e.g., between India and our Pakistani ally) he acknowledges America's difficult choices, dilemmas, and risks. Yet he simply rejects the "extreme" position—that our "military involvement in [any] regional nuclear wars is unwarranted."[45]

Guarding against proliferation falls within America's broadest objective of retaining its global primacy. Militarily, politically, and economically, "America will continue to have an interest in maintaining itself as the number one power in the world."[46] The goal itself is not at all new. Primacism's current distinctiveness stems from its preventive cast. In the past the focus was upon an immediate, pressing, identifiable challenger. Now it is upon any and all powerful states and possible coalitions, including U.S. allies and others who have not shown any aspiration to challenge U.S. predominance. Our power and overt determination are to discourage the emergence of any such ambitions; our protective commitments are to render security-motivated power strivings unnecessary. The strategy has been portrayed as competitive and cooperative. Demands, demonstrations of resolve, insistent leadership, deterrence, and forceful measures are complemented by reassurance, alliance commitments, shared interests, and common endeavors. Yet the latter are largely contingent, dependent upon others not denying our leadership or setting out to challenge us as the "premier global power."[47]

According to the Pentagon's 1992 draft paper on defense-planning guidance for the 1990s, "Our first objective is to prevent the reemergence of a new rival . . . that poses a threat on the order posed formerly by the Soviet Union . . . [Besides the latter] there are other potential nations or coalitions that could . . . develop strategic aims and a defense posture of region-wide or global domination. Our strategy must now refocus on precluding the emergence of any potential future global competitor."

This adversarial emphasis is tempered by protective commitments. "The U.S. must show the leadership necessary to establish and protect a new order that holds the promise of convincing potential competitors that they need not aspire to a greater role or pursue a more aggressive posture to protect their legitimate interests . . . [The United States] will retain the pre-eminent responsibility for addressing selectively those wrongs which threatened not only our interests, but those of our allies or friends."[48] The latter are clearly to remain in their subsidiary places.

This two-pronged primacist strategy was publicly supported by President Bush. It was given its first concrete post–Cold War expression in the administration's negative reactions to France and Germany's military integration. Their "Eurocorps," initially consisting of some forty-thousand troops, to include those of other countries after 1995, is designed for contingencies in which NATO would not be willing or able to intervene. Washington did not at all welcome Chancellor Helmut Kohl and President François Mitterand's announcement of a "process of building European unity which will include eventually a policy of common defense." NATO, which provides our only formal leadership seat at any European table, is to remain the region's exclusive military organization.[49]

Primacism's adversarial policies include the preservation of overwhelming military superiority, a forward presence to deter, balance, and defend against the emergence of Eurasian and regional hegemons, military intervention to protect weak states, nuclear weapons targeted upon opponents, and despite the improbability of their use in regional conflicts, a studied ambiguity on this score when facing aggressors armed with weapons of mass destruction. Along with the assertive promotion of U.S. interests, these policies are to demonstrate the resolve to ward off any challengers; our manifest determination is to discourage aspiring challengers from thinking that they can succeed.[50]

Assertiveness tempered by a protective activism comes through in Samuel Huntington's enumeration of our "specific interests" in negating the "emergence of a political-military hegemonic power in Eurasia." Confronting and successfully competing with Japan economically is foremost. In addition, America and NATO are to prevent the "reimposition of Soviet or Russian military or political control in Eastern Europe," while also helping to democratize and develop the successor states of the USSR. The United States is to "limit German power in the new Europe" by working with Britain, France, and others to constrain its domination of European-wide organizations, while also "encouraging German involvement in NATO and European international organizations." Washington is "to promote [the] evolution of the European Community in the direction of a looser, purely economic entity with broader membership rather than a tighter political entity with an integrated foreign policy," while also "entangling" the major powers in regional and global multilateral institutions.[51]

Adversarial geoeconomic policies feature an "admixture of the logic of conflict with the methods of commerce—or, as Clausewitz would have written, the logic of war in the grammar of commerce." Edward Luttwak elaborates upon these policies. In the new era "not only the causes but also the instruments of conflict must be economic. If the commercial quarrels [between the United States and Japan, Germany, and the European Community] do lead to political clashes, as they are now much more likely to do with the waning of the imperatives of geopolitics, those political clashes must be fought out with the weapons of commerce: the more or less disguised restriction of imports, the more or less concealed subsidization of exports, the funding of competitive technology projects, the support of selected forms of education, the provision of competitive infrastructures, and more."[52] Over and above striving for absolute economic gains, we need to be greatly concerned with relative ones as well; more material wealth for the United States is unacceptable if Japan and Europe's economic growth is yet faster.[53] The primacists see a several-sided challenge in Japan's economic might. Besides the risk to our economic well-being via the loss of markets, jobs, and profits, for Huntington, Japan could threaten the nation's security if it takes the lead in developing "militarily important technologies." Its greater economic power also "means an increase in [its] influence and a relative decline in American influence."[54]

Being number one is surely desirable. The absence of major challengers is obviously most advantageous in ensuring America's overall security. However, it is one thing to partake of the fruits of a readily available position of predominance. It is quite another to exaggerate the need for across-the-board superiority, to sidestep the costs of exercising and maintaining political-military primacy, and to ignore the ways in which efforts on behalf of primacy make its retention more problematic.

The primacist exercise is saddled with several difficulties. Remaining the premier global power and partaking of the benefit depend upon somehow being able to circumvent several contradictions between the security and economic realms and within them.

The security prescription derives from realist theory. States struggle to enhance their power and security. Relative gains and losses are crucial. States that are satisfied with their absolute gains, those that do not compete effortfully, or who lose out in the competition are subject to the will of the strong, suffer security deflations, or both. These generalizations point to primacist policies. They also go a long way in negating them, especially for the United States because of its power and strategic immunity. For according to realist theory, states generally balance against rather than bandwagon with those that are stronger and threatening. As expressed by the contemporary dean of the realist school, "overwhelming power repels and leads others to balance against it."[55] Facing a globally assertive America whose lead in military technology is assured under any security strategy, an already powerful Japan, Germany, Russia, China, Iraq, Iran, and possibly a unified Europe and a Moslem coalition would look squarely to their "national interests." The determined exercise, and possibly the expansion, of their power, becomes imperative; America's pressures are to be warded off. Primacism could well intensify the very challenges it is designed to deter.[56]

It could be argued that primacism negates these counterproductive tendencies by way of reassurance—its benign, mutually protective side. But not only is the latter largely contingent upon others accepting the United States as number one, in realist theory reassurance is overshadowed by conflicting interests, relative gains, and power-seeking imperatives. Even the major powers' common security interests are subject to the competitive concerns of who gains more and who pays less in supporting their mutual endeavors. There is a great difference between allies working together in furthering common interests and their laboring under U.S. auspices in doing so. Major and regional powers are not about to take kindly to Washington's insistent unilateral leadership, their overt or muffled relegation to a subordinate position even in their own regions, and their ties of military dependency. Even while facing the common Soviet threat, and with Washington allowing for a good deal of cheap riding militarily and economically, its political-military leadership engendered resentments and independent actions on the part of major allies.

Along with the United States, Germany and Europe collectively, Russia, and Japan have an abiding interest in curbing nuclear spread. If not absolutely necessary in all regards, their support is certainly advantageous. The Nuclear Nonproliferation Treaty and the International Atomic Energy Agency need to be shored up, the sale of nuclear components and facilities needs to be curbed, and economic sanctions against likely proliferators may well be necessary, as might military strikes against overtly hostile ones on the cusp of a nuclear capability. Yet alliance support for U.S. efforts and actions becomes less likely because of resentments of U.S. leadership cast in terms of primacy. Despite the great and cheap success of the Persian Gulf War, many who supported the U.S.-led coalition quickly became disenchanted with its self-serving "new world order."[57] That experience makes a comparable coalition less likely. Moreover, to insist upon the overarching importance of the military balance and to maintain a highly favorable one are of no help in slowing proliferation. Others can only be encouraged to build up their nuclear armories. Military and political primacism is likely to engender the self-assertiveness, national pride, and possible hostility that foster nuclear ambitions—in and of themselves and as covering justifications. Washington's protective commitments might well dampen these tendencies. However, arguments have already been made that alliance reassurances are downgraded in the absence of a common threat after the Cold War.

On the economic side, there is first of all an incompatibility between the facts and primacism's decidedly competitive policies. Just as we exaggerated the relative strengths of the Soviet Union and the bevy of communist threats, so too with today's economics. It is an enormous jump from underscoring the competitiveness of trade relations with the industrialized countries to great concerns about the United States "coming in second." Japan's gross domestic product is just 40 percent and Germany's slightly more than 20 percent of America's. Only that of the European Community as a whole is comparable to our own.[58] Chapter 9 not only sets out a large number of U.S. competitive leads and advantages; it also sharply deflates the arguments about America's relative decline. Primacists manage to downplay the fundamental fact of trade theory: The relative gains of others do not compromise our own absolute gains. The U.S. growth rate would not be adversely affected if others managed to exceed it. In fact, along with the resulting expansion of trade relations, faster growth abroad usually abets efficiency, price, and quality improvements at home. This is certainly not to suggest that the terms of trade—most especially Japan and Europe's departures from free and fair trade practices—are of little consequence. But they should not be allowed to obscure the basic aspects of trade relations, which can produce mutual gains. Besides, U.S. growth rates depend first and foremost upon domestic policies, from dealing with the federal budget deficit to restoring the nation's physical and social infrastructure. Those policies are not of an adversarial kind.

An assertive economic diplomacy is certainly needed vis-à-vis Japan and Europe. Yet it is not clear that it will be pursued in the consistent, concerted manner that is required. As with the past applications of strategic internationalism, economics may be displaced by political-military imperatives. Primacism calls for us to lead others, maintain mutually protective relations, and act together in dealing with regional violence, aggression, and nuclear spread. At the same time, pressures and retaliation are to be employed when it comes to trade and trade-related issues. The allies will obviously resist reshaping their economic policies to conform with U.S. interests in free and fair trade; their resistance and counterpressures will more or less deeply fracture alliance relations. Given the priority that we have invariably assigned to political-military issues, will Washington be willing to pay the price—the price of divisiveness—in concertedly pressuring Japan and Europe on behalf of our economic interests? The likelihood of minor fissures in alliances was such a daunting security prospect that Washington deferred pressure throughout the 1970s and 1980s.[59] The severity and immediacy of security concerns have certainly declined since 1990. Yet they still remain eminently prominent in the primacists' short- and long-range strategic lexicon.

If security concerns do not make for economic self-deterrence, the primacist strategy engenders the reverse problem, that of an overbearing economic exercise. Across-the-board assertiveness is more likely to deepen resistance to trade reforms than to bring them to fruition. In addition to the sharp resentments of Washington's political-military leadership, others stem from an unvarnished geoeconomic approach on trade issues. Nor is this just a matter of likely failure, due to more intense resistance of strong economic competitors. Their counterpressures would also translate into counterproductive results. The most likely eventualities include the Group of Seven's refusal to continue with the coordination of their financial and foreign-exchange policies, the obstructive bureaucratic regulation of imports from the United States, informally sanctioned cutbacks of U.S. imports, the demise of previously negotiated caps on exports to the United States, if not also the raising of nontariff barriers, new import quotas, and protectionist spirals tending toward trade wars. To a greater or lesser extent each of these reactions would detract from America's material well-being and economic growth. If taken all together, they detract from America's economic security.

Whatever its security benefits abroad, political-military primacy is hardly a free economic good at home. True, the negative impact of military spending upon economic growth has often been much exaggerated; at certain junctures it has done more to spur growth and international competitiveness. But adverse effects have exceeded the beneficial ones by a significant margin.[60] At a minimum, political-military primacy does not pay economically. A widespread military presence on the ground, a dozen aircraft carrier battle groups around the world, a favorable military balance within several regions, force-projection capabilities, and the occasional intervention are not about to foster economic growth. And the temporal conjunction of higher defense budgets and certain macroeconomic conditions could turn out to be decidedly hurtful for the economy.

These criticisms go a long way in deflating the justifications for striving to retain across-the-board predominance. The national strategy promotes primacism's security and economic objectives and promises more at much less cost and risk.

Efforts to discourage possible contenders and counter actual challengers to U.S. primacy are unnecessary and counterproductive for U.S.

security. It was argued previously that a nonengaged America would have been strategically immune when facing the global communist threat. Those arguments surely take on yet more weight in the absence of a major rival. In discussing the tailoring of activist security policies to the other side's presumed intentions, it was seen that adversarial policies in facing a defensively motivated opponent can turn it into a more threatening one. By extension, efforts to keep others in their secondary positions can engender the very ambitions that are to be negated. The previous parts of this chapter considered the globalized credibility exercises and competitive nuclear policies of the past. With only minor emendations, the arguments regarding their superfluousness and ineffectiveness become all the more compelling under the prevailing conditions, in which the United States remains the world's single superpower. And the later chapter on strategic mismanagement identifies the diversity of inadvertent security deflations stemming from the pursuit of primacism and any other variant of adversarial internationalism.

Under the national strategy, the alliance concerns and the attendant constraints that Washington has consistently imposed upon itself in pursuing U.S. economic interests fall by the wayside. The national strategy positively encourages an assertive diplomacy on trade issues. To divorce economic from security issues and to abrogate alliances affords Washington full scope for doing what is necessary. It is able to apply leverage, lay down credible threats, and carry out proportional acts of retaliation, which effectively capitalize upon the country's exceptional economic endowments. In all the talk of economic interdependence and American dependencies, it is all too often forgotten that interdependence is a two-way street. In some major respects others are considerably more dependent upon us; we are less economically vulnerable than Europe and Japan. While America's economic security is not at risk, the United States is not so well positioned to be able to rely upon an exclusively adversarial strategy for bringing about trade reform—that of a primacism that would not just further heighten the economic counterpressures of others but fuel them with nationalist stirrings and strivings. The generally most effective strategy in dealing with states with whom we have both conflicting and common interests pays close attention to both. Europe and Japan are not just our chief economic rivals; outside of North America they are also our chief trading partners. Thus the need for an affirmative diplomacy alongside an assertive one—the economic hallmark of the concurrent foreign policy.

America's disengagement ensures at least two economic outcomes. Burden-sharing disparities with equally wealthy allies, defense subsidies to a Europe and Japan that can well afford to protect themselves, become history. Burden-sharing excesses into the late 1990s look like they will total some $50 billion a year. We are currently spending more than eight times as much on the military as is any one of our allies, about 60 percent more than the Group of Seven industrial powers taken together. Eliminating these disparities is most unlikely to have as pronounced a positive impact upon U.S. competitiveness as has been claimed. But to eliminate burden-sharing inequalities is to recapture a huge amount of forgone economic welfare. Primacists are silent on this score. The exercise of political-military leadership and the continuing tendency to see the world as more threatening than our allies see it hardly help remedy burden-sharing excesses.

Disengagement permits a radical, 50 percent reduction in military spending. With economic growth depending heavily upon private and public investments, these enormous savings could be put to productive uses. Annual defense savings on the order of $100 billion are telling on three counts. They add to the nation's material well-being, its absolute economic gains. They improve upon its international competitiveness, its relative gains as they speak to our economic (and any military) security interests. And they address the conventional wisdom about military power now being more often trumped by economic power as it affects the nation's security.

Chapter VI

MAXIMIZING CONCILIATION:
REASSURING THE CHALLENGER

THE SECURITY OF status quo states is endangered not only by revisionist, aggressive opponents, but also by those with largely benign intentions. The rivalry and its hazards are real, although neither side is intent upon threatening the other. The contender's defensive needs bring on, continue, or exacerbate conflictual relations. Whether it be done confidently or out of desperation, he builds up his military forces, extends his sway, and relies upon some combination of swaggering, terrorism, and wars. A nation's security can thus be assured by reassuring powerful and weak contenders alike that they are not, in fact, the focus of threatening ambitions, that the guardian state is not animated by hostile or expansionist objectives and that its military configuration is not distinctly offensive.

Up to this point there is no divergence among hawks, doves, and eagles in principle. However, hawks regularly deny benign motivations on the part of those who challenge an evidently status quo America. Reassurance is thus variously irrelevant, fruitless, counterproductive, and decidedly dangerous. Doves are convinced of the contender's safety-first imperative, defensive motivations, if not also of his beleaguered self-perceptions. Continuous efforts are thus essential to demonstrate our nonthreatening aims and to highlight the prevalence of shared interests. Eagles maintain an agnostic position with regard to intentions. On the oft borne out possibility that they are of a defensive kind, reassurance becomes advantageous or even crucial. It is most effectively pursued by way of minimally activist policies.

In assessing the effectiveness of activist policies of reassurance this chapter fully accepts the underlying premise of conciliatory internationalism. The comparisons are developed on the latter's high ground, its understanding of the challenger's conflictual behavior as deriving from vulnerability and fear, "needs and weaknesses," rather than from ambitions and a "search for opportunity."[1] He is presumed to be basically mistrustful of America's aims and convinced that our capabilities and those of our allies are overtly threatening. The opponent may also subscribe to the positional goals of greater respect and influence. But just as revisionist aims predominate over positional aims in hawkish interpretations of intentions, in dovish ones—and on this chapter's premises—defensive concerns are taken to be far weightier than any other goals.

Eagles, like many doves, appreciate that reassurance is often an inordinately difficult exercise. Defensive anxieties and needs may derive from hard-to-dispel beliefs and unchangeable realities: the guardian's past and current actions, the rivals' conflicting interests, the opponent's geostrategic vulnerabilities, military disadvantages, and economic weaknesses, and from the distortions brought on by worst-case thinking, ideological convictions, cultural biases, and psychological tendencies. There are also the common difficulties in communicating any important messages—the irrelevant "noise" and complexities involved in sending and receiving them. It is "hard enough to communicate straightforward and gross threats,"[2] and allaying the rival's suspicions and anxieties could well constitute a yet more formidable undertaking. A good deal of "discrepant" information must not only get through to the opponent, it needs to be sufficiently persuasive to overcome the resistance of preexisting convictions. Moreover, it could well be harder to influence the mind-set of an insecure than an ambitiously revisionist state; for potential losses tend to be more salient than possible gains of comparable magnitude.[3] Thus, for a contender who is "motivated by what he perceives as defensive concerns, the incentive to use force in order to avoid loss may be even stronger and more urgent than an offensively motivated state's desire to achieve gains."[4]

Working on these premises, conciliatory internationalism gets down to the activist and interactive work of a great project, of doing all that is possible to create a hardy climate of predictability, trust, shared interests, accommodation, and nonthreatening competitiveness. Its realization depends upon an array of public declarations to external and internal audiences, informal discussions, high-level meetings, negotiating initiatives and efforts, formal and informal understandings, treaties, and regime building. Agreements are to grow out of some combination of evenhanded proposals, mutual compromises, one-sided concessions, hard bargaining, side payments, and technical labors. In their substance they address territorial issues, limits on strategic and conventional weapons, confidence-building measures, troop deployments and movements, rules of conflict avoidance, crisis management procedures, verification and compliance arrangements, constraints on the use of force, arms exports, and trade flows.

While there is obviously much to be said for conciliatory engagement, there are no a priori doctrinal reasons or practical dictates for reassurance to take a thoroughly activist form. Actions do speak louder than words. But so do inactions. Conciliatory activism can help manage conflictual relations. Yet a minimal activism practically obviates conflicts from the outset and avoids the exacerbation of those that do emerge. Unilateralism has been regularly associated with adversarial internationalism. However, there is no reason why it cannot constitute a central component of a reassuring exercise. In point of fact, it is all the more certain, compelling, and comprehensive than bi- and multilateralism precisely because it does not depend upon the assent of others.

According to the *fourth doctrinal tenet*, a national strategy communicates messages that are maximally reassuring, far more so than those of conciliatory internationalism. Because almost all national policies are unilateral, they have an "automatic," immediate, and continuous impact. Their being practically unconditional makes for clear, consistent, and compelling reassurance. Most being comprehensive and consequential, they translate into "forceful" reassurance and avoidance of conflict. To be sure, there is room for some bilateral and multilateral agreements. Certain accords can add to a national strategy's security-enhancing promise. But they are to be compatible with it, neither infringing upon the design of a national military configuration nor requiring political-military actions beyond the core perimeter. In fact, the compatible accords partake of one of nonengagement's doctrinal tenets, that of an agnostic orientation toward the other side's intentions. The accords' effectiveness does not depend on the opponent's intentions.

The first part of this chapter highlights the special reassuring impact of a national strategy's unilateralism and unconditionality, the second that of its great scope and consequentiality. Both parts draw comparisons with conciliatory internationalism's recent practice and full potential. The third section discusses the bilateral and multilateral accords that add to the national strategy's security-enhancing potential while remaining compatible with it.

I

The unilateralism of a national strategy, the avoidance of political-military relations with the rival, includes a distinct disinterest in the usual arms reduction and territorially centered accords. Unconditionality goes yet further. Reassuring national policies are not contingent upon the expectation that contenders will reciprocate. For instance, unconditional "arms control by example" is not premised upon the other side following suit, although its doing so is certainly welcome. Nor do reassuring national policies depend on anything more than a truly minimal standard of good behavior, that the opponent does not take threatening actions against the narrow core perimeter.

Presumptively correct policies—accommodating ones in the case of a defensively motivated rival—can obviously do more for the nation's security the more consistently, and sooner they are put into effect. Unilateralism and unconditionality make for "automaticity": As soon as a decision is made, without depending or waiting upon others for their assent, it is translated into practice. A decision is nearly tantamount to full implementation. Policies put into practice speak louder than words, plans, and efforts, in this instance, declarations of shared interests and peaceful intentions, negotiating proposals, and successful attempts to work out accommodative accords. Because they take hold right away, national policies provide for more immediate security than those that involve several steps before their (full) impact is felt. Although disengagement may not quickly convince a benignly motivated opponent of our nonthreatening aims and capabilities, it is almost bound to have the immediate effect of dampening conflict.

In contrast, conciliatory internationalism usually requires a considerable interval prior to its full implementation. There are the time-consuming demands of working out the provisions of formal agreements. Work on the SALT I and SALT II treaties began six years before they were signed; negotiations on the 1991 Strategic Arms Reduction Treaty (START) began in 1982. Arms reduction accords then require several more years for the cuts to be made, seven years in the case of START's full implementation. In the meantime, technology can outpace politics. While arms accords are arranged, a perhaps more destabilizing weapon system than the one that is to be limited may be developed and tested.[5]

A national strategy can have a reassuring impact when conciliatory engagement is largely stymied. A benignly motivated opponent is sometimes unwilling to sign defensively designed or other accommodative proposals. They are thought to detract from the opponent's security, or advance it but less so than America's. The contender rejects the proposals because they place equal quantitative limits on its qualitatively inferior weapons, squander his conventional advantages in protecting himself via an offensive strategy, do not address asymmetric military configurations in their units of account, require disclosures of capabilities and weaknesses, equate the size of America's forward deployments with the rival's close-by core deployments, ignore the greater number and power of U.S. allies, or depreciate the challenger's relative influence and prestige. A defensely motivated Soviet Union could have had just such reasons for turning aside Washington's proposals for strategic arms limitations, conventional force reductions in Europe, and on-site inspection and force transparency arrangements.

There are also circumstances in which the rival appreciates the security-heightening advantages of accommodative agreements yet rejects them because of domestic constraints or external ones outside the purview of the rivalry. A defensively motivated USSR might have subscribed to American proposals but for one or more considerations largely unrelated to the United States. The withdrawal of some forces from Eastern Europe ran up against the need for a fulsome military presence to insure

Moscow's political dominance in the region. Reductions in long- and intermediate-range missiles were unacceptable because of the conflict with a China possessing nuclear weapons and a huge army. The stabilizing restructuring of nuclear forces was not pursued because of the "sunk costs" in the heavy, land-based MIRVed missiles and the additional costs of substituting submarine-based missiles and single-warhead ICBMs. These and other security-enhancing possibilities were unacceptable to those within the military-industrial complex, the internal security services, and the Party who were unwilling to give up the valued domestic by-products of an extensive and intensive superpower rivalry.

Unlike the free hand of a national strategy, conciliatory internationalism is sometimes made less compelling, if it is not also heavily constrained, by allies who oppose accommodation. Because U.S. security depends upon them, their opposition can negate the dampening of conflictual relations with the common opponent. Throughout the Cold War Bonn would not even consider the building of nonthreatening, exceptionally effective fortifications along the East German border because they would have symbolically reinforced the division of the two Germanies. Saigon's opposition to the peace negotiations with Hanoi delayed our withdrawal from Vietnam. Seoul's lobbying efforts helped thwart the Carter administration's intended withdrawal of U.S. troops from South Korea. Taiwan's demands diluted our attempts at a full reconciliation with the People's Republic of China on several occasions during the second half of the Cold War. Acting on their own, allies have sorely exacerbated the Soviet-American rivalry. The French-British-Israeli invasion of Egypt brought on the Suez crisis, and Israeli intransigence toward the end of the 1973 Mideast war brought on another. Numerous Third World clients manipulated our fears of—and thus increased our hostility towards—leftist, radical, and Marxist movements.

Being nearly unconditional, a national strategy should be inordinately compelling. Adopting a nonthreatening political-military posture without requiring anything in return should revise the rival's image of the guardian state. The national strategy does not hinge upon his disengaging abroad; it is not contingent upon his shifting toward a defensive military configuration at home. The challenger need not even forgo most efforts to expand his territorial influence-control and military capabilities. The embrace and maintenance of national policies are only dependent upon a truly low standard of good behavior: No challenges to the core perimeter and no expansive actions that are sufficiently ambitious and successful to jeopardize the core's strategic immunity. Moreover, a national strategy allows the contender "world enough and time" to put a reassuring interpretation to the test and for us to pass the test. Its unconditionality offers the secure latitude for him to adopt a wait-and-see attitude. He need neither sign constraining accords nor decide upon expansive moves in fending off an American threat. He can safely allow himself to be reassured over time.

In contrast, conciliatory engagement is almost invariably conditional. All but the most radical and risky of dovish designs, such as an unconditional weapons freeze and unilateral nuclear disarmament, feature various quid pro quos, expectations, and contingencies. They are thus rarely if ever decidedly reassuring, not all that compelling under the most common conditions, and not at all so under others, as with the use of unnecessary weapons as bargaining chips.

A conciliatory internationalism that goes substantially more than halfway in meeting the contender's security or other interests can, of course, have a significant reassuring impact. Yet it is still delimited. Even one-sided concessions are usually dependent upon his acceptance of other, less than palatable, conditions. Accommodative offers shaped by conceptions of fairness and equal security should prove compelling, if similarly interpreted by the other side. But designs based on the principle of parity may be less than they seem once their contextual significance is taken into account. Little if anything can be inferred about the guardian state's benign intentions from accords that are patently self-interested, as in the case of those governing the management of nuclear crises. The most common negotiations have both sides probing and maneuvering in striving for that exquisite point at which an advantageous agreement for themselves is just barely acceptable on the other side of the table. They can engender mutual respect and well-crafted accords that are sustainable over the long haul, without, however, doing all that much in dispelling mistrust.

Negotiated agreements can diminish reassurance by eliciting problems of interpretation and compliance.[6] It is no easy matter to write up comprehensive stipulations and clear-cut specifications. Even arms control treaties featuring precise technical definitions contain the occasional provision that is susceptible to different readings. Accords that limit certain kinds of conflictual behavior and provide for conflict-avoiding procedures are almost sure to include some ambiguous wording, possibly purposefully vague language to paper over irresolvable differences. Verification provisions and capabilities have their share of gaps and uncertainties. Some mutually supplied data on conventional arms and troop deployments can be questioned with regard to their authenticity and conformity with the prescribed counting rules. Compliance becomes uncertain and suspicions of purposeful cheating are hard to allay when the signatories are pressing up close to the edges of what is prohibited. Most understandings are reached during reasonably good times; the signatories anticipate an adherence to their spirit. In light of excessive expectations and unforseen circumstances comes the all-too-easy, subsequent conclusion that they or their spirit have been violated.

Detente, conciliatory internationalism's highwater mark during the Cold War, bears out these observations. The 1972 Basic Principles Agreement was to curtail the superpowers' hazardous competition. The 1973 Agreement on the Prevention of Nuclear War called for immediate consultations in dealing with potential crises. The ambiguity necessarily built into the vast project of regulating a global political-military competition was exposed before the diplomatic ink had dried. Many on the American side (but not the Nixon administration) accused Moscow of violating both agreements: It failed to inform Washington in a sufficiently explicit way that its Egyptian ally was about to launch a surprise attack against Israel. American recriminations were met by Soviet countercharges of propaganda mongering that helped sour detente.[7]

The Basic Principles Agreement stated that "differences in ideology and in the social systems of the U.S. and the USSR are not obstacles to the bilateral development of normal relations based on the principles of sovereignty, equality, noninterference in internal affairs and mutual advantage." These principles were operationalized, so to speak, in the two sides' unspecified pledges to forgo the "use or threat of force," to "do their utmost to avoid military confrontations," to "negotiate and settle differences by peaceful means," and to desist from "efforts to obtain unilateral advantage at the expense of the other, directly or indirectly."[8] Not surprisingly, these comprehensive provisions were interpreted very differently. Washington read them to mean that the Soviets would end their military support for national liberation movements and clients throughout the Third World. Moscow did not at all recognize such broad restrictions, as in Secretary General Brezhnev's insisting upon its "equal rights to meddle" in the Third World. Problems of interpretation and compliance were not even avoided with respect to detente's widely applauded strategic arms agreements, despite their being detailed, technically cut-and-dried accords. From the late 1970s through the mid-1980s the Soviets were accused of a sizable handful of violations. Most of the accusations turned out to be unwarranted.[9]

Agreements are almost always negotiated on the assumption that the conditions that made for their mutual acceptability will continue to prevail and that future relations will not deteriorate. But times change. Additional states have become part of the rivalry, others have changed sides, new issues have arisen, and technological developments and economic trajectories have unhinged the military balance. Treaty provisions that were seen to be mutually advantageous could then perversely become the source of constraining imbalances, frictions, and instability.

Military buildups and preparations appear far more threatening when they overstep existing accords than in their absence. In the former case defensive actions generate the "stereotypical escalation of tension that 'spiral' theorists worry about." In the latter they "could seem more innocent or ambiguous," with the response being "determined according to the merits of the balance of power rather than the legal order of allowed armament." With some exaggeration, Richard Betts goes on to make a similar point about apparently risk-free inspection, transparency-heightening, and crisis management agreements. In the run-up to a confrontation, they "could just as easily have a counterproductive effect as a dampening one, since the effect of abrogating *during* the crisis could seem much more threatening." An anxious state that revokes self-defense restraints and intrusive inspections would be seen as preparing to strike first.[10] Had there been a European crisis in the 1980s, it could have escalated as one or both sides thought it necessary to redeploy their forces at once, as with previous Soviet interventions in Eastern Europe. For doing so would have contravened the confidence-building agreements that required notification of all large-scale troop movements well ahead of time.

Having highlighted the reassuring potency of unconditional unilateralism and bilateralism's relative weaknesses, what of the latter's strengths? Matthew Bunn, the editor of *Arms Control Today*, set out five advantages of bilateralism over unilateralism with respect to weapons issues and inferentially to other kinds as well. He did so in 1991 despite "the walls of superpower confrontation collapsing and [with] both East and West cutting back their military forces without benefits of agreements."[11] The arguments for arms accords should be all the more telling and consequential with regard to conflictual times and issues.

"First, signed and ratified international agreements, locking in reductions, make reversal less likely," as with President Reagan's "efforts to undo the unlimited-duration Anti-Ballistic Missile Treaty (proving to be) politically impossible." Second, an agreement's verification provisions "ease the task of confirming that reductions have in fact taken place, of detecting reversals in time to respond; and of predicting the future size and capabilities of potential adversaries' military forces. In contrast, unilateral measures alone can be misinterpreted, thus undermining the trust they were intended to foster. Recent confusion over exactly what the Soviets are doing with the equipment being withdrawn from Europe is a case in point." Third, "building a new security system for Europe will not only require cutbacks in forces but also international organizations to manage, inspect, and report." Creating and sustaining them requires the negotiating "sweat of diplomats' brows."

These three claims revolve around a central consideration—predictability broadly conceived. Agreements constrain future departures, provide adequate warning of any that do occur, and confirm both adherence to and violations of their provisions. Predictability is clearly crucial in building trust. Albert Carnesale and Richard Haass's comprehensive review of the Cold War arms control record concludes with the overall "modesty of what it has wrought." Still, they are most impressed with its contributions in placing the rivalry on a fairly predictable and thus stabilizing basis. "The historical record tends to support the contention that arms control negotiations and outcomes serve to reduce uncertainties in the estimates and projections that each participant makes about the other's forces. . . . the enhancement of predictability may well be the principle contribution of the arms control experience."[12]

Nonengagement provides at least as much reassuring predictability as a signed, sealed, and verified bilateralism. As a fully comprehensive accommodating strategy and as an unconditional one at that, the opponent can expect it to endure. It is not about to be jettisoned except under truly trying conditions, that of the opponent challenging the security of the core. It is unlikely to be modified except by his putting a sharp dent in our strategic immunity. There is a great substitute at hand for the predictability instilled by the verification and information-sharing provisions of negotiated accords. Nonengagement is about as open, as fully transparent, as any strategy can be. Noninvolvements beyond the core and the distinctly defensive military configuration are intended to be and are readily recognizable as such. Secrecy pertains largely to research and development, intelligence-gathering capabilities, and some weapons capabilities.

The fourth and fifth arguments for bilateralism's negotiated agreements are demonstrably weak. "They can channel reductions in directions that are most conducive to overall stability. Purely unilateral cuts are likely to be driven more by economics than by a concern for the security of one's neighbors, and the most threatening weapons are not always the most expensive."[13] This claim is completely untenable apropos of a national strategy, whose distinctly defensive design is doctrinally derived rather than economically driven. And arms accords were not especially impressive in curtailing the "the most threatening weapons." In fact, weapons ceilings and reductions have occasionally encouraged the development and deployment of other, less stabilizing weapons.[14] SALT I and II did just that by allowing for improvements in missile accuracy and for the MIRVed launchers, the most threatening weapon of the Cold War in fostering first-strike fears and preemptive incentives. Thomas Schelling— a founder of arms control studies who is not known for advocating conciliatory giveaways—proposed that we simply eliminate the MIRVs along with all other land-based missiles. "If we unilaterally dismantled [them], we would instantly deprive a large part of the Soviet land-based missile force of its raison d'etre. . . . While it is nice to do these things by negotiated agreement with the Soviet Union, it might be a more impressive step to do it unilaterally and suggest that the Soviets do likewise."[15] And it should be recalled that the single most important stabilizing arms contribution, the building of untargetable submarine-launched ballistic missiles circa 1960, was a unilateral one on both sides.

Lastly, formal accords "provide a framework conducive to deeper cuts, allowing each party to justify further reductions by pointing to negotiated cutbacks in the threat it faces."[16] Yet having already carried out radical arms reductions, a nonengaged America would not have any reason to carry out others. Nor is it evident why unilateral cuts would be less likely to encourage the opponent to make additional ones. In fact, the reverse is more likely. The earliest agreements almost invariably deal with weapons and numbers that are easiest to negotiate and verify. They have then brought out the difficulties in agreeing upon subsequent reductions.

II

National policies of reassurance are truly impressive in their scope and consequentiality. They feature a distinctly defensive military configuration and an exceptionally narrow security perimeter, and a diversity of critical inactions fall within their compass. A nonengaged America does not maintain political-military alliances, issue more than the bare minimum of deterrent threats, intervene in regional conflicts, treat secondary issues as tests of resolve, use sticks to weaken or carrots to detach the rival's allies, supply his external and internal opponents with material support, strive for military superiority or offensive advantages, carry out provocative military deployments and maneuvers, attempt to exhaust the challenger economically in an arms competition, or commit acts of economic punishment and coercion against it.

These exceptionally encompassing and consequential inactions send compelling messages of reassurance. Because nearly all national policies are evidently self-denying ones for the United States, the suspicions of most opponents should be allayed. Minimally activist policies obviously go a very long way in curtailing conflictual interactions. Avoidance of conflict is a more consistent and powerful guarantee of reassurance than most efforts at conciliation. Moreover, the great scope of self-denying national policies extends well beyond conciliatory internationalism's usual projects, to something like global reassurance. They relate to those states that are not (yet) mistrustful of the United States, to the small ones that do not figure (much) in the conciliatory project, to those governments with whom formal accords are politically impracticable, and to the terrorist, guerrilla, religious, and other "ultra" political movements for whom negotiating with Washington is unacceptable. At this time various parts of the huge Moslem world fall into each of these categories.

In principle, conciliatory engagement could be almost as wide-ranging and consequential. It could comprise mutual nonengagement territorially and radical arms accords, including complete or near-total nuclear disarmament down to a few hundred weapons. But during the Cold War most dovish analysts maintained that the (near-) complete elimination of nuclear weapons is positively dangerous. It would increase the probability of conventional war, encourage suspicions of cheating, prompt a rapid and thus destabilizing nuclear buildup if these suspicions or the conflict became extensive, and generate preemptive temptations during a crisis or limited war.[17] Just about any unambiguous, genuinely constraining, and verifiable agreements of great scope and consequence are barely imaginable except after they are no longer needed, when the conflictual issues have been buried. On paper, the Basic Principles Agreement did come close to serving as a substitute for mutual nonengagement by addressing most of the territorially centered hazards of the rivalry. But as already noted, it was soon sorely strained, engendered additional mistrust and anger on both sides, and then quickly unraveled. The START II treaty cut strategic weapons by 75 percent and eliminated the most destabilizing MIRVed missiles, but it was signed three years after the Cold War's demise.

In practice, conciliatory internationalism did not approach the scope and consequentiality of a national strategy during the superpower rivalry. Most Soviet-American accords dealt with secondary arms limitations; they did not begin to fulfill the overlapping criteria on which such agreements are judged. For advocates of mutual security, "what most needs to be 'cut' are the threats that each side perceives in the other's strategic forces."[18] For dovishly inclined nuclear strategists, the forces making for assured destruction are to be preserved while eliminating counterforce weapons—those that look to be offensive in number and design, have war-fighting purposes and a preemptive potential.[19] For those concerned with conventional deterrence and defense, effective arms control entails the elimination of offensive weapons, restrictions on provocative troop maneuvers, and the provision of transparency and other confidence-building measures.[20] Taken together, these criteria are at one with "the classical approach to arms control" as it was developed in the 1960s.[21]

The 1972 Anti-Ballistic Missile Treaty stands out as exceptionally consequential, the only one to ban the testing and deployment of a thoroughly new kind of weapon. It helped prevent what might have turned into a conflict-exacerbating offensive and/or defensive arms race. Some ten years later it also helped head off the "Star Wars" population shield that caused Moscow so much consternation. For a defensive weapon that could fully protect the United States from a ragged Soviet second strike could also be integral to an American first-strike threat. But even the ABM treaty was at least partly superfluous. The ground-based interceptors of the 1970s were judged insufficiently effective to warrant either side building the two antimissile sites that were permitted by the treaty. The various spaced-based designs of the 1980s for protecting the population were widely seen to be highly porous and readily rendered ineffective by simple means (e.g., depressed-trajectory submarine-launched missiles) that were already available to the Soviets. Both kinds of defenses could at best protect only some number of land-based missiles.

The SALT I and SALT II aggreements covered nearly the entire strategic weapons spectrum: land-based and submarine-launched ICBMs, single- and multiple-warhead missiles, air-launched cruise missiles, and long-range bombers. Yet the most that can be said about both agreements is that they introduced a measure of predictability by putting a (high) quantitative cap on the arms race. They did little more than ratify the current nuclear armories, along with their plans for modernizing and expanding them. The 1972 SALT I agreement even allowed for the American MIRV buildup and Soviet deployment of these anxiety-provoking weapons. And with so many weapons packed into the MIRVed launchers, U.S. warheads increased from five thousand to ten thousand and the Soviets' from four thousand to eight thousand during SALT I's short life span.[22]

The 1979 SALT II ceilings were minimally constraining.[23] In fact, both sides were permitted to place additional warheads on MIRVed launchers. During SALT II's official five-year life span American warhead numbers increased from about ten thousand to thirteen thousand, the Soviets' from eight thousand to ten thousand.[24] The agreement also allowed each side to deploy one new missile, modernize another, and improve the submarine and bomber legs of the strategic triad. The United States deployed an accurate counterforce missile on its new Trident II submarines, the ten-warhead MX missile, and a penetrating bomber. President Reagan could thus well afford to abide by the unratified treaty despite his publicly railing against its supposed one-sidedness.

Three major agreements were completed between 1987 and 1991. The 1987 Treaty on Intermediate Nuclear Forces (INF) was unprecedented in banning an entire class of existing weaponry, all ballistic and cruise missiles with a range between three hundred and three thousand miles. It thereby eliminated twenty-six hundred weapons, most of them Soviet and recently deployed, and some destabilizing American ones capable of attacking Soviet C3I centers from Western Europe over exceptionally short flight times. The treaty was also unprecedented in featuring on-site inspections to verify the weapons' destruction and the closing of production facilities. The 1990 Conventional Forces in Europe Treaty accomplished what Washington had been trying to achieve throughout the Cold War. It equalized the balance of conventional forces in Europe. It did so primarily by reducing the Warsaw Pact's heavy offensive forces: tanks, armored personnel carriers, and mobile long-range artillery. Along with the destruction of fourteen thousand Soviet, six thousand East European, and two thousand NATO tanks, a still larger number of heavy Soviet weapons was redeployed at a safer distance east of the Ural mountains. Compliance with these provisions was also subject to strict verification arrangements. The 1991 Strategic Arms Reduction Treaty involved a 30 percent cutback across the strategic spectrum. Its counting rules required a shift away from land-based MIRVs. On-site inspections and other verification requirements made for high transparency and thus predictability. Still, the weapons ceilings only took the rivals back to their 1982 levels, when the negotiations began.

Despite what they wrought on the ground and in the air, these three treaties do not constitute a strong case for negotiated arms control. It is one thing to achieve consequential agreements during an ongoing rivalry when they are most needed in dampening its hazardous pursuit. It is quite another for the opponent to sign onto conditions laid down by the United States while the rivalry was already cascading downward to a capitulatory conclusion. With the Soviets avidly seeking to improve East-West relations from a position of manifest weakness—after publicly acknowledging that severe domestic debilities necessitated a curtailment of the military competition—the agreements did more to signal the end of the rivalry than to help end it.

The Conventional Forces in Europe Treaty, easily the most consequential of the three, came to fruition almost twenty years after its negotiation became part of the mutual and balanced force reductions talks. It was finalized in 1990, one year after Moscow announced plans for the unilateral withdrawal of 500,000 troops from Eastern Europe, and when the Warsaw Pact had become nearly defunct, with East Germany having come over to the NATO side. On *Time* magazine's blunt account of START, any reassuring impact must have been minimal. "On almost every major question in START, the U.S. demanded, and got, its own way. . . . Gorbachev is tacitly accepting a position of overall *in*feriority, at least in the near term, since he is giving up right away much of the U.S.S.R.'s principal strength, which is in land-based ballistic missiles, while allowing the U.S. to keep its own advantages in bombers, cruise missiles and submarine weapons." Despite the appearance of strategic equality, Gorbachev was "presiding over the capitulation of the Soviet Union in the cold war."[25]

This then is the reasoning and the record for maintaining that a unilateral, unconditional, wide-ranging, and consequential national strategy can accomplish far more than conciliatory internationalism in avoiding conflictual relations with a defensively inclined contender. But before an opponent is reassured, before taking the strategy at its face value, he will surely assess other interpretations. He need not be extraordinarily mistrustful of U.S. intentions; security imperatives alone are sufficient for a deliberate skepticism. However, a benign understanding should prevail over alternative interpretations—if not fully, then largely so, if not immediately, then over a few years, if not among those who see us as the "great Satan," then with nearly all other opponents.

Nonengagement could be interpreted in a way parallel to that in which many Americans viewed Moscow's conciliatory behavior—as a deceptive stratagem to convince the other side to let down its guard and curtail territorial and military expansiveness. Moscow's understanding of nonengagement as such a machination would have been most plausible in the 1960s. At the start of the decade the Soviet Union was still held up as a political and economic model to be imitated by much of the Third World. At its close, the Soviets had achieved strategic parity. Once our dissembling led the USSR to forswear its expansionist opportunities and military potential, Washington would exploit its strong suit of economic hegemony. By manipulating trade and investment flows, capitalizing upon the multinational corporations' expanding influence, and controlling the World Bank and the IMF, the United States would contain the Soviet Union by weakening socialist regimes in the Third World. Nonengagement's defensive military configuration could have been seen as a cheap, nuclear-reliant strategy capable of deterring the USSR, and as sufficient to destroy it several times over.

Such an interpretation would have had to overcome several telling objections. Moscow would have had to convince itself of far more than deceptive diplomatic and tactical military ploys, but of a deceptive rationale for a strategic sea change. Would Washington go to such historically unheard-of lengths? And this without first trying out such other possibilities as negotiated concessions in lulling the Soviets into a false sense of security? Moscow would have had to believe that our thinking took this naive, unpromising, and risky form: Nonengagement would succeed in fooling a Kremlin whose own cunning was acknowledged in Washington; Soviet restraints would eventuate in a substantially more advantageous "correlation of forces" than one resulting from the full-blown prosecution of the Cold War; and the United States could reconstitute its alliances, take up the adversarial cudgels, and put them to decisive use before Moscow could compensate for the deception. Moreover, by the 1960s Soviet ideology had significantly revised its portrayal of the United States as being fully dominated by a unified capitalist class. Thus the requirements of secrecy, conspiracy, and political control in carrying out a truly grand deception would have looked most unpromising.

A national strategy might also have been construed as a manifestation of American weakness, a decline in political will and material wherewithal. Such an interpretation does not ascribe malign intent to the United States, but the absence of a benign motivation would cut into nonengagement's reassuring impact and allow for a strategic reversal under more favorable circumstances in the future. The Soviets would have found a declinist interpretation most plausible during the 1970s. America was divided and demoralized by Vietnam, reeling from the Arab oil embargo, looking somewhat economically exhausted, and toward the end of the decade it was beginning to bemoan its decline—all at a time when the USSR was at its strategic zenith and apparently profiting from its "geopolitical momentum" in the Third World. A national strategy might then have been seen as the product of international constraints, domestic political limits, and capitalist contradictions.

But Moscow would still have had to explain why a global withdrawal and a vast military retrenchment were carried out unilaterally and uncon- ditionally. Why not try to negotiate mutual disengagement or arrange spheres of influence that would leave the United States in a much stronger relative position? Moscow would have recognized that we had more than enough bargaining chips—many more and far more powerful allies and equal strategic power—with which to strike such a deal. There is also a very different kind of rejoinder to an interpretation of disengagement as the product of weakness. A national strategy is not only premised upon an appreciation of the privileged position afforded by our strategic im- munity. There is literally nothing in the isolationist tradition, the coun- try's history, or our foreign policy culture to suggest that we would dis- engage out of weakness. The strategically self-confident foundations of disengagement would certainly have become visible to Moscow through all manner of behavioral expressions.

On one other possible interpretation, nonengagement appears as a more or less malign opportunism. It is affordable and adventitious. Be- cause of the challenger's external setbacks, domestic debilities, or both, he is no longer able to mount a serious challenge. The United States could then maintain its dominant position without the expense of an adver- sarial strategy, avoid the risks of pressuring a beleaguered opponent into a desperate gamble, while waiting in the wings to deliver some sort of coup de grace. This understanding of nonengagement would have been most convincing to the Soviet Union during the 1980s, when it was ac- knowledging its economic crisis and institutional sclerosis.

Although Soviet weaknesses would allow for a retrenchment and re- laxation on America's part, why would they translate into a unilateral, unconditional, thoroughgoing disengagement? Since the Soviets were still nuclear equals and supporting Third World clients, nonengagement would have allowed for a long-term respite, for their eventual recupera- tion. The curtailment of pressurized adversarial policies alone would have avoided the risks of cornering an exhausted, wounded Russian bear in its nuclear lair. The Soviets would also have had to explain why a putatively hostile America did not seek additional satisfaction and credit by loudly applauding their decline and imminent defeat.

Regarding each skeptical interpretation a national strategy still allows the contender to put the United States to the test and for us to pass the test. Its unconditionality offers the opportunity for him to adopt a wait-and-see attitude. He need not sign onto constraining accords or rely upon expansive moves in fending off the perceived American threat. He can safely allow himself to be reassured over time.

III

Although nonengagement is much more efficacious than conciliatory engagement even on the latter's own turf, bilateral and multilateral agreements can supplement it on two conditions. The accords must be compatible with a national strategy. They neither cramp a military posture that maximizes deterrence and defense, nor obligate political-military involvements outside the core perimeter. And given the enormous compass of the national strategy's reassuring and conflict-avoiding policies, the accords must have a niche in which to make a difference. It is not enough to negotiate for the sake of negotiating, to generate warm atmospherics, or to prepare the ground for possibly useful agreements down the road.

Agreements that satisfy these conditions should be considered part of a national strategy. For they all conform to one of its doctrinal foundations, an agnostic posture regarding the other side's intentions. Appropriate accords do not detract from America's security even if the opponent is aggressively motivated; they may well add to it whatever his intentions. Such accords are also at one with the strategy's centrist position on the firmness-flexibility continuum. Despite their divergent understandings of Soviet intentions, most hawks and doves have favored those accords that are compatible with the national strategy and capable of enhancing the security of a nonengaged America whatever Moscow's aims.

There is little doubt about the utility of direct communications under pressing circumstances, when they can defuse crises by clarifying the nature of clashing interests, threatening movements, and unintended encounters. Sparked by the Cuban missile crisis, Washington and Moscow agreed to set up the hotline link between them. It was modernized in 1971 and again in 1984, providing for cable, radio, and satellite linkages capable of simultaneously transmitting full-page texts and maps on multiple teleprinters. American and Soviet leaders reportedly used the hotline to exchange messages on at least three occasions, during the 1967 Arab-Israeli war, the 1973 Middle Eastern war, and the 1980 Polish crisis.

Greater predictability was an advantageous consequence of arms limitation accords. However, their verification and transparency-heightening provisions can stand alone, without being joined to arms ceilings and reductions. They may well be easier to negotiate and more reassuring without restricting military deployments. Most confidence-building accords are of this kind. Their monitoring provisions can mitigate worst-case thinking and preparations, reassuring both sides that the other is not preparing for some unpleasant surprise, not building distinctly offensive weapons, and not striving for some military advantage. A nonengaged America would certainly want to underscore its nonaggressive intentions by demonstrating its nonthreatening military posture, the close monitoring of the other side's capabilities and deployments concomitantly heightening the confidence accorded to our own. In this regard the START agreement stands as a model to be replicated. Its verification provisions include "regularly updated data exchanges; twelve types of on-site inspections; continuous monitoring of mobil ICBM production plants; cooperative measures to facilitate reconaissance satellites; and a commitment not to interfere with National Technical Means of intelligence collection, including a ban on the denial of ballistic missile flight data."[26]

The exceptionally narrow core perimeter of the national strategy nearly obviates the need for conflict-avoiding accords pertaining to most of the world's landmass, but that still leaves certain possibilities in space, airspace, and international waters. The Limited Test Ban Treaty (LTBT), which was negotiated by the superpowers and Great Britain in 1963 and now has over a hundred signatories, prohibits nuclear testing in the atmosphere, in outer space, and under water. While limiting tests to deep underground sites was primarily intended as the first in a series of arms control accords, its secondary rationale is relevant here. It prevented contamination of the environment by radioactive fallout, as well as any pollution and environmental conflicts resulting from atmospheric explosions.[27] Prior to the 1972 Agreement on the Prevention of Incidents at Sea, the U.S. and Soviet navies frequently disrupted one another's formations, occasionally collided, trained their radar-activated guns on one another, and harassed each other with naval aircraft flying directly at the other side's ships. The treaty was signed on an understanding of how easily such incidents could raise international tensions, result in immediate combat, and even escalate toward war. Its conflict-avoiding provisions reaffirm the international rules of the road, restrict most forms of harassment, and require communications at sea and advance notice of close-quarters naval exercises. Disruptions, near collisions, and harassment declined dramatically after 1972.[28]

The United States has the obvious goal of preventing the spread of weapons that could be used against it. The Nuclear Nonproliferation

Treaty (NPT) came to fruition in 1968 after Washington and Moscow realized that it was not in their interests for others (including allies) to acquire the weapons. The nuclear-capable signatories of the NPT agreed not to help them to do so; by now nearly 150 nonnuclear signatories have pledged not to acquire or build the weapons. Despite possible appearances to the contrary, the NPT does not contravene the national strategy's narrow core perimeter. In fact, it could be seen as a form of nuclear nonengagement, reinforced by the nuclear nonengagement of others. And while binding the signatories with regard to the transfer and acquisition of nuclear capabilities, there is no obligation for us to carry out political, economic, or military actions against violators and nonsignatories.[29] The Missile Technology Control Regime was signed in 1989 by seven Western suppliers of rocket technologies; they were subsequently joined by the Soviet Union and several others. In 1993 the United States, Russia, and some 120 other states signed a treaty banning the production, sale, stockpiling, and use of chemical weapons. Most of those that already have such capabilities agreed to the terms of regular and "challenge inspections" by a new organization working for the prohibition of chemical weapons. Like the NPT, these accords take the form of a nonengagement that does not obligate punitive actions beyond the core perimeter.

Along with the post–Cold War START II treaty, these agreements are worth preserving. Some should be strengthened and extended.[30] Indeed, the nonproliferation regime's inspection procedures practically cry out for improvement. If nuclear spread does proceed, it would be useful to build upon the 1971 Accidents Measures Agreement (AMA)—the superpowers' pledge to heighten their organizational and technical safeguards against the unauthorized use and accidental detonation of nuclear weapons. An extended accord might involve U.S. technical assistance in sharing the command destruct mechanism employed on test missiles.[31] Washington could also provide potential nuclear rivals with satellite photography data for purposes of reassurance. As with the LTBT restricting nuclear tests to underground sites, other possible multilateral accords shade off into a far broader definition of national security. A national strategy could indirectly foster multilateral ones for protecting us against potential environmental and health hazards.[32]

Chapter VII

MINIMIZING STRATEGIC MISMANAGEMENT: AVOIDING INADVERTENT SECURITY DEFLATIONS

INADVERTENCE HAPPENS. Mismanagement is always possible. Potential minor and major security deflations stem from misconceptions, misunderstandings, miscalculations, mistakes, misbehavior, and other "malfunctions of minds and machines." Inadvertent possibilities have been attributed to careless decision making, psychological distortions, decisional biases, information gaps and intelligence failures, jumbled communications, organizational constraints, breakdowns in command and control arrangements, ambiguous directives and insufficient guidance of middle-level officials, their purposeful disobedience, and sheer accidents. Mismanagement has also been explained by the (all too full) fulfillment of preestablished decision-making arrangements, standard operating procedures, and both centralized and dispersed organizational responsibilities and routines.

Since the Cuban missile crisis took us near the nuclear brink, diplomatic historians, political scientists, newspaper columnists, and government officials have focused upon the hazards of inadvertence.[1] Doves and most hawks assumed that if a nuclear war were to befall the country, it would almost certainly emerge out of a superpower confrontation and its miscalculated, uncontrolled, or accidental escalation. The salient historical model was no longer just World War II, purposefully initiated by Germany and Japan. The transformation of a localized Balkan crisis into World War I was interpreted as the most tragic of largely unintended wars. It has been explained by Germany's having preciously little choice in backing up its single ally despite Austria-Hungary's patently excessive demands upon Russia's Serbian ally, the fears inspired by the expectations that victory would go to the side whose arms were fielded first and fastest, and the rigid comprehensiveness of the mobilization plans, which precluded a partial, defensive mobilization.

The explanations of inadvertence range from the equivalents of a Greek to a Christian tragedy. The security deflation may be comparable to the Greek kind, virtually foreordained from the outset, if not by the gods, then by the geographic givens of a difficult-to-defend common border, an inexorable science and technology imparting a decisive advantage to the offense, or a fanatically driven opponent. Alternatively, inadvertence can be more like an avoidable Christian tragedy, one that would not have occurred if different individuals—less sinful or otherwise less fallible ones—were making and implementing the decisions.

Here the appropriate focus is upon the strategic middle ground. A security strategy can hardly alter what is structurally given. A strategy has little if any bearing upon the qualities of the particular individuals who happen to be its managers. However, a strategy is a matter of more or less appropriate choice. It can make decisions and their implementation sorely problematic, not just for "average" national security managers but for the most talented ones as well.

Thus the questions: To what extent are inadvertent security risks attributable to the strategies themselves? More importantly for present purposes, how does a national strategy compare with adversarial and conciliatory internationalism in precluding inadvertence?

The great diversity of explanations of inadvertence needs to be given a manageable order. A simple, comprehensive scheme is suggested by the three inclusive components of effective security management. Policy options are formulated and decisions are made in a cognitively well-considered manner. They are based upon the open-minded examination of—and only of—the available options' security costs and benefits. And the decisions are made and implemented in a controlled manner. Departures from this rational policymaking model entail cognitive, psychological, and uncontrolled inadvertence. This chapter relates their likely emergence to the alternative strategies' doctrinal and policy centerpieces.

Cognitive mismanagement refers to the security risks and deflations brought on by the failure to fulfill the responsibilities of "quality" decision making—the careful consideration of the relations between ends and means and the latter's second- and third-order consequences. Insofar as cognitive inadvertence derives from the strategy at hand, it is due to the latter's difficult decisional requirements. It tends toward the complex and demanding, rather than the simple and easy. National security officials must confront formidable choices. The strategy's successful decisions hinge upon the availability of extensive and reliable information. And the strategy entangles its managers in incompatible ends and means.

Effective decision making involves considerably more than the careful assessment of the available options. It also entails their open-minded consideration, the absence of any nonconscious and thus patently irrelevant motivations. Psychological inadvertence refers to the nonconscious influences that distort rationally—realistically and relevantly—grounded decisions. Unconscious beliefs, emotions, biases, wants, and needs help shape decisional perceptions and assessments with little or no self-awareness of their impact. Strategic inadvertence of a psychological kind occurs insofar as the prevailing doctrine and attendant policy situations facilitate the activation of nonconscious influences, encourage their behavioral translations because of a substantive match between policy and psychology, and increase the frequency with which the latter comes into play.

Uncontrolled inadvertence refers to the failures of high-ranking officials to regulate the behavior of others. Just about all discussions of a loss of control are focused upon military officers. However, there is no reason for this limitation. Mismanagement could just as easily involve failures to implement the highest officials' aims by other relevant actors, including civilians and allied governments. Managerial regulation involves both positive and negative control, insuring that others act on directives as intended and do not act contrary to their prohibitions. The sturdiness of control declines insofar as a given strategy discourages regulatory oversight by high-ranking officials. Control capabilities also vary with the pressures that a strategy imposes upon high- and midlevel officials.

Having grouped the various accounts of inadvertence and noted how they are affected by strategic variations, we can invoke the *fifth doctrinal tenet*. A national strategy cannot be improved upon in avoiding the risks of inadvertence. It is more successful than strategic internationalism in preventing cognitive, psychological, and uncontrolled mismanagement, much more effective than the adversarial variant and substantially more effective than the conciliatory in guarding against inadvertent security risks.

Some clarification is called for since this proposition could easily subsume the second doctrinal tenet: With strategic internationalism's dependence upon the problematic identification of the challenger's intentions, it is imbued with a powerful potential for strategic inadvertence by adopting excessively adversarial or conciliatory policies. The interpretation of intent may be wide of the mark because of demands for extensive, highly reliable information, with uncertain and plausibly divergent interpretations also allowing nonconscious biases and motivations to come into play. The overlap is readily resolved in two ways. In accord with some other conceptions of inadvertence, the fifth proposition is limited to policy formation and implementation, thereby excluding any mistaken choices of an overarching hawkish to dovish strategy. Alternatively, the present proposition is based on the same working assumption as the previous two. Strategic internationalism's presumptively correct identification of the opponent's intentions as agressive-defensive consequently allows for the comparison with the national strategy on other grounds.

I

A national strategy entails few risks of cognitive inadvertence. To exaggerate somewhat, nonengagement approximates a self-executing strategy, given its minimal activism. The strategy's chief managerial responsibilities are relatively easy to fulfill. On the one hand, policymakers and intelligence analysts must avoid lassitude, overconfidence, and carelessness in assessing the continuing scope and potency of the immunity-enhancing conditions. On the other hand, they should foresee the adverse second- and third-order consequences, along with the "slippery slope" risks, of activist modulations. Immediately advantageous, cheap, and easy involvements could turn nasty, costly, and long.

Cognitive demands, especially difficult policy choices, are mitigated by two of the strategy's great advantages. Minimal political-military activism means that decision makers are not confronted with hard choices regarding scarce resources and means. Difficult trade-offs—between investment in long-term economic security and short-run military security, between the allocation of defense dollars to new weapons or current readiness—are largely obviated. So too is the resolution of the incompatibilities and outright contradictions among policies of deterrence, defense, and reassurance. The structural and perceptual security dilemmas are relatively simple to overcome. The narrow core perimeter allows for the design of a force posture that is maximally effective for deterrence and defense, as well as being defensively distinctive. Just about any challenges to the core are relatively easy to meet considering America's decisive military and political advantages in and around it. The demands of dealing with nuclear and other kinds of terrorism remain formidable, but they are less severe insofar as a nonengaged America is its less frequent target. The absence of allies removes the exceptionally hard demands of extended deterrence. A national strategy is thus left with one set of difficult decisions: How to go about making the graduated shift from strategic engagement to nonengagement. Yet even the complexities of disengagement are currently much allayed in the absence of a powerful global rival.

In comparison, the avoidance of cognitive inadvertence within an international strategy presents formidable complexities and demands. Nearly all rivalries and most of their specific interactions take the form of mixed-motive games. They feature a combination of opposing and shared interests in the context of mutual dependency and uncertainty, which is to say, particularly difficult-to-manage relations of conflict and cooperation. Both sides are continuously manipulating costs, risks, and rewards—bargaining with each other directly and indirectly, with greater or lesser trust, in good and not such good faith, with or without bargaining chips. They are doing so not just to attain the best possible outcomes in everything from sharp confrontations to minor arms agreements, but also to avoid ending up with the worst, rather than the second- or third-best outcomes. And this is all taking place in a thoroughly interactive world: Each side's optimum course depends upon a correct assessment of how the other will respond, while simultaneously trying to influence that choice by instilling expectations about its own likely course. Interactions are of the "He thinks that I think that he thinks" kind, which is also to say that they involve considerable uncertainty.

Managing a hawkish, dovish, or mixed strategy thus requires considerable acuity in navigating through Thomas Schelling's demanding strategic world—working through the "spiral of reciprocal expectations," thinking ahead several steps in a "theory of interdependent decisions," knowing when to signal, bluff, double-cross, make believable promises, strike deals, arrive at tacit understandings, lay down credible threats, and possibly rely upon the "rationality" of apparently "irrational behavior."[2] Richard Nixon was judged to be an "extraordinarily astute" international politician, Henry Kissinger a "brilliant geostrategist," and both were recognized for their thoroughgoing "geopolitical realism." They still failed to realize their goals of containment, reconciliation, and arms control. Their version of detente quickly deteriorated into its acrimonious demise, engendered yet more mutual mistrust, failed to ward off Soviet incursions and gains in the Third World, proved ineffectual in linking strategic arms and expansionist issues, and produced a virtually meaningless SALT I treaty, one that simply ratified yet higher weapons ceilings and did nothing to curtail the MIRVed missiles that constituted the Cold War's most destabilizing weapon.

Most activist measures depend upon extensive, unambiguous, and reasonably certain information. Yet Richard Betts is certainly not alone in maintaining that "intelligence failures are inevitable." According to experienced analysts, "estimating is what you do when you do not know"; in many situations "it is inherent . . . that after reading the estimate, you will still not know."[3] Providing for both reliable and usable intelligence analyses is problematic. "To the degree they reduce uncertainty by extrapolating from evidence riddled with ambiguities, analysts risk oversimplifying realities and desensitizing the consumers of intelligence to the dangers that lurk within the ambiguities; to the degree that they do not resolve ambiguities, analysts risk being dismissed by annoyed consumers who see them as not having done their job." Prescriptions for procedural reforms that "address specific pathologies introduce or accent other pathologies." And still more effective procedures "cannot fully compensate for the predispositions, perceptual idiosyncrasies, and time constraints of political consumers." Thus the need to "live with fatalism."[4]

The diversity of intelligence failures comes through in this partial listing. The massing of Chinese armies in the days before their onslaught against U.S. forces in Korea was undetected. Expectations of a massive uprising against Castro triggered by the U.S.-sponsored Bay of Pigs invasion were wildly exaggerated.[5] Were it known that Moscow might be intending to deploy some seventy missiles in Cuba, "then both public diplomacy (in drawing the unacceptable line at that level or somewhat lower) and private deliberations about American responses might have led to a satisfactory outcome that avoided the atmosphere and the risks of a superpower showdown."[6] The CIA's pessimistic assessments of the ground war in South Vietnam were contradicted by the army's, while the civilian analysts' negative assessments of the bombing runs against the North diverged sharply from the air force and navy's. In 1978 the CIA reported that "Iran is not in a revolutionary or even a 'pre-revolutionary' situation." After the Jaleh Square massacre ("Black Friday") the CIA still maintained that the shah would "remain actively in power over the next 10 years," leaving Washington completely unprepared for the Iranian revolution and its anti-Americanism.[7] Throughout the Cold War Washington exaggerated Soviet strategic capabilities and their impending improvements, the size and health of the economy, and mass support for the regime. And the failure to destroy all of Iraq's nuclear capabilities was due to intelligence shortcomings, not to the inaccuracies of the bombing runs and missile attacks.[8]

The managers of an activist strategy must regularly come to grips with trade-offs, incompatibilities, and contradictions among means and ends. Mitigating the policy dilemmas may require extraordinary judgment and perspicacity. Is it best for presidents to be alerted to risks and uncertainties, or (as Secretary of State Dean Acheson insisted) "should they be given confidence" to act quickly and decisively?[9] Should rapidly unfolding developments be dealt with instantaneously, or should a response await a thorough exploration of all the options and their second- and third-order repercussions? How are immediate defense needs to be stacked against the possibility of military and economic overextension down the road? Where is the line to be drawn between bolstering deterrence and defense for allies and ironclad security assurances that they can exploit for their own purposes? How are simultaneous deterrent and reassuring actions to be made clear, believable, and compelling? How design conciliatory proposals that are meaningful, fair, verifiable, and acceptable to both sides?

Some of these questions take on special significance in the midst of strategic internationalism's occasional confrontations. Analyses of crises and deterrent duels show that the most successful approach usually integrates complex elements of firmness and flexibility, a hard line to demonstrate resolve tempered by a "sensitivity" to and "tacit cooperation" with the challenger in meeting his specific security needs.[10] This delicate determination is made more difficult by diplomatic and military incompatibilities. Confrontations limit the "possibility of transforming military force and threats of force into a highly refined, exquisitely managed, discriminating instrument of diplomacy and crisis bargaining." At the same time, "efforts to impose the operational requirements of crisis management on the management of military force will often exacerbate the latent tension between competing diplomatic and military considerations."[11] It is difficult enough to assess the trade-offs between the safety of U.S. forces and the assertion of the U.S. position in managing some coercive duels. It may also require a rare knowledge (or the scarce opportunity to acquire it as needed) of the intricate military rules of engagement, such as the sometimes fine line between permissible defense in "hot pursuit" and retaliation.[12] Then there are the incompatibilities between acting with alacrity and deciding with more extensive information at hand. Constraints of time imposed upon analysts and decision makers eventuate in bits and pieces of intelligence information being viewed myopically rather than contextually. "The bewildering array of data, reports, and oral briefing" cannot be adequately digested, unless they happen to form a manifestly coherent pattern (or play into preexisting beliefs).[13]

II

There is no reason to suppose that the managers of a national strategy have fewer or weaker nonconscious motivations than their internationalist counterparts. However, the latter have a substantially greater propensity to commit psychologically motivated errors. Internationalism's decision-making demands generate some special incentives to act on nonconscious motivations, its doctrinal guidelines activate them, and its policy thrust increases the frequency with which such distortions come into play.

It was just seen that the intellectual complexities and judgmental demands of activist strategies can make for cognitive inadvertence. Some of those demands also foster psychological inadvertence. When decision makers see themselves as having preciously little in the way of policy choices, bereft of any feasible and desirable options, they have a tendency to avoid cognitive strains and emotional anxieties. This tendency often translates into wishful thinking, "bolstering," and "defensive avoidance." When faced with policy dilemmas, situational trade-offs, and uncertainties about outcomes, security managers are prone to exaggerate the effectiveness of the least bad option. They are also motivated to inflate the relevance and success of past and preferred policies, concomitantly ignoring or explaining away their debilities.[14] Given their activist imperatives, the veritable need for decisions, internationalist policymakers are particularly susceptible to these nonconscious departures from rational decision making.

When decisions are required of officials who find themselves in unfamiliar, complex situations about which they have inadequate information—situations that necessarily arise in managing global containment—they tend to rely upon oversimplifications. According to the social psychologists' schema theory, they are barely aware of how or why the unknown and unfamiliar becomes understandable. Deborah Larson's study of the ways in which America's highest officials arrived at their early containment decisions brings out the distorting effects of "scripts" and metaphors. A script is a "stereotyped sequence of events," a causal "chain of captioned scenes telling a story. . . . A simple form of script might consist of one scene setting up the situation (such as communists attack free-world nation) joined to another illustrating the outcome (United States intervenes to prevent communist takeover)." Scripts are applied with little or no thought given to their possible variations from current circumstances and their causal connections. "Foreign policy makers simply react as they have responded to similar situations in the past." So too with metaphors. In trying to understand ambiguous events and decide among their uncertain interpretations, decision makers try to match up what they are "experiencing to a preconceived schema describing analogous situations in the past. . . . Sometimes the resemblance is only metaphorical. Still a metaphor may help make the unfamiliar intelligible and understandable."[15]

The managers of any security strategy are commonly resistant to reviewing and questioning the effectiveness of "their" policies. Doing so may result in substantial costs to their political interests, professional reputations, public images, and private egos. Beyond conscious resistance there is also the nonconscious kind. The personal costs being manifestly irrelevant to the making of "good" security policy, their salience is denied. The managers of an international security strategy have some special investments in the correctness of their policies and are thus more psychologically resistant to acknowledging any excessively firm, flexible, or activist measures. They have the deep satisfaction of being involved in and helping to shape worldwide developments, the rewards of shouldering great responsibilities, pride in continually making important decisions, the recognition stemming from highly visible decisions, and the gratification of hard work and hard worrying in serving the country's security needs. In addition there are the bureaucratic and institutional interests that are imbued with distinctively activist policy biases. Self- and organizationally-interested beliefs in the appropriateness of larger budgets, greater internal autonomy, "higher" policy roles, and more extensive responsibilities—these interests can best be realized by way of activist policies. They are not about to be readily diluted by assessing the latter's seeming successes or recognizing their failures. Taken together, these are weighty conscious and nonconscious investments in the unquestioning effectiveness and continuation of effortful, if not still more activist, policies.

In part the Korean intervention was apparently due to the nonconscious influence of strategic activism. Prior to the North Korean invasion "*all* the major strategic schools, factions, and bureaucracies warned against being dragged into this kind of a war in the years—even months—before its outbreak."[16] The interventionist option had previously been coolly considered and rejected several times, yet the highest officials immediately embraced it upon learning of the invasion. The nonconscious attractions of direct and forceful military action apparently blocked out all considerations other than the Munich analogy, despite Korea's being a "small peninsula leading nowhere." This interpretation is reinforced by the availability of another containment option, indeed a better one on the acknowledged possibility that the North Korean attack was a feint to tie down U.S. forces far from the Soviet Union's real and inestimatably more important target in Western Europe.[17] Jack Snyder believes that the United States might well have achieved "the main benefits of the war without having fought it at all . . . it could have accepted the loss of South Korea but then shored up its positions in Europe and Japan by directly increasing its economic subsidies and military deployments in those core areas. This should have achieved the desired (deterrent and reassuring effects) on the psychology of the Soviets, Europeans, and Japanese."[18]

The heady attractions of successful activism then translated into overconfidence and closed-mindedness, a depreciation of the other side's capabilities, and an insensitivity to its paramount security interests. Having routed the enemy, the war's objective was extended beyond the successful defense of the South to the unification of the two Koreas. Not to move into North Korea was somehow taken to be tantamount to weakness, even as inadequate resolve comparable to the appeasement of Munich.[19]

Beijing sent diplomatic messages and used minor military moves to signal that it would intervene if U.S. forces moved into the bordering areas of North Korea. They were discounted on the over-confident assumption—General Douglas MacArthur's in particular—that China's army would not intervene against America's high-powered forces, and if this proved incorrect, they would be no match for U.S. air power. Washington was insensitive to China's readily discernible security needs: No capitalist forces on or near its border. London's often-suggested option of leaving a twenty-mile buffer zone, as opposed to moving right up to the Yalu River within easy reach of important economic targets, was not seriously explored until four days before the final offensive was launched. The likelihood of Beijing's not believing that our war aims did not extend into China was largely ignored. "To the extent that the issue was raised at all, MacArthur's offensive gained first priority over any alternative political-military options. No authoritative voice called for postponement of the offensive, either pending further information on Chinese capabilities and intentions or in order to probe for a negotiated settlement. Last but not least, the Joint Chiefs of Staff were unwilling or unable to define what course of action would follow should the offensive fail."[20] The massive Chinese attacks for which U.S. forces were totally unprepared brought on the longest retreat in America's military history. Well over half our casualties were inflicted in this now much bigger and longer war, one that ended where it could have ended almost three years before, along the defensible "narrow waist" of Korea's North-South border.

Inadvertence derives from the consonance between a strategy's doctrinal guidelines and some fairly common nonconscious biases; the latter inadvertently inform the formers' policy expressions. No type of bias is more important or frequently salient than the policymakers' misperceptions of the rival and the rivalry, nearly all of which have been elucidated in Robert Jervis's *Perception and Misperception in International Politics*.[21] Although he did not take note of it, taken all together they form a distinctive pattern: They exaggerate the need for and effectiveness of additional activist measures, mostly adversarial ones. For among the other misperceptions none points in the opposite direction; and the remaining ones are "silent" on this score in not having any special activist implications.

Policy makers who spend a great deal of time drawing up a plan or making a decision commonly think that the message they wish to convey will be clear to the receiver. Since they are aware of what is to them the important pattern in their actions, they often feel that the pattern will be equally obvious to others, and they overlook the degree to which the message is apparent to them only because they know what to look for. With decision makers not being in the habit of doubting the effective transmission of their messages, if the challenger does not respond as wished the problem must derive from *his* aims, values, and mind-set. This perceptual bias has little applicability to the managers of a national strategy; they do not draw up elaborate plans and continuously send threatening or accommodating messages. It does apply to the internationalist security managers' constant, painstaking consideration of activist options, and the detailed design of announcements, dispatches, offers, signals, and subtle warnings. What they conveyed may not have been interpreted as it was intended. In particular, tacit and "mixed" communications that combine firmness and flexibility may be poorly conveyed, ignored due to other political "noises," misunderstood in their complexity. But believing

the reverse, the opponent's unsatisfactory reaction or nonresponse requires that more be done—the sending of yet more or more compelling
messages. They may be warranted. They could also constitute activist
overreactions, excessively hard-line policies that exacerbate the conflict
or unduly soft ones that communicate weakness.

Decision makers tend to inflate the extent to which unwelcome, expansive, and outrightly hostile actions are seen to derive from the opponent's
intentions and specific aims, from within himself, as it were. In contrast,
his welcome inactions and cooperative behavior are seen to be the result
of the decision makers' own previous actions. This perceptual bias has
little relevance for the managers of a national strategy. Not being much
concerned with most of the opponent's actions and agnostic with respect
to his intentions, they do not go about deciphering and disentangling the
explanations. Internationalist security managers overlook the explanations of his "misbehavior" that may be (largely) unrelated to his aims,
those that are due to his own inadvertence, relations with third states, and
America's (apparently) threatening behavior. They are then prone to
adopt overly adversarial measures of deterrence, coercion, or punishment. Similar results are likely to stem from another frequent misperception: When governments are honest and open in proclaiming their peaceful and defensive (or revisionist) aims, they usually believe that their
veracity is accepted by others. America's opponents may take its peaceful,
nonthreatening proclamations at face value, but then again they may not.
On the former's nonconsciously exaggerated premise, there are then
"good reasons" to opt for additional or more adversarial measures,
thereby inadvertently exacerbating the conflictual issues and interactions.

To some extent the frequency of psychological inadvertence is situa-
tionally determined. A given strategy is more or less likely to place decision managers in those time-pressured, anxiety-producing situations in
which their thinking and actions are given to being nonconsciously disfigured. Dangerous confrontations and regional wars are, of course, more
frequent when pursuing an internationalist rather than a national strategy. Alexander George has set out a dozen decisional tendencies that can
have a direct effect on crisis instability. Half of them involve nonconscious blockages and biases.

1. The search for relevant options tends to be dominated by past experience
   . . . a fall[ing] back on familiar solutions that have worked in the past,
   whether or not they are appropriate to the present situation
2. A reduced receptivity to information that challenges existing beliefs
3. Increased stereotypical thinking
4. A reduced tolerance for ambiguity leading to the cut off of information
   search and premature decision

5. The belief that one's own options are quite limited
6. The belief that the opponent has it within his power to prevent an impending disaster.[22]

Some of these nonconscious influences were arguably salient in the midst of several Cold War confrontations: numbers 1 and 5 in the decision to intervene in Korea; numbers 2, 5, and 6 in sending U.S. forces right up to the Korean-Chinese border; numbers 1 and 5 in planning to use nuclear weapons to defend Quemoy and Matsu (the tiny pieces of "worthless rock") if China invaded them during the Taiwan Straits crises; numbers 3, 4, and 5 among those members of the Excom who advocated air attacks and an invasion of Cuba at the outset of the missile crisis; numbers 2 and 5 in continuing the Vietnam War for six years after it was known that no more than a cosmetic political settlement was possible; numbers 4 and 6 in mistakenly condemning Moscow for having violated the 1962 Cuban agreement by deploying a "new" brigade and offensive weapons on the island; and numbers 2 and 4 with regard to the Contras' actions in Nicaragua.

The literature on political psychology and decision making identifies some additional nonconscious paths toward strategic mismanagement.[23] Some imply the greater prominence of these tendencies among internationalist security managers. But not a single generalization points to their greater salience or more frequent activation among the managers of a national strategy.

III

Uncontrolled security deflations may be brought on by the failures of high-ranking officials to control the behavior of those upon whom they depend for the execution of their aims. The sturdiness and scope of control capabilities are especially salient with respect to the actions of friendly states and those of U.S. military commanders in the midst of tense confrontations and nuclear alerts.

Without political-military dependents or dependencies, a nonengaged America averts the alliance risks of uncontrolled inadvertence. These are more or less built into strategic internationalism in its having to contend with the "security dilemma in alliance politics."[24] Because allies are deemed unequivocally necessary to insure America's security, they need to be placated. Because their actions can detract from our security, they need to be controlled. The two imperatives become all the more incompatible the more that security needs make it necessary to reassure and placate allies, and/or the more that the allies' interests diverge from our own. Despite America's predominant power and the allies' dependence upon it during the Cold War—despite serving as their chief protector, patron, and paymaster in the common anticommunist cause—Washington still failed to maintain sufficient control on numerous occasions.

A less than complete listing begins in 1956. The Suez crisis was brought on—to Washington's complete surprise and utter consternation—by the joint British-French-Israeli invasion of Egypt. With some political and financial muscle, the United States did compel them to end the war, but not without Moscow first engaging in a little nuclear saber rattling and making some major political gains in the Middle East. In the late 1950s and early 1960s we failed to move the Diem government of South Vietnam toward political, legal, and economic reforms that were to dilute the communists' ideological appeal. In the 1960s the Alliance for Progress was to head off leftist and Marxist gains by providing Latin American governments with substantial economic aid, conditioned upon their carrying out political, tax, and land reforms. They managed to take the money without discernibly changing their ways. Toward the end of the 1973 Mideast War Israel ignored the cease-fire arranged by Washington and Moscow. It continued to attack an encircled Egyptian army, with the Soviets then threatening and preparing to airlift troops into the area. The crisis was resolved with U.S. nuclear forces being placed on alert status as a deterrent and Israel being strong-armed into a cease-fire. At about the same time the peace negotiations with Hanoi were dragged out until Washington made sufficient concessions to obtain Saigon's acceptance of the accords. Without major post–Cold War challengers to U.S.-led alliances, without the perceived presence of a shared threat, Washington's ability to influence alliance behavior becomes all the more problematic. Even the common threat of Libyan terrorism left Washington stranded. The Europeans rejected an oil embargo to compel Tripoli to extradite those suspected of destroying the Pan Am plane over Scotland in which more than two hundred people died.

Inadvertent security deflations can stem from inadequate control over U.S. forces in the midst of crises, standoffs, limited military actions, and prewar tensions. Misunderstandings, miscommunications, mistakes, and misbehavior vary with the sturdiness of command and control capabilities, along with the demands imposed upon them and the frequency with which they are put to high-pressured tests. The highest officials are unable to exercise sufficient positive control over the (precise) deployments and movements of military units, and/or negative control in preventing those actions that diverge from their aims and directives. These risks are clearly minimized by a national strategy. The narrow core markedly reduces the extent to which central command responsibilities need to be dispersed. The strategy's nuclear policies, featuring slow response times and measured retaliatory responses, allow for greater control. Minimal activism sharply circumscribes the frequency with which the highest officials' control capabilities need to be exercised and thus put to a strenuous test.

An activist strategy demands much more extensive control capabilities. It is also burdened with the trade-offs between positive and negative control, as when military actions are always to be executed on orders to do so and never to be undertaken in their absence.[25] The managers of a wide-ranging, sometimes fast paced, and occasionally confrontational strategy have good reasons to delegate command authority—those of circumstantial adaptability, flexibility in response to evolving events, and rapid reaction times. But to devolve authority is to risk unintended, uncontrolled devolutions. What is deemed appropriate at the center could diverge from what is advantageous, required, mismanaged, purposefully rejected, or accidentally obviated on the spot. In addition, forward troop deployments and their movements during tense situations increase the hazards of opposing forces unintentionally running into one another, of forceful reactions running beyond the formalized (or intended) rules of engagement, and of weapons being accidently fired in the fog and heat of crisis situations.

The U.S. side of the Cuban missile crisis is a close approximation of a most likely case for the exercise of effective central control. Yet under exceptionally propitious conditions several hazardous developments still escaped the crisis managers' supervision. President Kennedy, his brother Robert, and Secretary of Defense Robert S. McNamara have been held up as the very model of modern crisis managers in safely getting the Soviets to withdraw their missiles from Cuba. There is no doubting their thorough and detailed involvements and close supervision of events as Soviet ships were steaming toward the American blockade line—not surprisingly, since Kennedy reckoned the chances of war to be about one out of three. Moreover, Washington did not have to stretch its command and control capabilities geographically, and it enjoyed overwhelming local and strategic superiority.

The president ordered our nuclear forces to be placed on alert status. But he did not authorize or expect the head of the Strategic Air Command (SAC) to send the message "in the clear," to disregard the normal, less provocative encoded channels. The secretary of defense looked into the navy's standard operating procedures for laying down a blockade. What would it do and not do in protecting U.S. ships from the opponent's ships and in disabling and searching cargo ships? When McNamara sought the answers so as to exercise detailed supervision of the blockade, the chief of naval operations ushered him out of the command center. Not having received the information about the navy's procedures for dealing with submarines in the blockade zone, the Excom was apparently aghast to learn that these called for their harassment with depth charges. One

Soviet submarine may have been forced to surface and another was damaged.[26]

During the crisis the air force remained wedded to its routine. Unbeknownst to the Excom, it continued its scheduled flights over the North Pole to detect any radioactivity from Soviet nuclear tests. A U-2 plane accidentally strayed into Soviet airspace—near a missile field that would have been one of the first targets of an American strike. Soviet fighters took off to attack the U-2; American fighters with nuclear weapons aboard were launched from their bases in Alaska to rescue the lost pilot. Two dangers were skirted. The U-2 found its way back before the two sides' interceptors met in the air. Moscow did not react to the U-2 overflight as it might well have—as a last-minute reconnaissance mission prior to an American attack.[27] Prearranged mobilization plans called for SAC to take over the armed missiles and the test and training sites at Vandenberg Air Force Base. Yet one ICBM (without a nuclear warhead) was still somehow launched on a regular test flight in the middle of the crisis. In the absence of satellite intelligence capabilities at the time, Moscow probably did not know of the flight. Yet a poorly timed ICBM test launch in a crisis after those capabilities were in place would have immediately alerted Soviet warning systems and possibly been misinterpreted as the initial part of an attack.[28]

Over the course of the Cold War the United States adopted rapid operational retaliatory policies that placed greater and greater burdens upon the control of nuclear forces. For Schelling the "premium on haste" was the single greatest danger of nuclear war; the possibility of "accidental or inadvertent war" was exclusively tied up with the "crucial premise" of the need to strike back immediately. "It was hard to imagine how anybody would be precipitated into full scale war by accident, false alarm, mischief, or momentary panic, if it were not for such urgency to get in quick."[29] Until the early 1970s U.S. retaliation was to occur immediately (i.e., within minutes) after a Soviet first strike befell the United States. During the next decade U.S. forces were to be launched while America was under attack, after the first few missiles had exploded. And after the doctrine for fighting nuclear war was fully developed, the missiles were to be launched on tactical warning—on radar and satellite indications of an incoming Soviet attack. With rapid retaliation having priority, the incompatibilities between positive and negative control were resolved in favor of the former.

Thus there was never a significant time gap between a Soviet attack and the authorization of an American response. According to the earlier ("dovish") doctrine—the assured destruction of civilian targets—a time-urgent response was required, but not to "prevail" at the end of the ensuing holocaust. It was designed to bolster the credibility of the deterrent threat. If Moscow thought that the president would take the time to con-template if, when, and where to retaliate, it might surmise that he would come to a safe conclusion: No military purposes would be served by oblit-erating Soviet population and industrial centers, concomitantly ensuring the destruction of U.S. cities. During the last phase of the Cold War we relied upon the most sensitive control option of launch on tactical warn-ing, which might have proved mistaken. Holding off for just a few min-utes between the first warning and the Soviet missiles' first impact would presumably have "lost" us the nuclear war due to the destruction of nearly all our land-based missiles. "Strategic organizations expected[ed] to receive retaliatory authorization within minutes after the initial detec-tion of missile launches. That expectation [was] so deeply ingrained that the nuclear decision process [was] reduced to a drill-like enactment of a prepared script, a brief emergency telecommunications conference whose purpose is to get a decision from the national command authority before the incoming weapons arrive."[30]

The timing and control considerations—and much of the targeting policy—of Bruce Blair's proposal for "no immediate second use" co-incide with those of a national strategy. The authority to retaliate against the Soviet Union would have been withheld for at least twenty-four hours. Instead of destroying time-urgent missile silos, one or more parts of the military and economic infrastructure would have been targeted. Besides enhancing stability by not posing an apparent preemptive threat, Blair's proposal would have helped insure against partly accidental war, curtailed the risks of inadequate negative control, and bolstered positive control. It speaks to the essence of nuclear decision making—decision making that "should not be relegated to reflexes and brief drills, but should instead be regarded as a careful deliberative exercise of national leadership that could take days or longer . . . a decision on nuclear retali-ation should not be forced on officials before they have had a chance to assess actual damage, evaluate Soviet political and military objectives, define U.S. security interests, and determine the role of nuclear weapons in promoting those interests. These matters cannot be given adequate consideration in a matter of minutes or hours."[31]

Uncontrolled nuclear inadvertence was also a distinct possibility due to the Reagan administration's high-risk maritime strategy, its plans for cutting off the dispersal of Soviet missile-launching submarines near the Barents Sea during a serious crisis.[32] There was also a potential hazard "on the ground." America's theater nuclear weapons in Europe were to serve as a strong deterrent in a crisis, and in the event of an attack, to deter the Soviets from (fully) exploiting their conventional successes. The theater nuclear weapons could best be protected by dispersing them before and during a war. Yet doing so heightened the chances of their uncontrolled and accidental use. Rather than remaining in controllable centralized sites where they were vulnerable to sudden air attacks and sabotage by Soviet Spetzna commandos, in a prewar situation they were to be dispersed to maximize their survival. At the outset of a war they were to be placed in the hands of hundreds of military commanders. Some of these hands could easily have turned out to be less than controllable and controlled—with the weapons being primed for immediate use, shifted around to avoid missile and aircraft strikes, enemy forces moving toward and possibly around them, and the destruction of some NATO units being imminent unless they were fired immediately.

Having set out the many actual and potential instances of cognitive, psychological, and uncontrolled strategic inadvertence, what of the basic fact that the very worst did not happen? Except for the Cuban and Berlin crises between 1958 and 1962, we never even came close to the nuclear brink. Still, on the arguments of this chapter, not only would a national strategy have further curtailed the risks of the very worst and all others; these would have been significantly more prominent but for the fortunate circumstances of having the USSR as our chief rival.

However much Sovietologists and national security experts differed about other matters, including the crucial issue of Moscow's intentions, they nearly all agreed that the Soviet Union was exceptionally risk averse. The leadership's political culture featured a great reluctance to push ahead when the payoff was uncertain, to accept high-stakes gambles involving the possibility of a big loss, and a willingness to retreat to avoid defeat if resistance proved stronger than anticipated.[33] This risk-averse culture presumably took on yet greater salience regarding nuclear war. Soviet strategic forces were never placed on alert status during a crisis, the nuclear warheads were kept at some distance from their missile launchers, and the former were placed under the guard of the separate internal security forces. During the Berlin crises circa 1960, the Soviets did not exploit their local military advantages. Having insured themselves against West Germany's acquisition of nuclear weapons, they retreated by building the Berlin Wall to keep the East Germans and others from escaping. Although the Cuban missile deployment was an inordinately risky undertaking, this was the one such case. It was partly offset by Khrushchev's careful management of the crisis and his not exploiting the local Soviet advantage in Berlin to compensate for America's in the Caribbean. Moreover, the Politburo subsequently forced him out of office partly because of what was called his "hare-brained scheme."

The United States is unlikely to be so fortunate in the future. Although other challengers may be imbued with a decidedly risk-avoidance culture, few if any have been accorded such an interpretation. The USSR's thousands of nuclear weapons, many indestructible ones, and fairly sturdy command, control, and intelligence network made for a reasonably high degree of nuclear imperviousness vis-à-vis the United States. In contrast, "small" nuclear states must contend with the high exposure of both their weapons and command, control, and intelligence arrangements.[34] This combination of culture and structure, as it were, could engender nuclear threats, swaggering, first-strike temptations, and preemptive actions, with all their built-in possibilities of inadvertence.

PART TWO

Beyond the Security Realm

SECURITY STRATEGIES are considered first and foremost in terms of their performance and promise in safeguarding the nation's highest values from purposeful external threats. This is what they are intended and expected to do. In addition, security strategies have decided consequences outside the security realm—if not by design, then unintentionally, if not directly, then tangentially, if not immediately, then over time. And while the protection of the nation's highest values obviously comes first, a strategy's consequences for the nation's various extrasecurity values constitute patently important evaluative standards, all the more so at present—in the absence of a major security threat.

The second part of this book considers each of America's extrasecurity values that have been or could be significantly affected by the alternative security strategies. It compares the national and international strategies as they affect our ideal and material values, abroad and at home. Chapter 8 considers the strategies' contributions to the realization of the country's liberal, peaceful ideals within and between states. Chapter 9 compares their impact upon the nation's external economic relations and economic well-being at home. Chapter 10 focuses upon America's domestic political ideals: the government's responsiveness to Congress, respect for civil liberties, and adherence to the laws. And one part of the final chapter takes up America's desired standing in the world—preeminent, strong, principled, self and other regarding. There are no other substantial extrasecurity grounds in choosing between the alternative strategies.

Each chapter comes to the same conclusion: A national strategy promises considerably more than strategic internationalism in fulfilling the nation's extrasecurity values. (Unlike the five strategic propositions, these chapters' claims are separate ones; they do not relate to one another despite their similar conclusions.) In some respects the national strategy promotes our extrasecurity values "directly" at home. In others it does so by allowing for and heightening the effectiveness of U.S. foreign policy. The concurrent foreign policy that reconfigures isolationism takes the form of a three-track design: The minimally activist security strategy, in and of itself, and as it relates to a moderately ambitious idealistic activism and an assertive and affirmative economic diplomacy. As for the historical isolationists' extrasecurity arguments and predictions, these turn out to be regularly justifiable and frequently warranted by contemporaneous and subsequent developments. Where they were wide of the mark, their claims were usually fashioned in an extreme, possibly rhetorical manner.

And while the concurrent foreign policy diverges from the historical isolationists' outright rejection of idealistic activism, their critique of liberal internationalism still helps make the case for the pursuit of a principled, moderated liberal project alongside a national strategy.

The last chapter has a very different aim. Here it is shown that the concurrent design matches up with the country's foreign policy culture, more so than any other grand design. It can thus be viewed as a distinctly American foreign policy, with all that this implies for its widespread political appeal and possible adoption.

Chapter VIII

AMERICA'S INTERNATIONAL IDEALS

FROM THE LATE eighteenth century to the present there has been no denying America's liberal international ideals of maintaining and extending peace among and within states, national self-determination, political liberty, economic freedom, human rights, and democracy. Since 1900 America has been divided on whether and how extensively to go abroad in furthering these ideals. These divisions continue to cut across those having to do with the protection of the nation's security. Bringing the various levels of idealistically inspired and security-centered activism together finds historical isolationists advocating minimal levels of both. Liberal internationalists are their opposites in supporting activist policies in both realms. Realist internationalists favor few if any idealistic endeavors alongside substantial security efforts. There is a fourth position. The concurrent foreign policy brings together a moderated liberalism with a minimally activist security strategy.

This moderated liberal project is thoroughly principled, endowed with a diversity of hard and soft means, autonomously fashioned and advanced, and exclusively other regarding in its motivations. Although it does not include moral guidelines, or a moral calculus about when and where to become involved, its idealistic activism rarely strays beyond what is deemed right and proper to a reasonably impartial group, including the major powers who have criticized past U.S. contraventions of international law and self-serving security ventures. The project is enabled by a nearly full complement of means with which to compel, accommodate, and buy off those who are contemplating or engaging in illiberal practices. It is markedly autonomous in that liberal policies derive from liberal values; neither the choice of means nor their tactical deployments are shaped by the goal of providing for the nation's security. The project is solely focused upon our international ideals rather than being joined with, pursued alongside of, or justified by any security imperatives.

At one and the same time the concurrent foreign policy's liberal project is moderated and at least as activist as that of liberal internationalism. Being exclusively focused upon America's international ideals, it is delimited by what is deemed possible, by the variety of recalcitrant conditions that can negate even the most effortful and promising liberal designs. Liberal internationalism has obviously been highly activist. But its security imperatives, interests, and wants have done far, far more than its idealistic aims in eliciting activist measures—whether gauged in terms of their frequency, scope, costs, or risks. With the partial exception of the Wilsonian crusade to make "the world safe for democracy," the United States has never gone abroad in anything like an ambitious manner solely, primarily, or even largely on behalf of a liberal cause in and of itself. At his inauguration John F. Kennedy promised that the United States would "pay any price, bear any burden, meet any hardship, oppose any foe to assure the survival and the success of liberty." These words, the vaulting expression of Cold War liberalism, were spoken on two implicit assumptions: The cause of liberty is at one with the nation's security; the United States would only further the former in decidedly costly or risky ways insofar as its security was also involved.

With the crucial caveat that it is still marginally motivated and potentially much constrained by security concerns, in principle a post–Cold War liberalism has emerged that is broadly at one with the moderation of the liberal project. It endorses a policy of low-risk, limited interventions on behalf of peaceful, democratic, human rights and humanitarian causes—where intervention can make a difference. Without precluding unilateral actions, they should be of a multilateral kind, the burdens shared by the UN, NATO, the Organization of American States, or other regional coalitions. In addition, U.S. governmental agencies are to continue their hands-on assistance programs in the cause of democratization. The efforts of the National Endowment for Democracy, the Agency for International Development, and the State Department's human rights division can only make a marginal difference in most countries. Yet in some the difference could turn out to be decisive, and a whole host of minor contributions can add up to a major one.[1]

With these clarifications in mind comes this chapter's central claim: The conjunction of the liberal project with a national strategy has promised and still promises more than any other foreign policy in protecting and promoting America's international ideals. Contrary to the claims of full-blown isolationism, liberal activism can have an overall, decidedly positive impact. Contrary to the claims of realist internationalism, a moderated idealism does not infringe upon the nation's security when the latter is more than adequately insured by a minimally activist security strategy. The crucial comparison—and the focus of this chapter—is with the liberal internationalism whose double-barreled activism is said to maximize the country's security and ideal interests. To be clear, the promise of the concurrent dispensation should not be exaggerated. No security strategy, no foreign policy, can do all that much to vindicate America's liberal values. The past, present, and future world features too many unyielding conditions, too much opposition, too many sorely complex ethical circumstances for the United States—alone or along with others—to make a huge difference more than occasionally and a significant one consistently. But this is hardly to render what can be done minimally consequential or to downplay the considerable advantages of the concurrent dispensation.

The case for the concurrent foreign policy, for the relative effectiveness of pursuing our ideals alongside a national strategy, is developed in three parts. The first section of this chapter considers the historical isolationists' total rejection of idealistic activism. It shows their claims to be regularly reasoned and reasonable, often fully warranted. Yet in large part their arguments can be reconstituted in favor of a strategic isolationism that not only allows for a principled liberal activism, but one that also bolsters its effectiveness. The second part reviews and interprets liberal internationalism's record after 1945. It is thoroughly mixed in having variously advanced, ignored, and distorted America's ideals. Where our security and ideal interests were seen to coincide, the consequences were often benign. The malign consequences are primarily attributable to a perceived divergence of interests. A minimalist political-military activism thus allows for the autonomously fashioned, principled pursuit of liberal ends. The third part addresses the efficaciousness of such a project relative to that of liberal internationalism. With their hard and soft capabilities being just about the same, and with the concurrent dispensation being advantaged in just about all other regards, it holds out a greater promise of success at any one time and over time.

I

The historical isolationists rejected security involvements as unnecessary, ineffective, and harmful. In something of a parallel fashion they argued against going abroad to vindicate America's ideals. These could best, indeed only, be advanced by our serving as a model to be emulated. Attempts at their active vindication would not only dampen its luminosity as a guiding liberal beacon, but the efforts would be variously ineffectual, unprincipled, and counterproductive. And without repeating parts of the historical discussion in chapter 2, it is not just security-driven involvements, but also idealistically inspired ones, that can put the country's highest values at risk.

The isolationists' idea of America as an exemplar is a secularized version of Puritan New England as a "City upon the hill." Expressed only somewhat less confidently than John Winthrop's belief that "the eyes of all people are upon us" is this passage from George Washington's Farewell Address: "It will be worthy of a free, enlightened, and at no distant period a great nation, to give to mankind the magnanimous and too novel example of a people always guided by an exalted justice and benevolence." On his inauguration Thomas Jefferson advised against "entangling alliances" for both security and idealistic reasons. Rejecting nefarious, conflict-generating entanglements would set an example for other peaceful countries. Shunning political-military involvements would allow America to perfect its republican institutions, its special form of self-government, thereby setting an example for liberty-seeking peoples.[2]

In the early 1820s there was considerable enthusiasm for helping the Greeks in their nationalist struggle against the Ottoman Empire by extending them diplomatic recognition. It prompted Secretary of State John Quincy Adams to offer the most eloquent of elaborations upon America as an exemplar. "Wherever the standard of freedom and independence has been unfurled, there will America's heart, her benedictions, and her prayers be. But she goes not abroad in search of monsters to destroy." To intervene even under the "banners of foreign independence" would involve the United States in "wars of interest and intrigue, of individual avarice, envy, and ambition, which assume the color and usurp the standard of freedom. The fundamental maxims of her policy would insensibly change from liberty to force." The ideals of "freedom and independence" would be replaced by an "imperial diadem, flashing in false and tarnished luster, the murky radiance of dominance and power." America thus has no choice but to "recommend the general cause with the countenance of her voice and the benignant sympathy of her example."[3]

After the failed European revolutions of 1848, Louis Kossuth arrived in the United States to make a searching plea for help in the Hungarian cause against the Austro-Hungarian Empire. Henry Clay responded by maintaining that liberty can be better served by Americans keeping their "lamp burning brightly on this Western Shore, as a light to all nations, than to hazard its utter extinction, amid the ruins of fallen or falling republics in Europe."[4] On another issue the power of example was thought to be so great by John C. Calhoun that he claimed still more for a posture of "masterly inactivity." "If we remain quiet . . . and let our destinies work out their own results, we shall do more for liberty, not only for ourselves but for the example of mankind, than can be done by a thousand victories."[5]

Most nineteenth-century isolationists were not so naive to believe that the country's liberal values would be vindicated solely by our serving as an exemplar. Were the shimmering model to inspire others to do their part, brutal and even failing empires were not about to fall all that easily. Were the beacon to guide others in fashioning republican institutions, these could not always be successfully transplanted in "foreign soil." Secretary of State Adams took this position even in defending the Monroe Doctrine. European rule was not to be reimposed among the Latin American countries that had shaken it off, yet he did not envisage "any prospect that they will establish free or liberal institutions of government. . . . Arbitrary power, military and ecclesiastical, is stamped upon their education, upon their habits, and upon all their institutions."[6] But whatever its impact, the appeal of the American model would be maximized by having all ambitions and energies focused inward.

The Spanish-American War and the annexations that followed it caused a moral maelstrom among the isolationists. The war was a jingoistic, bellicist exercise; the annexation of Puerto Rico, Hawaii, and the Philippines betrayed the country's much prized principles of self-determination and liberty. The isolationists who formed the Anti-Imperialist League insisted that no standard of morality could justify one people imposing itself upon another or telling it how to live politically. They thoroughly rejected the annexations as part of America's civilizing mission, viewing this justification as a patina, a conceit, and a distortion of American values. William Graham Sumner of Yale gave a speech titled "The Conquest of the United States by Spain." Having beaten Spain militarily, "we are submitting to be conquered by her on the field of ideas and policies. . . . If we believe in liberty, as an American principle, why do we not stand by it? Why are we going to throw it away and enter upon a Spanish policy of domination and regulation?"

Sumner predicted that the "most important thing that we shall inherit from the Spaniards will be the task of suppressing rebellions." By not allowing the Filipinos to found the republic that they had already proclaimed, the United States forced them to fight for their independence. As many as 200,000 were killed or died in the war-induced famine. Bringing his anti-imperial ethics together with his psychology, William James was led to revise the latter. The recent conduct of an America that he had thought morally better than other countries had shown human nature to be the same everywhere: "At the least temptation all the old military passions rise, and sweep everything before them." Nor could such a country serve as a beacon, a model for others to emulate. Carl Schurz maintained that "our great mission, to further the progress of civilization by enhancing the prestige of democratic institutions, [would be] seduced by false ambitions and by running headlong after riches and luxury and military glory . . . down the fatal slope into vice, corruption, decay and disgrace."[7]

Woodrow Wilson's isolationist opponents did not question the sincerity of his belief that the spread of democracy would be abetted by U.S. entry into World War I. But they insisted that the European war actually had nothing at all to do with democracy. Whatever the political unsavoriness of Germany under the Kaiser, it was unacceptable to join Britain and France, who were themselves plutocratically governed, imperialist states. In speaking against Wilson's war resolution, Senator Robert

M. LaFollette predicted that a better world would not be brought into being by fighting alongside countries that had long been addicted to the ways of the "old order." To become aligned with Britain would lend support to an empire, as well as "a hereditary monarchy . . . with a hereditary land system, with a limited and restricted suffrage for one [class] and a multiple suffrage for another, and with grinding industrial conditions for all wage-workers." Not one of the allies "has done as much for its people in the solution of municipal problems and in securing social and industrial reforms as Germany." LaFollette then went considerably further in pointing to the operations of "financial imperialism" in the wealthy and "weaker undeveloped" countries of the world as "the underlying cause of [the war] which has converted almost all of Europe into a human slaughter pen." Another leading Progressive, Senator George W. Norris, applied this incipient Leninist theory of international relations to America's interventionist motives as these were instilled by Wall Street. Americans were being pushed and pulled "into war upon the command of gold," when they "ought to remember the advice of the Father of our Country and keep out of entangling alliances."

The isolationists were far from alone in opposing Wilson's idealistic quest for U.S membership in the League of Nations. Most of the senators who rejected it were internationalists. And their central argument coincided with the isolationists': The League would prove ineffective in keeping the peace, sorely infringe upon America's freedom of action and sovereignty, and by joining it we would become caught up in the Europeans' affairs and they in ours. The isolationist case against membership went on to contrast the League's idealistic objectives with the Europeans' military and imperial rivalries. America would be disfigured as a model by working with them on the League's Council.[8]

The great majority of isolationists held no brief for Nazi Germany. Many were shocked by German fascism and expansionism. Senator Robert A. Taft detested every one of the German government's actions after Hitler assumed power. Senator Burton K. Wheeler spoke of his "horror" over the Nazi treatment of German Jews. Senator Hiram Johnson maintained that "No one could wish more ardently than I do for the defeat of Hitler." Former president Herbert Hoover deplored the sufferings of occupied Europe, which "cry out to the sympathy of every decent man and woman." Still, isolationists justified their opposition to U.S. interventionism in one or more of several ways relating to America's liberal ideals.

Much of the isolationist case against European involvements during the 1930s revolved around the disillusionist memories and lessons of World War I. America's entry was a grievous, unmitigated mistake. We had in fact, or at least in effect, gone to war on behalf of king, czar, aristocracy, colonial office, and capital, helping to perpetuate them in the face of democratic opposition. The opening of the diplomatic archives revealed that it was not just Germany, but also Britain, France, and Russia who were responsible for World War I. Under the chairmanship of Gerald P. Nye, the Senate investigation of the munitions industry reinforced the widespread belief that the United States had been enmeshed in the European conflict by the American bankers who made loans to Britain and by Britain itself. Writing as the country's preeminent historian, Charles Beard sought to expand upon the economic motivations underlying World War I: Wars in general, and a future one in particular, are to be understood as the product of self-serving material interests and well-applied pressures, domestic and international. The widespread belief that the last war did not bear upon the nation's international ideals was deepened by its outcome. Wilson's crusade for peace and democracy was emasculated by the French and British in negotiating the Treaty of Versailles. Its iniquities facilitated the rise of Nazism and justified rearmament and the reoccupation of the Rhineland.

Some isolationists who were shocked by German fascism and expansionism still assumed that underneath the surface of events, the patina of ideology, and the cloak of propaganda, nations are not all *that* different. If they are not comparable in the degree to which self-seeking goals drive their foreign policies, they are all sufficiently self-interested to preclude the drawing of clear-cut, one-sided moral distinctions. German and Italian aggressiveness was pressing up against a Britain and France that had already been through their expansionist phases. Russia's communist ideology, totalitarian dictatorship, and agreement with Germany for the dismemberment of Poland (the Molotov-Ribbentrop pact) made it evident that the brewing European conflict was not about democracy and freedom. After the 1940 German invasion of Russia our quasi alliance with Stalin further highlighted the irrelevance of liberal ideals to the European war.

The isolationists who did draw a viable moral distinction were at one with the others in believing that American involvement would neither avert war nor help solve the world's problems. In *Saving America First* a prominent New Deal lawyer acknowledged that the troubles of other people "cannot but cause deep sorrow to any decent American, [yet] we can do nothing of substance to solve the basic problems of Europe— except to insure a sane and flourishing civilization in America." In *Giddy Minds and Foreign Quarrels*, Beard contended that idealistic internationalism was a delusion, that Roosevelt's "quarantining" of aggressors in order to influence developments in Europe and Asia could not possibly bring about a change in their foreign policies or alter the circumstances of other peoples. Over and above constituting an enormous, virtually ineffective sacrifice, some isolationists believed that American entry into the war would help further international evils. Besides rescuing France and Britain's archaic empires, it would facilitate the extension of Soviet communism. The Molotov-Ribbentrop pact showed that the Soviets wanted to sit on the sidelines and then spread communism throughout Europe at the war's end. They argued that Stalin's dictatorship was yet harsher than Hitler's, while the apparently ecumenical appeal of communism made it the greater threat over the long run. After the German invasion of Russia, America's defeat of Germany would simply make Europe "safe for communism."[9]

In 1943, when Washington was planning for a postwar world, Senator Robert A. Taft offered a liberal critique of the emerging grandiose internationalist design. It would be "completely contrary to the ideals of the American people and the theory that we are fighting for liberty as well as security. It is based on the theory that we know better what is good for the world than the world itself. . . . Other people simply do not like to be dominated, and we would be in the same position of suppressing rebellions by force in which the British found themselves during the nineteenth century." Whatever America's good intentions at the outset, power, military alliances, and far-flung economic interests will translate into a self-interested imperialism. "Our military forces will work with our commercial forces to obtain as much of the world trade as we can lay our hands on. . . . How long can [allied] nations restrain themselves from using a [preponderant] force with just a little of the aggressiveness of Germany and Japan? Potential power over other nations, however benevolent its purposes, leads inevitably to imperialism."

As the Cold War took shape, isolationists extended this critique and took yet stronger exception to policies that contradicted the nation's liberal ideals. One congressman depicted the Truman Doctrine as a "crusade [to] tell everybody in the world how to live" and doubted that "God approves of such egoism." Contrary to Truman's idealistic rhetoric about defending freedom wherever it is threatened by external aggression or internal subversion, U.S. actions belied the principle of self-determination. America was becoming not just an accessory, but an agent of imperialism in opposition to peoples seeking national independence, mocking its self-portrayal as the proponent of liberty. In taking over "the British program of suppression" and supplying military equipment to the French forces combating Ho Chi Minh's guerrillas—"the people who are struggling for liberty"—we were earning the hatred of Asia. Referring to the growth of economic and military assistance programs, Republican William Jenner asked his Senate colleagues: "What will the American people say when . . . [they] find themselves for another 20 years financing policies of British, French, Portuguese, and Belgian imperialism—policies of exploitation and oppression against which the very fiber of their being rebels?" Others objected to a NATO that would entangle the United States in the unpalatable policies of five empires.

It was also said that containing communism would turn this country into the guarantor of dozens of corrupt authoritarian regimes, only starting with the immediate beneficiaries of the Truman Doctrine. Greece was ruled by a venal, right-wing oligarchy that carried out mass arrests and executions to counter the leftist insurgency; the Turkish dictatorship had flirted with the Axis and the Allies as each side appeared victorious during World War II. The Truman Doctrine's globalized promise of aid prompted this prediction from one isolationist congressman: "Every corrupt government in the world which has fastened itself on the backs of the people will raise the cry of communism to get money from the United States to keep itself in power." Besides associating with ethically unacceptable regimes, the United States was actively serving their interests. Nationalist China, the most glaring example, was not only run by an oligarchy as a "private racket." Chiang Kai-shek was presiding over the starvation of millions and the murder of thousands of Taiwanese.

A minority of isolationists, Taft in particular, went on to insist that the extension of our ideals as universal norms surely required consistency. Yet U.S. policies constituted a double standard of international conduct. The Soviets had as much right to be in Iran as the British; Soviet demands for rights of free passage through the Dardenelles were in accord with the right of all nations to the freedom of the seas; Washington could hardly protest against the presence of Soviet troops in Iran and Manchuria as long as American troops were in China; Soviet actions should not be loudly condemned while remaining silent about the (sometimes forceful) reimposition of European colonial rule. In addition, the assumption of a special position in Greece and Turkey hardly allowed the United States to object to Russian domination in Eastern Europe. An America that was trying to dislodge the Soviets from their immediate defensive perimeter there must accept the Soviets' equal right to meddle in Latin America. Not just they, but we too were acting in an imperialist manner.

Compared to their absolute rejection of external involvements after World War I, a goodly number of isolationists more or less reluctantly condoned some measure of idealistically inspired activism after World War II. They gave some credence to the democracies' susceptibility to the Soviet threat, subscribed to a normatively abiding anticommunism, and allowed their paternalistic attachments to China to come into play. Most isolationists favored membership in a United Nations governed by pro-American majorities in the General Assembly and the U.S. veto in the

Security Council. Looking toward the future, Taft maintained that international peace ultimately depended upon "an international law defining the duties and obligations of nations . . . international courts to determine whether nations are abiding by that law . . . [and] joint armed forces to enforce that law and the decisions of that court . . . It is quite true that the United Nations Charter as drafted does not yet reach the ideals of international peace and justice which I have described, but it goes a long way in that direction."[10]

On this recounting of isolationist strictures against liberal activism, they were regularly reasoned and reasonable, often fully warranted. While this review does not place them on the idealistic high ground, it raises them well above the low ground to which they have been commonly relegated by contemporaneous and subsequent critics—their depiction of isolationism as an exercise in self-interestedness. To subscribe to "America first" was to be motivated by a self-regarding nationalism, a materialistic domesticism, partisan calculations, the hyperpatriotism of social mobility, and foreign loyalties in the case of the German- and Irish-Americans prior to both world wars.[11]

The isolationists did, of course, "turn their backs on others." But from this it does not follow that they were ethically unawares, insensitive, or jaundiced. Their claims were sufficiently persuasive to cast considerable doubt upon their depiction as exclusively self-serving. During the Republic's first years its minimal power precluded support for France without putting its own security at direct risk. During the nineteenth century American power was too limited to have any significant effect upon European struggles for national self-determination. When U.S. power was first "projected" at the beginning of the twentieth century, it was the isolationists who criticized their own government for its idealistic lapses and distortions. Prior to World War I the isolationists made a convincing case for the limits of our capabilities for furthering liberal goals that were not shared by others. As for the years before World War II, it should not be forgotten that the Holocaust, which later exposed the full evil of the Nazis, was as unimaginable for the internationalists as it was for the isolationists. During the postwar years the isolationists showed a healthy respect for what America could not accomplish globally, appreciating the ways in which our efforts would inadvertently be disfigured by their exclusively anticommunist focus.

Moreover, the condemnation of the isolationists as self-interested requires a comparison—a comparison with the putatively other-regarding or principled motivations of the internationalists. True, the advocates of assistance for revolutionary France, the Greeks, and the Hungarians were genuinely inspired by the ideals of liberty, self-determination, and human rights. But during the first half of the twentieth century the internationalists' external involvements were primarily motivated by America's own security concerns.

The only "ideals" that justified the Pacific annexations and the brutalities in the Philippines were imperialist and racist. The cause of making "the world safe for democracy" did its part in leading us into World War I. Yet national security concerns and those of national pride and power were at least as influential. Opposition to membership in the League of Nations was by no means limited to the isolationists. The internationalists who prided themselves on their realist conception of the national interest were also opposed, and for the same basic reason: America's security interests would only be diminished by becoming entangled with others. The threat to American security was of overriding importance for the internationalists before World War II with regard to both Europe and Asia. The Truman Doctrine's support for Greece and Turkey was solely security centered, rhetorically globalized in the language of helping free peoples so as to obtain congressional funding. Marshall Plan aid and NATO were primarily designed to preserve America's first and most important line of defense against the Soviet threat. Despite the U.N.'s authorization, the Korean intervention was exclusively undertaken as a credibility-enhancing security venture.

How then does this assessment of historical isolationism comport with the concurrent foreign policy's liberal project—the sharpest departure of a reconfigured isolationism from the isolationism of the past and present?

Isolationists have regularly turned aside the obligation to help others who are in need of our help on the basis of three empirical arguments. Each partakes of a hardy element of validity; each is also one-sided, exaggerated, or incomplete. First, foreign involvements have impaired and can detract from the nation's security. However, this claim hardly applies to all idealistically motivated actions, while the liberal project's moderation and the country's strategic immunity guard against nearly all serious security risks. Second, it is said that liberal actions are variously unsuccessful, counterproductive, and disfiguring to the liberal values they putatively promote. There is no shortage of evidence to support these claims. But as also seen in the following section, liberal internationalism can be credited with a goodly share of successes, and the failures and distortions are largely attributable to the confluence, the simultaneous pursuit of liberal and security objectives. Third, America as a liberal exemplar alone has inspired others. However, given America's great power and the great expectations engendered by its liberal internationalism and rhetoric, the model is sure to lose its lustre and appeal unless some resources, influence, and leverage are employed on behalf of others.

In short, much can be said for splitting apart isolationism's two halves and for reconstituting one of them. The isolationist tradition need not be fully rejected. It can be reconfigured in the form of a minimally activist security strategy that allows for and bolsters an affordable, principled, singularly focused, and thus a reasonably effective liberalism.

II

Whatever its adversarial, centrist, or conciliatory thrust, liberal internationalism's distinctive feature is an activism motivated by security and realism conjoined in doctrine and policy. America's resources and advantages are to be put to extensive liberal uses.[12] Activist efforts advance the international ideals of peace and nonaggression between states and economic freedom, political liberty, human rights, and democracy within them. Their realization helps bolster America's security since democracies rarely if ever go to war with one another.

The success of internationalism's liberal project thus hinges heavily upon the concurrence of its dual aims and policies—their parallelism, conformity, and mutuality. There are two criteria with which to assess its success. In the absence of security concerns the United States should still undertake liberally inspired projects. Where both aims come together, the idealistic ones are not ignored or distorted, but rather protected and promoted. Liberal internationalism falls short on both counts, most clearly so on the former.

The disparity between security- and liberally-motivated activism is truly striking. Where security interests have not come into play, post-1945 America has no more than occasionally pursued liberal ends in and of themselves. There have, of course, been numerous instances of humanitarian assistance, food and medical aid for the victims of natural disasters and wars, and economic aid has occasionally been given to some poor countries without any expectation of its serving our national interests. But beyond these there were quite possibly only four instances in which predominantly liberal values drove U.S. policy. The United States supported Israel around the time of its establishment for the sake of world Jewry and for Israel as a small, embattled state, the only democracy in the Middle East. An idealistically inspired Jimmy Carter placed human rights squarely on the world agenda. And in the post–Cold War era, Washington mounted military operations to restore democratic rule in Panama and to pacify and feed famine-afflicted Somalia. Even if this is an incomplete list, it is easy to see how the moderated liberal project of the concurrent foreign policy is decidedly more activist than that of a putatively ambitious, idealistically inspired liberal internationalism.

The issue is more complicated where both security and ideal interests have been at stake. When they were seen to be convergent, our ideals have been well served, exceptionally so when great security imperatives were involved. On the other hand, where the two interests were seen to diverge, liberal values were regularly betrayed. This pattern cannot simply be explained away by the higher priority assigned to the nation's security. The critical factor is the global definition accorded to the latter and the extraordinarily sensitive conception of the threats to it. Liberal values were distorted even when secondary and tertiary security interests in peripheral areas were seen to be somewhat impaired.

In reviewing the realization of our ideals during the first half of the Cold War Samuel Huntington offered the arch claim of liberal internationalism: "Any increase in the power or influence of the United States in world affairs generally results . . . in the promotion of liberty and human rights in the world."[13] While others have made comparable assertions supported by few examples, he provides extensive evidence in the form of more than a dozen diverse cases from 1945 to 1975. Unlike others whose evidence is less than relevant or interpretively strained, he provides cases where American "power or influence" did further "liberty and human rights." Yet the claim still needs to be much revised for the years before and after 1975.

Huntington's dozen cases only include those in which security and ideal interests were not seen to diverge. In all but two of them there was not even a perceived challenge to U.S. security interests. There was none with regard to the democratization of the former Axis states after World War II. German, Austrian, Italian, and Japanese governments and politics were transformed; the changes were well grounded by way of American constitutional engineering, economic reforms, and economic aid. All this was readily affordable in security terms given the near absence of any threats from communists or radicals within the former Axis states. Their popular support was insignificant in Germany, Austria, and Japan. The Communist Party of Italy won 31 percent of the votes in the 1947 elections, but it was kept well away from the levers of power in not obtaining a single seat in Italy's conservative governments. During the late 1950s Washington tried to mitigate military rule and repression in several Latin American countries: in Peru, Colombia, Venezuela, and the Dominican Republic. In none of them was there a guerrilla, Marxist, or leftist threat. Throughout the long association with South Korea there were never any trade-offs between U.S. security interests and Washington urging its authoritarian governments to curb their repressive actions. South Korea has invariably been intensely anticommunist.

In Huntington's two other cases, Marxist and radical movements were mounting serious challenges to regimes with which we were closely allied. By the early 1950s the Philippine army had still not defeated the sizable communist-led Huk insurgency. Rather than doing more to put down the guerrillas and their supporters, Washington tried to win them over by adopting the kind of "positive" counterinsurgency doctrine that had just proved successful for the British in dealing with the communist rebellion in Malaya. It helped guarantee a free election in which "its" presidential candidate ran on a genuinely liberalizing platform. After Magsaysay's electoral victory Washington encouraged the implementation of political and economic reforms up to his accidental death.

In the early 1960s the Cuban revolution had a powerful impact throughout much of Latin America. Inspired and aided by Fidel Castro, peasants, workers, and several leftist insurgencies challenged rural oligarchies, urban elites, and military rulers. Rather than working to put down the former while supporting the latter, the potential contradictions between our security and ideal interests were overcome by the then widely accepted academic ideas of economic and political development. Communist and radical challenges could be negated because "all good things" come together through economic modernization. By assisting and pushing for economic growth Washington could help increase wealth and literacy, resulting in the expansion of the middle classes committed to centrist and reformist policies, and thus democracy and political stability. These economically engendered changes would foster anticommunist proclivities, power, and policies. This was the rationale underlying the Alliance for Progress, which supplied generous amounts of economic aid ($22 billion over ten years) to Latin American governments conditional upon their proceeding with political, land, and tax reforms. The conditions were rarely enforced or met. Washington found itself endorsing a handful of military regimes that supplemented the civilian ones.

U.S. policies in the Philippines and Latin America were temporary and sui generis. Elsewhere between 1945 and 1975 the appearance of Marxist, radical, populist, and nationalist movements, and even some inordinately vague threats to a regime, elicited a perceived contradiction between security and ideal interests. With the former prevailing, they eventuated in thoroughly illiberal policies in more than a dozen instances—instances that Huntington does not refer to.

In 1953 the CIA engineered the overthrow of Iran's democratically elected prime minister, a nationalist who was about to take over the American and European oil companies. The shah and his authoritarian regime were put into place. The following year the CIA organized a coup against Guatemala's "radical" government. Its successor repealed universal suffrage and land reform legislation and murdered thousands of peasants. Washington encouraged and was prepared to assist the 1964 coup that overthrew Brazil's democratically elected president and ushered in twenty-five years of military rule. In 1965 U.S. marines intervened in the Dominican Republic to prevent a popularly elected government from assuming office. And this not because it itself was Marxist or radical, but because it had radical support. Not a critical word was heard from Washington when the military aborted the beginnings of constitutional government in El Salvador in 1972, nor a year later when Ferdinand Marcos rewrote the constitution to make himself president of the Philippines for life. In 1973 Washington backed the political groups and military officers who unseated Chile's democratically elected, socialist president. From the 1960s onward American policies worked against Marxist and nationalist guerrilla groups in southern Africa, first in their struggle with Portugal, which was trying to retain Angola and Mozambique as colonies, and then in their conflicts with rival (pro-Western) political and guerrilla movements. The security and internal stability rationale led Washington to provide regular doses of symbolic, political, economic, and military support to all manner of dictators. Some of the most repressive ones were embraced, including the shah in Iran, Mobutu in Zaire, Suharto in Indonesia, and military governments in Chile, Bolivia, Guatemala, and Honduras.[14]

The Cold War years since 1975 should be especially revealing in considering the practice of liberal internationalism. Presidents Carter and Reagan were both strongly committed to an idealistic activism. In coming to office neither saw any incompatibilities between the latter and strategic internationalism. And they subscribed to very different strategies for furthering America's security and ideal interests.

During the first part of his administration Jimmy Carter created great expectations for America's human rights campaign. He once referred to it as the "soul of our foreign policy." Universally defined, globally applicable ideals were to be actively vindicated solely for idealistic reasons. Within months of the administration's inauguration human rights were accorded a high place on the world's agenda. A new set of yardsticks was publicly employed in documenting and judging a government's political abuses. Carter's legislative initiative allowed us to join the world boycott of Rhodesian chromium as a way of bringing down the minority white government. He forestalled the military president of the Dominican Republic from stealing the 1978 election; the dispatch of U.S. warships underlined the serious repercussions if the votes for the popular candidate were not honestly counted. In 1978–79 military aid to Somoza's Nicaraguan dictatorship was cut off while it was trying to put down the Sandinista insurgency. Military aid was suspended and some loan requests to the World Bank were denied due to the gross human rights violations perpetrated by military dictatorships in El Salvador, Argentina, Uruguay, and Chile. Knowing that they were next, Guatemala and Brazil "rejected" further aid. Military supplies were funneled to the Afghan guerrillas, who were fighting the Soviet invaders. And multilateral diplomacy was used to pressure the Soviet Union and some Third World regimes who were engaging in human rights violations. Thousands of political prisoners were freed in Latin America, Asia, and Eastern Europe. Here was an upright human rights posture, one that was also reasonably even-handed toward violators among allies and opponents.

Overall, however, the Carter administration's actions were cautious and tentative, decidedly limited in their substantive content and geographical range. Congressional legislation required the cessation of economic and military aid to governments "engaged in a consistent pattern of gross (human rights) violations." Yet the administration characterized relatively few in these terms. Aid was not cut off to some (e.g., the Marcos regime in the Philippines) by citing the provision that allowed for exceptions under "extraordinary circumstances." If Washington were engaged in a determined human rights effort, there should have been a statistical association between economic and military aid on the one hand, and a country's human rights record on the other. There was no such correlation. It did not emerge when the extent and types of rights violations were differentially assessed by the State Department's country reports, Amnesty International, or Freedom House.[15]

The disjunction between Carter's liberal aspirations and their various policy translations was heavily mediated by security concerns. At the outset he said that "we are now free of that inordinate fear of communism which once led us to embrace any dictator who joined us in that fear." Liberalizing ventures would no longer be hobbled after disabusing ourselves of this exaggeration. But Secretary of State Cyrus Vance soon appraised the possibilities of aid cuts to human rights violators in a contingent manner: "In each case we must balance a political concern for human rights against economic and security goals."[16] It was only in Latin America that the balance was struck in favor of human rights. This also happened to be the only region that did not elicit security concerns. In the late 1970s Latin America did not feature a single "credible threat to United States security . . . [and none] to threaten stability-oriented (American) officials. No government was moving to the left, no government was threatening the continued dominance of liberal capitalism."[17] Only as the Somoza dictatorship was falling apart in 1979 did the positive attitude toward the Sandinista insurgents give way to concerns about their pro-Cuban and pro-Soviet proclivities. The administration then sought something less than a Sandinista victory, an outcome featuring the dictator's removal and formally free democratic elections, but also their likely "dilution" by preserving Somoza's notorious National Guard.[18]

As one of the world's most visibly repressive rulers relying upon one of the most efficient secret police forces, the shah of Iran should have been a chief focus of the human rights campaign. (He was during the presidential campaign.) However, Iran was also a crucial ally, a barrier to any Soviet movement into the Middle East and the chief U.S. police-man in the region. The conflicting considerations were consistently resolved in favor of U.S. security. The administration supplied Iran with arms at the previously criticized level; Carter and Vance tried to down-play the human rights issues almost from the outset. When they were raised by Congress and the State Department's new human rights bureau, the administration overtly reassured the shah of U.S. support. To the extent that the issue of liberalizing reforms was raised, it was less often pushed upon him than suggested in a by-your-leave fashion. Washington was not permitted any contacts with the regime's opponents, either Moslem moderates or secular socialists. As late as November 1978, three months before the shah's fall, all policy options other than those that supported his continuing rule were treated as "inadmissible." In the midst of the crisis Washington's reformist messages were still usually couched in such terms as "when possible" or "as you see fit." Carter rejected the arguments for supporting a moderate antishah coalition until the very end.[19]

By the midpoint of Carter's tenure serious human rights efforts were hard to discern, overridden by developments in Nicaragua, Iran, and by the Soviet invasion of Afghanistan. The geopolitical stakes were such that the administration ended up arguing for military and economic aid to some fully secure military regimes in Latin America.[20]

In taking office the Reagan administration denounced its predecessor's human rights policies as ineffectual, inconsistent, and dangerous. They had little or no impact except to penalize valuable allies for their authoritarian practices, ignored the far more flagrant abuses of communist totalitarianism, and consequentially detracted from the nation's security. In its first year the new administration overcorrected by praising rather than penalizing allies.

> Secretary of State Alexander Haig proclaimed "dramatic, dramatic reductions" in human rights abuses in Chile, Paraguay, Argentina, and Uruguay while they were still under brutal military rule; Ambassador Jeane Kirkpatrick praised the "moral quality" of the government of El Salvador at a time when its army and death squads were killing thousands; and President Reagan asserted that then President Rios Montt of Guatemala was "totally dedicated to democracy" and that complaints of human rights abuses by [his] government were a "bum rap."[21]

In dealings with adversaries, the administration pretended there was no incompatibility between the promotion of American security and ideal interests. The Reagan doctrine "repealed" the Brezhnev doctrine that did not allow for a communist country to leave the fold and asserted our right to intervene against nondemocratic governments. It sought to bring security and ideal interests together in a mutually reinforcing manner. Democracy and human rights were to be extended among threatening Marxist states by lending military, financial, and other kinds of aid to ongoing insurgencies aiming to destabilize and overthrow them.[22]

The Reagan doctrine failed to overcome the contradictions in the joint enterprise: because of its security-weighted aims and the political characteristics of the anti-Marxist groups that were being supported, the liberal values were consistently betrayed. Along with South Africa, Washington supported Jonas Savimbi and his UNITA guerrillas who were trying to unseat Angola's relatively open regime, which was under the protection of Cuban troops. The administration's portrayal of UNITA as a "democratic force" was belied by its composition as a minority tribal movement, the thousands of politically indiscriminate atrocities it carried out, and its organization along Leninist lines of "democratic centralism."

It was one thing for the Reagan administration to try to undermine Vietnam's post-1979 occupation of Cambodia and the Heng Samrin government it installed. It was quite another to do so by supporting the genocidal Khmer Rouge. This was the very same Khmer Rouge, with the infamous Pol Pot still at its head, whose rule over Cambodia between 1976 and 1978 featured the murder of a million people, many of them bludgeoned to death in the "killing fields" to save ammunition. Vietnam was seen as more of a threat to U.S. security interests than an inward-looking Khmer regime in control of Cambodia. China was also a factor as a powerful anti-Soviet ally. Given the conflict between Vietnam and China, American and Chinese interests thus converged on support for the Khmer Rouge. Thailand was not pressed to block the single route of crucial Chinese supplies to the Khmer Rouge, and perhaps was tacitly encouraged to permit the continuing flow. With both the Khmer Rouge and the Heng Samrin government claiming diplomatic recognition for Cambodia/Kampuchea at the United Nations, Washington voted for the former and against aid to the latter. Only after masses of gruesome evidence had been unearthed and publicized did the State Department reluctantly acknowledge that an act of genocide had previously been perpetrated by the Khmer Rouge.

In Afghanistan the Reagan administration continued its predecessor's policies of funneling arms to the guerrillas who were fighting the Soviet army. Security interests were pursued with clean hands against an aggressor on behalf of national self-determination. But while Soviet forces were being withdrawn and after their departure military assistance was continued in what was now a very different kind of conflict. Washington supported the Moslem guerrillas—one fundamentalist faction was led by the "Afghan Khomenei"—in their civil war against a moderate Marxist prime minister.

In Nicaragua we worked for the overthrow of a minimally abusive Marxist regime, one that greatly raised the nation's literacy levels and reduced concentrations of land ownership. The Contras whom we armed and financed "systematically engaged in the killing of prisoners and the unarmed, including medical and relief personnel; selective attacks on civilians and indiscriminate attacks; torture and other outrages against personal dignity; and the kidnapping and harassment of refugees."[23] What was documented by America's Watch was hardly unknown to the Reagan administration, which characterized the Contras as "freedom fighters" and "founding fathers" comparable to America's eighteenth-century revolutionaries. Besides providing material support, the CIA advised them on the use of terrorist tactics; the administration undermined the scheduled 1984 elections and opposed those proposed by Costa Rican president Oscar Arias, whose efforts won him the Nobel Peace Prize.

Central America received special attention from the Reagan administration in support of and alongside the Contra effort. Throughout the 1980s military and economic aid was afforded the brutal regime in Honduras and the murderous one in Guatemala. Along with our silence about their abuses, this was the price the administration was willing to pay for the logistic support they provided the Contra operation. That operation was originally justified by the light military supplies that Nicaragua's Sandinista regime was funneling to the reformist and Marxist insurgents in El Salvador. Trained and financed by the United States, the Salvadoran army committed thousands of human rights abuses: the massacre of peasants, the murder of church officials, and the torture of civilians. Over the course of the 1980s Washington consistently denied its detailed knowledge of the atrocities committed by the military and civilian death squads that were closely linked to the government. The worst atrocity was carried out by a U.S. trained battalion that slaughtered an entire village, including its children. When the story surfaced in 1981, American officials dismissed it as guerrilla propaganda. Congress was not to have the information with which to decertify U.S. aid to the Salvadoran government. As late as 1990 U.S. military officers were training Salvadorans associated with the death squads.[24]

The 1983 invasion of Marxist Grenada went well beyond the Reagan doctrine. There was no anti-Marxist insurgency to support. The invasion was intended to demonstrate U.S. resolve to Havana and Moscow, that need being crystallized after the precipitous withdrawal of the marines from Lebanon. The administration's mock legal justification was sharply criticized by Prime Minister Margaret Thatcher—a stalwart friend of Reagan's—as the leader of the Commonwealth, of which Grenada was a part.[25] On the other hand, the invasion did result in the installation of a durable democratic regime.

The demise of communism relieved most of the security imperatives that had constrained and disfigured post-1945 liberalism. Yet in an approximation of a unipolar world without a major rival in sight, under the Bush administration each divergence between security and ideal interests still led to the latter's disfigurement.

In June 1989 the Chinese army attacked the 100,000 demonstrators for political reform and democracy in Tiananmen Square. Several thousand were gunned down. The massacre was followed by mass arrests, executions, and a nationwide crackdown upon the "democracy movement" that could have affected the political lives of one-quarter of the world's population. Yet other than the mild sanction of suspending military exports and exchanges, the Bush administration's responses were obsequious. It opposed Congressional demands for economic sanctions involving most-favored-nation trading status, high-technology trade, guarantees to businesses investing in China, and loans from international financial institutions. When the House of Representatives voted 390 to 25 to enable Chinese students to remain in America, the administration carried out a full-press lobbying campaign in the Senate, where the president's veto was sustained by a four-vote margin. And the administration took several initiatives, symbolic and economic, to conciliate a Beijing that insisted upon Washington's responsibility for the fraying of bilateral relations. The administration did not even hint at the possibility of using China's most-favored-nation trading status as a deterrent, of making it conditional upon the regime's subsequent human rights record. In Bush's vague words, just about any show of firmness would adversely effect "our long-term interests" and the "important and enduring aspects of this vital relationship."[26] He could only have been referring to China's usefulness as a counter to the USSR, despite the collapse of communism, and to the potential commercial value of the Chinese market.

The Iraqi case involves considerably more than the United States organizing the UN coalition that went to war against Saddam Hussein. It extends back into the 1980s, outside the Cold War context, when Saddam was courted as an ally to counter the Iranian fundamentalism that was seen as a major threat to U.S. security interests in the Middle East. Saddam was treated as their chief regional bulwark—to the extent of our supporting an aggressor state, a brutal violator of human rights, and one with evident nuclear ambitions. Soon after Iraq launched its unprovoked attack upon Iran, Washington provided it with some $3 billion in guaranteed farm credits that helped sustain the war effort, military intelligence on the disposition of Iranian forces, and the occasional "use" of U.S. naval ships by way of attacks upon Iranian targets in the Persian Gulf. After the war ended in 1988, Hussein unleashed his army upon the Kurds, including poison gas attacks on some of their villages. The Senate was sufficiently outraged to vote 87 to 0 in favor of sanctions against Iraq. It was subsequently overturned by the Reagan administration's national security arguments. The Bush administration went out of its way to reassure Baghdad of its support, to the extent of criticizing the Senate for its overwhelming 1990 vote to cut off further Export-Import Bank loan guarantees because of Iraqi human rights violations. Between 1985 and the 1990 invasion of Kuwait Washington granted 162 export licenses with direct weapons applications.[27] Besides being directly at odds with our publicly avowed nonproliferation policies, as seen in chapter 10, the Bush administration knew that Iraq was striving for a nuclear capacity.

The war against Iraq was fought to vindicate our security and ideal interests. The former involved "regional stability" and stable oil supplies and prices, the latter an end to Saddam's brutal rule. The two sets of objectives converged on the restoration of Kuwaiti independence, nuclear nonproliferation, and the punishment of an aggressor as a deterrent to others. The security objectives were all realized, including those that overlapped with the liberal ones. The single exclusively liberal aim was not. Overthrowing Saddam would probably have entailed large casualties in fighting his powerful, well-trained Republican Guard units.

The Bush administration that did so much to disfigure liberalism before the war did not do nearly enough on its behalf after the victory, here again because of security considerations. The United States stood by as tens of thousands of Shiites and Kurds were killed. And this despite the promise of help implied by our encouraging them to overthrow Saddam during the war. Washington adhered to its announced policy of nonintervention in Iraq's internal affairs while the autonomy-seeking Shiites in the south were attacked by helicopter gunships and tanks, and a little later, as two million Kurds fled to the north to escape the army's attacks. Only after many of them froze to death in the mountains did the administration reluctantly take any action. It sought and readily obtained a UN Security Council resolution that authorized the protection of Iraqi minorities. The Kurds were provided with a secure zone outside the uninhabitable mountains and humanitarian relief. By then it was too late to protect the Shiites from Saddam's army. Only condolences were sent to the victims after the Bush administration studiously avoided the issue for eighteen months.

These passive betrayals cannot be explained by an inability to overthrow Saddam. Protecting the Kurds and Shiites would have required only the extension of the no-fly zones for Iraqi fixed-wing aircraft to include helicopters and the creation of secure zones to keep out Iraqi tanks and troop concentrations. But while complete domination of the skies and a largely open country allowed for both, they ran counter to U.S. security interests. Maintaining the bulwarks against Iranian-led Islamic fundamentalism and good relations with allies came first. To protect the

Shiites would have benefited Iran and been seen as a threat by nonfunda-
mentalist Saudi Arabia. Had the Kurds been helped, their heightened nationalism would have caused greater difficulties for Turkey with its own
Kurdish minority. If the Shiites and the Kurds attained some regional
autonomy, especially if this eventuated in Iraq's partition, there would
have been a power shift toward Iran and Syria (the other U.S. security
threat in the region) and against Saudi Arabia.

In campaigning for the presidency, Bill Clinton spoke the language of
a reasonably ambitious liberal project, as in his call for a "global democratic alliance" to enlarge the area of freedom. "Now that we don't have
to worry about Moscow, we can finally give content to our saying that
human rights is central, we can help in all kinds of humanitarian ways
where we couldn't before because we feared war with the Soviets." In his
inaugural address Clinton proclaimed that force should be used when the
"conscience of the international community is defied." The president and
his top aides insisted that the United States will continue to be "engaged"
and to take the "lead."[28] However, there is still a striking inhibition, now
from economic as well as security interest concerns. As in the past, ideal
interests alone are insufficient to energize U.S. policy except in the case of
low-risk, low-cost peacekeeping efforts that do not conflict with any significant security interests.

During the Clinton administration's first year and a half it fell well
short of its liberal rhetoric, and this despite the absence of any situations
that posed a contradiction between America's security and ideal interests.
Before coming to office Clinton promised to reverse Bush's policy of ignoring China's abysmal human rights and arms proliferation record because of the need for a counterweight to the Soviet Union. But he extended China's most-favored-nation trading status for yet another year,
announcing only that any further extension would be conditioned on
some unspecified human rights improvements.[29] Apparently trade interests now rivaled security interests. On the other hand, a nearly $1 billion
ban on high-technology sales to China was put in place as punishment
for China's selling sensitive missile technology to Pakistan in violation
of the Missile Technology Control Regime, which Beijing had agreed to
adhere to. Clinton continued Bush's practically toothless economic embargo against Haiti's military rulers, who had prevented the installation
of its popularly elected president. Only six months later did he obtain
UN approval for the oil embargo, which came close to effecting the democratic transition, yet he blinked when the military reneged on the settlement and murdered thousands. As for the Moslems of Bosnia, Clinton
said that "you can't allow the mass extermination of people and sit by
and watch it happen." Washington talked publicly about air strikes
against the Serbs—a moderated intervention in a case of genocide—

unless they halted their military operations against Sarajevo and the other Muslim "safe havens." But those words had little teeth until April 1994 when a more explicit threat of air strikes led the Bosnian Serbs to loosen their noose around two cities. And then Clinton still did not press to lift the U.N. arms embargo against Bosnia, which could otherwise have much better defended itself. And when the Somalia operation got off the humanitarian track momentarily, resulting in the deaths of eighteen U.S. soldiers, Clinton allowed that the United Nations was generally over-extended in its peacekeeping operations and set a deadline for the with-drawal of U.S. forces.

III

The previous section's conclusions raise two overlapping questions about the relative promise of liberal internationalism and the concurrent foreign policy. To recognize the former's benign and malign policies since 1945 is to ask whether the latter's principled efforts alone could have and can further liberal causes. To appreciate the extent to which political-military activism was primarily driven by security considerations is to ask whether liberal ends can be better served despite and because of their absence within the concurrent dispensation. Both questions are about means, ef-fectiveness, and consequences.

The concurrent design can better further America's ideals for a variety of reasons. It turns the United States into a more attractive model to be emulated, makes for greater moral leadership, does more to help activate the United Nations as an enforcement agency, and allows it to mitigate regional security disputes. Moreover, the concurrent dispensation affords nearly the same diversity of means as liberal internationalism, while put-ting them to much more frequent and tactically effective liberal uses.

America as an exemplar has inspired and guided others. It is the world's oldest, best-known democracy, as well as the largest and one of the most successful free market economies. The United States will almost certainly remain the world's preeminent nation, with its unparalleled complement of attractions and endowments. Referring to the post–Cold War era, an arch realist was led to observe that the "prospect of a world in which the American example and the influence of American institu-tions and values might decline, let alone become irrelevant, has never seemed more remote."[30]

Isolationists have reason to highlight the power of example and to bemoan its derogation under internationalist auspices. Ted Carpenter writes that the "impact of the U.S. model can be potent. Many of the demonstrators in the streets of East European cities (in 1989) and in Tiananmen Square looked to the American system for inspiration. But the source of that inspiration was America's reputation as a haven for the values of limited government and unalienable rights, not Washington's $300 billion-a-year military budget and its network of global military bases."[31] Its reputation has been disfigured by numerous illiberal warts and blemishes. "The potential impact of the democratic example of the United States is vitiated by U.S. practices in the Third World. A pervasive stench of hypocrisy exists when the world's leading democracy embraces an assortment of petty dictators" and some systematically abusive and exploitative rulers, earning us the "enmity of long suffering populations."[32]

This critique does not, however, necessarily lead to Carpenter's isolationist conclusions, but to the concurrent foreign policy. America's luster as a model would be heavily tarnished by a rejection of liberal activism. For the best-endowed, most powerful nation in the world to turn its back on others would surely be seen as an inordinate act of collective selfishness. And this all the more so because others have developed great expectations of the United States because of its pronouncements, commitments, and actions. The potency of the model thus hinges upon the exercise of *principled* power and influence. Whether our liberal ideals are respected and emulated, or rendered irrelevant and disparaged, depends on our going abroad for the right reasons in the right ways. And America's moral leadership might just approximate a necessary condition for making many others aware of and at least willing to condemn illiberal practices. If the world's most powerful state and its leading democracy is not genuinely committed, why should others be?

Because America's international ideals have been merged with its own security concerns, liberal commitments were not taken to be genuinely inspired. Leading the "free world" was not seen as an exercise in moral leadership. The single significant exception—the first year of Jimmy Carter's presidency—constitutes a telling case for the concurrent design's divorce of the two policy realms. Mostly by words alone, by the genuinely inspired force of example, he vitalized the human rights movement that had been a minor current in world politics. "Because we are free, we can never be indifferent to the fate of freedom elsewhere . . . our commitment to human rights must be absolute."[33] Within months of this inaugural declaration the international environment was altered as human rights were placed "on the world's agenda—and on the world's conscience."[34] The International League for Human Rights reported that its concerns "had for the first time become a subject of national policy in many countries," as well as "the focus of discussion in international organizations and of greater attention in the world media. A most significant factor in this has been President Carter and the U.S. human rights policy."[35] Other presidents have articulated their liberal visions, some with far greater eloquence, without having had anything like a comparable impact. Only Carter did so on principle alone. If one president's idealistic words, sincerely spoken, reinforced by only one threatening action and some dozen suspensions of foreign aid can have such an effect, there follows this almost ineluctable conclusion: The concurrent foreign policy could do much more to sustain America's moral leadership.

Not so paradoxically, the argument is reinforced by President Bush's active promotion of a "new world order," a world in which "the rule of law supplants the rule of the jungle . . . in which nations recognize the shared responsibility for freedom and justice . . . where the strong respect the rights of the weak." The idealistic phrase entered the common international vocabulary. The vision was backed up with impressive UN diplomacy, resulting in overwhelming support for military action against Iraq, followed by a quick victory on the part of predominantly U.S. forces. Despite these most favorable conditions, the attractions of the new world order were quickly dissipated. At best, the promise of America's moral leadership and its invigoration of the United Nations were seen to be what they actually were, the product of an unusually close coincidence of its security and ideal interests. In many quarters the moral rhetoric was taken to be a gloss, the organization of the anti-Iraqi coalition a pretext for using the United Nations to achieve U.S. objectives in the Gulf. And in some quarters the operation as a whole—before, during, and after the war—was seen to be an exercise for promoting U.S. dominance under UN auspices. Thus, instead of abetting America's moral leadership and a new world order centered around the United Nations, there was a heightened wariness regarding any future UN ventures led by the United States.[36]

There is no doubting that the United Nations cannot succeed without strong, constructive U.S. leadership, while the United States needs the UN to manage and promote a fair international division of labor and burden-sharing arrangements.[37] UN secretary general Boutros Boutros-Ghali made a related claim. "My message is that it is in the interest of the United States to preserve the identity and the minimum credibility of the United Nations. Otherwise, you must be prepared to be the policeman of the world—with all those advantages and disadvantages."[38] It is also clear that the United Nations has been enfeebled as an enforcement agency. Except for the defense of South Korea under nominal (and partly fortuitous) UN authorization and the Persian Gulf War, the organization has been regularly ineffectual in acting against aggressors, human rights transgressors, nuclear proliferators, and political movements and governments who have reneged upon peace keeping and humanitarian aid agreements.

Besides furthering U.S. moral leadership within the United Nations, the concurrent design has some special contributions to make in ameliorating the conditions underlying its enfeeblement as an enforcement agency, the two major stumbling blocks to the organization of its collective power.

The first is the organization's divisiveness. It was stymied by the numerous American and Soviet vetoes in the Security Council; there and in the General Assembly it was rendered asunder by the rival East-West blocs. Only with the end of the Soviet-American rivalry was the United Nations able to mount eighteen peace keeping and humanitarian operations, some of them much more demanding than the earlier ones. Cast backward in time, the national strategy approximates a functional equivalent of the Cold War's demise. Removing many of the divisive political-military issues from Soviet-American relations and thus also from the UN agenda, the organization would have been better positioned to act as a reasonably successful enforcement agency. And whether the Soviet Union was aggressively or defensively minded, as an overtly peaceful superpower it would have had an incentive to demonstrate its responsibilities. Looking ahead, a minimally activist security strategy should negate other debilitating divisions. It would allay the tendency to conflate Islamic fundamentalism with Islam as a civilization, to turn both into an enemy.[39] Otherwise a bloc of two dozen member states might be ranged against the United States, the West, or both. If it turned into a political, military, or economic rivalry with Europe, Germany, and Japan, striving to maintain U.S. primacy would divide the nations who have the most to contribute to the UN's effectiveness.

Free riding summarizes the other major explanation for the United Nation's ineffectualness. Potentially overwhelming capabilities are not organized into collective power because few members see the benefits to themselves as outweighing their individual contributions. The benefits many derive from most enforcement actions are usually unaffected by the costs and risks of their individual contributions. Member states are thus most reluctant to bear their equitable shares—yet less so when others are willing to take up the extra burdens.

The free rider problem can be mitigated by decreasing the overall costs and risks of enforcement actions; more member states will find their burdens to be fair and affordable to the extent that they are diminished. By not dividing the United Nations or hardening and broadening its divisions, the concurrent design lowers the overall burden of collective action, thereby fostering equitable contributions. The targets of enforcement actions are more likely to be vulnerable, single, politically and ideologically disparate states—more easily deterrable targets, as it were. The free rider problem could also be ameliorated insofar as the many states that have counted on security and political-military assistance from the United States can no longer do so. They can only request it as erstwhile allies and clients under the concurrent dispensation, thereby giving them something of an incentive to support the United Nations at Washington's urgings. Their doing so could elicit side payments, stand them in good stead in other circumstances, and enhance their reputations as cooperative partners. The free rider problem can also be allayed insofar as the major players have particularistic incentives to further the realization of collective goals. With the organization's preeminent member acting and contributing in a principled, liberally focused manner, the major powers are likely to have some interest in doing likewise. Maintaining or elevating their international standing, their prestige, reputations, and influence, could be served by cooperating (or "competing") with the United States in organizing the United Nations' collective power as an enforcement agency.

Since the end of the Cold War it has been increasingly recognized that the threats of nuclear and conventional weapons can often best be mitigated on a regional basis. Much of what has just been said suggests that a nonengaged America could play a relatively effective part in mediating and (telescopically) monitoring nuclear proliferation and conventional force developments in the Middle East, South Asia, and East Asia. Without America's security interests at stake, it is in a potentially good position to help reconcile those of other states, alone or jointly with other outside powers.

The concurrent dispensation has a diversity of potentially effective means of influence at its disposal for promoting America's ideals. Almost all of its rewards and punishments are identical to those of liberal internationalism. The two foreign policies offer America's good offices in the mediation of conflicts, political and economic incentives for one or both sides to discontinue their unacceptable behavior, and military forces for multilateral and unilateral peacekeeping and peacemaking operations. Both allow for public condemnations, calls for international investigations, the withdrawal of ambassadors, and the refusal to recognize governments that come to power by unacceptable means. And both foreign policies can wield the impressive economic sanctions at America's disposal.

Economic sanctions are all too often depreciated.[40] The most extensive and systematic investigation of their effectiveness, based on all of some one hundred cases since 1914, found them to be at least moderately successful more than a third of the time.[41] This number is not insignificant in and of itself. It becomes more so by a comparison with the effectiveness of the hardest kind of power. The use of military threats for purposes of extended deterrence was successful a little more than half the time between 1900 and 1980.[42] Since 1945 the United States has been in an especially good position to employ sanctions effectively. Its unrivaled armory includes the imposition of import restrictions and embargoes into the world's largest market, discontinuation of most-favored-nation trading status, restrictions on high-technology exports, the cutoff of economic aid, the abrogation of governmental incentives and guarantees for American firms investing abroad, and a central position within the World Bank, the International Monetary Fund, and the UN economic agencies from which to deny loan and aid applications. Nearly all states are in a decidedly weak position to retaliate against the use of these sanctions; economic dependencies run far more strongly toward the United States. Moreover, from what was just said, from its high moral ground the concurrent design can heighten the effectiveness of multilateral sanctions by encouraging a larger number of states to enact them.

The concurrent dispensation's available means are relatively limited in two regards. It calls for weapons sales and military aid only where they promote, and allows for them only when they are not injurious to, international security. Liberal internationalism features much milder restrictions so as not to curtail the number of political friends and the defense capabilities of allies and clients. The provision and suspension of military transfers are thus less extensively available as rewards and punishments. Still, the gap is not especially consequential as it bears upon liberal outcomes. For as seen below, liberal internationalism's greater openhandedness in the way of arms transfers has been offset by its constraints in using them on behalf of liberal causes.

At first glance there is a great difference with respect to the hardest of power capabilities. The concurrent dispensation deploys roughly half the military forces of liberal internationalism. But the differential is of little if any consequence in furthering the liberal agenda. The downsized land and air forces still wield the world's most advanced weaponry; the navy remains easily the world's largest. These forces could be overwhelmingly effective against many states and most political movements in setting up blockade lines and carrying out missile attacks and air strikes. Depending on the literal and metaphorical contours on the ground, U.S. interventions could involve intelligence collection, communications help, medical supplies, logistic support, as well as the military services' special forces and regular troops. The sufficiency and variable effectiveness of U.S. forces may in any case be less affected by their size than by the various conditions that permit a military solution in the first place. The force levels of the Korean, Vietnam, and Persian Gulf Wars could barely be met by the concurrent dispensation. Yet these actions were respectively undertaken solely, almost entirely, and primarily for security reasons. Neither foreign policy calls for unilateral military endeavors on such a great scale solely on behalf of our ideals. And the likelihood of multilateral contributions increases under the auspices of the concurrent design.

Endowed with about the same influence resources as liberal internationalism, the concurrent design puts them to markedly more frequent
and effective uses. Absent all manner of security interests, the United
States is much more autonomous, in translating our liberal aims into policy, rather than deterring ourselves or letting others dissuade us from
doing so. Liberal power is most effectively used when the choice of means
and tactics is governed by the conditions that mediate their impact, the
relevant circumstances at hand. Put differently, deciding when, how, and
in which combinations to use what kinds of punishments and rewards is
unconstrained by security interests.

The concurrent design's autonomy renders all liberal means potentially applicable to all manner of states. Threats, pressures, sanctions, and
force can be directed at those who are no longer allies and clients. And
they know what America knows, that the withdrawal of valued benefits
and the execution of hurtful actions are often readily affordable in the
absence of political-military considerations. Many border on the costless.
America's credibility is thus high, often sufficient for threatened penalties
to obviate the need to inflict them. Short of forceful actions, negative
sanctions can be directed at political-military challengers. America's strategic immunity and strategic nonengagement radically diminish the opponent's effective retaliatory capabilities and opportunities. A positive approach of quiet diplomacy, negotiations, compromise, and rewards is
also affordable. A nonengaged America does not put its resolve and credibility on the line beyond the narrow security perimeter. It need not be
concerned that the appearance or realities of partially accommodating an
opponent in a liberal cause will be interpreted as weakness. Tactically, the
concurrent design can employ firm, flexible, or mixed measures depending upon their likely liberalizing efficaciousness. Not being locked into a
supportive relationship with allies, pursuing neither an adversarial nor a
conciliatory strategy vis-à-vis opponents, the United States could choose
the mixture of firm and flexible tactics that has proved most successful in
resolving other kinds of conflicts.[43]

Liberal internationalism does not allow itself recourse to anything like
this frequent, varied, and idealistically focused use of influence resources.
Allies are much too important to be discomfited, no less antagonized.
There is almost always some security reason—military, geostrategic, political, or symbolic—not to press them to abide by liberal tenets. Over the
course of the Cold War Washington hardly ever applied determined, sustained pressure upon an ally or client to improve its human rights record,
end its suppression of ethnic and religious groups, move toward democracy with dispatch, or forgo its development of nuclear weapons. When
Washington held out the possibility of negative sanctions, it did so
hesitantly. Except for restrictions on U.S. investments in South Africa,

sanctions usually varied between well-circumscribed and wrist-slapping exercises. Tactics verged on the irrelevant when there was so little to manipulate.

In dealing with political-military opponents, internationalists of a hawkish variety insist upon the need to demonstrate a continuously high level of resolve. To try to negotiate away their illiberal practices, especially if some rewards are involved, could diminish the credibility and thus the potency of crucial deterrent threats. For internationalists of a dovish stripe the contender needs to be reassured, which usually negates the use of hard measures. They would be taken as expressions of our hostile intentions, if not also as attempts at destabilization. Strategic internationalists of a centrist kind allow for the mixture of firm and flexible means that are generally most successful. However, the combination's adoption depends not nearly so much upon its liberalizing promise, as upon the unrelated adoption of a centrist security strategy. It is largely by way of happenstance, the more or less fortuitous fit with the circumstances at hand, that the kinds of liberalizing efforts allowed for by an internationalist security strategy might prove effective. This is seen in the half-dozen wide fluctuations in Jewish emigration from the Soviet Union between the early 1970s and late 1980s. Moscow consistently allowed larger numbers of Jews to emigrate in the wake of centrist policies on arms control and trade matters, and just as consistently cut back on their numbers in the aftermath of hawkish policy shifts.

What then is to be lost in disengaging? Absent a strong security interest, the United States does not now promote liberal causes that entail high costs and risks. While liberal internationalism occasionally calls for great exertions up to the level of major war on behalf of security and ideal interests combined, when the former predominate, they may have decidedly unhappy consequences for the latter. The United States has fought three regional wars since 1945. Whatever the security arguments about the Vietnam and Persian Gulf Wars, little if anything can be said about their liberalizing consequences—and a great deal about the hundreds of thousands of lives lost and the sufferings of countless others in each of them. The Iraqi case is especially telling considering the quick, easy, and overwhelming victory. Over the past two years civil war and "ethnic cleansing" in the former Yugoslavia has been of the greatest concern. The United States would almost certainly have been much involved had the country broken apart during the Soviet-American rivalry, but not necessarily for the good. Absent the rivalry, America has stayed well out of harm's way, thereby highlighting liberal internationalism's activist limits in the absence of a security imperative. In the end, the concurrent dispensation's moderation, its recognition of limits, does not make for a less activist idealism than that of liberal internationalism.

Deprived of U.S. defense commitments, some countries may have much less with which to deter and defend against possible aggression. However, most countries balance against threats, internally by building up their own strengths, externally by forming alliances, or both. For the United States to disengage will thus usually prompt them to make up for most or all of the U.S. contribution. Cheap riding is no longer an option. What was said about Western Europe in chapter 3, that it could and would have generated the effective military capabilities to replace American ones, also applies to many others even though they do not have its great resources. These are not necessary since their threatening opponents do not begin to approximate the former Warsaw Pact in power. The concurrent dispensation sometimes involves the arming of weaker countries, helping to redress the military imbalance for states that are sorely threatened. They are sold or given arms, possibly including the world's most capable ones, with more being rushed to them if they are attacked. This is how Israel's security was insured during the Cold War; the Arab states now having lost the political-military backing of their Soviet patron, there is substantially less need for U.S. support. U.S. security guarantees served as nuclear inhibitors for some (but not other) allies in the past. In chapter 5 it was argued that alliances will do much less to curb nuclear temptations in the future. Absent a common opponent that made U.S. commitments sufficiently reassuring, alliances become a wasting asset for stemming nuclear proliferation.

Whatever the remaining gaps between the contributions of the concurrent dispensation and liberal internationalism, they are more than filled by two summary considerations. These are the latter's illiberal consequences, as set out in the previous section, and the former's advantages as delineated in the present one. Thus, while again acknowledging the distinct limits of any foreign policy in a large, disordered, recalcitrant, divisive, and violent world, the concurrent dispensation still holds out the greater promise of liberalizing and peaceful successes.

Chapter IX

THE NATIONAL WELFARE

THE PREAMBLE to the Constitution assigns the government the responsibility to "provide for the common defense" and "promote the general welfare." There is no doubting that any design to achieve the former also bears upon the latter. Every security strategy has significant consequences for the nation's welfare. The consequences may entail benefits and losses, costs and opportunity costs; they may be of a short-term and long-term kind, direct and indirect in being mediated by the economy and the political process; and they may be played out domestically and internationally. This chapter considers all the national-welfare values that have been, could have been, and might be affected by the national and international security strategies.

The national strategy promises the maximum possible contribution to the national welfare, a markedly greater one than any variant of strategic internationalism. It cannot be improved upon as it affects each of the material and social values that have been or could be affected by any security strategy. This claim applies "directly" at home. Abroad, the national strategy does more to bolster the most promising economic diplomacy, the assertive and affirmative economic internationalism of the concurrent foreign policy.

The historical isolationists addressed most of the country's welfare values: Extensive and profitable trade relations, economic development, financial stability, economic growth, low taxes, and (to some extent) the public funding of social programs. Their arguments, warnings, and predictions are reviewed and assessed in the following section. Since the 1970s isolationists and many internationalists have been highly critical of Western Europe and Japan for their cheap riding as allies and their less than free and fair trade practices. Besides making for extra financial costs and commercial losses in any single year, they have contributed to America's quasi-chronic economic ills and relative economic decline. The second section examines these claims from the perspective of an alliance-free national strategy and the concurrent foreign policy. Since the Vietnam War isolationists and many internationalists have bemoaned high defense budgets for slowing economic growth, hindering international competitiveness, cutting into social programs, and for imposing other opportunity costs. The final section assesses these and some related claims.

I

In his stately valedictory, Washington was not above discussing commercial relations and profits. He was much concerned that these would be uncertain and limited if the United States allowed itself to become part of a European alliance. Only a politically and militarily neutral posture would allow for fulsome trade. "Harmony, liberal intercourse with all nations, are recommended by policy, humanity, and interest . . . even our commercial policy should hold an equal and impartial hand . . . diffusing and diversifying by gentle means the streams of commerce, but forcing nothing . . . in order to give to trade a stable course, to define the rights of our merchants, and to enable the Government to support them."[1] This did not, of course, preclude the use of force to protect our shipping and commerce. At the beginning of the nineteenth century American neutrality and navigation rights were secured by naval actions against French, British, and Barbary pirate ships.

During the nineteenth century strategic isolationism was virtually unquestioned in its bestowal of great welfare benefits: profits abroad and economic development at home. Geopolitical and commercial interests were at one; a low political-military profile abroad made for free and extensive trade. Secretary of State John Quincy Adams viewed the "Principle of mutual treatment upon a footing of equality with the most favored nation . . . [as] the great foundation of our foreign policy." Absent the demands of an expensive military establishment, and not being taken up with or politically divided by foreign policy (i.e., European) issues, the country's energies could be concentrated upon economic expansionism and development in North America. As late as 1885 few Americans took exception to this part of President Cleveland's inaugural: "The genius of our institutions, the needs of our people in their home life, and the attention which is demanded for the settlement and development of the resources of our vast territory dictate the scrupulous avoidance of any departure from that foreign policy commended by the history, the traditions, and the prosperity of our republic."[2]

When isolationism was first set aside in any major way, economic and security interests were about equally salient. Commercial expansionism and strategic internationalism were linked together by way of the Pacific annexations that were to serve as way stations for the China trade and by a world-class navy for protecting them and our spheres of economic interest. The isolationists of the day objected to these developments with several national-welfare claims.

Possibly influenced by, but in any case consistent with Adam Smith's *The Wealth of Nations*, the members of the Anti-Imperialist League

argued that colonies are at best commercially superfluous. Distant annexations have consistently afforded their owners only inconvenience, expense, and unfulfilled expectations. Instead of "trade following the flag,"
it is the laws of economics that determine commercial success. Profitable
markets depend upon the price and attractiveness of the products; America's being sufficiently competitive, it becomes unnecessary to seize and
rope off markets. Colonies are also expensive to administer and protect.
With the Pacific outposts laying America open to sudden attack, the
maintenance of forces strong enough to guard them and the occasional
war to defend them would bring on a heavy tax burden and discourage
industry. Senator Carl Schurz noted that America alone of all the major
states has an "advantage of incalculable value. We are the only one not
under any necessity of keeping up a large armament on land or water for
the security of its possessions, the only one that can turn all the energies
of its population to productive employment." Moreover, to go abroad is
to dilute domestic priorities. For the anti-imperialists this meant less attention being accorded to the vital issues of the cities and the corporate
trusts.[3]

The incompatibilities between strategic internationalism and the nation's welfare were central to the Progressives' case against American intervention in World War I. Senators George W. Norris and Robert LaFollette led the fight against intervention in the expectation that it would
derail economic reform. The mounting political challenge to the powers
of "Wall Street," the "monopolies," and the "money trusts" would
whither away as the nation's attention turned to war. Others went further. The "vested interests" were charged with purposefully leading the
country into war so as to abort the progressive reforms. Most opponents
of intervention predicted that economic dislocations and depression
would follow in its wake.[4] Some socialists and trade unionists feared the
emergence of a kind of fascism dominated by bankers and large corporations. This would become a country in which strikes were outlawed, the
state dictated every worker's activities, and they would live on subsistence
wages.

The New Deal isolationists of the mid-1930s harkened back to the
results of World War I: It had moved economic reforms off the political
agenda and derailed the economy. The current depression obviously demanded the government's full concentration upon measures to alleviate
the economic and social plight of millions. For liberals and conservatives
alike, higher military expenditures with or without war were expected to
inhibit economic growth. After 1939 the conservative isolationists were
most anxious about internationalism's dire impact upon the country's
material well-being. Capitalism was imperiled, as full-scale mobilization

was bound to bring on inflation, price and wage controls, compulsory unionization, and a wartime socialism that would remain in place after the war was over. War thus spelled national bankruptcy and the collapse of a productive capitalism. At a minimum Roosevelt's interventionism was seen as an indirect political attempt to foist undesirable and costly New Deal reforms upon the country.[5] The postwar isolationists were convinced that the country's economic interests abroad were minimal or not at risk. Any threat to the nation's welfare lay elsewhere. In Senator Taft's words, "nothing can destroy this country except the overextension of our resources." With virtually all isolationists subscribing to a strict fiscal conservatism, many expected military and foreign aid expenditures to have grievous consequences. Economic prosperity would be unattainable, American taxpayers would suffer enormously, and the financial drain could bankrupt the country. Some recalled Lenin's (supposed) boast that the Soviet Union would force the United States to spend itself into the ground. Senator Wherry warned against the Truman Doctrine's globalism: "We cannot underwrite the staggering commitments to rearm and rebuild the rest of the world which is still outside the Russian sphere, and remain a sound, solvent, and free people." Others predicted that client states would make starkly anticommunist appeals. Their strategic and political resonance for Washington would result in its doing far more than its share in financing real and exaggerated defense needs around the world.

Isolationists differed as to whether the billions in Marshall Plan aid would be wasteful, whether a socialist Europe would turn out to be a "leaky barrel." (One congressman thought that U.S. aid would be counterproductive even if used productively: The Europeans' economic recovery would undermine American businesses and jobs as they became serious economic competitors.) In any case, the billions of dollars earmarked for Europe should instead be devoted to domestic needs, such as the building of more classrooms, higher teacher's salaries, and greater support for the elderly. Taft bemoaned the effects of military spending in curtailing "progress on every kind of education, social welfare, and many other matters in which Americans are vitally interested."[6]

This 150-year record is mixed. Isolationist claims were variously warranted, partly so, and mistaken. Nineteenth-century isolationism maximized the country's trading opportunities and allowed for a concentration of energies upon its economic development. The movement toward economic and social reforms was not derailed at the beginning of the twentieth century, but World War I did have this effect. Reading what was said about America's strategic immunity in chapter 3 alongside the anti-imperialist position supports that position and that of the post-

1945 isolationists who claimed that a global strategy was not needed to safeguard our economic interests abroad. The isolationists were right in predicting that entry into World War I would bring on a recession, yet grievously mistaken in foreseeing internationalism's adverse financial and economic consequences early in the century, before World War II, and after it. As seen below, their concerns about higher taxes and lower social expenditures resulting from an increasingly globalized containment strategy were partly justified.

This is not a poor record, especially since the isolationists' national-welfare claims were almost invariably reasoned and reasonable. They were furthest off the mark in insisting upon the negative economic consequences of military and foreign aid expenditures. However, those assertions were consistent with the fiscal conservatism that was the prevalent kind of economic thinking during the first half of the twentieth century. Most internationalists also subscribed to it with regard to domestic governmental expenditures, while somehow setting it aside or accepting its consequences when it came to defense spending. A comparable point applies to the infamously protectionist Smoot-Hawley tariff. The 1929 financial crisis and the beginning of the Great Depression led isolationists and internationalists alike to support it.

II

Strategic internationalism is expensive. It is all the more so when equally wealthy allies do not contribute their fair share of military forces to the common defense, when additional American contributions are thus needed to make up for the shortfalls. From the late 1960s to the last years of the Cold War an increasing number of internationalists have criticized NATO Europe for something between cheap riding and free riding on American contributions to their own security. Joined by isolationists in the 1980s, some internationalists claimed that the burden-sharing shortfalls made for huge budget deficits, our trading partners' competitive advantages, and slow growth rates. The comparable charges leveled against Japan were far fewer and less bitter. Its protection absorbed only a small part of U.S. defense expenditures, and after 1960 we wanted it to be no more than a "civilian power."

Considering the relevant numbers and the notion of fair contributions, just how much have burden-sharing disparities cost the United States? What is it about American alliance relations that accounted for the shortfalls and likely future ones? The answer to the latter question also relates directly to Europe and Japan's unfair trade practices, whether the abrogation of alliances would have and would help move them toward trade reforms.

Early on during the Cold War, when the European states were poorly off compared to the United States, they committed themselves to the principle of equitable burden sharing. Toward its close, when their total and per capita GNPs were at about U.S. levels, Washington was still trying to cajole them into contributing more. At their 1952 Lisbon meeting the NATO leaders agreed that alliance forces should equal those of the Soviet bloc and that national contributions should be made according to an equitable military division of labor. Each country would provide what it could most easily provide. America was to supply the nuclear deterrent, air power, and some naval forces; the West Europeans obligated themselves to provide the bulk of ground forces. But the NATO countries could not agree upon the necessary troop levels until 1978, when they signed onto modest 3 percent annual increases in defense spending. And then only Britain and France (and America) met their obligations. Ten years later Washington was still unsuccessfully asking NATO Europe to contribute more to its own defense.[7]

Toward the end of the Cold War, when NATO Europe's total GNP and the per capita GNPs of some allies were higher than our own, the United States was spending nearly twice as large a proportion of its GNP on defense as NATO Europe: over 6 percent versus 3.5 percent, while Japan devoted little more than 1 percent of its GNP to the military. On a per capita basis, each American contributed $1,100 to the defense budget, the average European less than $300, and the Japanese $200.[8] The disparities can be reduced by figuring in the rental value of the land given over to U.S. bases, the host nation contributions to the maintenance of the forces, and the higher troop costs of the American volunteer force relative to Europe's conscript forces. But taken together these considerations still have no more than a secondary impact upon the differentials.

The basic European reply and that of many Atlanticists in this country did not get into the account books. It denied the appropriateness of the comparisons that were just drawn; our larger defense expenditures are only relevant in part. For it was we ourselves who decided that it was necessary to undertake the great burdens of quasi-global containment on our own exaggerated strategic calculations. Those extra or unnecessary expenditures should therefore not be part of a comparison with Europe's defense outlays.

This is a reasonable position, certainly so from the vantage point of a national strategy. The most important numbers thus become America and Europe's expenditures on the defense of Europe, the 60 percent of U.S. defense spending devoted to that mission and NATO Europe's total defense expenditures. On this comparison every American still contributed more than twice as much to Europe's protection as the average European. Even on the data presented by two analysts who disagree with the burden-sharing criticisms, we spent more on Europe's defense than the Europeans themselves—indeed a third more so, the United States assuming 57 percent of the costs and Europe 43 percent.[9] According to the closest student of NATO finances, the appropriate response to the imbalance in the 1980s would have been a 50 percent reduction in U.S. troops stationed in Europe at an annual saving of $67 billion.[10] Moreover, consideration should be given to the American expenses of extended deterrence, the strategic missiles, bombers, and submarines whose primary mission was that of negating a Warsaw Pact attack. Half of these costs translated into $30 billion a year. And the Europeans who saw little or no reason for America's far-flung Third World commitments were silent with regard to the expenses born by the United States in protecting "their" Persian Gulf oil and shipping lanes.

It is then hardly unreasonable to suggest that we subsidized NATO Europe at the level of roughly $80 billion a year. This number has been and will be reduced in the 1990s, just possibly down to about $50 billion a year. But proportionally America's expenses do not look like they are about to decline significantly. The lower ones come from reductions in U.S. and allied defense expenditures. Whether considering the annual $80 billion excess in burden sharing during the 1980s or a $50 billion one for the 1990s, it clearly constitutes an enormous amount of forgone national welfare. Whatever the parts of these sums that would have been or might be devoted to public or private uses, invested or consumed, alliances with equally wealthy states entail some decidedly extra welfare costs.

This is the central conclusion. It stands without having to subscribe to the arguments that the burden-sharing inequities have been sorely detrimental to economic growth and competitiveness. The annual $67 billion shortfall on the Atlantic side calculated by David Calleo is said to have contributed substantially to our budget deficits, with these helping to bring on financial instability internationally, inflationary pressures, and thus slow economic growth. At the tail end of the Cold War he allowed how it is "absurd that the United States should be bankrupting itself, and destabilizing the world economy, by trying to sustain a balance against the Soviets that could almost exist without [its being in Europe]."[11] According to another kind of argument, America's picking up a disproportionate share of the allies' security costs has allowed them to invest more in their economies, increase productivity, and concentrate upon commercial research and development. Our economic competitiveness has consequently been impaired.[12] These far-reaching claims are supported by economic logic and some inferential comparisons. Yet the huge size of the American, European, and Japanese economies may easily have overwhelmed the effects of the burden-sharing disparities. There are also other explanations for America's flagging economy and lowered competitiveness: the allies' trade practices and America's low savings rate.

There is a standard collective- (or public-) goods explanation for burden-sharing disparities. Alliance benefits, protection from the common threat, are indivisible. Their distribution is no more than minimally affected by any one state's contributions to the common defense. As such, all have a strong incentive to curtail their financial and military burdens. This is a necessary part of the explanation, but it does not indicate which states end up bearing disproportionate costs and why they do so.[13]

The other part of the explanation involves variations in security dependencies, varying assessments of the common threat, and variable interests in particularistic, country-specific benefits. As these were played out across the Atlantic they point to an America that chose to assume disproportionate burdens because of its practice of strategic internationalism. That we chose to do so is indicated by a "reversal" of alliance dependencies. They should have allowed the United States, if anyone, to be the cheap rider. It was the allies who were directly confronted by the huge Warsaw Pact forces. We had the enormous security benefits of great distance from the threat, overwhelming naval superiority, and a huge nuclear arsenal. Yet no administration—as opposed to occasional congressional minorities—did more than make doctrinal arguments and requests in trying to elicit increased military contributions from Europe to rectify the conventional imbalance.

Despite Europe's much greater alliance dependencies and its highest values being directly at stake, the United States made itself more dependent on Europe. It did so by consistently adhering to assessments of the common threat that were distinctly more threatening than Europe's. From this side of the Atlantic the Soviet Union was seen as an ideologically motivated, extraordinarily ambitious global power. On the other side it was generally taken to be a less dangerous, more manageable great power, one whose political and security interests could almost certainly be satisifed well short of a Warsaw Pact invasion. America's sharply etched conception of the threat made for an inordinate sensitivity to alliance divisiveness; even minor diplomatic fissures would detract from the necessary cohesiveness in confronting the Soviets. Burden-sharing issues were consequently not pursued in anything like an assertive manner. Washington never said (or officially implied) that some U.S. troops would be withdrawn from Europe unless it did more for its own protection. And clearly something like this was required. Because of the Europeans' moderated view of the Soviet threat, they were not about to act solely upon Washington's requests or urgings.

America has derived some particularistic, exclusive benefits from NATO. As ally-in-chief it has enjoyed the right to appoint NATO's military commander, disproportionate say in political-military matters, considerable influence regarding out-of-area issues, as well as the trappings of high international status. Neither America's predominant position nor its benefits were disputed during the first half of the Cold War. Both have been increasingly questioned since then. Washington was unwilling to put them in any jeopardy. To make insistent burden-sharing demands was to raise the real possibility of embarrassing failures of leadership, the exposure of Europe's diminishing dependence on the United States, its unwillingness to do Washington's bidding.

Washington has recently become much concerned with retaining its position in Europe. NATO provides our single formal seat at the head of (and at) any European table. Keeping it made for a negative reaction to a considerable burden-sharing improvement, the Bush administration's criticism of the Eurocorps being formed by France and Germany. Because the corps is designed for military and humanitarian interventions that NATO as a whole is unwilling to undertake, and because it is intended to be enlarged with additional members and troops that would rival NATO's, it could easily undercut America's position in Europe. Chancellor Helmut Kohl aptly responded to Washington's criticisms of the Europcorps with a burden-sharing barb: "The Americans often tell us we must do more for our security. This corps should be reason for celebration."[14]

What then of the likelihood of the alliance disproportionalities continuing well into the post–Cold War era? They would be rectified if a security threat emerged that was seen to be similarly serious in America and Europe, if the United States did not rush in to take the lead, and if it were demonstrably unwilling to do more than its share.

The United States is currently spending "more than eight times as much on the military as any other member of the Group [of Seven] industrial powers. Indeed, it spends 60 percent more than all the other G-7 countries combined." Ted Carpenter goes on to question whether a post–Cold War America "really has many times over the security interests of Germany—or France, or Britain, or Japan—to defend."[15] There are no indications that the Bush or Clinton administrations asked themselves this question in their force planning for the late 1990s. Were a potential or actual threat to emerge in Washington's view, the Europeans would probably hold to a relatively diminished assessment of its immediacy and severity. If transatlantic assessments of a serious threat did converge, there is still the long record of our willingness to assume extra burdens. The expectations of its continuation would make for resistance to American demands, their credibility being put to the test before the allies agreed to do their share. Washington might not be sufficiently resolute to pass the test, especially after rushing in to meet the threat.

These considerations might appear to be belied by the first major test of burden-sharing propensities. Britain and France made significant military contributions to the coalition that fought the Persian Gulf War. Along with the Gulf oil producers, Germany and Japan financed our total war cost of $60 billion. However, there are some other relevant considerations. The United States rushed in. Within a few days of Iraq's invasion of Kuwait Bush announced that it "would not stand" and signed an executive agreement for the defense of Saudi Arabia. The coalition forces that defeated Iraq were overwhelmingly American. The amounts of the allies' contributions were agreed to before the war, at a time when it was expected to be far longer and costlier than it turned out to be. Moreover, Europe and Japan's economic security was at greater risk than America's. They are without any oil resources of their own, far more dependent on the Gulf's than is the United States. The anti-Iraqi cause merged security interests with a highly salient set of ideal interests, with Saddam constituting the perfect enemy. The latter condition is most unlikely to obtain in the future.

A central aspect of the burden-sharing discussion—America's decided reluctance to adopt an assertive posture due to the need for alliance unity—parallels the discussion of trade issues. Indeed, the single direct test of the alternative posture is not only indicative of the Europeans' past readiness to respond positively to burden-sharing demands, pressures, and threats. It is also suggestive of their willingness to respond to an assertive (and affirmative) economic diplomacy. Circa 1970 the Vietnam War forced a reduction in the U.S. forces stationed in Europe, and at the same time, the Senate came closest to passing the oft introduced Mansfield amendment requiring troop withdrawals from Europe unless the allies increased their military contributions. They reacted in the way in which cheap riders are supposed to react. During the 1970s NATO Europe enlarged its forces substantially, raising the proportion of military expenditures to GNP by half, and in the case of West Germany, more than doubled per capita defense spending.[16]

III

Since the late 1970s isolationists and internationalists have been vehemently criticizing the Europeans and the Japanese for their trade practices. They have not been free, given sizable nontariff barriers and some import bans; they have not been fair because of governmental subsidization, guidance, and coordination of export industries, along with occasional below-cost dumping. The profits of American companies have declined due to trade barriers hindering exports; domestic sales have run up against the special advantages of foreign competitors. Farms, firms, and jobs, good jobs in particular, have been lost. In addition, trade deficits are said to have had adverse effects upon interest rates and thus on budget deficits and economic growth.

America's trade problems continue to be seen as serious on the Atlantic side, considerably more so in the Pacific. Where the European Community maintains exceptionally high price supports for its relatively inefficient farmers, Japan's total ban on rice imports (partly lifted in 1993) eliminated an entire market for our far more efficient farmers. Where Europe and Japan have laid down nontariff barriers for an assortment of American exports, Japanese markets feature structural impediments— quasi cartels among suppliers, manufacturers, and retailers that can barely be penetrated by commercial outsiders. Where some European governments have afforded financial subsidies to their "national champions" in a few high-tech industries, Japan's Ministry for International Trade and Industry (MITI) has done this much and considerably more in helping all the huge manufacturing firms develop next-generation products and in restricting access to the domestic market until they have attained a dominant position within it. And where European governments and firms seek first and foremost to maximize profits and satisfy consumers, Japan pursues a quasi mercantilism whose chief goals are capital accumulation and the expansion of market shares.[17]

Political-military relations have affected trade relations with Europe and Japan in a singular manner: Strategic internationalism has allowed for our chief trading partners' less than free and fair trading practices. In one respect it is hardly surprising to find that the "high" politics of national security have been consistently assigned precedence over the "low" politics of international commerce. The former embraces the nation's highest values. However, as practiced by the United States, strategic internationalism has derogated economic interests to truly striking lows, at least until end of the Cold War. Up to the 1980s trade issues were not even considered "actionable" because of extrasensitive security concerns, or they were weakly addressed rather than effortfully confronted. For over forty years the Soviet threat was seen to be so great and immediate, allies so crucial, alliance strains so debilitating that commercial matters could not be allowed to intrude. No consideration was given to the allies' much greater security dependence upon the United States. Their having no where else to go was ignored. Close alliance relations were not to be jeopardized. Even trade demands, no less mild pressures and implicit retaliatory threats, were set aside.

During the 1950s and 1960s Washington not only accepted but encouraged trading developments that strengthened the allies at our expense. It supported the European Economic Community, which discriminated against U.S. exports, and tolerated Japanese protectionism and restrictions on foreign direct investment.[18] This was affordable while the U.S. enjoyed a favorable trade balance, a strong dollar, and healthy growth rates. But after 1970 America continued to subordinate its economic interests because of concerns for "the high politics of the global balance and the challenge of Soviet power."[19] Economists are not noted for emphasizing national security explanations when analyzing international trade patterns. Yet they have argued that this is the only way to understand the latter through the late 1970s. "American foreign policy focused on political rather than economic goals—often trading economic advantage, such as access to U.S. markets or technology, for political gains—driven by the perception that America's greatest threat was a political one from the Soviet Union."[20]

During the 1980s our low commercial interests underwent an upward policy revision. There was an official airing of grievances, the citing of chapter and verse of Europe and Japan's unacceptable practices, and in 1985 the dollar was devalued. The 1988 Trade Act added a "super" provision to section 30l that required the President to specify trade liberalization goals, identifying the "priority countries and practices" for investigation. However, more assertive declarations and implicit threats translated into little. The number of trade discrimination cases that were pursued in accordance with section 301 from 1975 to 1989 remained the same for Europe, hardly increased for Japan to a high of seven between 1985 and 1989, and averaged well under $200 million in export values.[21] Washington was insufficiently demanding or credible to move the Europeans to compromise on more than a few U.S. exports. Tokyo was somewhat more forthcoming. It agreed to permit American beef and citrus imports, to reduce tariffs on aluminum goods, cigarettes, and leather products, and to restrict automobile exports to the United States.

In surveying U.S. policy up to the Cold War's demise a former secretary of commerce maintained that "whenever 'economics' clashed directly with military 'security policy,' the U.S. *instinctively* opted to give precedence to the latter."[22] According to a high-ranking Commerce Department negotiator with Tokyo, Ronald Reagan was no different than other presidents. He too was unwilling to adopt an assertive posture on trade matters so as not to strain alliance relations. As long as national security continues to be "more important than trade we will always do poorly in trade. There will always be a [military] or a political interest that we do not want to endanger for the sake of some seemingly minor trade case."[23] Words alone, empty ones, suggested that international economic issues would take precedence over security concerns for the Bush administration. The record was so clear that a 1991 magazine story offered this prediction: The old argument about "push[ing] the Japanese too hard on imports" will probably continue to prevail despite the demise of the Soviet threat for fear that "the U.S. might lose its important strategic bases. . . . 'The Great Vacuum threat,' the possible break-up of the U.S.-Japanese alliance might leave a space to be filled by the USSR, China, or Japan itself."[24]

That prediction was not born out by the first full-fledged post–Cold War administration. For in its first year and a half the Clinton administration was not faced with any pressing security problems, none that required alliance cohesiveness. Strategic internationalism could then fortuitously remain in place while treating economic issues ("opening markets abroad") separately from political-military ones. Washington gradually turned from an affirmative to a more assertive economic diplomacy. At an April 1993 press conference with the visiting Japanese prime minister, President Clinton talked at length about "rebalancing our relationship" in a way that put economics at the forefront, concomitantly declaring that the "cold war partnership between our two countries is outdated."[25] Those words were followed by requests and demands involving increased Japanese purchases of U.S. goods and services and fulfillment of U.S. target shares of the Japanese market. However, there were still no pressures, no deadlines, no talk of restricting Japanese imports if the market-opening benchmarks were not realized.[26]

Assertiveness became prominent in July 1993 with the Congress legislating a December 15 completion deadline for the Uruguay round of the GATT negotiations that had been dragging on for seven years. If they were not satisfactorily concluded by then it was said that there would be no other progress on free trade, simultaneously allowing for the possibility of some protectionist policies. Short of threatening retaliation, the Clinton administration then put on a full-court economic press that resulted in what was probably the best achievable GATT agreement for the United States. Japan agreed to open up part of its rice market to imports, Europe is to phase back government subsidies and barriers for agriculture, cross-Atlantic tariffs were reduced by half and by an average of one-third for all 117 nations, quotas in farm goods, textiles, and finished apparel will be replaced by gradually decreasing tariffs, and intellectual property rights involving patents, copyrights, and trademarks are to be respected. In addition, a new organization was created to enforce the rules, one that was no longer stymied by the old unanimity rule. Washington did not get everything it wanted. There are still outstanding trade issues having to do with a diversity of government subsidies and the coverage of financial services, among others. But the results were a victory for the United States, one that should increase the national income of Americans by 1 percent, and keep the door open for the further liberalization of trade.[27]

Looking down the road, was the GATT agreement a one-time assertive success? Can the use of alliances as levers and strivings for across-the-board primacy do at least as well in furthering U.S. commercial interests? Does the United States—a nation in putative decline—have the exclusively economic wherewithal to resolve trade issues in its favor? Can it do so by pursuing an affirmative and assertive diplomacy? While these questions are addressed to the future, it should be emphasized that their answers have a critical bearing upon U.S. policies.

Perhaps it is time for the United States to put its alliance commitments to good economic use, offering to defend others "in return for economic favors."[28] Without anything like the extent and urgency of the Soviet threat in sight there is much less need for alliance cohesiveness. Divisions resulting from trade disputes should be far easier to contemplate. And the allies want the U.S. defense umbrella to remain in place, with Germany and Japan having extrasecurity interests for retaining U.S. troops on their soil and in their regions. Neighboring countries—in Central and Eastern Europe, and East and Southeast Asia—will be reassured that their security is not at risk, thereby allowing these two powerful, mistrusted states to extend their commercial activities and economic sway. Instead of alliances as usual, as self-imposed constraints, they are thus to become bargaining advantages.

This view of alliances as levers is not promising. It not only draws an exaggerated conclusion about alliance relations, it is also based upon a static future. True, U.S. alliance dependencies have markedly declined. However, Europe's and Japan's have declined at least as much with the demise of the Soviet threat, to which they were much more directly exposed. It is not at all clear that the allies would find Washington's political-military leverage compelling and credible. We would have to threaten the withdrawal of U.S. troops, if not the abrogation of alliances, and be prepared to act on it. This is not part of the conception of alliances as levers; it is precluded by the strategic internationalism within which it is embedded. Japan's and Germany's newfound independence and relative power will probably engender keener nationalist sensitivities and possibly a nationalist revivalism—a further devaluation of, resentment toward, or opposition to their status as American dependents. These developments will surely negate much or most U.S. leverage, even if America is not asked to go home. In fact, alliances could easily turn out to be doubly disadvantageous. Linking trade demands to politically sensitive alliance relations can only help heighten the nationalist sensibilities that sorely weaken America's bargaining position. Alliances could also become economic liabilities as the United States gives way on trade issues for the more important security imperative, the right to remain abroad militarily.

Partly incorporating alliances as levers, the primacist variant of strategic internationalism discussed in chapter 5 strives to maintain allies as secondary powers. Europe and Japan are to be kept down politically, militarily, and economically. Here the trade reform project is backed up by a readiness to demand, pressure, threaten, and retaliate. However, this merging of the economic and political-military spheres is counterproductive, both by heightening resistance to trade reform and by making resistance easier.

Whatever the propensities for the emergence of an intense, resentful, or sensitive nationalism, they will almost certainly be much heightened by purposeful U.S. efforts to maintain a position of across-the-board predominance. In this context U.S. trade pressures are less likely to move the allies toward trade concessions, more likely to engender a powerful nationalist resistance that moves them toward protectionism, retaliation, and possibly trade wars. Along with this singular drawback, on primacism's own logic America is disadvantaging itself by maintaining troops in and near Japan and Germany. As just noted, they currently want those troops in place as reassurance for others, to be better able to expand and deepen trade and investment links with neighboring countries. Japan and Germany's susceptibility to America's economic power, the need for its markets, will consequently be substantially diminished.

When considering the economic value of alliances it is eminently appropriate to ask whether they satisfy the crucial criterion of any economic project: Are the material benefits likely to outweigh the costs? Here the benefits are of two possible kinds. Alliances as more or less adversarial levers might be effective in helping to rectify less than free and fair trade practices. Alliances might also help preserve trade flows by heading off the instability, conflicts, and wars that would otherwise cut them off. These benefits are no more than possibilities; the alliance costs for their realization are certain. The maintenance of the Atlantic and Pacific security perimeter involves at least 40 percent of the defense budget, some $100 billion a year. With annual exports to Europe and Japan together running at about $170 billion, it is difficult to envisage the problematic benefits of alliances as levers surpassing the military costs of maintaining them. In chapter 3 it was seen that neither widespread instability nor regional wars would significantly impinge upon our trade flows. In any case, the low-odds benefit of preventing a level of conflict in Europe or Asia that would cut into our trade connections in some future year does not outweigh the certain $100 billion annual expenditure of trying to do so. Maintaining the capabilities to defend allies at a cost of one to two trillion dollars over the next ten to twenty years is much more likely to detract from than to contribute to the nation's economic welfare.

In contrast, the national strategy's minimalist political-military activism entails a sharp and strict separation between the security and economic realms. The abrogation of alliances maximizes the autonomy of economic ends and means in pursuing trade reform. Where alliance cohesion makes for economic self-deterrence, and alliances as levers and alliance primacy involve problematic and counterproductive means, the national strategy allows for and sustains the potentially most effective ones. The concurrent dispensation makes good and full use of America's economic power and advantages in market access negotiations, that is, up to the point at which they became overly adversarial. An assertive bilateral and/or multilateral diplomacy is necessary to move Europe and Japan toward trade reforms; the affirmative side minimizes the possibilities of their moving in the opposite direction.[29] Assertiveness features sustained demands, hard bargaining, calibrated pressures, resolute threats, and retaliation where necessary. On the affirmative side there is a willingness to put our own trade restrictions on the negotiating table, good-faith bargaining, a stress on shared long-run interests, cooperation in defusing domestic opposition to trade reform and building upon its political support, and the avowed rejection of retaliatory measures that extend beyond reciprocity.

The concurrent foreign policy does leave the United States without its political-military long suit. An exclusive reliance upon economic means may well appear less than sufficient given the size and endowments of the European and Japanese economies. Economic measures certainly look inadequate given all that has been written about America's relative economic decline. But they are not. The United States has been, is, and will continue to be endowed with impressive economic advantages. Even leaving aside its formidable structural power as mostly inapplicable in trade disputes,[30] there is good reason for a measured optimism regarding the realization of major trade reforms, more than that in obtaining important concessions.

The sufficiency of U.S. economic strengths is called into sharp doubt by the widely held view of our economic decline relative to Europe and Japan, of a marked downward shift in our share of gross world product, slower growth rates, unfavorable trade imbalances, huge budget deficits, and the loss of high-technology leadership and manufacturing jobs.[31] However, Paul Kennedy and the other declinists have greatly exaggerated the extent of the decline. They have also inflated its meaning, cause, and thus significance by misleading comparisons over time. Responding to the declinists' claims actually brings out America's economic strengths and stengthens the economic case for a national strategy.

An assessment of any change in relative economic standing should begin with a meaningful long-run comparison. How has America fared between 1941 and 1991, over the fifty-year course of all manner of economic developments? Most importantly, what does the comparison show with regard to Japan and Germany, whose postwar growth has done so much to inspire the declinist vision? The declinists have not addressed this question. And the data reveal not a descent but an ascent, a slightly faster long-term growth rate in the United States. Just prior to World War II the U.S. GNP was less than twice that of Japan's and Germany's together. In 1991 (with Germany reunified) it was more than twice theirs.[32] This comparison becomes yet more telling since the years before 1941 were hardly normal ones. The American economy was inordinately weak, Japan and Germany's were doing exceptionally well. We were still in the worst depression in our history. Their militarized economies had been growing rapidly, much more so than those of any of the industrialized countries.

There was a decline, a sharp one, between circa 1950 and circa 1970. America's generation of almost half the world's gross product dropped off by almost half, from 40 to 45 percent to 20 to 25 percent. However, this singular fact has little or no meaning when assessing America's absolute or relative, quantitative or qualitative economic performance and position. For the late 1940s and early 1950s baseline is decidedly inappropriate. Our fully mobilized economy was untouched by the enemy, while Europe's and Japan's economies were severely dislocated where they were not devastated. Nor are the differential growth rates of the 1950s and 1960s all that meaningful. Europe and Japan were growing rapidly while still getting themselves back to normality, back on their prewar feet. With our relative decline up to circa 1970 being part and parcel of the World War II effect, the declinist case hinges upon the years since then.

Joseph Nye looked at three crucial indicators of American economic power: Its percentage of world production, manufacturing, and technology-intensive exports. The data do not bear out the claim of a downward trajectory that was "continuous or precipitous . . . it was steepest from 1950 to 1973, the period often identified as the 'period of American hegemony.' American decline has been much more difficult to discern from 1973 to the present, which is often labelled the period of U.S. decline."[33] The U.S. share of the gross world product has not declined since 1970. It has remained within a narrow range of 22 to 25 percent. Standing at 23 percent as of 1991 makes it considerably more than twice that of Japan and well above three times that of the newly integrated Germany. While our less modern manufacturing industries in the rust belt have certainly suffered, the size of the manufacturing sector has not shrunk relative to the economy as a whole. Moreover, the proportion of the gross domestic product generated by the manufacturing sector's high-technology industries has been growing. It increased from 15 percent in 1981, to 23 percent in 1989, and to 27 percent as of 1992. This last figure is subtantially higher than the European Community's high-tech production as a proportion of manufacturing output (17 percent), and somewhat lower than Japan's (31 percent). Between 1980 and 1990 America's share of global exports of high-technology products increased in five out of eight high-tech industries.[34]

Among the indicators of economic strength perhaps the most important are the level and growth of productivity, the average value of output per worker. The American worker is easily the world leader, producing an average $49,600 in goods and services a year as of 1990, $5,000 more than that produced by German workers and $10,000 more than that of the Japanese. And over the last three years the productivity gap has been widening, even in the smokestack industries like steel, machine tools, and cars. Total exports, another yardstick of economic strength, increased twice as fast as world trade between 1970 and 1980. Market shares were restored in every manufacturing sector, with some returning to their "hegemonic" levels of the 1960s. Between 1980 and 1985 America's exports rose by nearly 9 percent a year, faster than Japan's 6.6 percent and Germany's 4.2 percent.[35]

The high-technology sector is regularly taken to be the centerpiece of the industrial economies. As of 1992, the United States was the leading producer in four out of six high-technology industries: aircraft, scientific instruments, computers and office equipment, and pharmaceuticals, lagging in communications equipment and electrical machinery. Our share of the global high-tech market stood at the same 37 percent in 1992 as in 1982, higher than Japan's 28 percent and the European Community's 29 percent in 1992. America remains far ahead in funding the research and development of the new technologies and products that are crucial determinants of national competitiveness. Its share of total industrial research and development performed among the OECD countries stood at 47 percent in 1990. The European Community's share was 30 percent and Japan's 21 percent.[36] Not surprisingly, then, French and Japanese newspapers have recently each run a long series on the new competitive threat from the United States.[37]

In their explanations for America's economic weaknesses the declinists discuss huge budget deficits, low investment rates, and educational deficiencies, and then hone in on the costs of what Paul Kennedy refers to as "imperial overreach." The underlying problem of the country's economy is to be found in an overly ambitious, overextended strategic internationalism. Military expenditures have been excessive in consuming so many financial, material, and scientific resources, resources that could otherwise be devoted to economic growth at home and competitiveness abroad. The policy prescription follows immediately: retrenchment, the shedding of some political-military burdens, implicitly about a 15–20 percent reduction in defense spending. Having exaggerated America's economic weaknesses, the declinists come up with a weak remedy—military savings of a little less than 1 percent of GNP. The declinists have identified part of the problem and its partial solution, but to get ahead of the story, the concurrent design can address the latter much more fully. A more assertive economic diplomacy along with the national strategy's 50 percent reductions in defense expenditures and their redirection can make a substantial difference for economic growth and competitiveness.

Economic power for bringing about trade reform should be considered in terms of the basic strengths of any industrial economy, its size, invulnerability, and leading edges. In size the United States is endowed with a truly impressive amount of market power. It sustains the world's largest corporations, generates nearly one-quarter of global GNP, and imports a half trillion dollars worth of goods a year. The American market is widely seen as our biggest bargaining tool, whether it is to be used in a balanced carrot-and-stick manner or primarily by way of deterrence and retaliation. Those who believe that it could and should be used on behalf of trade reform are found within every policy and economic school.[38] In fact, this position is supported in a recent Japanese bestseller. In the course of bemoaning Tokyo's (minor) trade concessions it acknowledged our current economic leverage over Japan and concluded that if we do not use it in a determined manner, we will lose it.[39]

Economic interdependence is a fact. All the industrialized countries are vulnerable up to a point. But the point differs, and the differences matter in the exercise of power. Favorable asymmetric dependencies are important in allowing for autonomous action, in reinforcing the credibility of demands and threats, and in staving off the actions of others. The United States is relatively invulnerable. It is also relatively powerful. For as shown by Albert Hirschman, the critical relations between trade and power revolve around the relative opportunity cost of change.[40] As the larger, more diverse, and more flexible economy, America can adjust more easily. It is thus less subject to external economic pressures and better able to make credible threats because the cost of their implementation is relatively low.

Compared to the European and Japanese economies, ours is more diversified, less dependent upon trade, more diversified in its exports, better supplied with natural resources, and less dependent upon crucial oil imports. Europe and Japan are without any oil. Japan has none of the natural resources, iron, bauxite, coal, and others of an industrial economy. Much of Europe's economic invulnerability stems from its integration; in its separate parts it would be decidedly vulnerable. The recent divisions over the Maastrich Treaty's provision for monetary union, Germany's 1992 interest rate increases that broke its implicit promise to support the European Monetary System, followed by Britain and Italy's beggar-thy-neighbor divergence from agreed-upon exchange rates indicate that Europe's economic integration cannot be taken for granted. Whether the problems stem from domestic economic difficulties or incompatible trading interests outside the European Community, there is now cause to worry about protecting past integrationist gains for some basic reasons stemming from the end of the Cold War.[41] At the same time the creation of the North American Free Trade Agreement can only improve upon our invulnerability.

America's financial invulnerability may appear problematic. Its relative decline is often dated from 1971, when we were "forced" off the gold standard; since then others could not be "forced" to hold onto their dollars. The unwillingness to finance the Vietnam War and the Great Society programs with current taxes and mounting balance-of-payments deficits triggered a great outflow of dollars. The financial crunch led President Nixon to close the gold window, formally ending the Bretton Woods regime, centered around our promise to exchange gold for dollars at a fixed rate.

In actuality, 1971 and subsequent developments underscore our financial invulnerability. Washington acted contrary to the interests of its chief trading partners by changing a basic rule of the international economy. It did so unilaterally, without so much as consulting them pro forma. And they still accepted the decision by holding onto their dollars. "To decide one August morning that dollars can no longer be converted into gold was a progression from exorbitant to super-exorbitant privilege; the U.S. government was exercising the unconstrained right to print money that others could not (save at unacceptable cost) refuse to accept in payment."[42] During the 1970s, it was easier to run a balance-of-payments deficit by exporting inflation. Europe and Japan's interests and actions in supporting the dollar as the world's chief currency have not waivered. An international economy operating largely in dollars continues to bolster America's financial invulnerability, to provide it with impressive structural power.

Concerns have recently appeared about America's financial vulnerability vis-à-vis Japan, of our becoming a prisoner of foreign capital. Japan has been the major purchaser of U.S. treasury bills and certificates of deposit, and of lesser concern, it has made substantial investments in American corporations and Japanese firms operating here. If the Japanese threatened to withdraw their capital, we would be exposed to rapidly rising interest rates and a drastic decline in the dollar, making for slower growth and higher inflation. Washington would also have a weak hand in tough trade negotiations with Tokyo.[43] Yet the purchase of government securities is an indication of the U.S. economy's viability and of considerable help in containing the effects of budget deficits. The introduction of Japanese capital into the manufacturing sector is a productive contribution to economic growth. Its withdrawal is not financially feasible. As for the possible threat to stop purchases of government securities, its impact on the economy is much exaggerated. In Japan's major recession of 1993–94 it sharply cut back on purchases of U.S. securities without any negative effect on U.S. interest rates or budget deficits. The threat itself would also be less than credible. To hurt the U.S. economy would be a very expensive proposition for a trade-dependent Japan, whose largest market absorbs nearly 30 percent of its exports.

As for the vulnerability concerns about the trade deficit, there are two reasons why it is not an especially persuasive measure of our economic health. How much a country buys abroad depends not just upon the attractiveness of the foreign products, but also upon its income. And America's income, its gross domestic product, has recently been rising faster than that of most other countries. Second, those who express alarm over the trade deficit of the last few years focus only on the figures that refer to goods that are traded internationally. Their significance is exaggerated by ignoring the service sector. For America's economic performance depends primarily upon the service industries, which now employ three-quarters of the workforce. Moreover, to some extent the trade imbalances were the product of discriminatory trade practices—the practices that strategic internationalism allowed for and that the concurrent foreign policy is designed to alter. Trade imbalances are also attributable to the allies' export of high-technology goods with possible military and intelligence-gathering applications to Eastern Europe and the USSR. Where Washington invariably adhered to agreed-upon strict export controls, Tokyo, Bonn, and Paris in particular allowed their nationals to export potential dual-use technologies. A 1987 study by the National Academy of Sciences concluded that export controls did not serve our economic interests. It put an annual $9.3 billion price tag on the losses suffered by the American companies who were barred from doing business with the Warsaw Pact countries. And that figure did not take into account subsequent commercial opportunities, the ways in which one-time exports make for additional long-term profits.[44]

Economic strength was powered by science and technology during the nineteenth century, very much more so during the twentieth; and it will presumably be yet more so in the next. This country's scientific and technological resources continue to translate into the discovery, design, and production of goods whose price, quality, and capabilities make them eminently competitive. And the United States is the leader in developing the cutting-edge technologies and products that will be crucial in the next century. These include computers, software, microprocessors, information storage and retrieval systems, telecommunications equipment, space satellites for exploring beneath the earth's surface, technology for deep seabed mining, as well as the biotechnology that could easily turn out to be the most crucial technology. The explanation for this preeminent position and the reason it will almost certainly be maintained is straightforward. America's scientific and technological capabilities, in numbers of Ph.D.s, their training, Nobel laureates, the number and quality of scientific journals, the size and equipment of research facilities, and registered patents, are unmatched. They cannot be matched, especially given the considerable American lead in funding industrial research and development.

IV

The previous two sections have considered the ways in which security strategies affect the behavior of others, and in turn the national welfare. Here the focus is exclusively domestic. It immediately conjures up the possible impact of defense expenditures upon economic growth rates and their certain opportunity costs, the trade-offs with public programs and private incomes. Another set of possible welfare consequences should also be considered: the political ones, the extent to which a security strategy affects space and priority on the partisan and governmental agendas that are accorded to the nation's welfare.

Insofar as defense expenditures have adverse effects upon the economy, they do so along one or more of several paths. Military spending brings on budget deficits and high interest rates that then inhibit noninflationary growth. Defense expenditures crowd out the private investment needed for short- and long-term growth. Weapons research and development draws off dollars, scientists, and engineers who would otherwise be put to more commercially productive uses in civilian research and development. Large defense budgets thereby detract from economic growth, raise unemployment levels, create inflationary pressures, and curtail international competitiveness.

The many scholars who have studied the connections between defense spending and economic performance have taken three different positions. There are those who maintain that there is a generally adverse relationship between them. Besides relying upon the economic reasoning that was just set out, their position is supported by sophisticated econometric analyses of the United States at different points in time and cross-national studies of other industrialized economies.[45] Using similar data and methodologies, other economists and political scientists conclude that military spending does not have generalized economic consequences and no generalizable one for the United States over time.[46] A third group takes a middle position. Defense spending does not regularly have negative economic consequences. Its effects are heavily dependent upon contextual conditions and substantive specifics. When these are taken into account, U.S. defense spending appears to have had something of a constraining effect from a macroeconomic perspective.[47]

This middle position is the most persuasive one. It rejects a consistent relationship between defense spending and economic performance. Adverse impacts of military spending are understood contextually, in ways that consider circumstantial variations such as size relative to GNP, the prevailing macroeconomic conditions, and the commercial applicability of military research and development. Relying upon these conventional reference points, it turns out that a national strategy promises more rapid economic growth than strategic internationalism.

As it impinges upon the economy's performance, defense spending has to "compete" with other variables, including some commonly more consequential ones, such as investment levels. Minor and moderate variations in the military budget, those that fluctuate around the 4 percent average of GNP devoted to defense since 1945, have consequently not had a significant economic impact. However, unusually high levels did have adverse consequences. During the Korean War, defense spending reached 12 percent of GNP and brought on a recession. Peaking at over 9 percent with the fighting in Vietnam, it helped fuel years of inflation and stagflation. The Reagan military buildup, with 6.5 percent of GNP devoted to defense at one point, helped raise federal budget deficits and the national debt to historic highs. A national strategy limited to 2 percent of GNP would have avoided these economic impairments. Its 50 percent reduction in average defense spending of $235 billion since 1950 totals some $6 trillion in 1990 dollars. These could have had a markedly beneficial impact on the economy's performance.

Variations in defense spending are, in effect, a form of fiscal policy. As such, the impact differs depending upon their fiscal correctness. Defense increases can inhibit economic growth by way of budget deficits, inflationary additions, and investment shortfalls. They can also accelerate growth by stimulating the economy along Keynesian lines. In reverse fashion, so too with defense cutbacks. The effects depend upon the prevailing macroeconomic conditions: Whether the economy is operating near full capacity or flagging, whether inflationary pressures are present or absent, and whether private investment capital is in large or short supply. As fiscal policy strategic internationalism then turns out to be a poor economic gamble. Levels of defense spending are shaped by security developments abroad. Their economic consequences are determined by economic developments at home. The odds of the two coming together in an economically beneficial manner are on the distinctly low side at any one point in time and over time. The national strategy's defense budgets do not make for an economic gamble. Given the exceptionally narrow security perimeter, few if any external developments call for variations in defense spending. Fiscal policy can thus be more fully shaped according to the immediately salient macroeconomic circumstances. Regularly low defense spending also allows for some greater scope in managing the economy. Countercyclical increases in governmental spending and tax reductions are less constrained than they are by strategic internationalism's far bigger military budgets.

Parts of the military budget generate future economic growth; others are unproductive. Its productivity depends upon the proportion allocated to research and development (R & D) and the degree to which military projects have commercial applications. In the 1950s and 1960s military-funded research was instrumental in developing the jet engines, computers, and semiconductors, which changed the shape of the economy. But spillover effects have declined as extraordinary military requirements in speed, precision, sensitivity, versatility, and durability moved beyond the commercial world's less stringent demands. Attaining the last 5 percent of a system's performance sometimes increased its cost by 30 percent. Compared to those of strategic internationalism, a bigger proportion of the national strategy's military budgets are devoted to R & D. It suffers minimal cuts, while 50 percent cuts are made in personnel and weapons procurement. (Weapons prototypes are built, but many or most of them can be left on the shelf absent current needs for their deployment.) With a nonengaged America having far less extensive and pressing military needs, R & D programs can be shifted in two productive directions. They can be more heavily concentrated upon the basic research that is too costly and risky to be undertaken by private firms, but that sometimes has enormous commercial payoffs. And more R & D dollars can be assigned to dual-use components and to the commercially crucial manufacturing technologies, the increasingly important assembly of components over and above the development of the components themselves. Doing so would improve "the nation's ability to produce high-quality, low-cost military equipment, in addition to contributing to the long-term competitiveness of the nation's industrial base."[48]

National security imposes material costs and opportunity costs that bear directly upon the nation's welfare. Assessing their extent begins with a simple bookkeeping question: What are the benefits that could be bought with a given number of defense dollars or in lieu of a particular military project? As a now almost quaint example, President Eisenhower elaborated upon the worth of a bomber. "The cost of one modern heavy bomber is this: a modern brick school in 30 cities. It is two electric power plants, each serving a town of 60,000 population. It is two fine, fully equipped hospitals. It is some 50,000 miles of concrete highways."[49] Since different groups would want to put defense savings to different uses, an assessment of opportunity costs is hardly this simple. A full accounting requires an answer to a difficult, perhaps unanswerable political question: Given differing interests among differentially powerful groups, what would the political process "produce" with a given reduction in defense spending?

Nothing like such an exercise is attempted here. It need not be for present purposes. The dollar differentials between the defense budgets of a national and an international security strategy are so large that they necessarily translate into a substantial welfare differential of one kind or another. With the differential coming to $115 billion in any average year and $6 trillion over the last forty-five years, it is manifestly substantial whether these amounts were devoted to publicly funded projects or tax savings, current consumption or investments. Half the 1990 defense budget, for example, might have been used to erase the budget deficit (satisfying conservatives and centrists), or to pay the bill for repairing the deteriorating stock of public housing, and to prevent privately owned low-income housing from being put to other uses (satisfying liberals). Alternatively, the savings could have paid for cleaning and modernizing the troubled nuclear weapons plants and upgrading the air traffic control system.[50] Half the approximately $230 billion defense budgets projected over the next ten years would amount to well over the estimated $1 trillion cost of fully renewing the country's physical and social infrastructure.[51]

Politically, a security strategy can cut deeply into the attention and concern afforded the nation's welfare. It may deflect and detract from a purposeful economic and social domesticism. It may also divide the country and distort the political process in ways that inhibit the pursuit of the national welfare.

A national strategy demands less space and priority on the partisan and governmental agendas than strategic internationalism. In not a single instance since 1945 have security needs lost out to domestic ones, even those with the highest priority. It has sometimes been difficult for domestic concerns to surface politically; much of the post-1945 partisan space has been filled with debates and charges about the Republicans' devotion to national strength versus the Democrats' commitment to peace. Incumbents and challengers have played down politically sensitive and contentious domestic issues in favor of national security as a valence issue, one to which no one is opposed. Presidents have been able to deflect politically inconvenient domestic needs and demands due to the appearance of globally disparate threats and their policies for meeting them. The popularity of presidents, and thus their immediate political interests and clout with Congress, has risen and fallen more in response to security-related than most domestic developments. Within the government the National Security Council, the Pentagon, the CIA, and the State Department have consistently overshadowed just about all the domestically focused agencies.

A national strategy is closely associated with and politically supported by a quiet confidence in the nation's security, the belief that just about whatever happens abroad will not prove harmful to the nation's highest values. Strategic internationalism often rests on very different political supports, those of specific fears, diffuse anxieties, and hatreds. The former does not produce, the latter can and has produced, political mistrust and bitterness at home. The various ways in which strategic internationalism has lent itself to the disfigurement of America's political ideals and government processes are the subject of the following chapter. Here it needs only to be noted that the political distortions have detracted from an economic and social domesticism in a singular manner. What was pervasive and pernicious during the McCarthy years was not uncommon and often politically potent for the next thirty to forty years. The ideas and supporters of economic and social policies involving greater governmental intervention and expenditures were associated with the enemy's socialist ideology and totalitarian regime. The early Cold War conflation of support for liberal economic and social policies with a lack of patriotism gradually diminished, yet its holdover still negated a full hearing and a fair debate on the policies' merits.

The absence of a major rival since the end of the Cold War has undoubtedly diminished the differential welfare consequences of the national and international security strategies. But in light of the strong connections between the strategic and welfare realms and the numerous welfare values that are subject to the former's influence, the differential will remain consequential.

Chapter X

LIBERAL, CONSTITUTIONAL, AND
LEGAL IDEALS

AMERICA'S IDEALS, liberal, constitutional, and legal, rank among its highest values. Taken together, they also define the national creed, what it is to be an American, our national identity. These political ideals have been articulated in the form of legally binding rules, normative declarations and exhortations, partisan promises, and national self-congratulations. They are found in the preamble to the Constitution and its Bill of Rights, the Declaration of Independence, and in countless Supreme Court decisions, presidential inaugurals, congressional addresses, national and local campaign speeches, July Fourth perorations, newspaper editorials, school texts, and scholarly books. America's liberal principles encompass democratic majoritarianism, minority rights, electoral accountability, the rights of free speech and assembly, political and economic freedom, political equality, constitutionalism, the rule of law, open debate, and the truthful conduct of governmental affairs.

A security strategy may be eminently successful in protecting our highest values from external threats yet still affect them adversely at home. At one time or another all but two or three of America's political ideals have suffered, on occasion egregiously and extensively, in the course of protecting them (and much else) from external challenges. This chapter considers the practice of national security as it affects the practice of our domestic ideals: To what extent, in what regards, through whose acts, and with how much justification?

The national strategy can do markedly more to insure adherence to and respect for America's liberal ideals than strategic internationalism, far more so than the adversarial variant. Where it does not immediately obviate, it discourages, their disfigurement. Strategic internationalism invariably has the powerful potential for and has frequently made for constitutional distortions, illegal transgressions, and political abuses. Its international ambitions and anxieties engender seductive appeals and easy justifications, political enticements and opportunities, official powers and institutional arrangements that allow the disfigurement of liberal principles. Moreover, all this is unnecessary on strategic internationalism's own doctrinal and policy premises. Neither the policy dictates and successes of strategic internationalism, nor its autonomous management by the executive, have necessitated public dissembling and deceit, constitutional and legal distortions, or intrusive and abusive internal security measures.

The first part of this chapter sets out the historical isolationists' counsels regarding the connections between the country's security policies and the practice of its political ideals. Sequentially they focused upon the republican virtues, public tolerance of political dissent, the protection of civil liberties, the preservation of economic freedoms, the government's adherence to legally and normatively binding rules, the opportunities for unfettered debate, and the maintenance of the constitutional balance of powers between Congress and the president. The isolationists' counsels and predictions regarding the alternative security strategies' benign and adverse consequences for our political practices were mostly warranted, all the more so after their political demise in the late 1940s. The second section categorizes the several dynamics by which strategic internationalism disfigured liberal political principles; none would have appeared with a national strategy in place. It then recalls the numerous occasions after 1945 on which those principles were contravened. The third section considers the principles' strategic significance. On the record there is little basis for maintaining that an autonomously managed internationalism was constricted by them; their disfigurement did not promote America's security even on strategic internationalism's own doctrinal assumptions. The chapter ends by looking into the future. Strategic internationalism will most probably continue to engender some illiberal practices. Insuring against them requires a national strategy.

I

George Washington was much exercised by the domestic divisiveness brought on by foreign involvements. The politics of the early Republic were inflamed by the European war; partisan passions divided Americans with an abiding attachment to Britain from those committed to revolutionary France. The Farewell Address begins with the warning that foreign involvements could eventuate in the decay of what later came to be called the republican virtues. When there is "Excessive partiality for one foreign nation and excessive dislike for another . . . Real Patriots, who may resist the intrigues of the favorite are liable to become suspected and odious." The valedictory concludes with the expectation that international aloofness will help "guard against the Impostures of pretended patriotism." Washington hoped that his counsels would help "control the usual current of passions," that they would "now and then recur to moderate the fury of party spirit."[1]

These concerns were widely shared by the leaders of the early Republic. Those who drafted the Constitution were keenly aware of the dangers that political-military involvements posed for the political freedoms to which they were committed. One of the only protections in the Constitution, as distinguished from the Bill of Rights, guards against unwarranted charges of treason being used to imprison those who oppose the government's policies. It was understood that national security claims could easily be used to curtail civil liberties by accusing citizens of working under the direction of a hostile foreign power. Jeffersonians discerned a historical pattern: The use of force abroad leads to the expansion of governmental power, its concentration within the executive, and the subsequent curtailment of domestic liberties. At the beginning of the nineteenth century James Madison was insisting upon what was a "universal truth" for many: "the loss of liberty at home is to be charged to provision against danger, real or pretended, from abroad."[2]

As with all other aspects of isolationist thinking, these counsels were not questioned throughout the nineteenth century. They were set aside circa 1900 as part of the justification for military might and colonial expansionism, most notably in Theodore Roosevelt's paeans to the "strenuous life" writ internationally. Only by confronting rivals militarily and taking up the burdens of governing lesser peoples could Americans maintain their vigorous character. "We cannot, if we could, play the part of China, and be content to rot by inches in ignoble ease within our borders." For Roosevelt, such an "unwarlike and isolated" America was "bound in the end, to go down before other nations which have not lost the manly and adventurous qualities. If we are to be a really great people, we must strive in good faith to play a great part in the world."[3]

Like all the isolationists who followed them, those of the early twentieth century stressed the contradictions between strategic internationalism and the preservation of our liberal political principles. They charged that the letter and the spirit of the Constitution had been warped in seizing the Philippines. President McKinley and Congress acted unconstitutionally since neither had the authority to annex territories that are not to become states, or to pass laws for colonial peoples that are not in strict accordance with those that apply within the United States. In the popular phrase of the day, "The Constitution follows the flag." Former president Grover Cleveland asserted that to abandon isolationism's landmarks would be to "follow the lights of monarchical hazards."

The arguments of the Anti-Imperialist League extended well beyond constitutional issues. For William Graham Sumner, "Expansion and imperialism are a grand onslaught on democracy . . . [They] are at war with the best traditions, principles, and interests of the American people." Militarism and expansionism favor "jobbery" in the colonies and at home. They also take "away the attention of the people from what the plutocrats are doing," which is critical since "plutocracy" is the "great foe of democracy." Carl Schurz spoke of the historical law according to which republics can avoid political decay only so long as they do not opt for the ways of empire. Senator Charles Sumner, another leader of the Anti-Imperialist League, spelled out the connections for America. Just as others who had taken up "adventurous policies of conquest or ambition," who had indulged "in the greed and lust of empire," the United States would first attempt to impose its rule on others, then be forced to arm against colonial rivals, eventuating in a large military establishment and a burgeoning government with bundles of patronage at its disposal. This concentrated power, and the exceptionally factious contention for its control, would make for a corrupt politics, displace the republican virtues, and ultimately threaten the people's liberties.[4]

Opposition to American entry into World War I came primarily from the political Left. It began with William Jennings Bryan, the leader of the Populists, resigning as secretary of state when Woodrow Wilson first moved the country toward intervention. "The great commoner" refused to lead the country into a war that was expected to engender a militarism thoroughly incompatible with popular government. Senator Robert M. LaFollette began his speech opposing Wilson's war resolution by pointing to a new "doctrine [that] has recently been promulgated by certain newspapers, which unfortunately seems to have found considerable support elsewhere, and that is the doctrine of 'standing back of the President,' without inquiring whether the President is right or wrong." Like the other Progressives he warned against the stifling of civil liberties, a theme that was amplified by Randolph Bourne, one of the few intellectuals who was not swept up by the war fever. He maintained that a holy war for democracy abroad would only result in Americans becoming more neglectful of their own democracy. It was already reeling under the onslaught of the "ideal of the state"—a state that organized "the herd offensively or defensively against another herd similarly organized." On the other side of the political spectrum, there were also fears that wartime government and politics would result in press censorship and the curtailment of civil liberties, along with distinctively conservative concerns about the loss of economic freedom and the emergence of socialism if the conflict continued for any length of time.[5]

On the left, opposition to European entanglements during the 1930s was partly prompted by a concern for the nation's liberal ideals as reinforced by the bitter memories of World War I. Civil liberties had been stifled. The Supreme Court upheld criminal penalties for those who spoke against the draft. The Sedition Act of 1918 made any word or act to "oppose the cause of the United States" a criminal offense. Eugene Debs, the Socialist Party leader, received a twenty-year sentence for speaking out against U.S. intervention. (He also received over a million votes in the

1920 presidential election while in prison.) Hundreds of thousands of isolationists, pacifists, and ethnic Germans and Irish were indicted, accused, or intimidated. Liberal isolationists expected that another war would eventuate in a worse performance, with regard to the stifling of civil liberties, the imposition of national censorship, and the intimidation of espionage laws. Robert M. Hutchins foresaw the "urge to victory annihilating tolerance." War, preparedness for war, and for some, even its anticipation, would trigger passionate fears and hatreds that would undermine liberal and humane values and their institutional safeguards. According to an editor of the *New Republic*, in hating the enemy there is "the danger of becoming like him ourselves. We shall fail to take the necessary steps at home to preserve and fulfill the democracy we are so eager to fight for." By 1940 the Roosevelt administration engaged in occasional acts of intimidation and efforts to link isolationism with Nazism.

Conservative isolationists maintained that war would provide additional reasons and excuses for governmental controls until, in former president Hoover's words, "all liberty—economic and personal and political—is lost." Whatever terms were used, "governments in business was Socialism, and government dictation was Fascism." And once in place, the regimentation of wartime would not allow for the postwar "demobilization of centralized power." Senator Robert A. Taft predicted that "war would destroy democratic government in the United States" and that it would not be restored after the war. "The additional powers sought by the President in case of war, the nationalization of all industry and all capital and labor . . . would create a socialist dictatorship which would be impossible to dissolve when the war ended."

The Republicans also opposed the manner in which Roosevelt was maneuvering the country into war. They charged him with acting unconstitutionally in taking a major step toward it. His trading of U.S. destroyers for American base rights in the British Caribbean was executed without congressional authorization, absent a precedent, and in violation of the Neutrality Act. In 1940 Roosevelt self-righteously condemned a German submarine attack against the American destroyer USS *Greer* and then called for the arming of merchant ships and a shoot-on-sight policy in the western half of the North Atlantic. His concealing the fact that the *Greer* was tracking German submarines and radioing their positions to British warships was taken as another example of presidential manipulativeness in distorting the constitutional balance. Roosevelt did obtain Congress's assent to the 1941 Lend-Lease Bill for supplying Great Britain. Taft voted against it in favor of a cash loan. The former allowed the president "to take us into the midst of the war, and once we are there his powers will be unlimited." The latter would not give him the excuse to convoy British ships carrying American supplies. Taft's basic credo was straightforward:

Only a strict constitutionalism would prevent the president from involving the United States to such an extent that the Congress might find it "impossible" to refuse a declaration of war.[6]

Between 1945 and 1950 isolationists were found almost entirely on the political right, among midwestern Republicans along with a sprinkling of southern Democrats. Their concerns for the nation's political principles were focused upon unrestrained presidential power. They opposed the Atlantic alliance (but not membership in the United Nations) because it entailed an "automatic" American involvement in the event of an attack, thereby depriving Congress of its constitutional war power. They criticized President Truman for deceiving the Senate in 1949, he having said that the ratification of NATO would not lead to the stationing of U.S. troops in Europe. Moreover, he had no right to deploy them without the congressional authorization that he did not ask for. Once they were deployed in Europe, the president alone could take us into a major war. Senate minority leader Kenneth Wherry asserted that the president's constitutional power to defend the country in the event of invasion "is being stretched into power for the President to order the armed services in peace-time anywhere in the world and into any situation. . . . If Congress surrenders its powers to determine whether American troops shall join an international army in Europe, it will have set a dangerous precedent for the President to assign American troops to any other spot on the vast perimeter of Russia."

When Truman was ordering the Korean intervention, Taft urged him to ask Congress for a joint resolution. The authority to defend South Korea would certainly have been extended to him. Taft maintained that his not requesting it was a usurpation of authority, one that "violated all the precedents which have been established as to the limitations of the President's power to make war." There is simply no legitimate "authority to use armed forces in support of the United Nations in the absence of some previous action by Congress dealing with the subject." Looking to the future, Taft argued, "If the President can intervene in Korea without Congressional approval, he can go to war in Malaya or Indonesia or Iran or South America."[7]

The historical isolationists' counsels and predictions were and were not warranted. Their catastrophic warnings of strategic internationalism eventuating in militarism, dictatorship, and the elimination of personal and economic liberties were obviously not borne out. And the disproportionate number of isolationists who were xenophobes, virulent nativists, and stark anti-Semites in the late 1930s is certainly a major blemish on the isolationist record. But it should not be sharply denigrated by focusing upon the disproportionately illiberal beliefs of isolationist supporters and leaders at one point in time. Doing so would verge on the equivalent of an ad hominem argument. The isolationists' concerns regarding governmental infringements of civil liberties, political attacks on the loyalties of those who opposed interventionist policies, and intense hostility toward those suspected of being less than fully "American" were substantially justified. (Taft was among the tiny group that opposed the internment of Japanese-Americans during World War II.) Their concerns about the constitutional deformations brought on by presidential unilateralism were partly warranted with respect to Roosevelt and fully so with regard to the Korean decision and its future import. The historical isolationists' warnings and predictions have come all too close to the mark since their political eclipse.

II

Compared to strategic internationalism's adverse effects upon America's liberal principles during the first half of the twentieth century, those of the second half were considerably more consequential. Since circa 1950 these ideals have been distorted in four distinct ways. It should be eminently clear that each would have been sharply curtailed or obviated with a national strategy in place.

Absent an effortful and often intense political-military rivalry, security issues would have been far less likely to elicit politically opprobrious domestic divisions. A strategically nonengaged America does not offer fertile ground for the unjustified, prejudicial identification of citizens, groups, and political causes with the rival and its ideology. It is not about to turn on its own out of (patriotic) hostility or loathing. In contrast, during the early Cold War years even politically quiescent individuals were defamed as "un-American" and "disloyal" for their past, perfectly legal associations. Later on many who criticized the methods of containment, particular interventions, and presidential claims and decisions had their patriotism impugned. During the Vietnam War its supporters were saddled with equally defamatory characterizations. Throughout the Cold War many on one side of the central domestic issues—those who advocated governmental economic and social interventions and expenditures—were insidiously depicted as "pink," socialist, and communistic.

Absent a security strategy that is inordinately sensitive to threats from abroad, there would have been little likelihood of exaggerating the threats from within. A nonengaged America that feels itself to be secure in the face of external developments is not given to inflating its internal security requirements. Under the auspices of strategic internationalism internal dangers were wildly exaggerated in their number and kind; not just actions, but words, beliefs, and ideas were seen to be threatening.

During the early phases of the Cold War, Congress, state legislatures and private associations abused the civil liberties of uncounted thousands of citizens in the name of national security. Throughout the Cold War presidents, executive departments, and law enforcement agencies did so. All but a truly miniscule number of suspected individuals were innocent of illegal activities.

Absent the vaunting responsibilities of a globe-straddling, interventionist strategy, the Constitution would not have been distorted. A nonengaged America does not offer the seductions, easy appeals, and problematic constitutional justifications for anything like the "imperial presidency." The framers of the Constitution arranged for checks and balances to govern the conduct of foreign affairs. In the classic modern phraseology, the Constitution presents the president and Congress with "an invitation to struggle for the privilege of directing American foreign policy."[8] But starting in 1950 the struggle was sharply diminished as Congress deferred to presidents and they deprived it of its major powers. "The Constitution could not easily sustain the weight of the indiscriminate globalism to which the Korean War gave birth. . . . [It] unbalanced and overwhelmed the Constitution." Arthur Schlesinger, Jr., was hardly alone in maintaining that the imperial presidency was the "creation of foreign policy."[9] The major impetus came from the national security side of foreign policy, with its focus upon Soviet and Communist strengths, crises, war, and preparations for war, and thus upon the need for presidential autonomy and power. Congress, the rest of the executive branch, the press, and the public were completely excluded in deciding upon each of America's major and smaller interventions.

Absent the imperial presidency and a strategy that closely links up America's immediate security with developments throughout the world there would have been little likelihood of a train of executive abuses culminating in the imperious presidency. A nonengaged America would not encourage officials to believe that their security assessments are sufficiently compelling and pressing to justify the use of thoroughly unprincipled or illegal means in implementing them. Starting in 1964—once the Cold War consensus had been shattered—presidents and executive officials avoided the struggle with congressional and political opponents by arrogantly exploiting the trust invested in them. They relied upon dissembling, preemptive actions, and quasi-legal and illegal means in subverting public accountability and the will of Congress, even contravening its legislation. Never before had unlawful and criminal acts centering around the nation's security reached the highest levels of government.

Chronologically, the post-1945 disfigurement of our liberal ideals begins with the transformation of the external communist threat into fears of an almost equally serious internal threat. It was seen to extend into the realm of ideas, beliefs, and associations. The loyalty program of 1947 led after 1950 to the frenzy and excess of McCarthyism and to its institutionalization in the bullying House Committee on Un-American Activities.[10]

The 1950 decision to intervene in Korea was the first great act of the imperial (not yet the imperious) presidency. It was the first time in U.S. history in which we went to war (formally a "police action") on a president's unilateral actions. And this in the absence of a prior commitment, on a completely unwarranted constitutional justification, and with the Congress almost certainly able and willing to authorize the intervention had it been asked to do so. After liberating South Korea President Truman adopted a second war aim of unifying the two Koreas without a congressional debate or authorization for sending American forces up the length of North Korea to the Chinese border.

Despite the resulting debacle, presidential unilateralism was not challenged over the next fifteen years. President Eisenhower authorized the CIA to engage in the covert overthrow of governments in Iran and Guatemala. Before ordering U.S. Marines into a possible combat situation in Lebanon he did ask for congressional authorization. It was quickly given in open-ended form. The "Eisenhower Mideast Doctrine" permitted the president to deploy troops as necessary, contingent only upon their request by a foreign government. President Kennedy ordered what was to be secret U.S. support for the overthrow of the Castro regime by way of the Bay of Pigs invasion. No questions were raised about his introduction of several thousand military advisers and troops into the communist insurgency in South Vietnam. None were raised when President Johnson ordered U.S. Marines into the Dominican Republic to prevent a popularly elected government from taking office.

The imperious presidency, with its manipulative to illegal actions, began in 1964 as serious doubts were being expressed about the continuing deployment of U.S. forces in Vietnam. It was turned into a massive intervention via Johnson's dissembling, if not outright deceitfulness. In 1964 he arrogantly exploited a minor incident in the Gulf of Tonkin to gain the political support and congressional authorization for waging full-scale war in South and North Vietnam.[11]

The almost unanimously approved Gulf of Tonkin resolution became legal warrant for putting and keeping up to 500,000 troops in Vietnam. The administration regularly used it to deny the need for a declaration of war or any other congressional authorization.

President Nixon's conduct and defense of the war extended to unconstitutional and criminal actions. Under his orders the air force secretly carried out the carpet bombing of Cambodia, and in 1970 he ordered a major invasion of Cambodia without consulting Congress and contrary to its clearly expressed desires for terminating the war. It was justified by the "right of the President of the United States under the Constitution to protect the lives of American men." But enemy forces in neutral Cambodia were hardly a threat to the withdrawal of American forces from Vietnam; nor were there any instances of the enemy fleeing into Cambodia with U.S. forces in hot pursuit. On Nixon's justification, the commander-in-chief powers and the constitutional conception of defensive war to repel sudden attacks against the United States were so widened that the president "could freely, on his own initiative, without a national emergency, without reference to Congress, as a routine employment of unilateral executive authority, go to war against any country that might in any conceivable circumstances be used in an attack on American forces."[12]

In 1971 the *New York Times* published the Pentagon Papers, a historical study of the Vietnam intervention that was completed in 1967. Nixon called their publication "a security leak of unprecedented proportions . . . [creating] a threat so grave as to require extraordinary actions." In response Nixon asked the courts to enjoin a newspaper from publishing the classified information in its possession, and activated a leak-plugging special investigations group within the White House. With CIA assistance, this "plumbers" unit conducted burglaries that the president justified as a "vital national security inquiry."[13]

Vietnam generated the most divisive foreign policy experience in American history and the most bitter divisions since the Civil War. The attacks upon the critics of the war included charges of personal cowardice, urgings to "love America or leave it," and accusations of abetting the killing of U.S. soldiers and America's defeat. Antiwar demonstrators were subjected to police riots and a shooting by the National Guard; antiwar groups were investigated, infiltrated, and harassed by the FBI. For their part, the critics' verbal attacks upon the Johnson and Nixon administrations were the most unremitting, vituperative, and merciless made upon any American government for its foreign policies. Public officials were besmirched as "imperialists," "pigs," "fascists," and "war criminals."

By 1973 Congress finally had enough of unbridled presidents. It passed the War Powers Resolution to ensure congressional consent to troop deployments into hostile circumstances, and it reduced presidential discretion in the conduct of covert intelligence operations with the 1974 Hughes-Ryan Amendment.

The new legislation was not challenged by the Ford and Carter administrations. Their security aims did not impel them to do so. Not so with Presidents Reagan and Bush. Their security aims were implemented via imperious actions that gutted the War Powers Resolution and contravened other legislation. The Reagan administration disfigured the country's political ideals in yet other ways.

In 1983 Reagan ordered 1,200 marines back to Lebanon for what started out as a three-nation peacekeeping operation. The marines came under sniper and artillery fire from Muslim militia units and often returned fire. About 50 of them died and another 100 were wounded. After successfully opposing congressional attempts to compel a withdrawal of the marines, Reagan attained a most favorable "compromise": The force could be kept in place for another eighteen months. This immediately became a pyrrhic success. The barracks bombing that killed 241 marines prompted Reagan to "redeploy" the force to offshore ships.[14]

On October 25, 1983 the United States invaded the island of Grenada in technical conformity with the War Powers Resolution. Reagan "consulted" Congress on the night of October 24, twelve hours before the operation was launched and after the implementing directive was signed. The prime minister of Great Britain was advised about the invasion before the president told the Speaker of the House of Representatives or the majority leader of the Senate. According to Reagan, the consultation was not more extensive because "we had little time and complete secrecy was vital to insure both the safety of the young men who would undertake the mission and the Americans they were about to rescue."[15]

The Nicaraguan story began in a constitutional manner. It ended with the exposure of the imperious presidency and the Iran-Contra scandal. In 1981 the House and Senate Intelligence Committees were informed that CIA funds would be used to finance five hundred Contras infiltrating into Nicaragua to interdict arms flows to the Marxist guerrillas in El Salvador. The Contras' actions were soon expanded to include sabotage raids on oil supplies, port facilities, and other Nicaraguan targets. Although the administration then acknowledged that the Contras' aims might be that of overthrowing the Sandinistas, *its* own purpose in aiding them only involved the interdiction of arms flows to El Salvador. The Intelligence Committees put a $24 million cap on Contra funding as of 1984, but it was readily circumvented. As late as 1985 Reagan still maintained that "we are not doing anything to overthrow the government of Nicaragua." Congress was not convinced. It passed the carefully crafted Boland Amendment to avoid any opportunity for its circumvention. The administration responded with unsavory efforts to win public support for the Contras and secret ones that negated the Boland Amendment.

With Reagan's at least implicit approval, two successive national security advisers (Robert C. McFarlane and Admiral John M. Poindexter) directed one of their staff (Colonel Oliver L. North) to circumvent the Boland Amendment and other legislation prohibiting military aid to the Contras. North coordinated the activities of the Contras, raised millions of dollars in funds from private citizens and other countries, sometimes with Reagan's help, and arranged for military supplies to reach them.

Arms were illegally sold to Iran, secretly contravening the Arms Export Control Act, which forbade sales to any country that was fostering terrorism. Millions in "profits" were then illegally funneled to the Contras. The highest CIA officials, Secretary of Defense Weinberger, and Elliot Abrams, assistant secretary of state for Latin American affairs, also helped with the supply operation while denying all before Congress in a cover-up to protect themselves and the president. The cover-up was coordinated by Edwin Meese, the attorney general, with the president's approval.[16]

The Reagan administration also distorted America's political ideals by using the national security rationale to justify domestic surveillance, intrusiveness, and harassment. In 1981 Reagan issued an executive order that authorized the CIA for the first time in its history to conduct surveillance operations within the United States of anyone who might possess "significant foreign intelligence," such as journalists, academics, and businessmen who had traveled abroad. It was also authorized to carry out undefined covert operations within the United States as long as they are not "intended" to influence "the political process, public opinion, policies or the media." The FBI's authority was expanded to gather intelligence from and on Americans at the request of the director of central intelligence and the National Security Council. The government took upon itself the right to investigate, tap telephones, and to break into offices and homes without a warrant so as to protect the country from foreign agents. None were ever discovered.[17]

Between 1982 and 1988 the FBI investigated the perfectly lawful activities of some six thousand U.S. citizens. These activities ranged from the maintenance of FBI files on a sixth-grader who wrote to foreign governments as part of a school project, to a major operation (COINTELPRO) focused upon opponents of the administration's Central American policies. Starting in 1983 the FBI carried out an intensive four-year investigation of the Committee in Solidarity with the People of El Salvador and similar groups in fifty-eight cities. Its clandestine counterintelligence efforts included the monitoring of church services, political speeches, and demonstrations of people who were not involved in, and probably were not even suspected of, any criminal or most broadly defined illegal activities. Not one such suspect was found. The FBI also harassed groups who offered sanctuary and aid to Central American refugees. *Time* magazine reported a "familiar" pattern: "desks are rifled, file cabinets searched, records apparently stolen or photocopied. Money and expensive equipment are usually left untouched. In six cities during the past 14 months, groups providing support and sanctuary for Central American refugees have been hit by burglaries, suggesting an organized campaign of harassment."[18]

President Bush continued his predecessor's policy of befriending Saddam Hussein to benefit from Iraq's balancing power vis-à-vis Iran. Saddam received financial aid and was allowed to import dual-use technologies. According to the law the latter could only be used for commercial purposes; according to the declared policy and legislation under which financial help was provided they could not be used for military purposes. There is reason to believe that Presidents Reagan and Bush, along with CIA and State Department officials, knew that the assistance that they pressed for and administered was being used by Iraq to acquire nuclear weapons and missiles. Under Reagan, many of the electronics and arms transfers were kept off the books, violating the law that Congress be kept informed. Besides pushing for yet more aid for Iraq after being alerted by his own defense and international-banking experts, Bush received a 1989 CIA report that concluded that "Baghdad has created complex procurement networks of holding companies in Western Europe to acquire technology for its chemical, biological, nuclear and ballistic missile programs." After the charges were publicly aired, the Commerce Department admitted tampering with documents to cover up the sale of military equipment to Iraq.[19] Bush acted deceptively and unlawfully to the extent that he knew of and furthered what Iraq was doing with U.S. dollars and technology.[20]

On August 2, 1990 Iraq overran Kuwait. On August 5, in the absence of any commitment to Kuwait, congressional authorization, or even consultation, Bush stated that the invasion of Kuwait "will not stand." On August 7 the secretary of defense announced that the United States would defend Saudi Arabia against Iraqi forces that were standing on its borders. Some 200,000 U.S. troops were dispatched to Saudi Arabia. Their deployment was reported to Congress within forty-eight hours as required by the War Powers Resolution. But Bush kept full control over the force by refusing to start the clock that required its withdrawal within sixty days unless congressional approval was forthcoming. The clock is to be started if and when hostilities are "imminent," but this was said not to be the case on the ground despite Bush's authorization of higher "danger" salaries for the troops. The clock should also be started if the troops are "equipped for combat," which no one denied. Yet Bush simply rejected this part of the War Powers Resolution by irrelevantly asserting that "their mission is defensive."[21] On November 8, again in a thoroughly unilateral manner, the president announced a doubling of U.S. forces to nearly half a million troops. Unless Saddam were to capitulate, this was the de facto decision for war. The huge force was out of all proportion for the defense of Saudi Arabia. It could not be left there for the year or more it would take for economic sanctions to have their possible effect on Iraq. It could not be brought home without hurting America's reputation for resolve and its standing as the collective-security organizer of the new world order.

Only in November—three months after the initial decisions—did Congress begin asking about the constitutional source from which the president drew his extraordinary power to bring the country to the verge of a major war without legislative approval. The administration offered two justifications. Bush stated that "many attorneys" had advised him that he has the "authority to fully implement the United Nations' resolutions." And Secretary of State Baker and Secretary of Defense Cheney argued that past presidents have used the armed forces on their own authority more than two hundred times. Both arguments are specious.

The resort to the UN's putative authority was already seen to be unwarranted with regard to the Korean intervention. Secretary Baker's testimony acknowledged its insignificance. He said that Security Council Resolution 678 permitted all necessary means to dislodge Iraq from Kuwait without, however, obliging the United States or the president to act upon the request for action. There are several problems with the two hundred precedents of presidential unilateralism. Congress did object to some of them. Nearly all involved clashes with pirates, cattle rustlers, brief naval actions, the protection of U.S. citizens, and other minor uses of force. Except for one, none were directed at significant adversaries or risked major casualties or wars. And as the single exception, Korea can hardly be used as a legal precedent, especially not after the enactment of the 1973 War Powers Resolution.[22]

Whether because the legal justifications did not stand public scrutiny, because Bush wanted Congress to take some political responsibility for the war, and/or because he was confident of its approval, in January 1991, five months after the first huge troop deployment, he asked for authorization under the War Powers Resolution. (Even then, on the next day, he insisted that legislative authority was unnecessary: "I don't think I need it.") The statutory authority passed in both houses of Congress, but only by a three-vote majority in the Senate. It probably would have failed except for Bush having unilaterally placed American troops in such a position that many or most believed the choices to be sorely limited. Commitments must be honored, U.S. resolve cannot be dissipated, the president's international standing should not be undermined.[23]

For all its other uses throughout the Cold War, red-baiting never found its way into the vocabulary of presidential candidates. Surely by 1992 it would seem to be a thing of the past. Yet in seeking reelection Bush tried to smear Bill Clinton's patriotism. And not just once or in one regard. Clinton was said to have absorbed European socialist ideas while studying at Oxford as a Rhodes Scholar. His health reform plan had the tenderness "of the K.G.B." Clinton was falsely accused of having written a letter in which he "condemned the whole [U.S.] military as immoral." Bush found it "impossible to understand how an American can demonstrate against his own country . . . in foreign soil" by protesting against U.S. policies in Vietnam. In any case, "It is wrong to demonstrate against your country when your country is at war." And then there is the attempt to imply something sinister about Clinton's tourist visit to Moscow while a student at Oxford. The president's deputy campaign manager allowed that Clinton might have been recruited as an "agent of influence" while in Moscow.

One of Bush's last presidential acts condoned several security-driven illegalities and generalized their justification. He pardoned former secretary of defense Caspar Weinberger and four other officials who were convicted or pleaded guilty to involvement in the Iran-Contra affair. The pardons also negated the independent counsel's full investigation of Bush's falsely denied knowledge of the Iran arms sales.[24] The principal public rationale for the pardon was the six men's "patriotism." Despite their having flaunted the Constitution, violated the laws, and covered up their actions by lies, their motivations were the primary consideration. Thus the conclusion: Officials may justifiably be able to act as they see fit in the belief that they are serving the nation's security.[25]

III

These then are the ways in which strategic internationalism has—and a national strategy would not have—directly and indirectly disfigured the Constitution, the rule of law, governmental accountability, and our political norms. But then it must be asked: What of the possible justifications of what was done in the name of national security? Executive transgressions of America's political principles in that cause, and that one alone, have often been defended. Only an autonomous executive can provide for the country's security when having to rely upon the utmost secrecy, confronting enormously powerful and insidious opponents protecting vital interests around the world, and doing so in a fast-paced and nuclear-armed world. The stakes are much too high to insist upon the consistent conformity to liberal principles. We cannot afford to adhere to them.

Starting with the defenders of Truman's unilateral Korean decision, America's security has been said to depend upon the executive, including the unfettered use and expansion of presidential powers and prerogatives, the secret operation of the national security agencies, and the conduct of internal security operations. With the country being subject to an instantaneous nuclear attack, aggressors capable of moving with great speed, and crises always on the horizon, the president must be able to act quickly and forcefully. He alone has the coordinated means, flexibility, and information to do so effectively. On certain occasions the demonstration of America's high resolve requires national unity in supporting the one President we have, who is seen to be *the* American decision maker by others. Internal security, rooting out those who are working to undermine the country from within, is always necessary, although unfortunately bound to be excessive on occasion. Congress has its national security part in helping to set the main directions of U.S. policy and in voting the necessary appropriations. But it should not strive for more than that. The legislature is an unwieldy institution, large, decentralized, and sometimes divided. Most members of Congress are uninformed about and not seriously involved with international developments, given to treating them in a parochial and partisan manner, and not to be trusted in keeping sensitive matters secret.

In principle all this may have a great deal of merit. Whether it does in practice depends upon the times and circumstances of executive autonomy and constraint. When and where were post-1945 presidents constitutionally, legislatively, or politically constrained in acting as they saw fit in dealing with conflict situations? How often were executive abuses necessary to allow for autonomous decisions, to avoid the restraints that would otherwise have been imposed upon them by public criticism, congressional opposition, and the laws? Bringing together the instances of constraint and those in which restraints were negated by the executive's transgressions should answer the crucial questions about their significance for the nation's security. Did the decisions that could not be taken detract from it? Did those that were implemented in an imperial and imperious manner promote it?

Crises, especially those that might spiral upward toward the nuclear level, entail the highest stakes. They require forceful responses, flexibility, and usually secret and rapid decisions. Presidents were, however, able to act autonomously in each of the seven confrontations with the Soviet Union—in the Middle East three times, Berlin twice, Cuba, and Afghanistan. They did not encounter any opposition to the substance of their actions or criticisms of their unilateralism: None when President Kennedy took the United States "to the brink" and President Carter threatened the use of nuclear weapons to ward off a Soviet advance beyond Afghanistan.

When strategic internationalism requires the introduction of massive U.S. forces, executive autonomy may be called for since immediate action is necessary, vital interests are at stake, and hundreds of thousands of American lives are at risk. A major intervention was deemed necessary on three occasions. The president acted unilaterally in each instance. In each he did so by traducing liberal principles. Yet his doing so to negate any political opposition to the deployment of U.S. forces was only necessary with respect to one of America's three regional wars.

Time was short with South Korean forces retreating under the on-slaught of a surprise attack, not enough to ask Congress to debate and vote on a declaration of war or the authorization to intervene. However, the exigencies did not stand in the way of consultations with the congressional leadership while working to have the UN Security Council adopt the resolution that called for intervention. Nor did an extraordinarily dubious requirement for the president to comply with the UN request for troops prevent him from asking Congress to ratify the decision immediately after its implementation. The Congress that alone has the authority to declare war was further denigrated by Truman's insistence that he would keep it informed out of political courtesy alone.

The unilateral scenario was then played out again, this time without any time constraints, in deciding to send UN-U.S. forces north of the 38th parallel. The executive alone transformed a defensive war into one that sought to unify the two Koreas. There was no doubting Congress's readiness to authorize the original intervention and the war's expansion. It was shocked by North Korea's blatant aggression, alarmed by its coming on the heels of the Soviet Union's complete domination of Eastern Europe, and convinced that North Korea was acting at Moscow's behest. When U.S. forces approached the 38th parallel, North Korea's were in full retreat, General MacArthur's Inchon landing caught them from behind, and China was not expected to intervene. Truman did not think that a request for congressional authorization would have been denied. The imperial presidency was unnecessary at the time of its inception.

Bush's imperial negation of the War Powers Resolution was similarly uncalled for by events abroad or circumstances at home. He could almost certainly have moved with the same despatch and then along the exact lines that he saw fit had he invoked it at the outset as required, rather than five months later. On the day of the Iraqi invasion of Kuwait, even before Bush's declaration that it "would not stand," Congress voted a resolution that condemned the attack. There was no criticism of the deployment of 200,000 troops to defend Saudi Arabia. Once the sixty-day limit was reached that would have required legislative authorization for a continued deployment, Congress would almost certainly have done so and most probably authorized the doubling of the U.S. force. Although numerous members of Congress objected to the unilateral, high-handed manner in which Operation Desert Shield was expanded into Operation Desert Storm, hardly any took exception to the expansion itself. In the weeks before the war Congress was divided on whether the forces should be used or remain in place until economic sanctions against Iraq could compel a withdrawal from Kuwait. Bush was correct in believing that Congress would vote him the War Powers authority to direct the force as he saw fit; for he had already committed the United States to Kuwait's liberation, and 400,000 troops could not remain in place for the duration.

Unlike the other two regional wars, the massive escalation of the Vietnam War and its subsequent expansion into Cambodia would almost certainly not have occurred absent imperious abuses. Prior to the Gulf of Tonkin incident there were serious doubts and mounting criticism of the U.S. involvement. In the 1964 presidential campaign both Johnson and Barry Goldwater won only plaudits for their promises to end it. Johnson was elected in part because of his greater dovish credibility on this issue. Thus without the dissembling and possible deceit that went into his presentation of the Gulf of Tonkin resolution, most probably nothing like 500,000 troops would have been sent to Vietnam. The widespread opposition that followed revelations of Nixon's unlawful bombing of neutral Cambodia indicates that it could not have been openly undertaken. Given Congress's express intent to end the war and the storm of opposition elicited by its expansion via the Cambodian invasion, it could only have been ordered in an imperious manner.

Besides crises and major wars, an effectively managed internationalism is thought to require executive autonomy in less dire but still demanding and crucial conflictual circumstances. Military and covert means are so sensitive that they frequently require secrecy, "deniability," and quick, possibly unpopular decisions. Presidents must be able to deploy and use U.S. forces and supply military aid in deterring aggression, defeating insurgencies, destabilizing hostile governments, countering terrorism, and rescuing U.S. nationals. Even with the net cast this widely, presidents were legislatively prohibited from acting as they saw fit on only three occasions since 1945. In 1973 Congress cut off all funds for U.S. forces in and military aid to the countries of Southeast Asia. In 1975 it prohibited any support for the anti-Marxist guerrilla movements operating in southern Africa. And in 1985 it cut off all direct and indirect assistance to the Nicaraguan Contras. In three secondary cases political and legal constraints were negated by imperial and imperious behavior—Reagan's continuing deployment of the marines in Lebanon, the invasion of Grenada, and aid to the Contras.

Two conclusions follow from this review. The post-1945 executive has had enormous constitutional, legal, and political latitude in preserving the nation's security. Presidents did not face any constraints in dealing with confrontations. They could have ordered and directed two of the three major interventions while abiding by the nation's political principles. They were legislatively prohibited from acting autonomously only on three occasions. Besides Johnson and Nixon's Vietnam decisions, on three other occasions they could only act as they saw fit by deforming the nation's laws and norms. On this record there is little basis for maintaining that the autonomous practice of strategic internationalism was or would have been substantially constricted by full respect for the nation's political principles.

The other conclusion is yet more telling. The restraints imposed upon the president did not detract from America's security; their transgressions did not promote it. Of the eight instances of congressional restraint and potential constraint, only the massive escalation in Vietnam was seen to be crucial to U.S. security. And that war inflicted immediate losses in lives and casualties without promoting our subsequent security. Thus the supposed incompatibility between the preservation of America's security and adherence to its political principles rests on only four, manifestly secondary to tertiary instances in which they were actually incompatible: Congress's prohibition of support for anti-Marxist guerrillas in southern Africa and Nicaragua, the continued deployment of twelve hundred marines in Lebanon, and the invasion of miniscule Grenada. In all but the first instance the War Powers Resolution was subverted.

A comparable conclusion also applies to the countless citizens whose civil liberties and due process rights were ignored, denied, and trampled in the name of national security. Very little needs to be said on this score given the patent absence of a justifiable security connection. America has had its few spies in and around the nuclear laboratories. But beyond that, where and how many? The extensive fears of subversive threats and disloyal actions—no less disloyal beliefs—fall between the hard to credit and the ludicrous. It is hard to exaggerate the disproportionality between what was done against so many and the emptiness of the charges and suspicions during the late 1940s and 1950s. The extent of the internal security threat in the 1960s and 1970s is apparent in the conclusion of a 1976 General Accounting Office report. On reviewing nineteen thousand open investigative cases it found that the subjects under surveillance were proposing or showing some potential for violence in twenty-three. When asked, the FBI was unable to provide Congress with any evidence that it had prevented a single act of violence through its surveillance programs.[26] In the 1980s the hundreds of federal agents who observed, investigated, and intruded upon the groups that opposed Reagan Central American policies did not find a single person to indict.

IV

Looking to the future, what can be said about the alternative security strategies' consequences for the gaps between America's political ideals and their practice? Does their preservation and rejuvenation depend more or less upon the adoption of a national strategy? Despite the past transgressions stemming from strategic internationalism, could it be conducted in a very different, liberally consonant manner? That it could and should be is suggested by what was just shown. Conformity with liberal principles does not contradict strategic internationalism's largely autonomous, time-constrained, and effective implementation by the executive. Nor do political ideals at all stand in the way of providing for the country's internal security. However, the liberal conduct and consequences of strategic internationalism depends upon one or another basic changes about which there is little or no reason to be optimistic. Only a national strategy or a close approximation to it promises to close the gap between principles and practices, ideals and institutional arrangements.

The post–Cold War world currently is and looks like it probably will continue to be far less threatening to America's security. If so and if recognized as such, strategic internationalism is unlikely to eventuate in more than occasional, probably minor political and official transgressions. Less anxious security concerns, less effortful security policies, less demanding decisional requirements, and less opposition to less costly efforts—these should sharply circumscribe its illiberal propensities.

On the other hand, the post–Cold War environment might not turn out to be all that much safer. Were there much greater safety it would not necessarily be interpreted as such. For relatively benign developments and patterns are not regularly recognized as such when viewed through strategic internationalism's doctrinal prism—its greatly magnified security sensitivities and inordinate standards of clear and sufficient security. A strategically engaged America may continue to come fairly close to expecting a world of its own choosing in security terms, concomitantly striving to remedy the shortfalls. There is also the short post–Cold War record to date. The one instance of a perceived security challenge, Iraq's invasion of Kuwait, called forth the usual behavior of the imperial presidency. Nor does the widespread condemnation of an earlier McCarthyism preclude the future abuse of civil liberties and the intimidation of citizens in the exercise of their political freedoms—when there is an "enemy" abroad.

Having been created and succored by strategic internationalism, the imperial presidency is not about to wane on its own—at least not without America's substantial strategic disengagement. Presidents will strive mightily to guard and exercise their post-1945 imperial prerogatives. For Congress to assert its constitutionally mandated place in the national security arena, concomitantly reigning in executive excesses, it must obviously have some strong incentives to do so. On most accounts of congressional politics—its preeminently local focus—they are decidedly unlikely. National security is the ultimate collective good, incapable of being disaggregated into the divisible goods of fifty states and nearly five hundred congressional districts. The possibilities of "credit-taking" legislation are minimal among 536 legislators. They are yet lower with regard to security issues. These are usually of less interest than domestic ones to constituents and feature preemptive presidential activity. Congress focuses upon the less divisive details of defense spending and cost overruns while ignoring issues of grand (and not so grand) political and military strategy. Reelection tactics often involve the avoidance of responsibility, which is not at all that difficult considering the president's high visibility in the security realm. Members of Congress can remain on the sidelines; after policy success or failure becomes evident, they can try to take some credit for the former and criticize the administration for the latter.

On the other hand, most members of Congress are more than reelection machines. They also have a sense of public responsibility, a conception of Congress as a coequal branch of government, and a commitment to the institution. The making of good public policy depends first of all upon their reelection. As committee members they have individual and corporate incentives for asserting themselves, as well as considerable powers, expertise, and large staffs with which to do so. A sizable number have an abiding interest in the conduct of foreign and security policy. Considerable oversight and assertiveness vis-à-vis the executive characterize the activities of the various foreign affairs, armed forces, and intelligence committees, as well as the security-focused subcommittees on appropriations and governmental operations. And since 1973 it has passed and strengthened framework legislation for regulating presidential actions involving military interventions, covert operations, executive agreements with foreign governments, and arms sales.

Other than in the War Powers Resolution, however, the 1970s framework legislation involves only information and communications, notifications and consultations. The "hard" requirement of prior authorization is notable for its complete absence. Legislative regulation of troop deployments, covert operations, executive agreements, and arms sales only requires the president to provide Congress with information about impending and current executive actions. He must variously consult with, report to, and send his findings to Congress publicly, or secretly to the leadership and Intelligence Committees. Although these requirements can deter executive excesses in anticipation of congressional and public criticism and serve as a component of political accountability, they are far from sufficient. Much of the information is to be held in high secrecy, in some instances it is impossible to monitor its accuracy, some actions do not obligate full disclosure of the surrounding circumstances, and not all that much is required in the way of explicit and truthful justifications with which to assess the decisions.

Although not as extensive as those that Congress suffered at the hands of the Johnson and Nixon administrations, the Reagan adminstration's abuses were certainly well above average. Here too Congress's response underscores the likely limits of its future actions. It passed one statute, the 1990 Intelligence Authorization Act. Its passage was prompted by the retroactive Reagan finding—signed fully one year after the fact—that authorized the secret arms sales to Iran, and to add insult to injury, supposedly allowed the use of governmental agencies and "private" and "unappropriated" funds for covert operations that were banned by Congress. The legislation involved only a marginal strengthening of the reporting requirements for covert action. And it still did not survive Bush's unpersuasive veto message. The act would have revised current statutes by requiring the president's written finding prior to all covert operations, the identification of all those within and outside the United States who are involved in it, and congressional notification before the operation is launched. The act made an exception for "extraordinary circumstances," like the rescue of U.S. hostages, in allowing the president "a few days" in which to inform the Intelligence Committees. But even this single notification reform was too much for Bush. According to the veto message it would somehow infringe upon the president's authority and "impair any Administration's effective implementation of covert action." The one specific criticism referred to the required congressional notification of U.S. requests for help from third parties: It could have "a chilling effect" on sensitive discussions with foreign governments. But this objection ignored a letter from the Intelligence Committees stating that preliminary discussions with third parties do not constitute such a request.[27] And Congress let the veto stand.

Neither circa 1970 nor 1990 did Congress even consider anything like a comprehensive framework that would facilitate, no less insure meaningful executive-legislative collaboration. Such a framework need not at all impair presidential provision for the nation's security or move him from the head of the national security table. According to one design, Congress would unify existing security statutes in a single charter, organize a small consultative group to advise and work with the president, establish its own legal adviser to oversee the national security apparatus, legislate rules to allow for "fast-track" responses to executive initiatives, and change the ways in which its appropriation powers are used so as to insure greater executive-legislative collaboration.[28] Without something on this order most attempts at congressional assertiveness will be too little or too late—and both in the case of presidential announcements that effectively commit the United States unless denied by Congress on pain of demonstrating our unreliability and perhaps weakness.

On this analysis only a national strategy or a close approximation to it can do more to insure that America's governing principles and political norms will be respected and preserved.[29] To view external developments through strategic internationalism's exceptionally sensitive, high-magnification lenses is likely to set up a replay of past transgressions. There are no visible domestic changes in the offing that indicate something other than a replay.

Chapter XI

AN AMERICAN FOREIGN POLICY

THIS BOOK has assessed the performance and promise of alternative security strategies as they bear upon the nation's security and extrasecurity values. This final chapter addresses the strategies' political attractiveness. No matter how well designed, how intellectually persuasive a security strategy and its attendant foreign policy may be, it must be compatible with the predominant foreign policy culture to be widely embraced and to enjoy support in the face of occasional setbacks. Strategy and politics are brought together here by way of the country's foreign policy culture, its externally focused behavioral dispositions. They encompass the generalized attitudes—values, norms, beliefs, and expectations—that speak to its position in the world, external goals, and the means for their realization. With cultural patterns constituting pervasive influences, laying the alternative foreign policy designs alongside them should reveal a great deal about the latter's current appeal, political potential, and effective management.

America's foreign policy culture is inordinately demanding in being deeply contradictory. The first half of this chapter interprets it in terms of four cultural dualisms. Analyzing the fit between policy and culture in the second part leads to this conclusion: A national strategy embedded within the concurrent design matches up sufficiently well with the country's predominant external orientations for it to be portrayed as America's characteristic foreign policy. At the least, the design is markedly more congruent with the political culture than the alternative foreign policy configurations—those of historical isolationism and realist and liberal internationalism in their adversarial and conciliatory modes. Insofar as both parts of the chapter are persuasive the concurrent foreign policy can be depicted as *the* American foreign policy.

I

Our foreign policy culture features a truly dialectical display of attitudinal polarities shifting over time in their leanings, dispersed among different parts of the population, and commonly embedded within the same individuals at the same time—with and without a suspension of their contradictions. There are the dualisms of isolationist domesticism and internationalist activism, the imperatives of realism and idealism, a sense of extraordinary power and the anxieties of weakness, expectations of consistent success and its achievement at no more than modest costs.

The grip of this culture may be all the greater insofar as it is reinforced by the dualistic form and substantive content of some pervasive domestic orientations. America's principal cultural interpreter was most struck by the enormous emphasis placed upon the accumulation of material goods, the relentless strivings and competitiveness behind their acquisition. Yet alongside this driving worldly culture Tocqueville also observed outbursts of evangelical fervor, religious spirituality, and periodic moral enthusiasm.[1] Some 150 years later Michael Kammen entitled his study of the country's historical and cultural roots *People of Paradox*. In the concluding chapter he summarizes the several dimensions of our "dualistic state of mind," including those with a foreign policy focus. "Americans have managed to be both puritanical and hedonistic, idealistic and materialistic, peace-loving and war-mongering, isolationist and interventionist, conformist and individualist, consensus-minded and conflict prone."[2] Louis Hartz portrayed American exceptionalism in terms of the "liberal tradition."[3] Rooted in domestic conditions and developments, it also has distinct and distinctive externally focused meanings. In severely encapsulated form, the tradition is characterized by the beliefs that "Change and development [abroad] are easy, all good things go together, radicalism and revolution are bad, distributing power is more important than accumulating power."[4] That all good things go together helps gloss over the contradictions among and within each of the dualisms. Samuel Huntington's cultural interpretation focused on the country's political ideals. Inordinately high expectations have regularly left great gaps with their institutional realization.[5]

Nearly all interpretations of the foreign policy culture highlight the isolationism-internationalism dualism.[6] On the one hand, military, political, and idealistic involvements have been considered superfluous, ineffectual, counterproductive, much too costly in blood and treasure, and outrightly dangerous. Their rejection was greatly reinforced by the powerful pulls of nationalism and unilateralism, continental development and economic growth, the domestic demands of major social and economic reforms, and a life of private normality and public virtue. On the other hand, with the emergence of great power the thoroughly activist culture has directed the country's energies far beyond the homeland. We have defined our security interests in a far-flung and then globally indivisible manner, taken the lead in trying to create a better world politically and materially, and engaged in exercises of national power, preeminence, and pride.

The isolationist-internationalist dualism has been depicted throughout this book. Not surprisingly, the collapse of the Soviet threat has elicited two opposite reactions among internationalists. Some formerly ardent cold warriors have embraced the now affordable "selectivity" principle in security matters, jettisoning the "unusual burdens" of the past to return to "normal times." Among the other turns toward isolationism that were noted in chapter 1, public opinion polls showed large majorities—74 percent in one instance—favoring considerably fewer foreign involvements so as to concentrate on domestic problems.[7] Other internationalists saw a safer environment and more opportunities within the UN for embarking upon liberal and humanitarian projects. According to one poll, 63 percent of the public favored an activism that is at least as extensive as that of the past, and in the wake of the Gulf War, 80 percent said that "the United States and the United Nations should take clear action to stop" dictators who are engaging in "rogue behavior." They are to be stopped from acquiring weapons of mass destruction, unnecessarily undertaking a major arms build-up, sponsoring terrorism, violating fundamental human rights, invading others, and supporting U.S. enemies.[8] For some internationalists the containment strategy was immediately replaced by strivings to insure across-the-board primacy vis-à-vis Japan and Germany into the future.

The realist-idealist polarity—the "fatal dualism" between power and morality[9]—cuts across the previous one. While idealism has engendered liberal activism, realism has fostered full-blown isolationism as well as strategic internationalism. Realism is exclusively concerned with national power, its constant preservation, exquisitely balanced calibration, regular exhibition, and often its extension. International anarchy, along with the will to power of some states and the defensive efforts of others, makes for an inherently dangerous world in which the only help is self-help. Thus the neglect of power, especially its overextension and "sentimental" expenditure in idealistic projects, is to court an immediate or not too distant security deflation. Idealism rejects this self-centered geopolitical exclusivism. The United States as a moral entity invariably has "duties beyond borders" to further the basic well-being of others. They are valued as human beings. A country with the ability to help is ethically bound to do so. Actions that have good outcomes are morally obligatory, especially on the part of a country that was founded on and continues to be governed according to the principles of universalized liberties and natural rights. Where other states have interests, America has interests and reponsibilities.[10] Realpolitik is not just unacceptably amoral because it has no higher aim than self-preservation. It is positively immoral when the dictates of power politics subvert international peace, human rights, democracy, self-determination, and international law.

Hans Morgenthau's *Politics among Nations*, whose first edition appeared in 1948, became the realist classic for the Cold War generation. A

few years later *In Defense of the National Interest* relied upon its guidelines in interpreting U.S. foreign policy as a "struggle" between opposing
conceptions of power and morality. "The illusion that a nation can escape, if it wants to, from power politics into a realm where action is
guided by moral principles rather than by considerations of power is
deeply rooted in the American mind. Yet it took more than a century for
that illusion to crowd out the older notion that international politics must
necessarily be defined in terms of power."[11] In George Kennan's *American Diplomacy, 1900–1950*, a new moralism and legalism were seen to
be predominant in these years.[12] Rather than being guided by a clear-eyed
understanding of the national interest, the Spanish-American War and
the Open-Door Policy were undertaken for "subjective and emotional
reasons" expressed in "high-minded and idealistic" terms. We went into
two world wars crusading against evil and then became disillusioned in
the face of intractable international realities. For Kennan the idealistically
framed globalism of the Truman Doctrine was far too undiscriminating
in its goals, scope, and means.

Morgenthau and Kennan strove to overcome the antinomies of power
and morality given the former's empirical and prescriptive centrality.[13]
No realist struggled as hard as Reinhold Niebuhr. In *Moral Man and
Immoral Society* the protestant theologian elaborated upon the differences between individual ethics and those of the group. He dissected the
"twilight zone" of morality and politics where national loyalty, patriotism, and the dichotomy between us and them become enduring obstacles to moral behavior abroad.[14] In the midst of World War II Niebuhr
portrayed Americans as naive "children of light" who would have to
learn some of the "wisdom of the children of darkness but remain free of
their malice."[15]

Niebuhr had worried about America not having the resolve to oppose
fascism; he defended the Truman Doctrine and containment. Yet he was
also duly suspicious of the disavowal of America's own will to power,
condemned its arrogant use, and exposed its evil consequences. He became alarmed by the expansion of the Korean War, the arms race, anticommunist messianism, and the "myth of national purity." The way in
which the Cold War was being prosecuted in the 1950s could bring about
"a dissipation of the Christian faith and its corruption by the mood of
self-congratulation and complacency to which a rich and powerful nation
is tempted, particularly when it is forced to engage in long conflict with a
foe, whose vices seem to prove our virtues."[16] The Vietnam War was
Niebuhr's most despairing time, as captured by this depiction of his
thinking: "To lose South Vietnam could possibly encourage further communist aggressions; to fight a war with no vision of democratic victory
would compromise the ideology of the Cold War and leave the country a
political disaster. It was a dilemma of power and morality, the will to

dominate and win and the desire to uphold values without which victory would be a squalid sham. . . . Too proud to admit a tragic mistake, America proceeded to bomb its way out of a situation it had not even reasoned itself into."[17]

Besides struggling with the fatal dualism—as with President Carter having to forgo his initial aspiration to turn the cause of human rights into the "soul" of U.S. foreign policy—it has also been set aside in different ways. The isolationists rejected the need for choice. Liberalism abroad could best be furthered by America retaining its political virtues at home and serving as a model for others. Theodore Roosevelt's determined insertion of the nation into great-power politics, Dean Acheson's insistence upon the primacy of means over ends, and Richard Nixon and Henry Kissinger's single-minded geostrategic calculations denied just about any room for principled considerations. Woodrow Wilson and Ronald Reagan had little trouble in simply equating morality with American power, the creed of "national innocence." Wilson asked "Am I an idealist?" and replied, "That is how I know that I am an American." His conflation of American power and morality was evident in urging intervention in Europe both to uphold our rights on the high seas and to "make the world safe for democracy." When the Navy bombarded and occupied Veracruz in 1914, he maintained that "the United States had gone to Mexico to serve Mankind." Reagan could not have expressed it better in justifying our efforts to unseat the Sandinista government. On the day that the administration rejected the World Court's jurisdiction regarding the CIA mining of Nicaragua's harbors he proclaimed Law Day in America, saying that "without law, there can be no freedom, only chaos and disorder."[18]

Writing of America's conduct of the Cold War, William Pfaff underscored its intellectual and moral confusion.

> Americans remain moralists, "globalists" in their fashion, prisoners of the progressive tradition, even as they chant the glories of American nationalism. We are not philosophical realists, willing to leave Russians, Nicaraguans, Cubans—or Afghans or Poles—alone if they would leave the United States alone. We are not philosophical pessimists, prepared to argue that international life is mean, and foreign policy a way to make the best of bad choices—in Michael Oakeshott's famous metaphor, to keep afloat in "a boundless and bottomless sea [where] there is neither harbor for shelter nor food nor anchorage, neither starting place nor appointed destination." There is an intense and even painful dissociation of the mind and moral sensibility from action, and the result is an attempt to escape.

Looking to the future, Pfaff discerns a possible solution in reverting to our "natural condition, which is isolationism. . . . Isolationism could be good for the country. The United States might find itself again."[19]

For some 150 years America's vision of its power and security was one of confident sufficiency, allowing for involvement in two world wars without fear, largely by choice rather than because of need. Since 1945 these beliefs have given way to a bifurcation tending toward the extremes, often among the same people. The country has been impressed with itself as history's most powerful, richest, technologically advanced nation, as "number one" in the world, the centerpiece of the international economy, straddling the globe as one of only two and now the only superpower. U.S. predominance has been taken for granted. Others have been expected to concede by right; we alone have the power to lead, and our leadership is imbued with the common interest. Despite the belief in America's relative economic decline and the now diminished importance of its military long suit, it is still "bound to lead."

At the same time we have experienced immediate weakness. After 1945 history caught up with a country that had previously been impregnable, barely challenged within and around its domain, and inordinately well endowed with power resources. It took up the internationalist cudgels without recognizing, no less assimilating, the fact that the presence of a powerful rival is the norm for any strategically engaged state. Sharp doubts, diffuse anxieties, and pronounced fears have consequently been expressed about the nation's position in the world, military capabilities, credibility, ideological appeal, and resource dependencies. Nixon's depiction of a hamstrung America as a "pitiful giant" had considerable resonance. That of an anxious, sometimes fearful giant was far closer to the mark over the course of the Cold War. Exaggerating somewhat, much of the country assumed itself to be safe only when most of the world was like America. This condition not having begun to be realized, the disparities have been turned into inflated threats despite both the power to ward them off and the security to ignore them.

The self-confident side of the "arrogance and insecurity dualism"[20] is well known. The depth and frequency of the weakness side has been much less appreciated. The "loss" of China in 1949 helped generate the most pervasive security fears in the nation's history, despite its manifest military and economic impotence vis-à-vis the United States. Besides China's expansionist threat, apprehensiveness was focused upon Marxist ideas. With these having begun to "invade" the homeland itself, came the fearful and fear-exploiting McCarthyism that thoroughly defaced the nation's politics. America saw itself as six feet tall, but during much of the Cold War the Russians were seen to be yet taller. The marked superiority of the U.S. position was not appreciated even though it was at least as advantaged as the USSR on all but two measures of potential and actual power, decidedly so on most of them. The criteria included strategic weaponry and invulnerability, force-projection capacities, naval power, the number, reliability, and military and economic might of allies, ideological appeal, international economic leverage, agricultural self-sufficiency, industrial output, economic growth rates, scientific and technological capacities, and the legitimacy and internal security of the regime. The Soviet Union was only advantaged in the size of its land forces and self-sufficiency in natural resources.

It is not necessary to be especially dovish in order to recognize the nation's insecure overreactions to Soviet nuclear advances. Despite our strategic superiority at the time of three of them and parity in the other, they triggered four "periods of peril": when the USSR exploded its first nuclear device, developed long-range bombers and thermonuclear weapons, deployed intercontinental ballistic missiles, and attained a hard-target-kill capability against our land-based missiles ("the window of vulnerability"). Robert Johnson identified the commonalties in our reactions. "A period of peril begins with Soviet acquisition of a new technological capability which creates a potential vulnerability for U.S. strategic forces at a date that is typically near at hand. . . . The emerging U.S. vulnerability is seen as undermining the American deterrent and as producing a general decline in American power if it is not promptly remedied. Because they will have checkmated our nuclear deterrent, the Soviets, it is assumed, will be emboldened, during the period of vulnerability, to take actions that previously involved unacceptable risks. Such actions may include surprise nuclear attack, employment of coercive diplomacy including nuclear blackmail, and the direct or indirect use of conventional force."[21] In a parallel vein, the launch of Sputnik in 1957 prompted anxieties about the Soviets' scientific-technological superiority, despite America's earth satellite being launched only a few months later.

The country's inordinate anxieties are clearly highlighted in comparative perspective, in contrasting America's reactions with those of its allies to the same security threats. Although they were much more closely exposed and vulnerable to communist expansionism, we have regularly been more concerned about its likely emergence and the power behind it. The "devil theory" of China was widespread in America during the 1950s and early 1960s, although barely known in Japan, South Korea, Pakistan, and Southeast Asia. It took years for Washington to pressure and cajole the Organization of American States into "recognizing" the Cuban threat under Castro. During the Vietnam War the nearby SEATO countries were less nervous about the threat to their security than was Washington for theirs and ours. Marxist Nicaragua and the radical insurgents in El Salvador prompted considerably more anxiety in America than among bordering and nearby Mexico, Costa Rica, Panama, Colombia, and Venezuela. Though the massive Warsaw Pact tank forces were positioned almost right up against Western Europe, in every disagreement about the danger of an invasion the NATO allies regarded it with greater equanimity. And we were consistently more anxious than the Europeans about the spread of neutralism, Soviet advances in the Third World, and the risks to Middle Eastern oil supplies.

Inordinate insecurities have also appeared outside the Cold War context. The long hostage crisis in which the lives of some fifty American diplomats were in the hands of Iranian "students" was sorely frustrating. Yet it also elicited an overreaction, a widespread sense of America's global weakness and decline, even more so than the Soviet invasion of Afghanistan that also occurred in 1979. Within and around the Bush administration, the newfound security stemming from the Cold War's demise was immediately followed by new concerns: the vague threats of instability, unpredictability, great uncertainty and latent danger, and vacuums of power. In Bush's words, "The enemy is unpredictability. The friend is stability." While some officials were concerned with a possible Japanese challenge to America's political-military primacy, others fretted that Japan would not become sufficiently activist to fill a looming power vacuum in East Asia.

According to the fourth dualism, the realization of the country's external goals is not only taken almost for granted. Their achievement is anticipated without having to bear more than modest costs—in blood, treasure, the absence of trade-offs among policy objectives, even in patience and understanding. What has proved itself domestically, and the collective self-confidence reinforced by those proofs, has been generalized far beyond the water's edge. With America having been "born free" and fairly easily and having enjoyed political stability and democracy, the continental expanse having proved to be conquerable and malleable, and national energies, innovativeness, and know-how having created unrivaled wealth, why should our external aims be any the less realizable or their realization more burdensome? Unlike the other dualisms, this one is not an antinomy, but rather the unrealistic expectation that America is to have it all, "the illusion of omnipotence" at a low price.

For the isolationist consensus of the nineteenth century and its post-1900 continuities the United States could fulfill its security, economic, and ideal interests with barely any external efforts. Wilson's Fourteen Points for securing peace, democracy, and self-determination in Europe and his collective-security solution for ending all wars were put forth almost entirely on promises alone. Analyses of international conditions and processes, their susceptibility to radically innovative principles, of the availability of the necessary will and power—these were most striking in their paucity. Wilson and many Americans simply put their trust in the benign aims, the long-run interests and thinking, and the unanimity of the major powers at the League of Nations. During both world wars it was widely believed that with total victory a long peace would arrive bolstered by international arrangements for disarmament, the outlawry of aggression, and collective security.

The first half of the Cold War witnessed a much-inflated confidence in simple economics. The Marshall Plan was eminently appropriate for Western Europe's physical and political restoration; the necessary structural and cultural conditions were already in place. But the economic and technical assistance rationale was then simply extended to Asia and later to Africa and Latin America. It was also very much extended on the cheap, since just about all the recipients received miniscule aid packages. Assuming change and development to be easy and that all good things go together, U.S. aid was to generate economic growth, which would then make for political stability, democracy, and social reform. These happy outcomes would in turn denude communism and radicalism of their appeals and cement alliance relations with the United States.[22] During the second half of the Cold War exaggerated expectations were placed upon eminently cheap, largely technical arms control accords. Their advocates assumed that agreements, in some measure negotiations alone, would have a substantial to decisive impact upon the underlying motivations, and conduct of a global ideological-political-military rivalry. Reassurance and good relations with the Soviet Union were to derive from mutually agreed upon high weapons ceilings that were usually in line with the superpowers' existing strategic armories and near-term plans. The sporadic disarmament and antinuclear movements supported radical solutions, but these were based solely upon vain hopes and the fear of a nuclear apocalypse.

Several administrations led us into four military actions and one tried to undertake a fifth. But what of the reactions to them? South Korea was successfully defended; starting in 1951 an "active defense" posture minimized U.S. casualties. Yet the standoff along the 38th parallel and the drawn-out peace negotiations elicited enormous disillusion and a record low level of public support for President Truman. That reaction was a factor in the Eisenhower administration turning to the threat of massive retaliation "at places and times of our choosing." We were not to become involved in another bloody and costly land war; nuclear weapons were relatively cheap and offered far more bang for the buck.

Shock, anger, and a sense of betrayal appeared well before the defeat in Vietnam was imminent. Nor were these reactions mitigated by President Johnson's decisions not to mobilize the reserves after the Tet offensive, not to cut back on the Great Society programs, and not to call for a tax increase to finance the war. The Reagan administration won loud plaudits for the invasion of Grenada, success being immediate and almost costless in lives. But at the height of his popularity the "great communicator" only won the support of a quarter of the population for some kind of limited intervention in Central America. Concerns about another Vietnam were too pervasive despite Reagan's stressing the proximity of the Marxist threat; the opposition to Contra aid alone was substantially prompted by the possibility of its leading us into another Vietnam. Mindful of the country's strong aversion to any less than immediately successful military action, Caspar Weinberger, Reagan's otherwise thoroughly hawkish secretary of defense, publicly listed the stringent criteria that would all have to be met before he would recommend an interventionist course.

There was an alternative to the land war against Iraq. It would most probably have attained all of America's avowed objectives except for the restoration of Kuwait's independence and Saddam Hussein's demise. The containment alternative would have included a continuing international economic embargo against Iraq, stationing a small U.S. land force and strike aircraft in Saudi Arabia, positioning missile-firing cruisers and aircraft carriers within striking distance of Iraq, and if necessary, having them destroy its missile and emerging nuclear capabilities. Such a policy was partly or largely rejected by the Bush administration for fear of popular impatience with a protracted conflict. Referring to this decision, it was noted that "The American people had never been happy with the policy of [long-term] containment, even when applied to the Soviet Union. That policy ill-fitted the national character, as its critics so often pointed out. If containment was accepted during the cold war, it was largely because the alternatives (often characterized as suicide or surrender) appeared so dangerous." At the end of the Gulf War, the concern for American casualties was of "critical importance in the decision to stop short in American war aims and to refuse (behind the shield of a disfigured doctrine of 'nonintervention') the arduous burdens of pacification."[23]

These four dualisms capture America's characteristic—and probably distinctive—foreign policy culture.

II

The concurrent design variously recasts, alleviates, reconciles, and matches up with the four dualisms. The alternative grand strategies diverge from them in some basic regards; in others they exacerbate the contradictions. Under a historical isolationist dispensation only the economic realm leaves room for America's activist dispositions; there are no opportunities to express its idealism. The latter also applies to realist internationalism, over and above its sometimes calling for policies that manifestly contravene America's liberal values. Realist, adversarial, and conciliatory internationalism foster inflated security anxieties and fears.

Liberal internationalism sets up America for intermittent disappointments and disillusions, frustrations and resentments, unpalatable attachments and high costs. Strategic internationalism cuts into America's material well-being, our having it all—by way of inequitable burden sharing with allies, high defense expenditures, diversions from the domestic agenda, and the security sensitivities that curtail an assertive economic diplomacy. All the variants of strategic internationalism deprive the country of its much valued domesticism.

Leaving the most basic isolationist-internationalist dualism for last, there is the realism-idealism polarity. The concurrent design bridges it from both ends. The national strategy was seen to be consistently at one with realist and adversarial internationalism's focus upon power capabilities and relations. Its necessary linchpin, the country's strategic immunity, accords close attention to our own power resources, those of the opponent and its allies, the possible targets of their expansionism, and the resources beyond the core perimeter that might be withdrawn from or used to hurt the United States. The encompassing power calculus of the immunity-enhancing umbrella is evident in the breadth of its components—those of insulation, invulnerability, impermeability, and imperviousness. In gauging their scope and potency full account was taken of all manner of direct and indirect security concerns—geographic, military, political, ideological, demographic, industrial, scientific-technological, export markets, oil, and other raw-material imports. America's strategic immunity was seen to hold up on realist and adversarial assumptions, those of the rival's great power and expansionist to hegemonic goals.

Besides preserving or heightening power capabilities, realist and especially adversarial internationalism are fixated upon the demonstration of resolve. Credibility is crucial in laying down deterrent threats, in bargaining from strength, and for maintaining alliances. A national strategy is hardly neglectful of power relations. Instead of choosing to define so many issues as tests of strength and resolve, and rather than thinning out American resources to pass those tests, it capitalizes upon the high ground of a narrow security perimeter.[24] It is here—unfettered by central arms control agreements—that the decided imbalance of capabilities and interests, of resolve and credibility, gives the United States overwhelming advantages in deterring and defending against virtually every kind of security-threatening encroachment. Neither widespread defensive outposts nor strategic superiority were seen to improve upon America's effective power at and around the core. And both are liable to detract from our security in predictable and inadvertent ways, certainly so through the lives lost in occasional military interventions.

Realist and hawkish engagement are so taken up with the exercise of power over others that, unlike the concurrent foreign policy, they pay the price of their exercising power over us. Power as a relationship includes more than getting others to do our bidding. It is all too often forgotten that autonomy also matters. A fully powerful state does not allow others to shape its policy agenda, goals, and the (costly) means for advancing them. Nor does it decline to translate its self-defined interests and values into determined policies to avoid antagonizing others. The United States has thus been something less than an autonomous, truly powerful state in devoting enormous material and human resources to the generation of political-military capabilities, expending them in interventions, and occasionally putting its security at immediate risk. While it is correct to say that we have chosen to make these sacrifices, it is more accurate to say that we have been constrained to do so by realist and adversarial assumptions about the wide-ranging indivisibility of security, power, and credibility. Moreover, self-deterrence has usually been the rule vis-à-vis allies and clients whose behavior has diverged from our international ideals, equitable burden sharing, and the principles of free and fair trade. By incorporating the two faces of relational power the concurrent configuration turns America into a powerful and autonomous state, one that consistently defines its own interests and values, without being beholden to others in deciding how to further them.

The realist-morality dualism is bridged from the other end by a principled idealism and a moderated liberal activism. Principle, prudence, and promise are its lodestars. The liberal project is not distorted by dependencies upon ethically odorous allies and not given to disfiguring liberal norms in its choice of means. America in the moderated service of exclusively liberal causes should come close to fulfilling the strongest medical injunction: "Do no harm." Counterproductive and unintended consequences are much less likely when idealistic goals are not pursued along with political-military ones, and when they are not overly ambitious in breaching the outer limits of the doable. Given the enormous difficulties in interpreting the aims and motivations of most challengers, there is the distinct possibility that they are largely benign. If so, a nonengaged America does not mistakenly subject the opponent to pressures, penalties, and punishing military actions. Nor does it thwart the rectification of its legitimate grievances. And being maximally reassured by the national strategy's conciliatory posture, challengers have little or no need to threaten, attack, or control other countries to protect themselves from the United States.

While accepting what cannot be achieved in the face of recalcitrant circumstances and intractable conditions, there is still much room for America to make a liberal difference. Besides unilateral military interventions under an uncommon concatenation of circumstances, the United States can take the lead in strengthening multilateral safeguards against nuclear proliferation, fostering democracy where the domestic conditions are propitious, protecting against extreme human rights abuses where sanctions (negative and positive) hold out some reasonable expectation of success, contributing to UN peacekeeping forces where the parties to the conflict are agreeable to their introduction, and opposing aggression where economic sanctions can have some real bite, air strikes are effective, or an overwhelming multilateral force can be mobilized. Multilateral actions—ad hoc, regional, or UN—are often the most effective, sometimes the only possible remedies. The United States is best positioned to mobilize multilateral ventures under the concurrent dispensation's auspices.

The national strategy directly addresses the post-1945 sense of extraordinary, unrivaled power punctuated by the severe doubts about its sufficiency that resulted in widespread insecurities. For 150 years isolationism was thoroughly consonant with and supportive of a deep confidence in the country's power and security. Even in 1941 there was no doubting the unconditional defeat of a Germany in control of almost all of Europe and of a Japan regnant in Asia. A national strategy should be able to take us "back to the future" in markedly mitigating, if not completely overcoming the strength-weakness dualism.

Instead of a highly exuberant power orientation whose actual, exaggerated, and imagined failures call up excitable anxieties, a national strategy offers the consistently well-grounded securities of strategic immunity. Rather than experiencing a sense of great-power superiority while overreacting to large and small contenders, there is a quiet assurance in the country's current and latent strengths. Compared to political-military muscle flexing, demonstrations of resolve, concerns with regional conflicts, and worries about minor military and political disadvantages, there is the evident demonstration of the nation's security via a purposeful, self-denying disengagement. As opposed to interpretive uncertainties about the opponent's intentions that risk excessively hawkish or dovish policies, the national strategy provides for steady, thoroughly compatible policies of maximally effective deterrence around the core and maximum reassurance. Instead of an America that considers itself constrained to lead while often having its leadership questioned, there are the abiding satisfactions of national autonomy, of an America that can say "no."

The sharp and swift shift in the national mood between 1979 and 1981 is indicative of the ease with which the strength-weakness dualism might be overcome. Much of America was insecure, feeling defensive, festering from the defeat in Vietnam, anxious about the Soviets' "geopolitical momentum" in the Third World, agitated by the impending "window of vulnerability," and practically flagellating itself during the hostage crisis in Iran. The national mood nevertheless underwent a sea change within a year of Reagan's ascension. We heard, "America is back," and we confidently embarked upon an adversarial contest with the "evil empire." And this quick U-turn occurred without any improvements in our power position. Some of the very same people, including the Committee on the Present Danger, who were most exercised by putative U.S. weaknesses in the late 1970s were talking about "spending the Soviets into the ground" a few years later.

America holds to the double-barreled expectation of consistent foreign policy successes and their realization through minimal to modest exactions of blood, treasure, material well-being, and patience. A national strategy promises the maximally attainable degree of security, markedly more than any type of internationalism with respect to each and every possible kind of rival, immediate threat, and long-run danger. A non-engaged America is not about to be drawn into a large or small war, generate a political-military or economic rivalry, inadvertently provoke or escalate a crisis, lose out in a deterrent or coercive duel, encourage an aggressor, negotiate a problematic arms control agreement, become caught up in a strategic or regional arms race, or suffer from the loss of trading partners, mineral supplies, and energy resources. The concurrent design's promotion of our economic and ideal interests cannot promise nearly as much. For here the United States must overcome recalcitrant conditions abroad. However, without widespread security concerns translating into self-deterrence and dependencies on others comes the greater use and efficaciousness of our impressive power, leverage, and influence—in furthering free and fair trade as well as international security, human rights, and democracy.

A minimal activism obviously makes minimal demands upon the country. The negation of most security concerns allows for a concentration upon domestic priorities and aspirations. The sustained dividend of a 50 percent military cutback can help generate economic growth and finance an assortment of public and private, social and material needs and aspirations. The nation's liberal principles and constitutional practices can be renewed as security-centered transgressions lose their honest justifications and rationalizing defenses. It becomes politically feasible to constrict imperious presidents, illegal behavior, dissembling, and secrecy at the highest levels of government. Civil liberties are not about to be abused due to security concerns.

The burdens of a moderated idealistic activism are no more than modest. On a yearly basis there is the financing of a discriminating, carrot-and-stick foreign aid program. Intermittent import embargoes might raise the price of some goods and export restrictions could hurt particular industries. The costs should be minimal since economic sanctions are almost certain to be directed against no more than a few countries at any one time. The occasional use of American troops will undoubtedly involve casualties. But given their selective, delimited use the losses will not begin to compare with those suffered in the course of past interventions. The costs are further minimized by the contributions of others, the concurrent design having several advantages in mobilizing the UN and regional powers in liberal and humanitarian causes.

Lastly, there is the isolationist-internationalist dualism. As isolationism reconfigured, the concurrent foreign policy matches up with most of one side of this polarity. The inclusion of some bilateral and multilateral security-centered accords, of which the most important ones make up the nuclear nonproliferation regime, are not inconsistent with isolationist thinking. The latter is fully at one with an assertive diplomacy on behalf of free and fair trade. The liberal project goes some way in meeting isolationist objections to involvements in other peoples' causes. Being moderated, principled, and exclusively focused upon feasible projects, it addresses the unacceptability of considerable sacrifices, the security-motivated betrayals of nominally liberal aims, and the omnipresent possibility of unintended consequences.

The concurrent design immediately runs up against a sharp difficulty in satisfying the other polarity. Since 1900 internationalism has regularly been most intensely animated by a national security rationale, invariably so since 1945. However, other motivations have not been in short supply, and they can be satisfied without bestriding the world politically and militarily. These include the pursuit of global economic interests, the fulfillment of idealistic obligations and ambitions, and a quest for national preeminence and leadership with their diffuse appeals of assertiveness and "action." The full complement and sheer weight of the country's material and financial resources insures it a leading, almost certainly the leading, position in the economic world and all of its most important institutions—the Group of Seven, GATT, the World Bank, the IMF, several UN agencies, and the conferences dealing with the environment and other global commons issues. Unfettered by security constraints, a determined economic diplomacy can come fully into its own in working with and pressuring formidable economic competitors. Internationalism and domesticism can become mutually reinforcing as defense savings and a concentration on American priorities foster economic competitiveness abroad.

Internationalist energies and ambitions can be more actively directed toward the advancement of liberal ideals within and among states once shorn of security-motivated concerns and constraints. The concurrent design's moderated aims still allow for a panoply of other-regarding responsibilities and opportunities for America to make a difference. Considering the lesser power and liberal activism of other states, the United States would still be number one, far more than an "ordinary country." The concurrent policy's internationalist appeals include national autonomy and national pride, self-respect and the respect of others, unrivaled power and a sense of inner strength, the free hand of unilateralism and a willingness to take a leading part in common endeavors, national assertiveness, and international cooperation.

Ronald Reagan's adversarial words and imagery of standing tall resonated throughout the country. There are, however, two ways of doing so. One posture involves standing up to rivals, standing upon the foundations of an enormous military buildup, and standing on the beaches of a miniscule, barely defended Grenada in a mood of national self-congratulation. The alternative posture is one of standing upright in conceiving and pursuing an independent foreign policy—in not permitting others to define what is and is not in our interest, what is and is not a setback; purposefully refusing to become caught up in the great efforts and minutiae of appearing strong in the eyes of others; focusing upon central interests rather than transforming peripheral matters into tests of resolve that must invariably be passed; saying no when implored by others to serve nominally common interests instead of making overt bids for predominance that are often resisted and rejected; not allowing the promotion of liberal ideals to be set aside and disfigured by highly inflated security needs and sensitivities; pressing and pressuring on behalf of free and fair trade instead of being self-deterred by concerns for alliance unity. An independent, inwardly secure, visibly self-confident country would not only be highly self-respecting; given our power, central interests, and liberal values it would also be potent and much respected, seen and treated as a globally preeminent country.

No grand strategy can fully address and fulfill the four cultural dualisms. Still, the concurrent design constitutes a very good fit with the nation's foreign policy culture, the best attainable one in form and substance and in mitigating its contradictions. It can thus be portrayed as America's characteristic foreign policy with all that this says about its extensive appeal, possible adoption, sustained implementation, and successful management. And this is no accident, not simply a fortuitous conclusion. For as seen in this concluding rehearsal of the advantages and attractions, benefits and compensations of a national strategy embedded in the concurrent foreign policy, they are indeed impressive—in and of themselves and compared to the alternatives.

NOTES

Chapter I

1. Michael Howard, "The Classical Strategists," in Alastair Buchan, ed., *Problems of Modern Strategy* (New York: Praeger, 1970), p. 47; Raymond Aron, "The Evolution of Modern Strategic Thought," in ibid., p. 15.

2. Frank N. Trager and Frank Simonie, "An Introduction to the Study of National Security," in Frank Trager and Phillip S. Kronenberg, eds., *National Security and American Society: Theory, Process, and Policy* (Lawrence: University Press of Kansas for the National Security Education Program, 1973), pp. 35–48.

3. Daniel J. Kaufman, Jeffrey S. McKitrick, and Thomas J. Leney, "A Conceptual Framework," in Daniel J. Kaufman et. al., eds., *U.S. National Security: A Framework for Analysis* (Lexington, MA: Lexington Books, 1985), pp. 18–19.

4. Barry Posen, *The Sources of Military Doctrine: France, Britain, and Germany between the Wars* (Ithaca, NY: Cornell University Press, 1984), p. 13.

5. Robert Jervis, "Realism, Game Theory, and Cooperation," *World Politics* 40, no. 3 (April 1988): 329. Also see Robert Jervis, *The Meaning of the Nuclear Revolution* (Ithaca, NY: Cornell University Press, 1989), pp. 217–18.

6. Thomas C. Schelling, *Arms and Influence* (New Haven: Yale University Press, 1966), p. 118.

7. Trager and Simeone, "Introduction," p. 36.

8. Kaufman, McKitrick, and Leney, "A Conceptual Framework," pp. 18–19.

9. Richard H. Ullman, "Redefining Security," *International Security* 8, no. 1 (summer 1983): 129–53. On page 133 a "threat to national security" is defined as "an action or sequence of events that (1) threatens drastically and over a relatively brief span of time to degrade the quality of life for the inhabitants of a state, or (2) threatens significantly to narrow the range of policy choices available to the government of a state or to private, nongovernmental entities (persons, groups, corporations) within the state." For much more circumscribed but still overly inclusive uses of the national security concept that cover all aspects of the country's physical well-being, see Barry Buzan, *International Relations* (Chapel Hill: University of North Carolina Press, 1983), and Jessica Tuchman Mathews, "Redefining Security," *Foreign Affairs* 68, no. 2 (spring 1989): 162–77.

10. See the critical review of the claims in Alan S. Milward, "Was the Marshall Plan Necessary?" *Diplomatic History* 13, no. 2 (spring 1989): 231–53.

11. Stephen E. Ambrose, *Eisenhower the President* (New York: Harcourt Brace, 1984), pp. 70–71, 86–91, 143–45, 454–56, 517–19, 625–26.

12. Paul Kennedy, *The Rise and Fall of the Great Powers* (New York: Random House, 1987). The declinist thesis is critiqued in chapter 9 below.

13. For the theory confirming power of "crucial" single cases, see Harry Eckstein, "Case Study and Theory in Political Science," in Fred I. Greenstein and

Nelson W. Polsby, eds., *Handbook of Political Science*, vol. 7, *Strategies of Inquiry* (Reading, MA: Addison-Wesley, 1975), 79–138.

14. Internationalist-isolationist opinion data from 1940 to 1988 are brought together in one time series in Thomas W. Graham, "Extended Deterrence and the Use of Nuclear Weapons," occasional paper no. 4, Center for Science and International Affairs, Harvard University, 1989, p. 24.

15. William Schneider, "The Old Politics and the New World Order," in Kenneth A. Oye, Robert J. Lieber, and Donald Rothchild, eds., *Eagle in a New World: American Grand Strategy in the Post–Cold War Era* (New York: Harper Collins, 1992), p. 63.

16. Robert W. Tucker, *A New Isolationism: Threat or Promise?* (Washington, DC: Potomac Associates, 1972).

17. Earl C. Ravenal, "The Case for Strategic Disengagement," *Foreign Affairs* 51, no. 3 (April 1973): 505–21. This article is expanded in *Never Again: Learning from America's Foreign Policy Failures* (Philadelphia: Temple University Press, 1978). Also see Earl C. Ravenal, "Counterforce and Alliance: The Ultimate Connection," *International Security* 6, no. 4 (spring 1982): 26–43; "The Case for Adjustment," *Foreign Policy* 81 (winter 1990–91): 3–19; as well as the articles cited in the third part of this chapter and the second part of chapter 2.

18. For one example, see Ernst B. Haas, "On Hedging Our Bets: Selective Engagement with the Soviet Union," in Aaron B. Wildavsky, ed., *Beyond Containment: Alternative American Policies toward the Soviet Union* (San Francisco: Institute of Contemporary Studies, 1983), 93–124.

19. Such a change is found in the time series data set out in Graham, "Extended Deterrence," p. 24. But see Eugene R. Witkopf, *Faces of Internationalism: Public Opinion and American Foreign Policy* (Durham, NC: Duke University Press, 1990), p. 26. There it is seen that isolationists—defined as those who "oppose militant internationalism" and "oppose cooperative internationalism"—continued to make up 22 percent of the population after 1974.

20. Ole R. Holsti and James N. Rosenau, *American Leadership in World Affairs: Vietnam and the Breakdown of Consensus* (Boston: Allen and Unwin, 1984), pp. 122–23.

21. Cited in Joshua Muravchik, *Exporting Democracy: Fulfilling America's Destiny* (Washington, DC: American Enterprise Institute Press, 1991), p. 46.

22. Melvyn Krauss, *How NATO Weakens the West* (New York: Simon and Schuster, 1986).

23. Charles Krauthammer, "Isolationism, Left and Right," *New Republic*, March 4, l985, p. 18.

24. John Marttila, "Public Opinion: Evolving Definitions of National Security," in Edward K. Hamilton, ed., *America's Global Interests: A New Agenda* (New York: Norton, 1989), pp. 300, 306; *Americans Talk Security: Serial National Surveys of Americans on Public Policy Issues*, National Survey no. 3, March 1988, p. 60; no. 8, September 1988, p. 56; no. 9, October 1988, p. 71, no. 15, March 1991, p. 42; Ronald H. Hinckley, *People, Polls, and Policymakers: American Public Opinion and National Security* (New York: Lexington Books, 1992), pp. 18–19; *Time*, October 7, 1991, p. 15 and October 14, 1991, p. 22; Edward Alden and Franz Schurmann, "Neo-Nationalist Fallacies," *Foreign Pol-*

icy 87 (summer 1992): 106; William Schneider, "Introduction: From Foreign Policy to 'Politics as Usual,' " in David A. Deese, ed., *The New Politics of American Foreign Policy* (New York: St. Martin's Press, 1994), p. xiv.

25. Ole R. Holsti and James N. Rosenau, "The Post–Cold War Foreign Policy Beliefs of American Leaders: Persistence or Abatement of Partisan Cleavages?" in Eugene R. Witkopf, ed., *The Future of American Foreign Policy*, 2d ed. (New York: St. Martin's Press, 1994), pp. 137, 139. For internationalist responses with majority support see p. 139.

26. William G. Hyland, "Setting Global Priorities," *Foreign Policy* 73 (winter, 1988–89): 22–38.

27. James K. Oliver and James A. Nathan, "Planning for the Most Likely Contingencies: The Foreign Policy Context," in Keith A. Dunn and William O. Staudenmaier, eds., *Alternative Military Strategies for the Future* (Boulder, CO: Westview Press, 1985); Colin S. Gray, *The Geopolitics of Super Power* (Lexington: University Press of Kentucky, 1988); Stephen M. Walt, "The Case for Finite Containment: Analyzing U.S. Grand Strategy," *International Security* 14, no. 1 (summer 1989): 5–49.

28. Colin S. Gray, "NATO: Time to Call It a Day?" *National Interest* 10 (winter 1987–88): 20–26.

29. Strobe Talbot, "The Delicate Balancing Act," *Time*, July 29, 1991, p. 32.

30. Charles William Maynes, "America without the Cold War," *Foreign Policy* 78 (spring 1990): 8, 13.

31. Robert W. Tucker, "1989 and All That," in Nicholas X. Rizopoulos, ed., *Sea Changes: American Foreign Policy in a World Transformed* (New York: Council on Foreign Relations Press, 1990), pp. 230–37.

32. Humphrey Taylor, "Polls, Politicians, and the Gulf War," *National Review*, May 13, 1991, p. 38; Lawrence Freedman and Efraim Karsh, "How Kuwait Was Won: Strategy in the Gulf War," *International Security* 16, no. 2 (fall 1991): 14.

33. Most of this agenda is set out by Richard J. Barnet and twelve other left-of-center political figures and writers in "American Priorities in a New World Era," *World Policy Journal* 6, no. 2 (spring 1989): 203–37.

34. Quoted in Morton M. Kondracke, "Make 'Em Pay," *New Republic*, October 12, 1987, p. 16. A few years later Gephardt urged the Democrats to adopt a "Strategic view of Economics" featuring governmental support for infant industries, discrimination against foreign products, and the aggressive promotion of exports. Alden and Schurmann, "Neo-Nationalist Fallacies," p. 113.

35. Alan Tonelson, "What Is the National Interest?" *Atlantic*, July 1991, pp. 37–38. Also see Tonelson's "A Manifesto for Democrats," *National Interest* 16 (summer 1989): 36–48, and "Clinton's World," *Atlantic*, February 1993, pp. 70–74.

36. Robert S. Greenberg, "The Winds of Change Battering Communism Tear Also at the Fabric of U.S. Conservatism," *Wall Street Journal*, November 16, 1989, p. A16.

37. J. B. Kelly, "America, the Gulf, and the West," *National Review*, October 15, 1990, p. 46.

38. Jeane J. Kirkpatrick, "A Normal Country in a Normal Time," *National*

Interest 21 (fall 1990): 40–44. However, Kirkpatrick has reverted back toward internationalism since the publication of this article.

39. Patrick J. Buchanan, "America First—and Second, and Third," *National Interest* 19 (spring 1990): 77–82. Also see Patrick J. Buchanan, "An America-First Foreign Policy," *Human Events*, May 2, 1992; Robert W. Merry, "Pat Buchanan's Push for 'America First,' " *Congressional Quarterly* 49, no. 47 (November 23, 1991): 3498; Gary Wills, "The Golden 'Blade,' " *New York Review of Books*, February 13, 1992, 22–26.

40. Earl C. Ravenal, "The Requisites of Containment," in Ted Galen Carpenter, ed., *Collective Defense or Strategic Independence? Alternative Strategies for the Future* (Lexington, MA: Lexington Books, 1989), p. 276; Ravenal, "The Case for Strategic Disengagement," pp. 506–7; Ravenal, "Europe without America: The Erosion of NATO," *Foreign Affairs* 63, no. 5 (summer 1985): 1034; Ted Galen Carpenter, "An Independent Course," *National Interest* 21 (fall 1990): 28–31; Carpenter, "The New World Disorder," *Foreign Policy* 84 (fall 1991): 24; Carpenter, *A Search for Enemies: America's Alliances after the Cold War* (Washington, D.C.: Cato Institute, 1992). Also see Doug Bandow, "Avoiding War," *Foreign Policy* 89 (winter 1993): 156–74.

41. Schneider, "From Foreign Policy to 'Politics as Usual,' " p. xiv.

42. Leslie H. Gelb, "Putting America First," *New York Times*, November 15, 1992, p. E19.

43. Lawrence J. Korb, "Shock Therapy for the Pentagon," *New York Times*, February 15, 1994, p. A21.

44. See for example Jonathan Clarke, "The Conceptual Poverty of U.S. Foreign Policy," *Atlantic*, September 1993, 54–66.

Chapter II

1. Albert A. Hirschman, *Exit, Voice, and Loyalty: Responses to Decline in Firms, Organizations, and States* (Cambridge, MA: Harvard University Press, 1970).

2. Brian Barry, Review of *Exit, Voice, and Loyalty*, by Albert A. Hirschman, *British Journal of Political Science* 4, no. 1 (January 1974): 91–95.

3. Joseph S. Nye, Graham T. Allison, and Albert Carnesale, "Analytic Conclusions," in Graham T. Allison, Albert Carnesale, and Joseph S. Nye, eds., *Hawks, Doves, and Owls: An Agenda for Avoiding Nuclear War* (New York: Norton, 1985), 206–22.

4. Nye, Allison, and Carnesale, "Analytic Conclusions," p. 213.

5. Richard K. Betts, "Elusive Equivalence: The Political and Military Meaning of the Nuclear Balance," in Samuel P. Huntington, ed., *The Strategic Imperative* (Cambridge, MA: Ballinger, 1982), p. 110.

6. Richard K. Betts, "Analysis, War, and Decision: Why Intelligence Failures Are Inevitable," *World Politics* 31, no. 1 (October 1978): 70.

7. Alan Tonelson advocates the "decoupling of America's security from that of its allies" while "keeping unfriendly foreign forces out of the hemisphere by using and threatening to use force unilaterally." See his "What Is the National Interest?" p. 37. Also see Ted Galen Carpenter, "Benign Realism: A New U.S.

Security Strategy in the Third World," in Ted Galen Carpenter, ed., *Collective Defense or Strategic Independence? Alternative Strategies for the Future* (Lexington, MA: Lexington Books, 1989), p. 220.

8. Trade disputes and economic diplomacy are thought to have a far greater impact upon America's prosperity than security. They are consequently discussed primarily in part 2 of the book, in chapter 9.

9. See especially the balanced, comprehensive assessments in Albert Carnesale and Richard N. Haass, "Conclusions: Weighing the Evidence," in Albert Carnesale and Richard N. Haass, eds., *Superpower Arms Control: Setting the Record Straight* (Cambridge, MA: Ballinger, 1987), pp. 342–55.

10. William W. Kaufman and John D. Steinbruner, *Decision for Defense: Prospects for a New Order* (Washington, DC: Brookings Institution, 1991).

11. James Chace, *The Consequences of the Peace: The New Internationalism and American Foreign Policy* (New York: Oxford University Press, 1992), p. 25.

12. Jeff Faux and Max Sawicky, "Defense Spending Should Be Decreased," in Carol Wekesser, ed., *American Foreign Policy: Options and Viewpoints* (San Diego, CA: Greenhaven Press, 1993), pp. 98–99.

13. Earl C. Ravenal, "A Strategy of Restraint," in Keith A. Dunn and William O. Staudenmaier, eds., *Alternative Military Strategies for the Future* (Boulder, CO: Westview Press, 1985), pp. 203–4; Ravenal, *Designing Defense for a New World Order: The Military Budget in 1992 and Beyond* (Washington, DC: Cato Institute, 1991), 62–79; Ravenal, "The Case for Adjustment," *Foreign Policy* 81 (winter 1990–91): 17–18.

14. "America's Peace Dividend: Income Tax Reductions from the New Strategic Realities," Cato Institute White Paper, August 7, 1990, part 1 by Ted Galen Carpenter and Rosemary Fiscarelli, "Defending America in the 1990s: A Budget for Strategic Independence," pp. 34–44; Ted Galen Carpenter, *A Search for Enemies: America's Alliances after the Cold War* (Washington, D.C.: Cato Institute, 1992).

15. Except for the base on Diego Garcia in the Indian Ocean, the possible loss of naval bases on foreign soil would entail only three to five days of extra "steaming" time every few months in reaching bases on U.S. territory. Some bases for repairing and supplying U.S. ships might be kept if doing so makes logistic—not "political"—sense, they being leased on a commercial basis without any obligation to defend an ally. Other substitute arrangements for forward naval bases are found in Michael E. O'Hanlon, *The Art of War in the Age of Peace: U.S. Military Posture for the Post–Cold War World* (Westport, CT: Praeger, 1992), pp. 37–40.

16. For the debate on the maritime strategy, see John Mearsheimer, "A Strategic Misstep: The Maritime Strategy and Deterrence in Europe," *International Security* 11, no. 2 (fall 1986): 3–57; and Linton F. Brooks, "Naval Power and National Security: The Case of the Maritime Strategy," *International Security* 11, no. 2 (fall 1986): 58–88.

17. This targeting doctrine is proposed in Earl C. Ravenal, "Counterforce and Alliance: The Ultimate Connection," *International Security* 6, no. 4 (spring 1982): 41–42. Also see Kenneth N. Waltz, "Nuclear Myths and Political Reali-

ties," *American Political Science Review* 84, no. 3 (September 1990): 731–45. Arguments for the elimination of land-based missiles are found in Charles L. Glaser, *Analyzing Strategic Nuclear Policy* (Princeton: Princeton University Press, 1990), pp. 261–67, 321–22; Thomas C. Schelling, "Abolition of Ballistic Missiles," *International Security* 12, no. 1 (summer 1987): 179–83; Stansfield Turner, "Land Based Missiles Are Obsolete," *New York Times*, December 29, 1992, p. A15.

18. Ravenal, "A Strategy of Restraint," pp. 201–2; Carpenter and Fiscarelli, "Defending America," pp. 22–23. The three thousand number is also proposed by Michael M. May, George F. Bing, and John D. Steinbruner, "Strategic Arsenals after START: The Implications of Deep Cuts," *International Security* 13, no. 1 (summer 1988): 90–133; and by Harold Brown, "Navigating the Security Sea Change," *Arms Control Today*, May 1990, 3–7.

19. Matthew Bunn allows that "there is little doubt that it is technically possible to defend the United States against a handful of long-range ballistic missiles launched by accident, a mad commander, or a Third World country." See "Star Wars Redux: Limited Defenses, Unlimited Dilemmas," *Arms Control Today*, May 1991, p. 15. Ravenal, "Designing Defense," pp. 68–70, is less enthusiastic about ABM defenses than Carpenter and Fiscarelli, "Defending America," pp. 30–33.

20. Michael Krepon, "Limited ABM Defense: A Prudent Step," *Arms Control Today*, October 1991, pp. 19–21.

21. Another is suggested in chapter 9 having to do with improvements in our economic competitiveness.

22. Terry L. Deibel, "Strategies before Containment: Patterns for the Future," *International Security* 16, no. 4 (spring 1992): 92–93.

23. For the historical background to Washington's valedictory—from the debates in England on its own detachment from continental affairs to the drafts offered by Alexander Hamilton and James Madison—see Felix Gilbert, *To the Farewell Address: Ideas of Early American Foreign Policy* (Princeton: Princeton University Press, 1961).

24. For the encomiums laid upon early isolationism by the realist internationalists, see Hans J. Morgenthau, *In Defense of the National Interest* (New York: Knopf, 1951), pp. 4–24; George F. Kennan *American Diplomacy, 1900–1950* (Chicago: University of Chicago Press, 1951), p. 11.

25. This and all other quotations from Washington's valedictory are taken from Gilbert, *To the Farewell Address*, pp. 144–47, which reproduces the version found in Victor Hugo Paltsits, *Washington's Farewell Address* (New York: New York Public Library, 1935.)

26. Cited in Ronald E. Powaski, *Toward an Entangling Alliance: American Isolationism, Internationalism, and Europe, 1901–1950* (New York: Greenwood Press, 1991), p. xvi.

27. Alexander DeConde, "On Twentieth-Century Isolationism," in Alexander DeConde, ed., *Isolation and Security* (Durham, NC: Duke University Press, 1957), p. 3; Gilbert, *To the Farewell Address*, p. 135. Also see Albert K. Weinberg, "The Historical Meaning of the American Doctrine of Isolation," *American Political Science Review* 34, no. 3 (June 1940): 539–47.

28. Cited in Robert Dallek, *The American Style of Foreign Policy: Cultural Politics and Foreign Affairs* (New York: Oxford University Press, 1983), pp. 34–35.

29. Robert L. Beisner, *Twelve against Empire: The Anti-Imperialists, 1898–1900* (New York: McGraw-Hill, 1968), pp. 218–38.

30. Robert C. Osgood, *Ideals and Self-Interest in America's Foreign Relations: The Great Transformation of the Twentieth Century* (Chicago: University of Chicago Press, 1953), p.17.

31. Foster Rhea Dulles, *America's Rise to World Power: 1898–1954* (New York: Harper and Row, 1954), p. 1. Also see DeConde, "On Twentieth-Century Isolationism," pp. 6–7.

32. Selig Adler, *The Isolationist Impulse: Its Twentieth-Century Reaction* (New York: Free Press, 1957), p. 29.

33. Harold Sprout and Margaret Sprout, *The Rise of American Naval Power, 1776–1918* (Princeton: Princeton University Press, 1939), pp. 326–28.

34. Cited in Howard K. Beale, *Theodore Roosevelt and the Rise of America to World Power* (Baltimore: Johns Hopkins University Press, 1959), p. 173.

35. Bernard Brodie, *War and Politics* (New York: Macmillan, 1973), pp. 344–45, 348, 361–62.

36. Cited in John A. Thompson, "The Exaggeration of American Vulnerability: The Anatomy of a Tradition," *Diplomatic History* 16, no. 1 (winter 1992): 24–26.

37. Morgenthau, *Defense of National Interest*, p. 29.

38. Osgood, *Ideals and Self-Interest*, pp. 376–80.

39. Robert M. Hutchins, "The Path to War—We Are Drifting into Suicide," in Arthur A. Ekirch, ed., *Voices in Dissent: An Anthology of Individualist Thought in the United States* (New York: Citadel Press, 1964), p. 273; Powaski, *Toward an Entangling Alliance*, pp. 71–87.

40. Bruce M. Russett, *No Clear and Present Danger: A Skeptical View of U.S. Entry into World War II* (New York: Harper and Row, 1972), p. 27–37, italics in the original. For a discussion of the possible dangers arising from Germany's development of the atomic bomb, see pp. 37–41. For later studies that document Britain's relative capabilities, see G. C. Peden, *British Rearmament and the Treasury* (Edinburgh: Scottish Academic Press, 1979); N. H. Gibbs, *Grand Strategy*, vol. 1 (London: HMSO, 1976); John J. Mearsheimer, *Conventional Deterrence* (Ithaca, NY: Cornell University Press, 1983), pp. 100–110.

41. Scott D. Sagan, "The Origins of the Pacific War," *Journal of Interdisciplinary History* 18, no. 4 (spring 1988): 893–922; Michael Barnhart, *Japan Prepares for Total War* (Ithaca, NY: Cornell University Press, 1987); Russett, *No Clear Danger*, pp. 440–62.

42. Richard K. Betts, *Surprise Attack* (Washington, DC: Brookings Institution, 1982), p. 42.

43. Sagan, "Origins of Pacific War," pp. 919–20, italics in the original.

44. Osgood, *Ideals and Self-Interest*, pp. 17–20.

45. Adler, *The Isolationist Impulse*, pp. 16–33.

46. Kenneth W. Thompson, "Isolationism and Collective Security: The Uses and Limits of Two Theories of International Relations," in DeConde, *Isolation and Security*, pp. 164–67.

47. Ted Galen Carpenter, "The Dissenters: American Isolationists and Foreign Policy, 1945–1954" (Ph.D. diss., University of Texas at Austin, 1980); Ronald Radosh, *Prophets on the Right: Profiles of Conservative Critics of American Globalism* (New York: Simon and Schuster, 1975), pp. 156–72; Justus D. Doenecke, *Not to the Swift: The Old Isolationists in the Cold War Era* (Lewisburg, PA: Bucknell University Press, 1979).

48. Carpenter, "The Dissenters," pp. 280, 337; Radosh, *Prophets on the Right*, pp. 176–77, 194; Doenecke, *Not to the Swift*, pp. 79, 239–40.

49. Carpenter, "The Dissenters," pp. 12–39, 244, 249–50, 289, 337; Doenecke, *Not to the Swift*, pp. 79, 239–40.

50. James T. Patterson, *Mr. Republican: A Biography of Robert A. Taft* (Boston: Houghton Mifflin, 1972), pp. 370–71, 436–38, 477–78; Henry W. Berger, "Senator Robert A. Taft Dissents from Military Escalation," in Thomas G. Paterson, ed., *Cold War Critics: Alternatives to American Foreign Policy in the Truman Years* (Chicago: Quadrangle Books, 1971), pp. 184–85.

51. But recall the major caveat noted in chapter 1 regarding the Soviets' early postwar military threat to Western Europe.

CHAPTER III

1. There are not any contradictions among the availability, scope, and potency of America's immunity-enhancing conditions. Without any trade-offs, there is considerable latitude (or "choice") regarding our reliance upon them. Any one of four possible pairs of conditions is sufficient for the country's immunity: Insulation-impermeability, insulation-imperviousness, invulnerability-impermeability, or invulnerability-imperviousness.

2. William Zimmerman, *Soviet Perspectives on International Relations, 1956–1967* (Princeton: Princeton University Press, 1969), pp. 253–54.

3. A comprehensive, if not somewhat inflated, list, includes Mongolia, Cuba, Nicaragua, Cambodia, Laos, North Korea, Vietnam, Syria, South Yemen, Ethiopia, Mozambique, Angola, Benin, and the Congo.

4. The most extensive discussion is found in Elizabeth Kridl Valkenier, *The Soviet Union and the Third World: An Economic Bind* (New York: Praeger, 1983).

5. Stephen T. Hosner and Thomas Wolfe, *Soviet Policy and Practice toward Third World Conflicts* (Lexington, MA: D. C. Heath, 1983), pp. 11–78; Robert H. Donaldson, "The Second World, the Third World, and the New International Economic Order," in Robert H. Donaldson, ed., *The Soviet Union in the Third World: Successes and Failures*, (Boulder, CO: Westview Press, 1981), pp. 358–83.

6. Richard E. Feinberg, *The Intemperate Zone: The Third World Challenge to U.S. Foreign Policy* (New York: Norton, 1983), pp. 136–38; Abraham S. Becker, "The Soviet Union and the Third World: The Economic Dimension," in Andrzej Korbonski and Francis Fukuyama, eds., *The Soviet Union and the Third World: The Last Three Decades* (Ithaca, NY: Cornell University Press, 1987), pp. 74–77, 85–86.

7. Roger F. Pajak, "The Effectiveness of Soviet Arms Aid Diplomacy in the

Third World," in Donaldson, ed., *Soviet Union in Third World*, pp. 384–408; Mark N. Kramer, "Soviet Arms Transfers to the Third World," *Problems of Communism* 36, no. 5 (September–October 1987): 52–68; *Discriminate Deterrence*, Report of the Commission on Integrated Long-Term Strategy (Washington, DC: U.S. Government Printing Office, 1988), p. 19. For the importance of East German and other palace guards, see Steven R. David, "Explaining Third World Alignment," *World Politics* 43, no. 2 (January 1991): 233–56.

8. Francis Fukuyama, "The Tenth Period of Soviet Foreign Policy," paper delivered at the national security conference held by the Center for International Affairs, Harvard University, June 1987, pp. 8, 11–12; Peter Shearman, "Gorbachev and the Third World: An Era of Reform?" *Third World Quarterly* 9, no. 4 (October 1987): 1093–1100.

9. These justifications for containment are fully set out in Stephen M. Walt, *The Origins of Alliances* (Ithaca, NY: Cornell University Press, 1987); Robert Jervis and Jack Snyder, eds., *Dominoes and Bandwagons: Strategic Beliefs and Great Power Competition in the Eurasian Rimland* (New York: Oxford University Press, 1991); John Lewis Gaddis, *Strategies of Containment: A Critical Appraisal of Postwar American National Security Policy* (New York: Oxford University Press, 1982).

10. For critical and empirical inquiries into dominoes and bandwagoning, see Kenneth N. Waltz, *Theory of International Politics* (Reading, MA: Addison-Wesley, 1979); Jervis and Snyder, eds., *Dominoes and Bandwagons*; Walt, *The Origins of Alliances*.

11. Stephen Goose, "Soviet Geopolitical Momentum: Trends of Soviet Influence around the World from 1945 to 1980," *Defense Monitor*, January 1989.

12. *The Military Balance 1976–1977* (London: International Institute for Strategic Studies, 1980), p. 71; Richard Sneider, *The Political and Social Capabilities of North and South Korea for the Long-Term Military Competition* (Santa Monica, CA: Rand Corporation, 1985), p. 44.

13. Ted Hopf, "Soviet Inferences from Their Victories in the Periphery: Visions of Resistance or Culminating Gains?" in Jervis and Snyder, *Dominoes and Bandwagons*, pp. 164–67.

14. Francis Fukuyama, "Soviet Strategy in the Third World," in Korbonski and Fukuyama, *Soviet Union and Third World*, pp. 27–31.

15. Stephen S. Kaplan, *The Diplomacy of Power: Soviet Armed Forces as a Political Instrument* (Washington, DC: Brookings Institution, 1981), pp. 661–62). The various studies that find Soviet influence to be distinctly circumscribed are reviewed in Joseph L. Nogee, "The Soviet Union in the Third World: Successes and Failures," in Donaldson, *Soviet Union in Third World*, pp. 438–52. For updates, see Rajan Menon, "Soviet Arms Transfers to the Third World," *Journal of International Affairs* 40, no. 1 (summer 1986): 59–76; S. Neil MacFarlane, "The Soviet Union," in Robert S. Litwak and Samuel F. Wells, eds., *Superpower Competition and Security in the Third World* (Cambridge, MA: Ballinger, 1988), pp. 67–71, 74; Harry Gelman, "The Soviet Union in the Less Developed World," in Korbonski and Fukuyama, *Soviet Union and Third World*, pp. 277–88.

16. Walt, *The Origins of Alliances*, pp. 225–27, and the studies cited there.

17. Walt, *The Origins of Alliances*, pp. 229–30, and the studies cited there.

18. Fukuyama, "Soviet Strategy," p. 35.

19. Richard E. Feinberg and Kenneth A. Oye, "After the Fall: U.S. Policy toward Radical Regimes," *World Policy Journal* 1, no. 1 (fall 1983): 208–9; Celeste A. Wallander, "Opportunity, Incrementalism, and Learning in the Extension and Retraction of Soviet Global Commitments," paper delivered at the annual meeting of the American Political Science Association, 1989, p. 4.

20. Mark N. Katz, *The Third World in Soviet Military Thought* (Baltimore: Johns Hopkins University Press, 1982); S. Neil MacFarlane, *Superpower Rivalry and Third World Radicalism: The Idea of National Liberation* (London: Croom Helm, 1985); Elizabeth Kridl Valkenier, "Revolutionary Change in the Third World: Recent Soviet Reassessments," *World Politics* 38, no. 3 (April 1986): 415–34; Francis Fukuyama, *Moscow's Post-Brezhnev Reassessment of the Third World* (Santa Monica, CA: Rand Corporation, 1986); Jerry F. Hough, *The Struggle for the Third World: Soviet Debates and American Options* (Washington, DC: Brookings Institution, 1986).

21. Max Jakobson, "Finland: Substance and Appearance," *Foreign Affairs* 58, no. 5 (summer 1980): 1034–44.

22. Christopher Layne, "Atlanticism without NATO," *Foreign Policy* 67 (summer 1987): 39.

23. Samuel P. Huntington, "The U.S.—Decline or Renewal?" *Foreign Affairs* 67, no. 2 (winter 1988–89): 93, italics added.

24. Paul H. Nitze, "Strategy in the Decade of the 1980s," *Foreign Affairs* 59, no. 1 (fall 1980): 87–88.

25. On the optimistic side regarding NATO's ability to withstand a blitzkrieg attack by the Warsaw Pact with conventional weapons alone, see John J. Mearsheimer, "Why the Soviets Can't Win Quickly in Central Europe," *International Security* 7, no. 1 (3–39; summer 1982): Mearsheimer, "Numbers, Strategy, and the European Balance," *International Security* 12, no. 4 (spring 1988): 174–85; William W. Kaufmann, "Non Nuclear Deterrence," in John D. Steinbruner and Leon V. Sigal, eds., *Alliance Security: NATO and the No-First-Use Questions* (Washington, DC: Brookings Institution, 1987), 43–90; Christian Krause, ed., *The Balance between Conventional Forces in Europe* (Bonn: Freidrich Ebert Stiftung, 1982); Paul Bracken, "The NATO Defense Problem," *Orbis* 27, no. 1 (spring 1983): 83–105; Barry R. Posen, "Measuring the Conventional European Balance: Coping with Complexity in Threat Assessment," *International Security* 9, no. 3 (winter 1984–85): 47–88. These analyses are criticized in Joshua M. Epstein, "Dynamic Analysis and the Conventional Balance in Europe," *International Security* 12, no. 4 (spring 1988): 154–65, and Eliot A. Cohen, "Toward Better Net Assessment: Rethinking the European Conventional Balance," *International Security*, 13, no. 1 (summer 1988): 50–89. The debate is continued with articles and correspondence in *International Security* 13, no. 4 (spring 1989): 54–179.

26. These standard figures may be found in Kaufmann, "Non-Nuclear Deterrence," p. 62.

27. This calculation is based on figures in *World Military Expenditures and Arms Transfers, 1987* (Washington, DC: Arms Control and Disarmament Agency, 1988), pp. 41, 81.

28. Robert J. Art, "Fixing Atlantic Bridges," *Foreign Policy* 46 (spring 1982): 70.

29. This calculation is based on figures in *World Military Expenditures, 1987*, pp. 44, 81.

30. Stanley R. Sloan, *Defense Burden Sharing: U.S. Relations with NATO Allies and Japan* (Washington, DC: Congressional Research Service, 1983).

31. *World Military Expenditures, 1987*, pp. 44, 50, 81.

32. David P. Calleo, "The American Problem," *Ethics and International Affairs* (1989): 237–38.

33. For an analysis of the navy's capabilities in protecting the sea-lanes during wartime, see William W. Kaufmann, *A Thoroughly Efficient Navy* (Washington, DC: Brookings Institution, 1987), pp. 73–83.

34. John C. F. Tillson IV, "The Forward Defense of Europe," *Military Review* 61, no. 5 (May 1981): 74.

35. Kaufmann, "Non-Nuclear Deterrence," p. 62. For another analysis of the high effectiveness and low cost of barrier defenses, see *U.S. Ground Forces and the Conventional Balance in Europe* (Washington, D.C.: Congressional Budget Office, 1988), pp. 38–43.

36. Robert W. Tucker, "Containment and the Search for Alternatives: A Critique," in Aaron Wildavsky, ed., *Beyond Containment: Alternative American Policies toward the Soviet Union* (San Francisco: Institute for Contemporary Studies Press, 1983), p. 81; Robert W. Tucker, *The Nuclear Debate: Deterrence and the Lapse of Faith* (New York: Holmes and Meier, 1985), p. 111. The most extensive and rigorous argument that nuclear superiority does not matter is found in Robert Jervis, *The Illogic of American Nuclear Strategy* (Ithaca, NY: Cornell University Press, 1984).

37. Robert H. Johnson, "Exaggerating America's Stakes in Third World Conflicts," *International Security* 10, no. 3 (winter 1985–86): 34–35.

38. Stephen Van Evera, "Why Europe Matters, Why the Third World Doesn't: American Grand Strategy after the Cold War," *Journal of Strategic Studies* 13, no. 2 (June 1990): pp. 21–22.

39. Jerome Slater, "Dominos in Central America: Will They Fall? Does it Matter?" *International Security* 12, no. 2 (fall 1987): 124–25; Lars Schoultz, *National Security and United States Policy toward Latin America* (Princeton: Princeton University Press, 1984), pp. 229–34, 249–67.

40. Schoultz, *National Security*, pp. 166, 173, 217–18. Most of the mid-to-high-level officials interviewed by Schoultz agreed with these statements.

41. Van Evera, "Why Europe Matters," pp. 22–23.

42. Michael C. Desch, "The Keys That Lock Up the World: Identifying American Interests in the Periphery," *International Security* 14, no. 1 (summer 1989): 86–121; Steven R. David, "Why the Third World Matters," *International Security* 14, no. 1 (summer 1989): 63–65.

43. *World Military Expenditures, 1987*, p. 54.

44. These data come from the Central Intelligence Agency, *Handbook of Economic Statistics, 1987* (Washington, DC: U.S. Government Printing Office, 1988). The size of the Third World economies have to be revised upward when relying upon the new purchasing power measures recently developed by the International Monetary Fund and the World Bank. In addition, India's rather than

Brazil's becomes the largest Third World economy. See *New York Times*, May 20, 1993, pp. A1, 8.

45. Stephen Van Evera, "The United States and the Third World: When to Intervene?" in Kenneth A. Oye, Robert J. Lieber, and Donald Rothchild, eds., *Eagle in a New World: American Strategy in the Post–Cold War Era* (New York: HarperCollins, 1992), pp. 115–16.

46. Joseph S. Nye and Robert O. Keohane, *Power and Interdependence: World Politics in Transition* (Boston: Little, Brown, 1977); Kenneth N. Waltz, "The Myth of National Interdependence," in Charles P. Kindleberger, ed., *The International Corporation* (Cambridge, MA: MIT Press, 1970), pp. 205–23; Bruce Russett, "Dimensions of Resource Dependence: Some Elements of Rigor in Concept and Policy Analysis," *International Organization* 38 (summer 1984): 481–99; and Stephen D. Krasner, "Oil Is the Exception," *Foreign Policy* 13 (spring 1974): 68–84.

47. There is a marked overlap between this conventional conceptualization of economic invulnerability and that of some analysts who stress America's vulnerability. See Bolslaw Adam Boczek, "Resource Rivalry in the Third World," in Robert W. Clawson, ed., *East-West Rivalry in the Third Word: Security Issues and Regional Perspectives* (Wilmington, DE: Scholarly Resources Press, 1984), pp. 184–86; Bodhan O. Szuprowicz, *How to Avoid Strategic Minerals Shortages: Dealing with Cartels, Embargoes, and Supply Disruptions* (New York: John Wiley, 1981), p. 286.

48. *Direction of Trade Statistics* (Washington, DC: International Monetary Fund, 1988), pp. 93, 139.

49. *Direction of Trade Statistics*, pp. 93, 139; David, "Why Third World Matters," p. 74.

50. For some illustrative specifics, see Feinberg, *The Intemperate Zone*, pp. 88, 109–10, and L. Harold Bullis and James E. Mielke, *Strategic and Critical Materials* (Boulder, CO: Westview Press, 1985), pp. 93, 130. For a general discussion of America's predominance in "structural power," see Susan Strange, "Toward a Theory of Transnational Empire," in Ernst-Otto Czenspiel and James N. Rosenan, eds., *Global Changes and Theoretical Challenges: Approaches to World Politics for the 1990s* (Lexington, MA: D. C. Heath, 1989), 161–76.

51. Jock A. Finlayson and David G. Haglund, "Whatever Happened to the Resource War?" *Survival* 29, no. 5 (September–October 1987): 403–15.

52. W. Wendall Fletcher and Kirsten Oldenburg, "How Technology Can Reduce U.S. Import Vulnerability," *Issues in Science and Technology* 2, no. 4 (summer 1986): 79, fig. 1. The information in this article comes from *Strategic Minerals: Technologies to Reduce U.S. Import Vulnerability* (Washington, DC: Office of Technology Assessment, 1985).

53. Feinberg, *The Intemperate Zone*, p. 117; Barry M. Blechman, *U.S. Security in the Twenty-First Century* (Boulder, CO: Westview Press, 1987), p. 49.

54. Fletcher and Oldenburg, "Technology Can Reduce," p. 79, fig. 1; Bullis and Mielke, *Strategic and Critical Materials*, pp. 115, 121, 172, 222.

55. Fletcher and Oldenburg, "Technology Can Reduce," p. 119; Feinberg, *The Intemperate Zone*, p. 118; Michael W. Klass, James G. Burrows, and Steven D. Beggs, *International Mineral Cartels and Embargoes: Policy Implications*

for the United States (New York: Praeger, 1980), p. 150; Michael Shafer, "Mineral Myths," *Foreign Policy* 47 (summer 1982): 159.

56. Simon D. Strauss, "Why the Strategic Stockpile Is Essential," *Issues in Science and Technology* 2, no. 4 (summer 1986): 89.

57. Strauss, "Strategic Stockpile," p. 87; Bullis and Mielke, *Strategic and Critical Materials*, p. 223; Shafer, "Mineral Myths," pp. 164–67.

58. S. Fred Singer, "NOPEC—the Future of Oil," *National Interest* 7 (spring 1987): 63.

59. Robert H. Johnson, "The Persian Gulf in U.S. Strategy: A Skeptical View," *International Security* 14, no. 1 (summer 1989): 124–25; Singer, "NOPEC"; the chapters by Morris Adelman, David Teece, Theodore Moran, John Lichtblau, and James Griffin in James Griffin and David J. Teece, eds., *OPEC Behavior and World Oil Prices* (London: Allen and Unwin, 1982).

60. Abbas Alnasrawi, *OPEC in a Changing World Economy* (Baltimore: Johns Hopkins University Press, 1985), p. 147.

61. Robert J. Lieber, "International Energy Policy and the Reagan Administration: Avoiding the Next Oil Shock?" in Kenneth A. Oye, Robert J. Lieber, and Donald Rothchild, eds., *Eagle Resurgent? The Reagan Era in American Foreign Policy* (Boston: Little, Brown, 1987), pp. 172–73; Alnasrawi, *OPEC*, pp. 156–59.

62. This calculation is based on the data in *Monthly Energy Review*, Energy Information Administration, April 1988, pp. 42–43.

63. Central Intelligence Agency, *Handbook of International Economic Statistics, 1992* (Washington, DC: U.S. Government Printing Office, 1992), p. 129; Lieber, "International Energy Policy," p. 171; Johnson, "Persian Gulf," pp. 139, 141, 146; *New York Times*, October 17, 1993, p. E4.

64. Lieber, "International Energy Policy," p. 171; *Monthly Energy Review*, April 1988, pp. 42–43; Robert L. Bradley, *The Mirage of Oil Protection* (Lanham, MD: University Press of America, 1989), p. 88.

65. *Washington Post*, August 15, 1990, p. A31. Les Aspin, chairman of the House Armed Services Committee, offered a similar assessment. "If we allow Saddam to control half the world's oil supply, he will control our economy—determining our rate of inflation, our interest rates, our rate of growth." Les Aspin, "Define Our Goals in the Gulf," *Washington Post*, August 10, 1990, p. A15.

66. William A. Niskansen, "Oil, War, and the Economy," in Ted Galen Carpenter, ed., *America Entangled: The Persian Gulf Crisis and Its Consequences* (Washington, DC: Cato Institute, 1991), p. 54.

67. David R. Henderson, "The Myth of Saddam's Oil Stranglehold," in Carpenter, *America Entangled*, pp. 42–44.

68. Christopher Layne and Ted Galen Carpenter, "Arabian Nightmares: Washington's Persian Gulf Entanglement," Cato Institute Policy Analysis, November 9, 1990, p. 2.

69. Peter R. Odell and Kenneth E. Rosing, *The Future of Oil: Resources and Use*, 2d ed. (New York: Nichols, 1983), pp. 24–26, 40–44; Doug Bandow, "The Myth of Iraq's Oil Stranglehold," *New York Times*, September 17, 1990; *New York Times*, October 17, 1993, p. E4.

70. Johnson, "Persian Gulf," p. 159. Also see Peter G. Peterson with James K. Sebenius, "The Primacy of the Domestic Agenda," in Graham Allison and Gregory F. Treverton, eds., *Rethinking America's Security: Beyond Cold War to New World Order* (New York: Norton, 1992), pp. 71–73.

71. *Vital Speeches of the Day*, October 15, 1992, p. 13. According to Chairman of the Joint Chiefs of Staff General Colin Powell, "As the only nation with the military capability to influence events globally, we must remain capable of responding effectively if the United States is to successfully promote the stability required for global progress and prosperity." Cited in *Defense Monitor* 21, no. 4 (1992): 2.

72. Van Evera, "Why Europe Matters," pp. 10–11; Robert J. Art, "A Defensible Defense: America's Grand Strategy after the Cold War," *International Security* 15, no. 4 (spring 1991): 41–42.

73. Van Evera, "Why Europe Matters," pp. 10–11.

74. Richard Ullman, *Securing Europe* (Princeton: Princeton University Press, 1991); Robert Jervis, "The Future of World Politics: Will It Resemble the Past?" *International Security* 16, no. 3 (winter 1991–92: 46–55; Stephen Van Evera, "Primed for Peace: Europe after the Cold War," *International Security* 15, no. 3 (winter 1990–91): 7–57.

75. John Mearsheimer, "Back to the Future: Instability in Europe after the Cold War," *International Security* 15, no. 1 (summer 1990): 5–56.

76. Robert H. Johnson, "Periods of Peril: The Window of Vulnerability and Other Myths," *Foreign Affairs* 61, no. 4 (spring 1983): 950–70.

77. Karl Lautenschläger, "The Submarine in Naval Warfare: 1901–2001," *International Security* 11, no. 3 (winter 1986–87): 94–140.

78. For the actual numbers and a look at the balance after proposed U.S. cutbacks, see Kaufmann, *A Thoroughly Efficient Navy*, pp. 7–9, 68–70.

79. Robert W. Tucker, *The Nuclear Debate*, p. 111.

80. See articles on "prospect theory" in special issue of *Political Psychology* 13, no. 2 (June 1992).

81. Thomas C. Schelling, *The Strategy of Conflict* (New York: Oxford University Press, 1963), pp. 21–66; Thomas C. Schelling, *Arms and Influence* (New Haven: Yale University Press, 1966), pp. 35–125.

82. Robert J. Art, "Between Assured Destruction and Nuclear Victory: The Case for the 'MAD-Plus' Doctrine," *Ethics* 95, no. 3 (April 1985): 512–13.

83. Additional evidence is found in chapter 11. Whenever the United States and its allies (who were much more exposed) to the communist threat disagreed about its seriousness, Washington saw it as more threatening.

Chapter IV

1. Robert Jervis, *Perception and Misperception in International Politics* (Princeton: Princeton University Press, 1978), pp. 53–113; Charles L. Glaser, "Political Consequences of Military Strategy: Expanding and Refining the Spiral and Deterrence Models," *World Politics* 44, no. 4 (July 1992): 497–538; Glenn H. Snyder and Paul Diesing, *Conflict among Nations: Bargaining, Decision Making, and System Structure in International Crises* (Princeton: Princeton University Press, 1977), pp. 297–310.

2. Graham T. Allison, Albert Carnesale, and Joseph S. Nye, eds., *Hawks, Doves, and Owls: An Agenda for Avoiding Nuclear War* (New York: Norton, 1985), pp. 209–14.

3. Alexander Yanov, "In the Grip of the Adversarial Paradigm," in Robert O. Crummey, ed., *Reform in Russia and the U.S.S.R.* (Urbana: University of Illinois Press, 1989), pp. 156–81; George F. Minde II and Michael Hennessey, "Reform of the Soviet Military under Krushchev and the Role of America's Strategic Modernization," in Crummey, *Reform in Russia*, pp. 182–206.

4. Representative writings of this kind of interpretation include Richard Pipes, *U.S.-Soviet Relations in the Era of Detente: A Tragedy of Errors* (Boulder, CO: Westview Press, 1981); Colin S. Gray, "Nuclear Strategy: The Case for a Theory of Victory," *International Security* 4, no. 1 (summer, 1979): 54–87; Colin S. Gray, *Nuclear Strategy and National Style* (Lanham, MD: Hamilton Press, 1986); Charles Tyroller, ed., *Alerting America: The Papers of the Committee on the Present Danger* (Washington, DC: Pergamon-Brassey, 1984); R. James Woolsey, "The Politics of Vulnerability," *Foreign Affairs* 62, no. 4 (spring 1984): 805–19. The chief governmental document that articulated the USSR's hegemonic drive is NSC-68, "United States Objectives and Programs for National Security," principally authored by Paul Nitze, printed in *Foreign Relations of the United States 1950*, (Washington, DC: U.S. Government Printing Office, 1977), 1:234–92.

5. Representative writings of this kind of interpretation include Louis J. Halle, *The Cold War as History* (New York: HarperCollins, 1967); Seweryn Bialer, *Stalin's Successors: Leadership, Stability, and Change in the Soviet Union* (Cambridge, England: Cambridge University Press, 1980); Seweryn Bialer and Joan Afferica, "Reagan and Russia," *Foreign Affairs* 61, no. 2 (winter 1982–83: 249–71; Dimitri Simes, "The Death of Detente," *International Security* 5, no. 1 (summer 1980): 3–25; Robert Legvold, "Containment without Confrontation," *Foreign Policy* 40 (fall 1980): 74–98; John Lewis Gaddis, "Containment: Its Past and Future," *International Security* 5, no. 4 (spring 1981): 74–102; Stanley Hoffmann, *Janus and Minerva: Essays in the Theory and Practice of International Politics* (Boulder, CO: Westview Press, 1987).

6. Representative writings of this kind of interpretation include George F. Kennan, *The Cloud of Danger: Current Realities of American Foreign Policy* (Boston: Atlantic Monthly Press and Little, Brown, 1977); Richard J. Barnet, *The Giants: Russia and America* (New York: Simon and Schuster, 1977); Richard J. Barnet, "Why Trust the Soviets?" *World Policy Journal* 1, no. 3 (spring 1984): 461–82; Ernst Haas, "Why Collaborate? Issue Linkage and International Regimes," *World Politics* 32, no. 3 (April 1980): 357–405; Randall Forsberg, "Confining the Military to Defense as a Route to Disarmament," *World Policy Journal* 1, no. 2 (winter 1984): 285–318; Robert C. Johansen, *The National Interest and the Human Interest: An Analysis of U.S. Foreign Policy* (Princeton: Princeton University Press, 1980).

7. The quotations are found in John Lewis Gaddis, "The Reagan Administration and Soviet-American Relations," in David E. Kyvig, ed., *Reagan and the World* (New York: Greenwood Press, 1990), pp. 19, 22, 28.

8. This background is taken from Richard K. Herrmann, "The Middle East and the New World Order: Rethinking U.S. Political Strategy after the Gulf War," *International Security* 16, no. 2 (fall 1991): 52 for the quote; Theodore

Draper, "The Gulf War Reconsidered," *New York Review of Books*, January 16, 1992, pp. 46–47; Richard Schofield, *Kuwait and Iraq: Historical Claims and Territorial Disputes* (London: Royal Institute of International Affairs, 1991).

9. Herrmann, "Middle East," p. 51.

10. Janice Gross Stein, "Deterrence and Compellence in the Gulf, 1990–91: A Failed or Impossible Task?" *International Security* 17, no. 2 (fall 1992): 149–55, 160; Elaine Sciolino, *The Outlaw State: Saddam Hussein's Quest for Power and the Gulf Crisis* (New York: John Wiley, 1991); John Bulloch and Harvey Morris, *Saddam's War: The Origins of the Kuwait Conflict and the International Response* (London: Faber, 1991).

11. Cited in Sciolino, *The Outlaw State*, p. 292.

12. Jack Snyder, "Science and Sovietology: Bridging the Methods Gap in Soviet Foreign Policy Studies," *World Politics* 40, no. 2 (January 1988): 167–70.

13. See the numerous studies cited in Carol R. Ember, Melvin Ember, and Bruce Russett, "Peace between Participatory Polities: A Cross-Cultural Test of the 'Democracies Rarely Fight Each Other' Hypothesis," *World Politics* 44, no. 4 (July 1992): 574, note 2.

14. "X," "The Sources of Soviet Conduct," *Foreign Affairs* 25, no. 4 (July 1947): 566–82; George F. Kennan, *American Diplomacy: 1900–1950* (Chicago: University of Chicago Press, 1951), pp. 89–91.

15. For the application of "everyday" attribution theory to the thinking and behavior of four American decision makers at the outset of the Cold War, see Deborah Welch Larson, *Origins of Containment: A Psychological Explanation* (Princeton: Princeton University Press, 1985).

16. The most penetrating discussion of the economists' reliance upon behavior as revealed preferences is found in Amartya K. Sen, "Rational Fools: A Critique of the Behavioral Foundations of Economic Theory," *Philosophy and Public Affairs* 6, no. 4 (summer 1977): 317–44.

17. On the possibility that the shelters were built by a leadership intent upon surviving a nuclear war, it has been argued that this still would not have influenced or been indicative of its peacetime intentions in challenging U.S. interests. See Charles L. Glaser, *Analyzing Strategic Nuclear Policy* (Princeton: Princeton University Press, 1990), pp. 236–38.

18. M. A. Salmon, S. Van Evera, and K. J. Sullivan, "Analysis or Propaganda? Measuring American Strategic Nuclear Capability, 1969–1984," unpublished manuscript, 1985, quoted in James H. Lebovic, *Deadly Dilemmas: Deterrence in U.S. Nuclear Strategy* (New York: Columbia University Press, 1990), p. 58.

19. James G. Blight, Joseph S. Nye, and David A. Welch, "The Cuban Missile Crisis Revisited," *Foreign Affairs* 66, no. 1 (fall 1987): 180–83. In reviewing the host of studies on the missile crisis, Richard Ned Lebow concludes that they are all "at best, clever speculations about Soviet [aims] consistent with a few established facts." "The Cuban Missile Crisis: Reading the Lessons Correctly," *Political Science Quarterly* 98, no. 3 (fall 1983): 456.

20. Alexander L. George, "The Cuban Missile Crisis," in Alexander L. George, ed., *Avoiding War: Problems of Crisis Management* (Boulder, CO: Westview Press, 1991), p. 224. A detailed defensive interpretation of the missile emplacements, based on Soviet sources and interviews with former Soviet officials, is

found in Richard Ned Lebow and Janice Gross Stein, *We All Lost the Cold War* (Princeton: Princeton University Press, 1994), pp. 19–109.

21. On this last point see chapter 7.

22. Jack Snyder, "Richness, Rigor, and Relevance in the Study of Soviet Foreign Policy," *International Security* 9, no. 3 (winter 1984–85): 89–108.

23. Snyder, "Richness, Rigor, and Relevance," pp. 95–97.

24. Robert Axelrod, *The Evolution of Cooperation* (New York: Basic Books, 1984).

25. George W. Downs, David M. Rocke, and Randolph M. Siverson, "Arms Races and Cooperation," *World Politics* 38, no. 1 (October 1985): 143.

26. Axelrod, *The Evolution of Cooperation*, pp. 138, 186–90.

27. Downs, Rocke, and Siverson, "Arms Races and Cooperation," pp. 141–42.

28. Daniel Druckman, "The Psychology of Arms Control and Reciprocation," in Bennett Ramberg, ed., *Arms Control without Negotiation: From the Cold War to the New World Order* (Boulder, CO: Lynne Riener, 1993), pp. 27, 35; Roger Fisher and William Ury, *Getting Together* (Boston: Houghton Mifflin, 1988), p. 201.

CHAPTER V

1. John Lewis Gaddis, *Strategies of Containment: A Critical Appraisal of Postwar American National Security Policy* (New York: Oxford University Press, 1982); Robert H. Johnson, "Exaggerating America's Stakes in Third World Conflicts," *International Security* 10, no. 3 (winter 1985–86): 32–68; Bruce W. Jentleson, "American Commitments in the Third World: Theory vs. Practice," *International Organization* 41, no. 4 (autumn 1987): 667–704.

2. Ernest May, *"Lessons" of the Past: The Use and Misuse of History in American Foreign Policy* (New York: Oxford University Press, 1973), pp. 52–86.

3. May, *"Lessons" of the Past*, pp. 52–86. William Stueck, *The Road to Confrontation: American Policy toward China and Korea, 1947–1950* (Chapel Hill: University of North Carolina Press, 1981).

4. Yuen Foong Khong, *Analogies at War: Korea, Munich, Dien Bien Phu, and the Vietnam Decision of 1965* (Princeton: Princeton University Press, 1992), p. 3.

5. John Lewis Gaddis and Terry Diebold, *Containing the Soviet Union: A Critique of U.S. Policy* (Washington, DC: Pergamon-Brassey, 1987), p. 3; Gaddis, *Strategies of Containment*, pp. 212–13. Also see George McT. Kahin, *Intervention: How America Became Involved in Vietnam* (Garden City, NY: Doubleday, 1987); Larry Berman, *Planning on Tragedy: The Americanization of the War in Vietnam* (New York: Norton, 1982).

6. Senator Gravel Edition, *The Pentagon Papers: The Defense Department History of United States Decisionmaking on Vietnam* (Boston: Beacon Press, 1975), 3:695, 700.

7. Henry A. Kissinger, "The Vietnam Negotiations," *Foreign Affairs* 47, no. 2 (January 1969): 218; *Public Papers of the Presidents: Richard M. Nixon, 1970* (Washington, DC: U.S. Government Printing Office, 1971), p. 409.

8. Khong, *Analogies at War*, p. 5.

9. Zbigniew Brzezinski, "Strategic Implications of the Central American Crisis," in Joseph Cirincione, ed., *Central America and the Western Alliance* (New York: Holmes and Meier, 1985), p. 109.

10. Thomas C. Schelling, *Arms and Influence* (New Haven: Yale University Press, 1966), pp. 124, 66. Also see Schelling, *The Strategy of Conflict* (New York: Oxford University Press, 1963).

11. Robert Jervis, "Deterrence Theory Revisited," *World Politics* 31, no. 2 (January 1979): 318–19.

12. Ted Hopf, "Soviet Inferences from Their Victories in the Periphery: Visions of Resistance or Culminating Gains?" in Robert Jervis and Jack Snyder, eds., *Dominoes and Bandwagons: Strategic Beliefs and Great Power Competition in the Eurasian Rimland* (New York: Oxford University Press, 1991), pp. 145–89.

13. Hopf, "Soviet Inferences," pp. 176–77.

14. Alexander L. George and Richard Smoke, *Deterrence in American Foregin Policy: Theory and Practice* (New York: Columbia University Press, 1974), p. 561.

15. Glenn H. Snyder and Paul Diesing, *Conflict among Nations: Bargaining, Decision Making, and System Structure in International Crises* (Princeton: Princeton University Press, 1977), pp. 187, 190. Italics in the original.

16. Paul Huth and Bruce Russett, "What Makes Deterrence Work? Cases from 1900 to 1980," *World Politics* 36, no. 4 (July 1984): 517–18. This finding does not show up in a later study using almost the exact same data set. But as confirmed by the null findings about the effect of alliances, this has to do with the introduction of a new independent variable that subsumes the effects of arms sales and trade. See Paul K. Huth, "Extended Deterrence and the Outbreak of War," *American Political Science Review* 82, no. 2, (June 1988): 436–37.

17. Huth, "Extended Deterrence," pp. 436–38.

18. Jervis, "Deterrence Theory Revisited," p. 316.

19. Schelling, *Arms and Influence*, p. 36.

20. Advocacy of the countervailing and later the nuclear-war-fighting strategy is found in Colin S. Gray, "Nuclear Strategy: The Case for a Theory of Victory," *International Security* 4, no. 1 (summer 1979): 54–87; Colin S. Gray and Keith Payne, "Victory Is Possible," *Foreign Policy* 39 (summer 1980): 14–27; Walter Slocombe, "The Countervailing Strategy," *International Security* 5, no. 4 (spring 1981): 18–27; *Report of the President's Commission on Strategic Forces* (Washington, DC: U.S. Government Printing Office, 1983). Official expressions of the strategy are found in Secretary of Defense Harold Brown, *Annual Report, FY 1980* (Washington, DC: U.S. Government Printing Office, 1979); Secretary of Defense Caspar W. Weinberger, *Annual Report, FY 1987* (Washington, DC: U.S. Government Printing Office, 1986).

21. The arguments are most fully developed in Robert Jervis, *The Illogic of American Nuclear Strategy* (Ithaca, NY: Cornell University Press, 1984) and Charles L. Glaser, *Analyzing Strategic Nuclear Policy* (Princeton: Princeton University Press, 1990). Also see Kenneth N. Waltz, "Nuclear Myths and Political Realities," *American Political Science Review* 84, no. 3 (September 1990): 731–45.

22. That these constitute all the justifications for strategic advantage may be appreciated by reviewing the most comprehensive discussion of U.S. nuclear policies and the debates surrounding them. See Lawrence Freedman, *The Evolution of Nuclear Strategy* (New York: St. Martin's Press, 1981). It should also be noted that McGeorge Bundy argues for the ineffectualness of our nuclear threats during the 1950s, the period of predominance, in "The Unimpressive Record of Atomic Diplomacy," in Gywn Pris, ed., *The Nuclear Crisis Reader* (New York: Random House, 1984), pp. 46–47; with regard to the Korean War so too does Roger Dingman, "Atomic Diplomacy during the Cold War," *International Security* 13, no. 3 (winter 1988–89): 72–75. Also see Gaddis, *Strategies of Containment*, pp. 168–73, and Richard K. Betts, *Soldiers, Statesmen, and Cold War Crises* (Cambridge, England: Cambridge University Press, 1977), pp. 106–7.

23. Marc Trachtenberg, *History and Strategy* (Princeton: Princeton University Press, 1991), p. 259.

24. Warner Schilling, "U.S. Strategic Nuclear Concepts in the 1970s: The Search for Sufficiently Equivalent Countervailing Parity," *International Security* 6, no. 2 (fall 1981): 63. Not so parenthetically, the Soviets' improved capabilities for fighting a conventional war in Europe did not make for bolder threats or actions. See Michael McGuire, *Military Objectives in Soviet Foreign Policy* (Washington, DC: Brookings Institution, 1987). Nor was there an association between "increased Soviet military capabilities and enhanced Soviet propensities to take risks." Hannes Adomeit, "Soviet Crisis Prevention and Management: Why and When Do the Soviet Leaders Take Risks?," *Orbis* 30, no. 1 (spring 1986): 42–43.

25. Richard K. Betts, *Nuclear Blackmail and the Nuclear Balance* (Washington, DC: Brookings Institution, 1987), pp. 14–15.

26. For the historical application of the claim over the course of the Cold War, see McGeorge Bundy, *Danger and Survival* (New York: Random House, 1988).

27. Trachtenberg, *History and Strategy*, p. 259.

28. Schelling, *Arms and Influence*, pp. 166–68.

29. Arnold Horelick, "The Cuban Missile Crisis: An Analysis of Soviet Calculations and Behavior," *World Politics* 16, no. 3 (April 1964): 387–88; Schelling, *Arms and Influence*, pp. 95–96.

30. Huth and Russett, "What Makes Deterrence Work?" pp. 517–18. Also see Huth, "Extended Deterrence," pp. 428–32.

31. Samuel P. Huntington, "Arms Races: Prerequisites and Results," in Carl J. Friedrich and Seymour E. Harris, eds., *Public Policy* (Cambridge, MA: Harvard University, Graduate School of Public Administration, 1958), pp. 41–86; Huntington, "The Renewal of Strategy," in Samuel P. Huntington, ed., *The Strategic Imperative* (Cambridge, MA: Ballinger, 1982), pp. 41–42.

32. Eric A. Nordlinger, "Prospects and Policies for Soviet-American Reconciliation," *Political Science Quarterly* 103, no. 2 (summer 1988): 201.

33. Betts, *Nuclear Blackmail*, p. 219.

34. Adomeit, "Soviet Crisis Prevention," pp. 42–43.

35. Barry M. Blechman and Stephen S. Kaplan, *Force without War: U.S. Armed Forces as a Political Instrument* (Washington, DC: Brookings Institution, 1978), pp. 127–29, 132.

36. The problems are discussed in Richard Ned Lebow, *Nuclear Crisis Management: A Dangerous Illusion* (Ithaca, NY: Cornell University Press, 1987); Bruce G. Blair, *Strategic Command and Control: Redefining the Nuclear Threat* (Washington, DC: Brookings Institution, 1985); Paul Bracken, *The Command and Control of Nuclear Forces* (New Haven: Yale University Press, 1983).

37. Freedman, *The Evolution of Nuclear Strategy*, p. 380.

38. Brown, *Annual Report, FY 1980*, p. 80. It may be noted that this statement lends further support to the argument made in chapter 2—that interpretations of the other side's intentions "drive" hawks and doves to their different policy perches.

39. Robert W. Tucker and David C. Hendrickson, *The Imperial Temptation: The New World Order and America's Purpose* (New York: Council on Foreign Relations Press, 1992), p. 36.

40. Robert J. Art, "A Defensible Defense: America's Grand Strategy after the Cold War," *International Security* 15, no. 4 (spring 1991): 30, italics added.

41. The patterns, facts, and possibilities of nuclear spread to "second tier" and "third tier" states are comprehensively set out in Leonard Spector, *Nuclear Ambitions* (Boulder, CO: Westview Press, 1990). For the security threats, see Lewis A. Dunn, *Controlling the Bomb: Nuclear Proliferation in the 1980s* (New Haven: Yale University Press, 1982), pp. 69–95; Thomas C. Schelling, "Thinking About Nuclear Terrorism," *International Security* 6, no. 4 (spring 1982): 61–77; Paul Leventhal and Yonah Alexander, eds., *Nuclear Terrorism: Defining the Threat* (Washington, DC: Pergamon-Brassey, 1986.) A recent update is found in "Fighting Off Doom," *Time*, June 21, 1993, pp. 36–38.

42. Michele A. Flournoy, "Nuclear Weapons and the Changing Security Environment," in Michele A. Flournoy, ed., *Nuclear Weapons after the Cold War* (New York: HarperCollins, 1993), p. 23.

43. These proposals are reviewed in Michael J. Mazarr, "Nuclear Weapons after the Cold War," *Washington Quarterly* 15, no. 3 (summer 1992): 190–91. As an example, see Walter B. Slocombe, "The Continued Need for Extended Deterrence," *Washington Quarterly* 14, no. 4 (autumn 1991): 157–72.

44. John Mearsheimer, "Back to the Future: Instability in Europe after the Cold War," *International Security* 15, no. 1 (summer 1990): 5–56.

45. Stephen Peter Rosen, "Regional Nuclear War: Problems for Theory and Practice," Olin Institute for Strategic Studies, Harvard University, December 1990.

46. Samuel P. Huntington, "America's Changing Strategic Interests," *Survival* 33, no. 1 (January–February 1991): 8.

47. Samuel P. Huntington, "Why International Primacy Matters," *International Security* 17, no. 4 (spring 1993): 68–83; Slocombe, "Continued Need for Deterrence"; Colin Gray, "Strategic Sense, Strategic Nonsense," *National Interest* 29 (fall 1992): 11–19; Charles Krauthammer, "What's Wrong with the 'Pentagon Paper'?" *Washington Post*, March 13, 1992, p. A25. Also see the references to the "maximalists" in Mazaar, "Nuclear Weapons," pp. 186–90.

48. *New York Times*, March 8, 1992, pp. A1, 14. In response to public criticisms, the revised version of this document downgrades the emphasis on deterrence. *New York Times*, May 24, 1992, pp. 1, 14.

49. Jonathan G. Clarke, "The Eurocorps: A Fresh Start in Europe," Cato Institute, *Foreign Policy Briefing*, December 28, 1992, pp. 2–3, 6.

50. See the studies cited in note 47 above.

51. Huntington, "America's Changing Strategic Interests," pp. 11–12.

52. Edward N. Luttwak, "From Geopolitics to Geo-Economics: Logic of Conflict, Grammar of Commerce," *National Interest* 20 (summer 1990): 19, 21.

53. For recent writings on the importance of relative economic gains and losses see the references in Michael Mastunduno, "Do Relative Gains Matter? America's Response to Japanese Industrial Policy," *International Security* 16, no. 1 (summer 1991): 77.

54. Huntington, "America's Changing Strategic Interests," pp. 8–10. Huntington's "Why International Primacy Matters" focuses yet more closely upon Japan. For an exceptionally thorough discussion of the possible, but greatly exaggerated, dependencies upon Japan for military and defense-related technologies, see Theodore H. Moran, "The Globalization of America's Defense Industries: Managing the Threat of Foreign Dependence," *International Security* 15, no. 1 (summer 1990): 57–99.

55. Kenneth N. Waltz, "America as a Model for the World? A Foreign Policy Perspective," *Political Science and Politics* 24, no. 4 (December 1991): 669. Also see Waltz, *Theory of International Politics* (Reading, MA: Addison-Wesley, 1979); Stephen M. Walt, *The Origins of Alliances* (Ithaca, NY: Cornell University Press, 1987); Jervis and Snyder, *Dominoes and Bandwagons*.

56. Relying on realist theory and historical parallels, Christopher Layne argues that unipolarity will not last, whatever efforts the United States makes on its behalf. See "The Unipolar Illusion: Why New Great Powers Will Rise," *International Security* 17, no. 4 (spring 1993): 5–51. Also relying upon realist theory, but without offering any predictions about the possible passing of American primacy, Robert Jervis questions whether the benefits warrant the effort to retain it. See "International Primacy: Is the Game Worth the Candle?" *International Security* 17, no. 4 (spring 1993): 52–67.

57. On this development, see chapter 8.

58. Central Intelligence Agency, *Handbook of International Economic Statistics 1992* (Washington, DC: U.S. Government Printing Office, 1992), table 2, p. 16. The data are based upon U.S. purchasing-power equivalents.

59. This pattern is reviewed in chapter 9.

60. The effects of defense spending upon economic growth in general and under varying macroeconomic conditions are discussed in chapter 9.

CHAPTER VI

1. Janice Gross Stein, "Reassurance in International Conflict Management," *Political Science Quarterly* 106, no. 3 (autumn 1991): 432. Among the studies that take insecurity to be a major cause of conflict and war, see especially Kenneth N. Waltz, *Theory of International Politics* (Reading, MA: Addison-Wesley, 1979). What Waltz leaves unsaid about the effects of declining power is covered in Jack Levy, "Declining Power and the Preventive Motivation for War," *World Politics* 40, no. 1 (October 1987): 82–107.

2. Robert Jervis, "Deterrence and Perception," *International Security* 7, no. 3 (winter 1982–83): 27.

3. Daniel Kahneman and Amos Tversky, "Choices, Values, and Frames," *American Psychologist* 39, no. 4 (April 1984): 341–50, and Amos Tversky and Daniel Kahneman, "The Framing of Decisions and the Psychology of Choice," *Science* 211, no. 4481 (January 30, 1981): 453–58. For references to other experimental studies and their applications to international politics, see Janice Gross Stein, "International Cooperation and Loss Avoidance: Framing the Problem," *International Journal* 47, no. 2 (spring 1992): 202–34; and Robert Jervis, "Political Implications of Loss Aversion," *Political Psychology* 13, no. 2 (June 1992): 187–204.

4. Paul Huth and Bruce Russett, "Testing Deterrence Theory: Rigor Makes a Difference," *World Politics* 42, no. 4 (July 1990): 487.

5. Bruce D. Berkowitz, *Calculated Risks: A Century of Arms Control* (New York: Simon and Schuster, 1987), pp. 90–135.

6. For a review of such problems by a sympathetic arms control participant, see James E. Goodby, "Can Arms Control Survive Peace?" *Washington Quarterly* 13, no. 4 (autumn 1990): 93–101.

7. Janice Gross Stein, "The Managers and the Managed: Crisis Prevention in the Middle East," in Gilbert Winham, ed., *New Issues in Crisis Management* (Boulder, CO: Westview Press, 1987).

8. Alexander George, "U.S.-Soviet Relations: Evolution and Prospects," in Richard Smoke and Andrei Kortunov, eds., *Mutual Security: A New Approach to Soviet-American Relations* (New York: St. Martin's Press, 1991), pp. 32–34.

9. For a complete review of the Soviet-American compliance record, see Gloria Duffy, *Compliance and the Future of Arms Control* (Cambridge, MA: Ballinger, 1988). The charges voiced by the Reagan administration are discussed in Jeanette Voas, "The Arms-Control Compliance Debate," *Survival* 28, no. 1 (January–February 1986): 8–31.

10. Richard K. Betts, "Systems for Peace or Causes of War? Collective Security, Arms Control, and the New Europe," *International Security* 17, no. 1 (Summer 1992): 35, 41, italics in the original.

11. Matthew Bunn, "Arms Control's Enduring Worth," *Foreign Policy* 79 (summer 1990): 151, 154–55. Based partly on some of the just-mentioned drawbacks of bilateral agreements, John Mueller appears to urge thoroughgoing unilateral reductions: "Just *do* it." Since the arms buildup did not involve written accords, neither does their builddown require them. However, Mueller's proposal is neither extensive nor unconditional. It "supposes *low* tension" between the rivals. This is, of course, when arms accords are easiest to realize and their achievements have the least to contribute to peaceful outcomes. See "Taking Peace Seriously: Two Proposal Proposals," in Robert Jervis and Seweryn Bialer, eds., *Soviet-American Relations after the Cold War* (Durham, NC: Duke University Press, 1991), pp. 267, 269.

12. Albert Carnesale and Richard N. Haass, "Conclusions: Weighing the Evidence," in Albert Carnesale and Richard N. Haass, eds., *Superpower Arms Control: Setting the Record Straight* (Cambridge, MA: Ballinger, 1987), pp. 355, 345–46.

13. Bunn, "Arms Control's Enduring Worth," p. 155.

14. Berkowitz, *Calculated Risks*, pp. 22, 28–29, 32, 40, 46–51, 55; Carnesale and Haas, "Conclusions," pp. 342–44.

15. Thomas C. Schelling, "Abolition of Ballistic Missiles," *International Security* 12, no. 1 (summer 1987): 180, 182. The same arguments have been put forward by a leading proponent of conciliatory internationalism. See Stanley Hoffmann, *Janus and Minerva: Essays in the Theory and Practice of International Politics* (Boulder, CO: Westview Press, 1987), pp. 343–44, 362.

16. Bunn, "Arms Control's Enduring Worth," p. 155.

17. For an extended elaboration of these risks, see Charles L. Glaser, *Analyzing Strategic Nuclear Policy* (Princeton: Princeton University Press, 1990), pp. 315–60.

18. Richard Smoke, "A Theory of Mutual Security," in Smoke and Kortunov, *Mutual Security*, pp. 91–109.

19. Glaser, *Analyzing Strategic Nuclear Policy*, 207–56, 315–60.

20. James E. Goodby, "The Stockholm Conference: Negotiating a Cooperative Security System for Europe," in Alexander L. George, Philip J. Farley, and Alexander Dallin, eds., *U.S.-Soviet Security Cooperation: Achievements, Failures, Lessons* (New York: Oxford University Press, 1988), pp. 144–72; John Maresca, *To Helsinki* (Durham, NC: Duke University Press, 1985); Johan Jørgen Holst, "Confidence-Building Measures: A Conceptual Framework," *Survival* 25, no. 1 (January–February 1983): 2–15.

21. Hedley Bull, "The Classical Approach to Arms Control: Twenty Years Later," in Uwe Nerlich, ed., *Soviet Power and Western Negotiating Policies* (Cambridge, MA: Ballinger, 1983), 2:21–30; Thomas C. Schelling, "What Went Wrong with Arms Control?" *Foreign Affairs* 64, no. 2 (winter 1985–86): 219–33.

22. Berkowitz, *Calculated Risks*, p. 21.

23. The positive case for SALT II is set out in Lloyd Cutler and Roger Molander, "Is There Life after Death for SALT?" *International Security* 6, no. 2 (fall 1981): 3–20. According to Michael McGuire's assumptions about Soviet plans in *Military Objectives in Soviet Foreign Policy* (Washington, DC: Brookings Institution, 1987), p. 240, SALT II probably led to a 40 percent reduction in the planned deployment of MIRVed Soviet ICBMs.

24. Berkowitz, *Calculated Risks*, p. 21.

25. *Time*, August 5, 1991, p. 22, italics in the original.

26. Spurgeon M. Keeny, "Arms Control during the Transition to the Post-Soviet World," in Joseph Kruzel, ed., *1993 American Defense Annual* (New York: Lexington Books, 1993), p. 181.

27. Ivo H. Daalder, "The Limited Test Ban Treaty," in Carnesale and Haass, *Superpower Arms Control*, pp. 19–20.

28. Sean Lynn-Jones, "The Incidents at Sea Agreement," in George, Farley, and Dallin, *U.S.-Soviet Security Cooperation*, 482–509.

29. For a discussion of the new interest in regional arrangements and inducements for controlling nuclear spread that do not involve the United States, see Brad Roberts, "From Nonproliferation to Antiproliferation," *International Security* 18, no. 1 (summer 1993): 166–70.

30. It should be possible for Washington and Moscow to renegotiate the ABM

treaty or abrogate it in a mutually acceptable manner to permit the building of "light," nonthreatening missile defenses that can guard against accidental launches and attacks by minor nuclear states.

31. Peter D. Feaver, "Command and Control in Emerging Nuclear Nations," *International Security* 17, no. 3 (winter 1992–93): 181–86; Gregory F. Giles, "Safeguarding the Undeclared Nuclear Arsenals," *Washington Quarterly* 16, no. 2 (spring 1993): 173–86.

32. The rationale for this claim is found in chapter 8. It brings out the national strategy's contributions to multilateral institutions that can foster international security in all its guises.

CHAPTER VII

1. Graham T. Allison, Albert Carnesale, and Joseph S. Nye, eds., *Hawks, Doves, and Owls: An Agenda for Avoiding Nuclear War* (New York: Norton, 1985); Kurt Gottfried and Bruce G. Blair, eds., *Crisis Stability and Nuclear War* (New York: Oxford University Press, 1988); Paul Bracken, *The Command and Control of Nuclear Forces* (New Haven: Yale University Press, 1983); Bruce G. Blair, *Strategic Command and Control: Redefining the Nuclear Threat* (Washington, DC: Brookings Institution, 1985); John D. Steinbruner and Charles A. Zraket, eds., *Managing Nuclear Operations* (Washington, DC: Brookings Institution, 1987); Richard Ned Lebow, *Nuclear Crisis Management: A Dangerous Illusion* (Ithaca, NY: Cornell University Press, 1987); Alexander L. George, ed., *Avoiding War: Problems of Crisis Management* (Boulder, CO: Westview Press, 1991); Wallace Theis, *When Governments Collide* (Berkeley and Los Angeles: University of California Press, 1980); Alfred C. Mauerer, ed., *Intelligence: Policy and Process* (Boulder, CO: Westview Press, 1985); Robert Jervis, Richard Ned Lebow, and Janice Gross Stein, eds., *Psychology and Deterrence* (Baltimore: Johns Hopkins University Press, 1985); Irving L. Janis, *Crucial Decisions* (New York: Free Press, 1989); Marc Trachtenberg, *History and Strategy* (Princeton: Princeton University Press, 1991); Barry R. Posen, *Inadvertent Escalation: Conventional War and Nuclear Risks* (Ithaca, NY: Cornell University Press, 1992).

2. Thomas C. Schelling, *Arms and Influence* (New Haven: Yale University Press, 1966), pp. 35–125; Schelling, *The Strategy of Conflict* (New York: Oxford University Press, 1963), pp. 3–80.

3. Richard K. Betts, "Analysis, War, and Decision: Why Intelligence Failures Are Inevitable," *World Politics* 31, no. 1 (October 1978): 61–89. The quotes from intelligence analysts are found on p. 69. Also see Glenn P. Hastedt, "Organizational Foundations of Intelligence Failures," in Maurer, *Intelligence: Policy and Process*. A more positive assessment of intelligence work, at least regarding its analyses in contrast with its use by decision makers, is found in Stan A. Taylor and Theodore J. Ralston, "The Role of Intelligence in Crisis Management," in George, *Avoiding War*, pp. 396–97.

4. Betts, "Analysis, War, and Decision," pp. 69, 84–85.

5. Trumball Higgins, *The Perfect Failure: Kennedy, Eisenhower, and the CIA at the Bay of Pigs* (New York: Norton, 1987).

6. James G. Blight, Joseph S. Nye, and David A. Welch, "The Cuban Missile Crisis Revisited," *Foreign Affairs* 66, no. 1 (fall 1987): 181–82.

7. Bruce W. Jentleson, "American Commitments in the Third World: Theory vs. Practice," *International Organization* 41, no. 4 (autumn 1987): 688–89.

8. Elaine Sciolino, "Iraq's Nuclear Program Shows the Holes in U.S. Intelligence," *New York Times*, October 20, 1991, p. A5.

9. Quoted in John D. Steinbruner, *The Cybernetic Theory of Decision* (Princeton: Princeton University Press, 1974), p. 332.

10. Richard Ned Lebow, *Between Peace and War: The Nature of International Crisis* (Baltimore: Johns Hopkins University Press, 1981), p. 22; Paul K. Huth, "Extended Deterrence and the Outbreak of War," *American Political Science Review* 82, no. 2 (June 1988): 423–43.

11. Alexander George, "Findings and Recommendations," in George, *Avoiding War*, p. 556.

12. Scott D. Sagan, "Rules of Engagement," in George, *Avoiding War*; Jack Levy, "Organizational Routines and the Causes of War," *International Studies Quarterly* 3 (1986): 209–11.

13. Taylor and Ralston, "Role of Intelligence," p. 404. Also see J. Philip Rogers, "Crisis Bargaining Codes and Crisis Management," in George, *Avoiding War*, pp. 428–29.

14. Richard Ned Lebow, "Miscalculation in the South Atlantic: The Origins of the Falklands War," in Jervis, Lebow, and Stein, *Psychology and Deterrence*, pp. 108–10, and the psychological studies cited there; Alexander George, *Presidential Decisionmaking in Foreign Policy: The Effective Use of Information and Advice* (Boulder, CO: Westview Press, 1980), pp. 25–35.

15. Deborah Welch Larson, *Origins of Containment: A Psychological Explanation* (Princeton: Princeton University Press, 1985), pp. 54–55. See the psychological studies cited there and in Rogers, "Crisis Bargaining Codes," p. 440, notes 29–32.

16. Jack Snyder, *Myths of Empire: Domestic Politics and International Ambition* (Ithaca, NY: Cornell University Press, 1991), p. 256, italics in the original.

17. Ernest R. May, *"Lessons" of the Past: The Use and Misuse of History in American Foreign Policy* (New York: Oxford University Press, 1975), pp. 81, 80–86.

18. Snyder, *Myths of Empire*, p. 262.

19. William Stueck, *The Road to Confrontation: American Policy toward China and Korea, 1947–1950* (Chapel Hill: University of North Carolina Press, 1981), pp. 253–55; Rosemary Foot, *The Wrong War: American Policy and Dimensions of the Korean Conflict, 1950–1953* (Ithaca, NY: Cornell University Press, 1985), pp. 86–89, 99–100. Contrary to conventional analyses, and on the basis of newly available sources, it has been claimed that China intended to intervene well before the U.S. move into North Korea, while we were still fighting in South Korea. See Thomas J. Christiensen, "Threats, Assurances, and the Last Chance for Peace: The Lessons of Mao's Korean War Telegrams," *International Security* 17, no. 1 (summer 1992): 122–54. Based on other new archival sources this revisionist interpretation is countered in Michael H. Hunt, "Beijing and the

Korean Crisis, June 1950–June 1951," *Political Science Quarterly* 107, no. 3 (1992): 453–78.

20. Alan S. Whiting, "The U.S.-China War in Korea," in George, *Avoiding War*, pp. 112–13. Also see Foot, *The Wrong War*, pp. 91–100; Lebow, *Between Peace and War*, pp. 149–64, 184–232. Alexander L. George and Richard Smoke, *Deterrence in American Foreign Policy: Theory and Practice* (New York: Columbia University Press, 1974), pp. 184–231 and the studies cited there show that the American decisions cannot be explained away by the "historically accidental" actions and position of General Douglas MacArthur.

21. Robert Jervis, *Perception and Misperception in International Politics* (Princeton: Princeton University Press, 1976).

22. Alexander George, "The Impact of Crisis Induced Stress on Decision Making," in Frederic Solomon and Robert Marston, eds., *The Medical Implications of Nuclear War* (Washington, DC: National Academy Press, 1986), p. 542.

23. William J. McGuire, "The Nature of Attitudes and Attitude Change," in Gardner Lindzey and Elliot Aronson, eds., *The Handbook of Social Psychology*, 2d ed., vol. 3, *The Individual in a Social Context* (Reading, MA: Addison-Wesley, 1969, 136–314; Irving L. Janis and Leon Mann, *Decision Making: Psychological Analysis of Conflict, Choice, and Commitment* (New York: Free Press, 1977); Philip G. Zimbardo, Ebbe B. Ebbeson, and Christina Maslach, *Influencing Attitudes and Changing Behavior* (Reading, MA: Addison-Wesley, 1977); Ole R. Holsti, "Foreign Policy Formation Viewed Cognitively," in Robert Axelrod, ed., *Structure of Decision: The Cognitive Maps of Political Elites* (Princeton: Princeton University Press, 1976), 18–54; Janis, *Crucial Decisions*; John D. Steinbruner, *The Cybernetic Theory of Decision*; the special issue of *Political Psychology* 13, no. 2 (June 1992), devoted to prospect theory; Larson, *Origins of Containment*.

24. For a wide-ranging analytical discussion, see Glenn H. Snyder, "The Security Dilemma in Alliance Politics," *World Politics* 36, no. 4 (July 1984): 461–95. For additional cases, see Jentleson, "American Commitments," pp. 690–94.

25. In addition to studies cited in note 1 of this chapter, see Sagan, "Rules of Engagement"; Levy, "Organizational Routines."

26. Raymond Garthoff, *Reflections on the Cuban Missile Crisis* (Washington, DC: Brookings Institution, 1987), pp. 101–2; Graham Allison, *Essence of Decision: Explaining the Cuban Missile Crisis* (Boston: Little, Brown, 1971). For a very different account, see Joseph F. Bouchard, *Command in Crisis: Four Case Studies* (New York: Columbia University Press, 1991), pp. 117–28.

27. Scott D. Sagan, *Moving Targets: Nuclear Strategy and National Security* (Princeton: Princeton University Press, 1989), p. 147.

28. Sagan, *Moving Targets*, p. 146; Garthoff, *Reflections*, pp. 38, 78.

29. Schelling, *Arms and Influence*, p. 227.

30. Blair, *Strategic Command and Control*, pp. 288. Also see Bracken, *Command and Control*; Peter Feaver, *Guarding the Guardians: Civilian Control of Nuclear Weapons in the United States* (Ithaca: Cornell University Press, 1992); Sagan, *Moving Targets*; Foot, *The Wrong War*, pp. 91–100; Lebow, *Between Peace and War*, pp. 149–64, 184–232.

31. Blair, *Strategic Command and Control*, p. 289.

32. John J. Mearsheimer, "A Strategic Misstep: The Maritime Strategy and Deterrence in Europe," *International Security* 11, no. 2 (fall 1986): 27–28.

33. Nathan Leites, *A Study of Bolshevism* (New York: Free Press, 1953); Alexander L. George, " 'The Operational Code': A Neglected Approach to the Study of Political Leaders and Decision Making," *International Studies Quarterly* 13, no. 2 (June 1969): 190–222; Hannes Adomeit, *Soviet Risk-Taking and Crisis Behavior* (London: Allen and Unwin, 1982); Dennis Ross, "Risk Aversion in Soviet Decision Making," in Jiri Valenta and William C. Potter, eds., *Soviet Decisionmaking for National Security* (London: Allen and Unwin, 1984), 237–51; Jack Snyder, *Myths of Empire*, pp. 228–29; Benjamin Lambeth, "Uncertainties for the Soviet War Planner, *International Security* 7, no. 3 (winter 1982–83): 141–43.

34. A recent discussion is found in Peter D. Feaver, "Command and Control in Emerging Nuclear Nations," *International Security* 17, no. 3 (winter 1992–93): 160–87.

Chapter VIII

1. This moderated liberalism is not only supported by erstwhile Cold War hawks and doves; in some instances they have reversed their former positions. Among many other similar statements, see Graham Allison and Robert P. Beschel, Jr., "Can the United States Promote Democracy?" *Political Science Quarterly* 10, no. 1 (spring 1992): 81–98; Larry Diamond and Marc F. Plattner, eds. "Capitalism, Socialism, and Democracy," special issue of *Journal of Democracy* 3, no. 3 (July 1992); Samuel P. Huntington, *The Third Wave: Democratization in the Late Twentieth Century* (Norman: University of Oklahoma Press, 1991); Tony Smith, "Making the World Safe for Democracy," *Washington Quarterly* 16, no. 4 (autumn 1993): 197–214. Also see the studies cited in note 12 below.

2. Felix Gilbert, *To the Farewell Address: Ideas of Early American Foreign Policy* (Princeton: Princeton University Press, 1961), appendix C, pp. 144–47; Michael H. Hunt, *Ideology and U.S. Foreign Policy* (New Haven: Yale University Press, 1987), pp. 21–22.

3. Cited in Alexander DeConde, "On Twentieth-Century Isolationism," in Alexander DeConde, ed., *Isolation and Security* (Durham, NC: Duke University Press, 1957), p. 3.

4. Cited in Ronald E. Powaski, *Toward an Entangling Alliance: American Isolationism, Internationalism, and Europe, 1901–1950* (New York: Greenwood Press, 1991), p. xviii.

5. Cited in Hunt, *Ideology*, p. 34.

6. John Quincy Adams, *Memoirs of John Quincy Adams* (Philadelphia: J. B. Lippincott, 1874–77), 5:324–25, cited in Greg Russell, "John Quincy Adams and the Ethics of America's National Interest," *Review of International Studies* 19, no. 1 (January 1993): 33.

7. Robert L. Beisner, *Twelve against Empire, The Anti-Imperialists, 1898–1900* (New York: McGraw-Hill, 1968), pp. 219–32; Robert L. Beisner, "1898 and 1968: The Anti-Imperialists and the Doves," *Political Science Quarterly* 85,

no. 2 (June 1970): 200–204; Stanley Karnow, *In Our Image: America's Empire in the Philippines* (New York: Random House, 1989); William Graham Sumner, "The Conquest of the United States by Spain," in Arthur A. Ekirch, ed., *Voices in Dissent: An Anthology of Individualist Thought in the United States* (New York: Citadel Press, 1964), pp. 172, 175–76.

8. Eric F. Goldman, *Rendezvous with Destiny: A History of Modern American Reform* (New York: Vintage, 1956), pp. 184–85; Robert M. LaFollette, "Speech on the Declaration of War against Germany," in Ekirch, *Voices in Dissent*, pp. 211–22; John Milton Cooper, *The Vanity of Power: American Isolationism and the First World War, 1914–1917* (New York: Greenwood Press, 1969), pp. 56–58, 87–98, 123–24, 134–42, 183, 197; Powaski, *Toward an Entangling Alliance*, pp. 8–11. The arguments of William Jennings Bryan and others, that America could contribute most as an exemplar of peace and democracy, held little sway. See Cooper, *The Vanity of Power*, pp. 123–24, 178.

9. Warren I. Cohen, *The American Revisionists: The Lessons of Intervention in World War I* (Chicago: University of Chicago Press, 1962); Robert C. Osgood, *Ideals and Self-Interest in America's Foreign Relations: The Great Transformation of the Twentieth Century* (Chicago: University of Chicago Press, 1953), pp. 371–73; Manfred Jonas, *Isolationism in America, 1935–1941* (Ithaca, NY: Cornell University Press, 1966), pp. 26–31, 82–84; Ronald Radosh, *Prophets on the Right: Profiles of Conservative Critics of American Globalism* (New York: Simon and Schuster, 1975), p. 128; Justus D. Doenecke, "American Isolationism, 1939–1941," *Journal of Libertarian Studies* 6, nos. 3–4 (summer–fall 1982): 203–204; Justus D. Doenecke, "The Anti-Interventionism of Herbert Hoover," *Journal of Libertarian Studies* 8, no. 2 (summer 1987): 315.

10. James T. Patterson, *Mr. Republican: A Biography of Robert A. Taft* (Boston: Houghton Mifflin, 1972), pp. 288–370; Justus D. Doenecke, *Not to the Swift: The Old Isolationists in the Cold War Era* (Lewisburg, PA: Bucknell University Press, 1979), pp. 63, 76–80, 240; Ted Galen Carpenter, "The Dissenters: American Isolationists and Foreign Policy, 1945–1954" (Ph.D. diss., University of Texas at Austin, 1980), pp. 146, 149–51, 247–48, 351, 393; Henry W. Berger, "Senator Robert A. Taft Dissents from Military Escalation," in Thomas G. Paterson, ed., *Cold War Critics: Alternatives to American Policy in the Truman Years* (Chicago: Quadrangle Books, 1971): pp. 172, 175; William Pfaff, *Barbarian Sentiments: How the American Century Ends* (New York: Hill and Wang, 1989), p. 11.

11. Selig Adler, *The Isolationist Impulse: Its Twentieth-Century Reaction* (New York: Free Press, 1957); DeConde, "On Twentieth-Century Isolationism," p. 225; Bernard Fensterwald, Jr., "The Anatomy of American 'Isolationism' and Expansionism, Pt. I" *Journal of Conflict Resolution* 2, no. 2 (June 1958): 111–39; Richard Hofstadter, "The Pseudo-Conservative Revolt," in Daniel Bell, ed., *The New American Right* (New York: Criterion Books, 1955) pp. 33–55; Samuel Lubell, *The Future of American Politics* (Garden City, NY: Doubleday Anchor Books, 1956), pp. 137–50.

12. For recent discussions of America's moral obligations from the Left and the Right, respectively, see Stanley Hoffmann, *Duties beyond Borders* (Syracuse: Syracuse University Press, 1988), and Joshua Muravchik, *Exporting Democracy:*

Fulfilling America's Destiny (Washington, DC: American Enterprise Institute Press, 1991). For a historical treatment of Wilsonian internationalism see Tony Smith, *America's Mission: The United States and the Worldwide Struggle for Democracy in the Twentieth Century* (Princeton: Princeton University Press, 1994). At bottom, idealist activism is commended or obligated by one or another of three kinds of ethical theories, currently conceived as theories of justice and virtue. There are those that focus upon absolute rules of moral conduct, the moral consequences of action and inaction, and the conformity or behavior with convention. The former two generally parallel Max Weber's "ethics of intentions" and the "ethics of responsibility."

13. Samuel P. Huntington, *American Politics: The Promise of Disharmony* (Cambridge, MA: Harvard University Press, 1980), p. 289.

14. Among the works that review most of these and some other comparable cases, see Stephen Van Evera, "Why Europe Matters, Why the Third World Doesn't: American Grand Strategy after the Cold War," *Journal of Strategic Studies* 13, no. 2 (June 1990), notes 94 to 109 on pp. 48–49; Peter J. Schraeder, "The Faulty Assumptions of U.S. Foreign Policy in the Third World," in Ted Galen Carpenter, ed., *Collective Defense or Strategic Independence? Alternative Strategies for the Future* (Lexington, MA: Lexington Books, 1989), 151–74. For a study that stresses the illiberal influence of economic interests that Washington has often viewed in security terms, see Jonathan Kwitny, *Endless Enemies: The Making of an Unfriendly World* (New York: Penguin Books, 1984). Two of the most revealing in-depth analyses of U.S. intervention are James A. Bill, *The Eagle and the Lion: The Tragedy of American-Iranian Relations* (New Haven: Yale University Press, 1988), and Stephen Schlesinger and Stephen Kinzer, *Bitter Fruit: The Untold Story of the American Coup in Guatemala* (Garden City, NY: Doubleday, 1982).

15. David Carleton and Michael Stohl, "The Foreign Policy of Human Rights: Rhetoric and Reality from Jimmy Carter to Ronald Reagan," *Human Rights Quarterly* 7, no. 2 (May 1985): 218–19. An account of the Carter administration's limited human rights efforts by a high-ranking official who was closely involved is found in Stephen B. Cohen, "Conditioning US Security Assistance on Human Rights Practices," *American Journal of International Law* 76, no. 2 (April 1982): 246–79.

16. *Human Rights in U.S. Foreign Policy: The First Decade, 1973–1983* (New York: American Association for the International Commission of Jurists, 1984), p. 21.

17. Lars Schoultz, *Human Rights and United States Policy toward Latin America* (Princeton: Princeton University Press, 1981), p. 372.

18. Van Evera, "Why Europe Matters," pp. 26–27.

19. Gary Sick, *All Fall Down: America's Tragic Encounter with Iran* (New York: Random House, 1985); Barry Rubin, *Paved with Good Intentions: The American Experience and Iran* (New York: Penguin Books, 1981).

20. For studies of the Carter U-turn on human rights, see Gaddis Smith, *Morality, Reason, and Power: American Diplomacy in the Carter Years* (New York: Hill and Wang, 1986), and Jerel A. Rosati, *The Carter Administration's Quest for Global Community: Beliefs and Their Impact on Behavior* (Columbia: University of South Carolina Press, 1987).

21. Cynthia Brown, ed., *With Friends Like These: The Americas Watch Report on Human Rights and U.S. Policy in Latin America* (New York: Pantheon, 1985), p. 233.

22. For favorable discussions of the Reagan doctrine and the administration's human rights accomplishments, see Laurence Whitehead, "The Imposition of Democracy," and Thomas Carothers, "The Reagan Years: The 1980s," both in Abraham F. Lowenthal, ed., *Exporting Democracy: The United States and Latin America* (Baltimore: Johns Hopkins University Press, 1991); Charles Krauthammer, "The Poverty of Realism," *New Republic*, February 17, 1986; Walter F. Hahn, ed., *Central America and the Reagan Doctrine* (Lanham, MD: University Press of America, 1987).

23. Morris J. Blachman and Kenneth Sharpe, "De-Democratising American Foreign Policy: Dismantling the Post-Vietnam Formula," *Third World Quarterly* 8, no. 4 (October 1986): 1302.

24. Clifford Kraus, "U.S. Aware of Killings, Kept Ties to Salvadoran Rightists, Papers Suggest," *New York Times*, November 9, 1993, p. A9; Tim Weiner, "Documents Assert U.S. Trained Salvadorans Tied to Death Squads," *New York Times*, December 14, 1993, pp. A1, 11.

25. The decision to invade Grenada is discussed in chapter 10 below.

26. For a review of Washington's reactions to and relations with Beijing in the months after the Tiananmen Square massacre, see Robert S. Ross, "National Security, Human Rights, and Domestic Politics: The Bush Administration and China," in Kenneth A. Oye, Robert Lieber, and Donald Rothchild, eds., *Eagle in a New World: American Grand Strategy in the Post–Cold War Era* (New York: HarperCollins, 1992), pp. 291–306.

27. *New York Times*, July 19, 1992, pp. A1, 22.

28. The quotes are found in Michael Kramer, "In Search of the Clinton Doctrine," *Time*, October 1993, p. 41; Paul Lewis, "Reluctant Warriors: U.N. Member States Retreat from Peacekeeping Roles," *New York Times*, December 12, 1993, p. A22.

29. R. W. Apple, "No Progress Seen as Clinton Meets with China's Chief," *New York Times*, November 20, 1993, pp. A1, 6.

30. Robert W. Tucker, "1989 and All That," in Nicholas X. Rizopoulos, ed., *Sea Changes: American Foreign Policy in a World Transformed* (New York: Council on Foreign Relations Press, 1990), p. 232.

31. Ted Galen Carpenter, "The New World Disorder," *Foreign Policy* 84 (fall 1991): 37–38.

32. Ted Galen Carpenter, "Benign Realism: A New U.S. Security Strategy in the Third World," in Carpenter, *Collective Defense*, p. 219.

33. For his earlier statements on human rights, see Jimmy Carter, *A Government as Good as Its People* (New York: Simon and Schuster, 1977), pp. 125–35, 172–80.

34. Arthur M. Schlesinger, Jr., "Human Rights and American Foreign Policy," *Foreign Affairs*. 57 (spring 1979): 503–26.

35. Quoted in Joshua Muravchik, *The Uncertain Crusade: Jimmy Carter and the Dilemmas of Human Rights Policy* (Lanham, MD: Hamilton Press, 1986), p. 214.

36. Mohammed Ayoob, "Squaring the Circle: Collective Security in a System of States," in Thomas G. Weiss, ed., *Collective Security in a Changing World* (Boulder, Colo.: Lynn Rienner, 1993), pp. 51–53. For some implications of our anti-Iraq policy in the United Nations that are consistent with the present argument, see Bruce Russett and James S. Sutterlin, "The UN in a New World Order," *Foreign Affairs* (spring 1991): 76–77.

37. Edward C. Luck and Toby Trister Gati, "Whose Collective Security?" *Washington Quarterly* 15, no. 2 (spring, 1992): 46.

38. Reported in Leslie H. Gelb, "The U.N. Chief's Dilemma," *New York Times*, December 31, 1992, p. A25.

39. Ghassan Salamé, "Islam and the West," *Foreign Policy* 90 (spring 1993): 22–37.

40. The scholarly concepts and political biases that have artificially deflated the effectiveness of economic sanctions are discussed in David A. Baldwin, *Economic Statecraft* (Princeton: Princeton University Press, 1985).

41. Specifically, "36 percent of the [103] cases overall" were found to be successful (p. 80). Economic sanctions were also found to be more successful against allies, "erstwhile friends and close trading partners," because of the high degree of trade linkages (pp. 84–86). Gary Clyde Hufbauer and Jeffrey J. Schott, assisted by Kimberly Ann Elliot. *Economic Sanctions Reconsidered: History and Current Policy* (Washington, DC: Institute for International Economics, 1985).

42. Paul Huth and Bruce Russett, "What Makes Deterrence Work? Cases from 1900 to 1980," *World Politics* 36, no. 4 (July 1984): 496–526; Paul K. Huth, "Extended Deterrence and the Outbreak of War," *American Political Science Review* 82, no. 2 (June 1988): 423–44.

43. Studies showing a combination of firmness and flexibility to be maximally effective include Richard Ned Lebow, *Between Peace and War: The Nature of International Crisis* (Baltimore: Johns Hopkins University Press, 1981) and Paul K. Huth, "Extended Deterrence and the Outbreak of War," *American Political Science Review*, June 1988.

CHAPTER IX

1. Felix Gilbert, *To the Farewell Address: Ideas of Early American Foreign Policy* (Princeton: Princeton University Press, 1961), appendix C, pp. 144–47.

2. Gregg Russell, "John Quincy Adams and the Ethics of America's National Interest," *Review of International Studies* 19, no. 1 (January 1993): 31; Foster Rhea Dulles, *America's Rise to World Power, 1898–1954* (New York: Harper and Row, 1954), pp. 20, 48–50.

3. Robert L. Beisner, *Twelve against Empire: The Anti-Imperialists, 1898–1900* (New York: McGraw-Hill, 1968), pp. 84–85; Michael H. Hunt, *Ideology and U.S. Foreign Policy* (New Haven: Yale University Press, 1987), p. 39; Carl Schurz, "Manifest Destiny," *Harper's New Monthly Magazine*, October 1893, p. 743, cited in Ronald E. Powaski, *Toward an Entangling Alliance: American Isolationism, Internationalism, and Europe, 1901–1950* (New York: Greenwood Press, 1991), p. xxi.

4. Alexander DeConde, "On Twentieth-Century Isolationism," in Alexander

DeConde, ed., *Isolation and Security* (Durham, NC: Duke University Press, 1957), pp. 17–20; Eric F. Goldman, *Rendezvous with Destiny: A History of Modern American Reform* (New York: Vintage, 1956), pp. 183–86.

5. Robert C. Osgood, *Ideals and Self-Interest in America's Foreign Relations: The Great Transformation of the Twentieth Century* (Chicago: University of Chicago Press, 1953), pp. 371–73; Manfred Jonas, *Isolationism in America, 1935–1941* (Ithaca, NY: Cornell University Press, 1966), pp. 82–84; Ronald Radosh, *Prophets on the Right: Profiles of Conservative Critics of American Globalism* (New York: Simon and Schuster, 1975), p. 128: Justus D. Doenecke, "Explaining the Anti-War Movement, 1939–1941: The Next Assignment," *Journal of Libertarian Studies* 8, no. 1 (winter 1986): 145–46.

6. Justus D. Doenecke, *Not to the Swift: The Old Isolationists in the Cold War Era* (Lewisburg, PA: Bucknell University Press, 1979), pp. 86, 116–17; Ted Galen Carpenter, "The Dissenters: American Isolationists and Foreign Policy, 1945–1954" (Ph.D. diss., University of Texas at Austin, 1980), pp. 139–40, 179, 188; James T. Patterson, *Mr. Republican: A Biography of Robert A. Taft* (Boston: Houghton Mifflin, 1972), pp. 477–78, 481.

7. For a summary of American requests and the minimal pressures behind them, see John R. Oneal and Mark A. Elrod, "NATO Burden Sharing and the Forces of Change," *International Studies Quarterly* 33, no. 4 (December 1989): 435–37. For the Europeans' few concessions to head off determined pressures and threats, see D. B. H. Denoon, "Conclusions," in D. B. H. Denoon, ed., *Constraints on Strategy* (Washington, DC: Pergamon-Brassey, 1986), pp. 197–99.

8. The most extensive data on burden-sharing issues are found in Gorden Adams and Eric Munz, *Fair Shares: Bearing the Burdens of the NATO Alliance* (Washington, DC: Center for Budget and Policy Priorities, 1988). Also see the study by the Congressional Budget Office, *Alliance Burden-Sharing: A Review of the Data* (Washington, DC: U.S. Government Printing Office, 1987).

9. Adams and Munz, *Fair Shares*, pp. 42–43, 74–75. For the claim that NATO Europe has not been free riding, see pp. 25–30.

10. David P. Calleo, *Beyond American Hegemony: The Future of the Western Alliance* (New York: Basic Books, 1987). Although their different methodology does not produce a dollar figure, the general conclusion is supported by Oneal and Elrod, "NATO Burden Sharing," pp. 445–47.

11. David P. Calleo, "The American Role in NATO," in Ted Galen Carpenter, ed., *NATO at 40: Confronting a Changing World* (Lexington, MA: Lexington Books, 1990), p. 214. Also see Calleo, *Beyond American Hegemony*. Comparable claims are found in Christopher Layne, "NATO and the Next Administration," in Edward H. Crane and David Boaz, eds., *An American Vision: Policies for the '90s* (Washington, DC: Cato Institute, 1989), pp. 150–51, and Alan Tonelson, "The Economics of NATO," in Carpenter, *NATO at 40*, pp. 101–8.

12. Ted Galen Carpenter, *A Search for Enemies: America's Alliances after the Cold War* (Washington, D.C.: Cato Institute, 1992), pp. 9–10; Layne, "NATO and Next Administration," pp. 150–51; Tonelson, "The Economics of NATO," pp. 101–2.

13. The original application of collective-goods theory to alliance relations is found in Mancur Olson and Richard Zeckhauser, "An Economic Theory of Alli-

ances," *Review of Economics and Statistics* 48, no. 3 (August 1966): 266–79. They argue that small countries will underspend because their contributions have especially little significance for their own or the common defense. This argument has been called into question as it applies to NATO by Richard Eichenberg in "The Myth of Hollanditis," *International Security* 8, no. 2 (fall 1983): 143–59.

14. This quote and those pertaining to Washington's public reasons for opposing the Eurocorps are found in Jonathan G. Clarke, "The Eurocorps: A Fresh Start in Europe," Cato Institute, *Foreign Policy Briefing*, December 28, 1992, Washington, DC, pp. 4, 6.

15. Carpenter, *A Search for Enemies*, p. 2.

16. Robert J. Art, "Fixing Atlantic Bridges," *Foreign Policy* 46 (spring 1982): 70; Todd Sandler and James C. Murdock, "Defense Burdens and Prospects for the Northern European Allies," in Denoon, *Constraints on Strategy*, pp. 61, 90. The latter study (unpersuasively) explains the changes in terms of NATO's new military doctrine of flexible response. The European increases might have been partly motivated by the modernization and enlargement of the Warsaw Pact forces. By the late 1970s the numerical imbalance was somewhat greater than in 1970.

17. For characterizations of Japan along these lines, see Chalmers Johnson, "Their Behavior, Our Policy," *National Interest* 17 (fall 1989): 22–24; Clyde V. Prestowitz, *Trading Places: How We Allowed Japan to Take the Lead* (New York: Basic Books, 1988); James Fallows, "Containing Japan," *Atlantic*, May 1989, p. 322. Also see Dennis J. Encarnation, *Rivals beyond Trade: America versus Japan in Global Competition* (Ithaca, NY: Cornell University Press, 1992); William S. Dietrich, *In the Shadow of the Rising Sun: The Political Roots of American Economic Decline* (University Park: Pennsylvania State University Press, 1992).

18. Michael Mastanduno, "Do Relative Gains Matter? America's Response to Japanese Industrial Policy," *International Security* 16, no. 1 (summer 1991): 81; Stephen D. Krasner, "American Policy and Global Economic Stability," in William P. Avery and David P. Rapkin, eds., *America in a Changing World Political Economy* (New York: Longman, 1982), pp. 29–48.

19. Joseph S. Nye, *Bound to Lead: The Changing Nature of American Power* (New York: Basic Books, 1990), p. 90.

20. Barry P. Bosworth and Robert Z. Lawrence, "America's Global Role: From Dominance to Interdependence," in John D. Steinbruner, ed., *Restructuring American Foreign Policy* (Washington, DC: Brookings Institution, 1989), p. 12.

21. Thomas O. Bayard and Kimberly A. Elliott, "'Aggressive Unilateralism' and Section 301: Market Opening or Market Closing?" *World Economy* 15, no. 6 (November 1992): 687, 689, table 2.

22. Peter G. Peterson with James K. Sebenius, "The Primacy of the Domestic Agenda," in Graham Allison and Gregory F. Trevorton, eds., *Rethinking America's Security: Beyond Cold War to New World Order* (New York: Norton, 1992), p. 58, italics added.

23. Prestowitz, *Trading Places*, p. 322.

24. "The Big Split: Special Report," *Fortune*, May 6, 1991, p. 41.

25. David E. Snager, "Head to Head with the Japanese," *New York Times*, April 18, 1993, p. E5.

26. Dan Goodgame, "Trading Punches," *Time*, June 21, 1993, p. 24; *New York Times*, July 10, 1993, pp. A1, 4.

27. For several articles detailing the GATT agreement, see *New York Times*, December 15, 1993.

28. Robert J. Art, "A Defensible Defense: America's Grand Strategy after the Cold War," *International Security* 15, no. 4 (spring 1991): 40–41; Fred Bergsten, *America in the World Economy: A Strategy for the 1990s* (Washington, DC: Institute for International Economics, 1988), pp. 68–69.

29. For a review of strategic trade theory in which outcomes of reciprocity and cooperation are closely associated with threatened retaliation, see Carolyn Rhodes, "Reciprocity in Trade: The Utility of a Bargaining Strategy," *International Organization* 43 (spring 1989): 272–82. Also see Michael Mastanduno, "Trade Policy", in Robert J. Art and Seyom Brown, *U.S. Foreign Policy: The Search for a New Role* (New York: Macmillan, 1993), pp. 155–60.

30. America's "structural power" is indeed impressive. Its military, economic, financial, and cultural pervasiveness and centrality elicit positive responses to U.S. interests from others by way of their anticipated reactions, adaptations, and imitations. On this argument most of our structural power would remain intact despite a political-military disengagement. However, the structural perspective does not have all that much bearing upon the likely outcomes of trade disputes. Once they, or any other conflict, become overt the determining factors mainly involve the exercise of relational power based upon the actors' power capabilities and strategies. For the delineation of America's structural power and the denial of its relative decline, see Bruce Russett, "The Mysterious Case of Vanishing Hegemony; or Is Mark Twain Really Dead?" *International Organization* (spring 1985); Susan Strange, "The Persistent Myth of Lost Hegemony," *International Organization*, (Autumn 1987); Susan Strange, *States and Markets* (New York: Basil Blackwell, 1988).

31. Paul Kennedy, *The Rise and Fall of the Great Powers: Economic Change and Military Conflict from 1500 to 2000* (New York: Random House, 1987); Robert Gilpin, *War and Change in International Politics* (New York: Cambridge University Press, 1981); Calleo, *Beyond American Hegemony*; Walter Russell Mead, *Mortal Splendor* (Boston: Houghton Mifflin, 1987); Immanuel Wallerstein, "The United States and the World 'Crisis,'" in Terry Boswell and Albert Bergesen, eds., *America's Changing Role in the World-System* (New York: Praeger, 1987), 17–23.

32. Paul Bairoch, "Europe's Gross National Product, 1800–1975," *Journal of European Economic History* 5, no. 3 (fall 1976): 322; Russett, "The Mysterious Case of Vanishing Hegemony," p. 212; Central Intelligence Agency, *The World Factbook 1991* (Washington, DC: U.S. Government Printing Office, 1991), pp. 113, 160, 325.

33. Nye, *Bound to Lead*, pp. 73–78. Also see Samuel P. Huntington, "The U.S.—Decline or Renewal?" *Foreign Affairs* 67, no. 2 (winter 1988–89): 76–96.

34. Central Intelligence Agency, *Handbook of International Economic Statistics, 1992* (Washington, DC: U.S. Government Printing Office, 1992), pp. 14, 16, 200; Raymond Vernon and Ethan B. Kapstein, "National Needs, Global Resources," in *Defense and Dependence in a Global Economy* (Washington, DC:

Congressional Quarterly Press, 1992), p. 13; National Science Board, *Science and Engineering Indicators, 1993*, pp. 160–61.

35. Bergsten, *America in World Economy*, p. 55; Sylvia Nasar, "The American Economy, Back on Top," *New York Times*, February 27, 1994, sec. 3, pp. 1, 6.

36. National Science Board, *Science and Engineering Indicators, 1993*, pp. 161–62, 168–69.

37. Nasar, "American Economy," p. 1.

38. For the full range of the economists' policy views on trade issues, see Robert Z. Lawrence and Charles L. Schultz, eds., *An American Trade Strategy: Options for the 1990s* (Washington, DC: Brookings Institution, 1990).

39. Akio Morita and Shintara Ishihara, *The Japan That Can Say No: The New U.S.-Japan Relations Card* (Kobunsha: Kappa-Holmes, 1989).

40. Albert Hirschman, *National Power and the Structure of Foreign Trade* (Berkeley and Los Angeles: University of California Press, 1945).

41. Josef Joffe, "The New Europe: Yesterday's Ghosts," *Foreign Affairs* 72, no. 1 (1992–93): 36–43.

42. Strange, "Persistent Myth," pp. 568–69. On the train of events and American calculations, see Joanne Gowa, *Closing the Gold Window* (Princeton: Princeton University Press, 1989).

43. Felix Rohatyn, "Restoring American Independence," *New York Review of Books*, February 18, 1988, pp. 9–10; Daniel Burstein, *Yen!* (New York: Ballantine Books, 1990), pp. 13–20.

44. Mastanduno, "Trade Policy," p. 158; Robert Kuttner, "How 'National Security' Hurts National Competitiveness," *Harvard Business Review* 69, no. 1 (January–February 1991): 141.

45. Robert W. DeGrasse, *Military Expansion and Economic Decline* (New York: M. E. Sharpe, 1983); Lester Thurow, "Budget Deficits," in Daniel Bell and Lester Thurow, *The Deficits: How Big? How Long? How Dangerous?* (New York: New York University Press, 1985); Kennedy, *Rise and Fall*, pp. 444–46, 532; Lloyd J. Dumas, "National Security and Economic Delusion," *Challenge* 30, no. 1 (March–April 1987): 28–33; Ronald P. Smith, "Military Expenditures and Investment in OECD Countries, 1954–1973," *Journal of Comparative Economics* 4, no. 1 (March 1980): 19–32; Karen Rasler and William R. Thompson, "Defense Burden, Capital Formation, and Economic Growth: The Systematic Leader Case," *Journal of Conflict Resolution* 32, no. 1 (March 1988): 61–86.

46. William K. Domke, "Fiscal Constraints and Defense Planning in Advanced Industrial Democracies," in Andrew L. Ross, ed., *The Political Economy of Defense: Issues and Perspectives* (New York: Greenwood Press, 1992), 23–40; David Gold, *The Impact of Defense Spending on Investment, Productivity, and Economic Growth* (Washington, DC: Defense Budget Project, 1990); Nils P. Gleditsch, Olav Bjerkholt, and Ådne Cappelen, "Military R & D and Economic Growth in Industrialized Market Economies," in Peter Wallensteen, ed., *Peace Research: Achievements and Challenges* (Boulder, CO: Westview Press, 1988), 198–215; Robert Eisner, "Macroeconomic Consequences of Disarmament," *Challenge* 34, no. 1 (January–February 1991): 47–50; David Greenwood, "Note on the Impact of Military Expenditure on Economic Growth and Performance,"

in Christian Schmidt, ed., *The Economics of Military Expenditures* (New York: St. Martin's Press, 1987), 98–103; Paul Dunne and Ron Smith, "Military Expenditure and Unemployment in the OECD," *Defence Economics* 1, no. 1, (1990): 57–73.

47. Aaron L. Friedberg, "The Political Economy of American Strategy," *World Politics* 41, no. 3 (April 1989) 381–406; Jacques Gansler, *Affording Defense* (Cambridge, MA: MIT Press, 1989); Charles A. Kupchan, "Empire, Military Power, and Economic Decline," *International Security* 13, no. 4 (spring 1989): 36–53; Charles A. Kupchan, "Defense Spending and Economic Performance," *Survival* 31, no. 5 (September 1989): 447–61; Alex Mintz and Chi Huang, "Defense Expenditures, Economic Growth, and the 'Peace Dividend,'" *American Political Science Review* 84, no. 4 (December 1990): 1283–95; Gordon Adams and David Gold, *Defense Spending and the Economy: Does the Defense Dollar Make a Difference?* (Washington, DC: Defense Budget Project at the Center on Budget and Policy Priorities, 1987); Steve Chan, "The Impact of Defense Spending on Economic Performance: A Survey of Evidence and Problems," *Orbis* 29, no. 2 (summer 1985): 403–34.

48. Jacques S. Gansler, "Needed: A U.S. Defense Industrial Strategy," *International Security* 12, no. 2 (fall 1987): 56. The case for the economically productive development and manufacture of military products is further elaborated in Jacques S. Gansler, "The Future Industrial Base," in Joseph Kruzel, ed., *1993 American Defense Annual* (New York: Lexington Books, 1993).

49. Eisenhower cited Ethan Kapstein, *The Political Economy of National Security* (New York: McGraw-Hill, 1992), p. 41.

50. These examples are based on figures in the *New York Times*, December 14, 1989, p. B18.

51. Such a design, largely financed by military cutbacks, is set out in Felix Rohatyn, "What the Government Should Do," *New York Review of Books*, June 25, 1993.

CHAPTER X

1. Felix Gilbert, *To the Farewell Address: Ideas of Early American Foreign Policy* (Princeton: Princeton University Press, 1961), appendix C, pp. 144–47.

2. Cited in Morton H. Halperin, "National Security," in Norman Dorsen, ed., *Our Endangered Rights: The ALCU Report on Civil Liberties Today* (New York: Pantheon Books, 1984), p. 281. In a more diffuse manner, Federalists and Republicans were fearful of political "contamination" stemming from friendly foreign entanglements. See Robert W. Tucker and David C. Hendrickson, *Empire of Liberty: The Statecraft of Thomas Jefferson* (New York: Oxford University Press, 1990), pp. 243–44.

3. Michael H. Hunt, *Ideology and U.S. Foreign Policy* (New Haven: Yale University Press, 1987), pp. 126–28.

4. Kenneth W. Thompson, "Isolationism and Collective Security: The Uses and Limits of Two Theories of International Relations," in Alexander DeConde, ed., *Isolation and Security* (Durham, NC: Duke University Press, 1957), p. 161; Robert Beisner, *Twelve against Empire: The Anti-Imperialists, 1898–1900* (New

York: McGraw-Hill, 1968), pp. 216–30; Hunt, *Ideology*, pp. 20, 48–50; William Graham Sumner, "The Conquest of the United States by Spain," in Arthur A. Ekirch, ed., *Voices in Dissent: An Anthology of Individualist Thought in America* (New York: Citadel Press, 1964), pp. 179, 185–86.

5. Alexander DeConde, "On Twentieth-Century Isolationism," in DeConde, *Isolation and Security*, p. 23; Ronald Radosh, *Prophets on the Right: Profiles of Conservative Critics of American Globalism* (New York: Simon and Schuster, 1975), p. 69; Hunt, *Ideology*, p. 135; Robert M. LaFollette, "Speech on the Declaration of War against Germany," in Ekirch, *Voices in Dissent*, p. 211; John Milton Cooper, *The Vanity of Power: American Isolationism and the First World War, 1914–1917* (Westport, CT: Greenwood Press, 1969), p. 110.

6. Ronald Schaffer, *America in the Great War: The Rise of the War Welfare State* (New York: Oxford University Press, 1991); Robert C. Osgood, *Ideals and Self-Interest in America's Foreign Relations: The Great Transformation of the Twentieth Century* (Chicago: University of Chicago Press, 1953), pp. 374–75, 379; Radosh, *Prophets on the Right*, pp. 124–25; Manfred Jonas, *Isolationism in America, 1935–1941* (Ithaca, NY: Cornell University Press, 1966), pp. 86–88; Robert M. Hutchins, "The Path to War—We Are Drifting into Suicide," in Ekirch, *Voices in Dissent*, p. 277; James T. Patterson, *Mr. Republican: A Biography of Robert A. Taft* (Boston: Houghton Mifflin, 1972), pp. 200–201, 234, 244–46; Henry W. Berger, "Senator Robert A. Taft Dissents from Military Escalation," in Thomas G. Patterson, ed., *Cold War Critics: Alternatives to American Foreign Policy in the Truman Years* (Chicago: Quadrangle Books, 1971), pp. 171, 187; Richard W. Steele, "Franklin D. Roosevelt and His Foreign Policy Critics," *Political Science Quarterly* 94, no. 1 (spring 1979): 15–32; Justus D. Doenecke, "The Anti-Interventionism of Herbert Hoover," *Journal of Libertarian Studies* 8, no. 2 (summer 1987): 318.

7. Ted Galen Carpenter, "The Dissenters: American Isolationists and Foreign Policy, 1945–1954" (Ph.D. diss., University of Texas at Austin, 1980), pp. 310–11; Justus D. Doenecke, *Not to the Swift: The Old Isolationists in the Cold War Era* (Lewisburg, PA: Bucknell University Press, 1979), p. 192; Radosh, *Prophets on the Right*, pp. 174, 185; Patterson, *Mr. Republican*, pp. 477–78; Ted Carpenter, "Global Interventionism and a New Imperial Presidency," Cato Institute for Policy Analysis, number 71, May 16, 1986.

8. Edward S. Corwin, *The President: Office and Powers* (New York: New York University Press, 1940), p. 200.

9. Arthur M. Schlesinger, Jr., *The Imperial Presidency* (Boston: Houghton Mifflin, 1973), pp. 168–69, 208; Louis Henkin, *Constitutionalism, Democracy, and Foreign Affairs* (New York: Columbia University Press, 1990), p. 33; Glenn P. Hastedt and Anthony J. Eksterowicz, "Presidential Leadership in the Post Cold War Era," *Presidential Studies Quarterly* 23, no. 3 (summer 1993): pp. 446–47. Also see Aaron Wildavsky, "The Two Presidencies," *Trans-action* 4, no. 2 (December 1966): 7–14.

10. John Lord O'Brian, "New Encroachments on Individual Freedom," *Harvard Law Review* 66, no. 1 (November 1952): 1–27; Arthur Sutherland, "Freedom and International Security," *Harvard Law Review* 64, no. 3 (January 1951): 33–416; Alan Theoharis, "The Threat to Civil Liberties," in Paterson, *Cold War*

Critics, pp. 266–68, 292–94. Among the many studies of McCarthyism, its national security connections are most extensively examined in David Wise, *The Politics of Lying, Government Deception, Secrecy and Power* (New York: Vintage Books, 1973).

11. Neil Sheehan, ed., *The Pentagon Papers as Published by the New York Times* (New York: Bantam Books, 1971), pp. 232–35.

12. Schlesinger, *The Imperial Presidency*, p. 192.

13. Schlesinger, *The Imperial Presidency*, p. 265.

14. Francis D. Wormuth and Edwin B. Firmage, *To Chain the Dog of War: The War Power of Congress in History and Law*, 2d ed. (Urbana: University of Illinois Press, 1989), pp. 219–22; Stephen Dycus, Arthur L. Berney, William C. Banks, and Peter Raven-Hansen, *National Security Law* (Boston: Little, Brown, 1990), pp. 235–36. For the details of the fighting and the American casualties, see David Locke Hall, *The Reagan Wars: A Constitutional Perspective on War Powers and the Presidency* (Boulder, CO: Westview Press, 1991), pp. 138–46.

15. Wormuth and Firmage, *Chain the Dog*, pp. 219–22.

16. Theodore Draper, *A Very Thin Line: The Iran-Contra Affair* (New York: Hill and Wang, 1991); Haynes Johnson, *Sleepwalking through History: America in the Reagan Years* (New York: Norton, 1991); George P. Shultz, *Turmoil and Triumph: My Years as Secretary of State* (New York: Scribner's, 1993). The Draper and Shultz books bring out the president's responsibility for the arms-for-hostages deal.

17. John Shattuck, "National Security a Decade after Watergate," *Democracy* (winter 1983).

18. Morton H. Halperin and Jeanne M. Woods, "Ending the Cold War at Home," *Foreign Policy* 81 (winter 1990–91): 136–37; Shattuck, "National Security"; *New York Times*, November 12, 1989, p. 39; *Time*, December 23, 1985, cited in Morris J. Blachman and Kenneth Sharpe, "De-Democratising American Foreign Policy: Dismantling the Post-Vietnam Formula," *Third World Quarterly* 8, no. 4 (October 1986): 1306. Also see Dorsen, *Our Endangered Rights*.

19. *New York Times*, July 19, 1992, p. A1; "What Bush Knew—and When," *Boston Globe* editorial, July 21, 1992, p. 16.

20. These and other illegalities, deceptions, and a cover-up are documented in Alan Friedman, *The Spider's Web: The Secret History of How the White House Illegally Armed Iraq* (New York: Bantam Books, 1993).

21. Michael J. Glennon, "The Gulf War and the Constitution," *Foreign Affairs* 70, no. 2 (spring 1991): 85–86, 97; Bruce Jentleson, "The Domestic Politics of Desert Shield: Should We Go to War? Who Should Decide?" *Brookings Review* 9, no. 1 (winter 1990–91): 27.

22. Doug Bandow, "The Persian Gulf War: Restoring the Congressional War Power," in Ted Galen Carpenter, ed., *America Entangled: The Persian Gulf Crisis and Its Consequences* (Washington, DC: Cato Institute, 1991), pp. 91, 101; Glennon, "Gulf War and Constitution," pp. 89–90.

23. Glennon, "Gulf War and Constitution," pp. 96–97; Mike Moore, "How George Bush Won His Spurs," *Bulletin of the Atomic Scientists* 47, no. 8 (October 1991): 26–33.

24. Draper, *A Very Thin Line*. For a summary of the widely accredited evi-

dence of Bush's part in the affair, see Jay Peterzell, "What Did Bush Know," *Time*, September 21, 1992, p. 24.

25. Taken yet further, this is the view of the pardon taken by Anthony Lewis, "George Milhous Nixon," *New York Times*, December 28, 1992, p. A22.

26. David Campbell, *Writing Security: United States Foreign Policy and the Politics of Identity* (Minneapolis: University of Minnesota Press, 1992), p. 185.

27. *New York Times* editorial, December 22, 1990, p. A26.

28. Koh, *The National Security Constitution*, pp. 153–81.

29. For a far broader analysis that supports the present one, see James M. Lindsay, "Congress and Diplomacy," in Randall B. Ripley and James M. Lindsay, eds., *Congress Resurgent: Foreign and Defense Policy on Capitol Hill* (Ann Arbor: University of Michigan Press, 1993), pp. 261–81.

CHAPTER XI

1. Alexis de Tocqueville, *Democracy in America*, 2 volumes (New York: Knopf, 1960).

2. Michael Kammen, *People of Paradox: An Inquiry concerning the Origins of American Civilization* (New York: Vintage, 1973), p. 290.

3. Louis Hartz, *The Liberal Tradition in America: An Interpretation of American Political Thought since the Revolution* (New York: Harcourt, Brace, 1955).

4. Robert Packenham, *Liberal America and the Third World* (Princeton: Princeton University Press, 1973), pp. 18–23.

5. Samuel P. Huntington, *American Politics: The Promise of Disharmony* (Cambridge, MA: Harvard University Press, 1980).

6. Gabriel A. Almond, *The American People and Foreign Policy* (New York: Harcourt, Brace, 1955); Frank Klingberg, "The Historical Alternation of Moods in American Foreign Policy, *World Politics* 4, no. 2 (January 1952): 239–73; Robert C. Osgood, *Ideals and Self-Interest in America's Foreign Relations: The Great Transformation of the Twentieth Century* (Chicago: University of Chicago Press, 1953); Richard Ullman, "The 'Foreign World' and Ourselves: Washington, Wilson, and the Democrat's Dilemma" *Foreign Policy* 21 (winter 1975–76): 99–124; Ronald H. Hinckley, *People, Polls, and Policymakers: American Public Opinion and National Security* (New York: Lexington Books, 1992); Ole R. Holsti and James N. Rosenau, *American Leadership in World Affairs: Vietnam and the Breakdown of Consensus* (Boston: Allen and Unwin, 1984); Eugene R. Witkopf, *Faces of Internationalism: Public Opinion and American Foreign Policy* (Durham, NC: Duke University Press, 1990). For a cultural study that does not discuss the isolationist-internationalist dualism, see Michael H. Hunt, *Ideology and U.S. Foreign Policy* (New Haven: Yale University Press, 1987).

7. *Time*, October 7, 1991, p. 15.

8. *New York Times*, October 11, 1991, p. A8; Alan F. Kay and Hazel Henderson, "Perceptions of Globalization, World Structures, and Security," *Americans Talk Issues*, Survey 17, March 1992.

9. E. H. Carr, *The Twenty Years Crisis, 1919–1939* (London: Macmillan, 1939), p. 302.

10. See the studies cited in note 6 above.

11. Hans J. Morgenthau, *In Defense of the National Interest* (New York: Knopf, 1951), p. 13.

12. George F. Kennan, *American Diplomacy, 1900–1950*, rev. ed. (Chicago: University of Chicago Press, 1984).

13. For discussions of the realists' ethical concerns and struggles see Joel H. Rosenthal, *Righteous Realists: Political Realism, Responsible Power, and American Culture in the Nuclear Age* (Baton Rouge: Louisiana State University Press, 1991); David Meyers, *George Kennan and the Dilemmas of U.S. Foreign Policy* (New York: Oxford University Press, 1989); Richard Fox, *Reinhold Niebuhr: A Biography* (New York: Pantheon Books, 1985); Ronald Steel, *Walter Lippmann and the American Century* (Boston: Houghton Mifflin, 1980); Greg Russell, *Hans J. Morgenthau and the Ethics of American Statecraft* (Baton Rouge: Louisiana State University Press, 1990).

14. Reinhold Niebuhr, *Moral Man and Immoral Society: A Study in Ethics and Politics* (New York: Charles Scribner's Sons, 1932).

15. Reinhold Niebuhr, *The Children of Light and the Children of Darkness* (New York: Charles Scribner's Sons, 1944), p. 41.

16. Reinhold Niebuhr, "'Favorable' Environments," *Messenger*, August 18, 1953, quoted in John Patrick Diggins, "Power and Suspicion: The Perspectives of Reinhold Niebuhr," *Ethics and International Affairs* 6 (1992): 157.

17. Diggins, "Power and Suspicion," p. 157.

18. The quotes are found in William Pfaff, *Barbarian Sentiments: How the American Century Ends* (New York: Hill and Wang, 1989), pp. 8, 10, 188. The ease with which Reagan could obviate the dualism between power and morality comes through clearly in this justification of his rollback doctrine. "The ultimate goal of American foreign policy is not just the prevention of war (with Marxist states) but the extension of freedom—to see that every nation, every person someday enjoys the blessings of liberty." *New York Times*, October 7, 1986, p. A1.

19. Pfaff, *Barbarian Sentiments*, pp. 188–89.

20. William Stueck, *The Road to Confrontation: American Policy toward China and Korea, 1947–1950* (Chapel Hill: University of North Carolina Press, 1981), p. 257.

21. Robert H. Johnson, "Periods of Peril: The Window of Vulnerability and Other Myths," *Foreign Affairs* 61, no. 4 (spring 1983): 952.

22. Packenham, *Liberal America*, pp. 25–110.

23. Robert W. Tucker and David C. Hendrickson, *The Imperial Temptation: The New World Order and America's Purpose* (New York: Council on Foreign Relations Press, 1992), p. 195.

24. It should not, however, be forgotten that some of the most prominent realists were much concerned with the superfluous and dangerous overextension of American power and commitments, what Jack Snyder has labeled "defensive realism." See his *Myths of Empire: Domestic Politics and International Ambition* (Ithaca, NY: Cornell University Press, 1991), pp. 12, 258–59.

Quemoy, 171

Ravenal, Earl, 16, 23, 24, 47
Reagan, Ronald: and arms control, 149, 153; and civil liberties, 251, 258, 261; and Contras, 115–16, 201, 272, 316n16; foreign policy of, 14–15, 199–201, 250–51; idealism of, 4, 197, 267, 318n18; internationalism of, 18, 23, 271–72; and Iraq, 203, 252; military policy of, 47, 236; and nuclear policy, 48, 123, 125, 175; and presidential power, 249, 257; and Soviet Union, 78, 97; and trade, 82, 83, 225; and U.S. confidence, 17, 276, 278
Reagan doctrine, 308n22
realism, 4; and idealism, 194, 263, 265–67, 273; internationalist, 184, 272–73, 274, 284n24, 318n24
realist-morality dualism, 274
realist theory, 136–37, 299n56
reassurance, 151–57, 163, 165, 168, 171, 275
Red Sea, 78
reform, 216, 217; political, 172, 195, 196, 199
religion, 71, 132, 151
Republican Party, 21, 22, 23, 24, 238, 244, 245, 314n2
reputational rationale: and credibility, 116–17, 118–19
research, 150, 231, 234–35; military, 49, 220, 236, 237; and strategic immunity, 65, 88–89
resolve, 168, 212, 255, 266, 273, 275, 278
Reston, James, 20
Rhineland, 117–18, 189
Rhodesia, 197
Rogers Peace Plan, 70
Romania, 98
Roosevelt, Franklin D., 57, 58–59, 189, 217, 244, 246
Roosevelt, Theodore, 52, 53, 54, 242, 267
Rosen, Stephen, 134
Rumania, 62
Russett, Bruce, 57, 58, 120
Russia, 53, 131, 135, 137, 159, 267; in World War I, 160, 189. *See also* Soviet Union

salami tactics, 93
Sandinistas, 35, 198, 201, 250, 267

Saudi Arabia, 21, 68, 204; oil from, 84, 85; and Persian Gulf War, 77, 223, 252, 256, 272
Savimbi, Jonas, 200
Saving America First, 189
Schelling, Thomas, 9, 116–17, 121, 150, 164, 174
schema theory, 167
Schlesinger, Arthur, 247
Schlesinger, James, 46
Schurz, Carl, 52, 187, 216, 243
security, internal, 258, 259
security, international, 210
security, national: and alliances, 146, 147, 282n7; and civil liberties, 24, 246–54, 255; and Congress, 260, 261; and credibility, 121; definitions of, 10–11; and economics, 141, 229, 283n8; and idealism, 183, 185, 190, 193–205, 211, 240–41, 254–58; and inadvertence, 171; and intentions, 37–39; and internationalism, 3, 183–85, 192, 193, 215, 273, 274, 277; and interventionism, 26; and isolationism, 185; and McCarthyism, 316n10; and military power, 88–91; and military spending, 236, 237, 238, 270; and national strategy, 4, 29–30, 276, 278; and nuclear weapons, 16; and presidential power, 257–58; and strategy, 7–8; threats to, 279n9; and trade, 224–26, 228; and unilateralism, 144–45
Security Council Resolution 678, 253
security dilemma, 43–44, 45–46, 102, 103, 163
security management, 160–77, 161
security perimeter: and agreements, 144, 157, 158, 159; boundaries of, 40–44, 78; and credibility, 113, 117, 120–21, 122; and idealism, 112, 211; and inadvertence, 163, 172; and internationalism, 35, 36, 113; and military power, 47, 122; and military spending, 80, 237; and national strategy, 3, 31, 39–41, 45, 144, 146, 150; and nuclear policy, 130; reassurance of, 151; and security dilemma, 46; and strategic immunity, 60–61, 63, 64–65, 88, 89, 91, 273, 275; trade within, 81, 82, 85, 228
security strategies, 9–10; and agreements, 157; and foreign policy culture, 263; and ideals, 240–62; and inadvertence,

Eric A. Nordlinger (1939–1994) was
Professor of Political Science at Brown University.
His works include *On the Autonomy of the
Democratic State* and *Soldiers in Politics*.